Three Athapaskan Ethnographies

Diamond Jenness on the Sekani, Tsuu T'ina and Wet'suwet'en,
1921–1924

Diamond Jenness

With a ᵗ·troduction by
B:

Rock's
Mills
Press

For ordering information, visit our website at
www.rocksmillspress.com or email us at
customer.service@rocksmillspress.com.

ISBN-13: 978-1-77244-010-2

Contents

The Sarcee Indians of Alberta, con't

Plates

Figures

The Carrier Indians of the Bulkley River

The Carrier Indians of the Bulkley River, con't

The Carrier Indians of the Bulkley River, con't

Figures

Three Northern Athapaskan Ethnographies: Diamond Jenness on the Sekani, Tsuu T'ina and Wet'suwet'en, 1921–1924

> History is the essence of innumerable biographies
> –Carlyle

"If I could divide myself into two persons," Diamond Jenness once confessed, "one of them would give his whole time to Eskimo archaeology and ethnology." And what of his other self, the one who didn't write the landmark ethnography *Life of the Copper Eskimos* (1922) or expand the temporal horizons of Arctic culture history by identifying Dorset and Old Bering Sea cultures? That would be the Jenness whose twenty-year career with the anthropological branch of Canada's Geological Survey turned him into one of the top rank generalists of his day, one whose investigations of indigenous peoples outside the Arctic—including intensive fieldwork among a half-dozen First Nations groups—continued to expand until they encompassed all of the country's culture areas. His synoptic *Indians of Canada*, pitched to a general readership and never out of print since the first edition appeared in 1932, testifies to the scope of these researches. As for depth, the trio of ethnographies reprinted here, each a foundational contribution to the field of northern Athapaskan studies, each an illustration of the day's disciplinary priorities, offer ample proof.

By way of introduction, the following pages roughly situate these seminal works in disciplinary and institutional context, explaining how Jenness, an Oxford-educated ex-pat New Zealander (1886–1969), came to undertake the pioneering researches on which his studies of the Tsuu T'ina (Sarcee) of Alberta, and of the Wet'suwet'en (Bulkley River Carrier) and Sekani in British Columbia, are based.

...

Domestic and foreign scholars and learned societies, notable among them the venerable British Association for the Advancement of Science, began calling on Ottawa to create an agency devoted to researching and preserving knowledge of the languages and cultures of first peoples in Canada in the 1880s.[1] It was not until an upsurge in nationalist sentiment accompanying the new century's dawn, however, that government finally took action. Passage of *The Geology and Mines Act* in 1907 set the stage, turning the formerly quasi-in-

---

1. For example, E.B. Tylor, "Opening Address [Section H]," *Nature* 31 (September, 1884), 453.

dependent Geological Survey, together with its affiliated natural history museum, into a branch of the newly organized Department of Mines, and broadening its research and curatorial functions to include building "complete and exact knowledge" of the dominion's anthropological and biological heritage.[2] Accordingly, the survey spawned two new divisions in 1910, each with a staff of specialists, a budget for field research and subsidiary activities, and an allotment of exhibition space in what was familiarly known as "the castle," the cavernous building, still standing on McLeod Street, housing the Victoria Memorial Museum, opened to the public one year later.

Having recently initiated a campaign to upgrade the survey's employment standards and do away with patronage, its director, Reginald Brock, sought to recruit a "scientific, [academically] trained ethnologist" to head up the new anthropological unit, oversee its collections, and implement comprehensive investigations across Canada.[3] Turning for guidance to Columbia University's Franz Boas, the reigning doyen of the American profession, the director was politely if pointedly informed that no Canadian fit the bill. Indeed, not one member of the country's small circle of anthropologists, avocational practitioners all, possessed the qualifications Boas believed the position, and the modern discipline, demanded: in brief, "firm grasp of the problems of comparative ethnology, of the method of linguistic inquiry ... [and] an intelligent appreciation of archaeological methods." In the circumstances, Brock's best bet was to look for candidates south of the border where a smattering of universities had been turning out graduates with advanced degrees, and research experience, since the 1890s. The most promising of them, in Boas's opinion, was his own protégé, Edward Sapir.[4] To the dismay of home-grown anthropologists who firmly believed that "birth right [conferred] automatic entitlement" to the prestigious post, the newly minted PhD, then twenty-six and a rising star in the field of linguistics, took up duties as founding chief of the Anthropological Division. Sapir would hold the position for fifteen years before decamping for the University of Chicago, in 1925.[5]

At its inception, the section's objectives were underscored by a sense of urgency, a reflection of the widely held belief that indigenous peoples and cultures in Canada (and globally) were fast disappearing under the relentless press of Western ideas and institutions, to say nothing of malnutrition and disease. "If ... information concerning the native races is ever to be secured and preserved," Brock wrote of the moment, "action must be taken very soon, or it will be too late."[6] Echoing that sentiment, Sapir cautioned his new employer

2. M. Zaslow, *Reading the Rocks: The Story of the Geological Survey of Canada 1842–1972* (Toronto: MacMillan, 1975), 257.

3. Geological Survey of Canada, *Summary Report of the Geological Survey for the Calendar Year 1909* (Ottawa: King's Printer, 1910), 8.

4. Boas to Brock, 9 May, 1910, cited in G. Avrith, "Science at the Margins: The British Association and the Foundations of Canadian Anthropology, 1884–1910." PhD Diss. (Ann Arbor: University Microfilms, 1986), 271.

5. *Ibid*, 271–72.

6. Geological Survey of Canada, *Summary Report of the Geological Survey for ... 1908* (Ottawa:

against allowing any "shortsighted policy of economy … [to] interfere with the thorough and rapid prosecution of the anthropological problems of the dominion. What is lost now," he warned, "will never be recovered again." With upwards of fifty groups identified for detailed study, many whose exposure to forces of assimilation—above all, the *Indian Act*, reserves, and residential schools—was already one or more generations deep, the new chief set about launching the program in his charge "hammer and tongs."[7]

In keeping with the research program Boas and his students implemented continent-wide after 1900, the new division's work had both descriptive and historical objectives, on the one hand, filling in the many gaps in knowledge of the cultures, languages, and physical traits of indigenous peoples within the dominion, and on the other, tracing their origins and affinities, and in the light of archaeological and ethnological evidence, reconstructing their development over time.[8] To these ambitious ends, a mix of academically trained and self-taught anthropologists, primarily from Canada and the United States, were recruited to conduct fieldwork. By the outbreak of World War I, the permanent staff had grown to six, with a seventh member on "outside service" in British Columbia. Twice that number were hired on temporary contracts. Indicative of the division's early success, in one year—1914—nine ethnologists and three archaeologists were engaged in as many projects. Equally telling, twenty monographs and papers were already published in a newly established anthropological series, and hundreds upon hundreds of artefacts had been accessioned into the Victoria Memorial's holdings.[9]

Detailed studies of Athapaskans rated high among the division's original priorities. A geographically far-flung ethno-linguistic family, their Canadian (i.e. northern) branch—Dene, in contemporary parlance—have deep roots in the continent's sprawling western subarctic, a region stretching from the lowlands west of Hudson Bay to the mountainous interiors of Yukon and northern British Columbia. Judging by the sparse entries on them in the compendious *Handbook of American Indians North of Mexico*, issued in 1907, they were one of the least well-known anthropologically of indigenous peoples anywhere in the country.[10] Available sources often drew attention to the seeming ease with which they borrowed elements of culture (other than language, toward which they were stalwartly conservative), from non-Athapaskan neighbours, sometimes fully remaking the cast of their societies in the process. Nowadays,

King's Printer, 1909), 9.

7. E. Sapir, "An Anthropological Survey of Canada," *Science* 34, no. 884 (1911), 793; "The Work of the Division of Anthropology of the Dominion Government," *Queen's Quarterly* 20, no. 1 (1912), 63–64.

8. Sapir, "Anthropological Survey," 791–93; see also F. Boas, "Ethnological Problems in Canada," *Journal of the Royal Anthropological Institute* 40 (1910), 529–39.

9. B. Richling, "Archaeology, Ethnology, and Canada's Public Purse, 1910–1921," In P. Smith and D. Mitchell, eds., *Bringing Back the Past: Historical Perspectives on Canadian Archaeology* (Gatineau: Canadian Museum of Civilization, 1998), 106–7.

10. F.W. Hodge, ed. *Handbook of American Indians North of Mexico* (Washington: Government Printing Office, 1907), 109–10.

this propensity is interpreted as highly functional, a trait enabling successful adaptation to novel social and natural conditions as varied as those found on the Chilcotin Plateau in central British Columbia, on the Albertan high plains, and at the farthest extent of Athapaskan territory, in the arid expanses of the American southwest. Long before anthropologists began thinking of cultures as adaptive strategies, however, Boas advanced what amounted to a psychological explanation, arguing that the constellation of traits associated with so-called "old Athapascan culture"—comparatively "simple social organization, simplicity of industrial life ... a general individualistic tendency ... [and] lack of great rituals which bring people together"—made them especially "susceptible to foreign influence."[11]

Sapir followed his mentor's lead in thinking that Athapaskan groups in marginal—that is, geographically isolated—regions such as the vast, western Arctic drainage, were more likely to have preserved traits approximating this reputedly elemental form of indigenous culture than were their compatriots in areas with culturally diverse populations. That prospect, and the light studying them would cast on the subsequent development of groups whose outward migrations brought them into contact with new, and sometimes starkly different, socio-cultural formations, convinced him that systematic fieldwork in this remote quarter was "probably the greatest single need of ethnological research in Canada."[12] Eager to get the ball rolling, he engaged James Teit, a long-time field associate of Boas and the division's newly appointed man on outside service, to research spatial, cultural, and historical relations among the so-called Nahani, a cluster of northern Athapaskan peoples whose cordilleran territories straddled the northwestern corner of his home province, British Columbia, and southern Yukon, beginning in 1912. One year later, Berkeley-trained J. Alden Mason signed a contract to widen the project's areal focus eastward with parallel fieldwork in the Mackenzie basin. Together, Sapir confidently declared before Mason ever took his first breath of boreal air, "we should be able to break the back of Athabascan ethnology."[13]And until the survey's war-imposed belt-tightening threw a wrench in the works in the mid-teens, it looked as if that goal was within reach.

Teit's investigations began with the Tahltan, a people he had observed in passing twice before on excursions through their backwoods home ground, up-river on the Stikine.[14] Travelling by way of Wrangel, on Alaska's inner coast, he put in six early autumn weeks with them at Telegraph Creek, a seasonal gathering place they had been using for decades. Though relatively brief, he made the most of his stay, verifying and adding to the published findings of previous

11. J. Van Stone, *Athapaskan Adaptations: Hunters and Fishermen of the Subarctic Forests* (Arlington Heights, IL: AHM Publishing, 1974), 125; Boas, "Ethnological Problems," 533–34.

12. Sapir, "Anthropological Survey," 792.

13. Sapir to Teit, 14 November, 1911; to Mason, 19 October, 1912; to Teit, 21 December, 1912 (Canadian Museum of History, Sapir Corres.).

14. J. Teit, "Notes on the Tahltan Indians of British Columbia," In B. Laufer, ed., *Boas Anniversary Volume: Anthropological Papers Written in Honor of Franz Boas* (New York: Stechert, 1906), 337–49.

ethnographic observers, the most recent of whom, George T. Emmons, visited the area in the summers of 1904 and 1906. He also recorded songs and myths, the latter, as with other elements of their culture, bearing the imprint of coast-derived influences absorbed from inland Tlingit neighbours.[15] Unlike Teit, Mason was a newcomer to northern landscapes and their indigenous inhabitants, having begun his career doing fieldwork in California and Mexico. As was the all-too-common plight of hinterland travelers in a day before commercial flight, he lost weeks journeying down the Mackenzie en route to Great Slave Lake. Even so, he still managed three solid months of research before turning homeward, gathering ethnographic and linguistic information from members of Tlicho (Dogrib), Deh Cho (Slavey), and to a lesser extent Denésoliné (Chipewyan) bands who were summering at forts Resolution and Rae, on the lake's eastern shores.[16] Buoyed by his colleagues' progress, Sapir drew up budgetary estimates for the 1915 field season that included funds for both men to return to their respective areas. But in what proved to be a foretaste of bigger troubles ahead, the onset of wartime retrenchment at the Geological Survey forced him to scrap an ambitious research plan that would have seen Mason overwinter with the Dene. Only Teit reached the field as intended, visiting the Tahltan for a second time at Telegraph Creek before shifting eastward into Kaska Dena (Kaska) territory, on the southern margins of Dease Lake. Regrettably, that turned out to be the last of his Nahani investigations, even deeper cuts to the division's already shrunken field budget killing his proposal to cross the border into Yukon the following summer.[17] And with that discouraging turn of events, the Athapaskan project—indeed, the best part of the Anthropological Division's scientific agenda, including publication—lapsed into a financially induced stupor, not stirring back to life until the early twenties when, by modest increments, the post-war purse strings began to loosen.

Determined to make up ground lost to the preceding half-decade of austerity, Sapir drafted Diamond Jenness, as of October, 1920, the division's newest full-time member and, arguably, its most experienced ethnographer, to help revive Athapaskan work.[18] Rather than having him retrace Teit and Mason's footsteps into the northern backcountry, however, Sapir chose an altogether different setting for his colleague's introduction to the Athapaskan field, and for his first Canadian fieldwork since his three year stint (1913–16) as ethnol-

15. Teit to Sapir, 2 November, 1912 (CMH, Sapir Corres.); "On Tahltan (Athabaskan) Work, 1912." *Summary Report of the Geological Survey … 1912* (Ottawa: King's Printer, 1914), 375–76; G.T. Emmons, *The Tahltan Indians*, University of Pennsylvania Museum, Anthro. Pubs. 4, no. 1 (Philadelphia, University of Pennsylvania Museum, 1911).

16. Mason to Sapir, 13 November, 1913 (CMH, Sapir Corres.); "On Work Among Northern Athabaskan Tribes, 1913." *Summary Report of the Geological Survey … 1913* (Ottawa: King's Printer, 1914), 375–76.

17. Sapir to Mason, 19 October, 1914; Teit to Sapir, 13 October 1915 (CMH, Sapir Corres.).

18. B. Richling, *In Twilight and Dawn: A Biography of Diamond Jenness.* (Montreal: McGill-Queen's University Press, 2012), 128–30.

ogist with the Canadian Arctic Expedition: the foothills of southern Alberta, location of the Sarcee reserve, now the Tsuu T'ina First Nation.

Up to this point, the division had paid scant attention to any of the dominion's plains-dwellers, the single exception being Wilson Wallis's 1914 research on the Dakota, a Siouan people settled near the town of Portage, west of Winnipeg.[19] Now, seven years on, Sapir's decision had less to do with catching up in a neglected culture area than with making the most of a still-inadequate research budget; for the price of sending one fieldworker to some far-flung corner of the western subarctic, both he and Jenness could visit the Tsuu T'ina at their reserve on the outskirts of Calgary. Delegating general ethnography to his junior, Sapir intended to concentrate on linguistics, part of a long-term project aimed at demonstrating the descent of Athapaskan, Haida, and Tlingit from a single language stock, one he recently dubbed Na-Dene.[20] Yet as sometimes happens to the best laid schemes, growing concerns over his wife's health prompted Sapir to remain behind. Jenness boarded the westbound train alone, left to his own devices in tackling the full gamut of Tsuu T'ina research, language and all.[21]

Despite looming on the horizon, momentous changes had yet to befall the Copper Inuit through the opening decades of the twentieth century, their independent existence virtually undiminished in the mid-teens when Jenness lived in their winter camps atop the sea ice, and stalked caribou with them across the soggy summer tundra. For the Tsuu T'ina, as for most First Nations from one end of the country to the other, the story was far different. Decades of illiberal treatment at the hands of government had exacted a crushing toll, their total population of 160—down from 450 in 1877, the year their leaders signed Treaty Seven—decimated by disease; residential schools alienating younger generations from their elders; customary ways living on in the memories of the reserve's oldest residents far more than in the rhythms of everyday life. These were the urgent conditions to which Brock and Sapir referred at the division's founding, and the motivation behind anthropology's comprehensive project of ethnographic salvage, a decades-long undertaking to document the continent's seemingly imperiled cultures and languages as they were before the deluge, not as they became afterward. Unlike the rare situation in Copper Inuit territory where an intact mode of life could still be observed at first hand, elsewhere a picture of that life had to be knitted together from the threads of oral memoir; each narrative was transcribed by the ethnographer as a rough equivalent of the historian's text. That's what American linguist Pliny Goddard did when he made limited inquiries during two pre-war visits to the reserve. And apart from collecting ethnographic specimens for the museum, it's precisely how Jenness kept busy over the summer months of 1921. With twelve

19. E. Sapir, "Field Work and Research," *Summary Report of the Geological Survey for ... 1914.* (Ottawa: King's Printer, 1915), 173–74.
20. E. Sapir, "The Na-Dene Languages, a Preliminary Report," *American Anthropologist* 17, no. 3 (1915), 534–58.
21. B. Richling, *Twilight and Dawn*, 163.

elders as teachers, he filled his notebooks with personal accounts of a once-autonomous Tsuu T'ina nation, their origins in the Peace River basin, reputedly as an offshoot of the Dunne-za (Beaver), and of the new existence they forged on reaching the high plains, one modeled on social and cultural conventions borrowed from Algonkian-speaking Siksika (Blackfoot) neighbours.

Faced with lots to do, relatively little time to get it done, and in Athapaskan, a language Sapir colourfully characterized "the son-of-a-bitchiest" to learn, Jenness cut to the chase and engaged John Whitney, his forty-something landlord and a fluent Sarcee speaker, to interpret and assist with the painstaking business of transcribing the elders' stories.[22] Spread over six weeks, their collaboration yielded a body of narratives replete with ethnographic and historical detail and personal rumination illuminating a world as it existed before Treaty Seven ushered in the reserve era. Sacred knowledge and its ritual expression figure prominently in the resulting monograph, a work regarded to this day as the standard treatment of Tsuu T'ina society, culture, and history. Missing from its pages, however, are musical transcriptions of 75 songs recorded with a borrowed phonograph, a fair selection of same performed by Whitney; apparently, they were omitted for want of a specialist to do the requisite musicological transcription. Absent, too, is any mention of language, a topic the author wisely entrusted to his more linguistically adroit colleague. "I spent two months among the Sarcee and did not know whether there was tone [that is, modulations of pitch affecting meaning] or not, and you discover it in one day!" he kidded Sapir, then in the midst of his own visit to the reserve, a visit postponed from the previous year; "Don't you think you had better take up Athapascan exclusively now instead of myself?"[23]

Initially baffled by the sounds of Athapaskan speech, Jenness was only slightly less so on hearing them again in dialects of the Dakehl (Carrier), a population spread across several hundred kilometers of cordilleran landscape in British Columbia's north-central interior. "Don't laugh too much over my phonetics," he wrote to Sapir, this time a bit sheepishly; "I am having plenty of trouble ... but feel a little more at home than when I went to Calgary."[24] All the same, after putting in five months of research—from early October 1923 to the end of February 1924—with the Wet'suwet'en, the westernmost branch of the Dakehl, he requested and received permission (and extra funding) to stay on in the field through spring to broaden his investigations. Distance ruled out visiting the Mackenzie valley, or ascending the Stikine. Instead, he settled on the Sekani as his next stop, a group no anthropologist had studied to this point, at least not at first-hand. From an ethnological perspective, their out-of-the-way territory in the Rocky Mountain Trench, near the headwaters

---

22. Sapir cited in R. Darnell, *Edward Sapir: Linguist, Anthropologist, Humanist* (Berkeley: University of California Press, 1990), 134; Jenness to Sapir, 3 July, 1921 (CMH, Sapir Corres.).

23. Jenness to W. McInness 15 December, 1937 (CMH, Jenness Corres.); Jenness to Sapir, 19 July, 1922 (CMH, Sapir Corres.).

24. Jenness to Sapir, 21 October, 1923 (CMH, Sapir Corres.).

of the Peace, held open the possibility, à la Boas and Sapir, that they retained more of the flavour of old Athapaskan ways than was evident among any of the peoples with whom he had worked thus far. Moreover, he relished the idea of journeying to their riverside settlements—forts McLeod and Grahame—by navigating a portion of the route celebrated explorer Alexander Mackenzie had followed in the 1790s on his successful search for an outlet to the Pacific. In the end, practicality prevailed over personal preference, the would-be adventurer hitching a ride aboard a Hudson's Bay Company barge hauling freight to its upriver posts. On the bright side, with departure from the docks at Prince George delayed by ice on the Parsnip River, he was able to fit in a few weeks of fieldwork at two eastern Dakehl reserves, Fraser Lake (Stellat'en) and Stony Creek (Saik'uz), both in the valley of the Nechako. As if local dialects didn't present problem enough, Chief Thomas, his interpreter, and main informant at Fraser Lake knew about as much English as Jenness did Dakehl. By chance, they found common ground in French, the ethnographer putting to use what he had learned in college, while his informant used a brand of pidgin introduced to the region's fur trade posts in the previous century courtesy of Métis voyageurs. How preposterous the scene would surely seem to onlookers conversant in "real French," he remarked in a letter to colleague (and Oxford classmate) Marius Barbeau, two grown men busily "jabbering and gesticulating in two horrible jargons."[25]

Speaking of Barbeau, it was he who had opened the door to his co-worker's researches among the province's Athapaskans in the first place; that happened in 1920, the year he began studies of the Tsimshian-speaking Gitxsan, of the Skeena River. A good portion of that season was spent at Hazelton, a village straddling the intersection of the Skeena and the westward-flowing Bulkley, the salmon-rich lifeline of Wet'suwet'en territory. "I am interested to learn that you are close to the Carriers," Sapir wrote from Ottawa, suggesting that if time allowed, it "would not be a bad idea ... to carry on some investigations with them as well ...." As usual, the linguist was eager to learn if "pitch accent"—that is, tone—featured in their speech. But ethnological details were equally welcome, Sapir regarding what was then the principal source on the Dakehl, the writings of late nineteenth-century Oblate missionary Father Adrien Morice, to be of uneven value, reliable enough on material culture and subsistence practices, but questionable on religious and ritual life. For his part, Barbeau was cool to the idea, having found in the nearby Gitxsan village of Kitanmax more than enough work to keep him busy for a good long while to come.[26] That's why Jenness's second stint of Athapaskan fieldwork began at Hazelton—actually, at Hagwilget (or Tse Kya), the Wet'suwet'en reserve located a few miles to the eastward, overlooking the lower Bulkley.

---

25. Richling, *Twilight and Dawn*, 182–85; Jenness to Barbeau, 3 May 1924 (CMH, Barbeau Corres.).

26. Sapir to Barbeau, 16 July 1920 (CMH, Sapir Corres.); Barbeau cited in L. Nowry, *Man of Mana: Marius Barbeau* (Toronto: N.C. Press, 1995), 196.

Much as circumstances had dictated on the prairies, here, too, fieldwork largely depended on interviews rather than direct observation. And in elder Felix George, a "veritable mine of information," Jenness was fortunate in finding an experienced interpreter and indispensable informant on local history and culture. Befuddlement over the nuances of phonology aside—"Are you holding up your hands in holy horror?" sums things up quite nicely— by late November his inquiries had already yielded substantial information about traditional social and political organization and customs, religion, and folklore, a body of ethnographic detail, he reported to Sapir, "as extensive as anything published by Morice."[27] More than a supplement to the scholarly cleric's findings, the material he obtained, coupled with the observations he had made in spring 1924 at Fraser Lake and Stony Creek, served as a corrective to Morice's tendency to ascribe to all Dakehl the ethnic traits he knew best from prolonged residence among the population of Fort St. James, a fair piece inland from Hazelton. This explains the priest's misjudgment of the extent to which the Wet'suwet'en had absorbed coast-derived, mainly Tsimshianic, ideas and practices, the result of sustained ties between them and their near-neighbours on the Skeena. Unlike conditions on the eastern flanks of Dakehl country where the impact of foreign influences, in Jenness words, had "not struck so deep," on the Bulkley they spawned a fully developed social formation modeled on (and dovetailing with) the Gitxsan system of matrilineal descent, phratric organization, inherited titles and crests, chiefly authority, and potlatch. Though less pronounced, those influences had also penetrated the overlapping spheres of religion, medicine, and myth, dimensions of intellectual culture whose eastern Dakehl analogues, by contrast, appeared to be "much more Athapascan in character."[28]

If his purpose in staying on in the field through spring was to get an even better sense of what Boas fashioned as "old Athapascan culture," then Jenness wasn't disappointed during his month-long stay in Sekani country. His first stop, Fort McLeod, was then home to some seventy people; one hundred more resided at Fort Grahame. While continuing to wrest a living from the land, scarcely a generation had passed since their forbears, originally divided among two southern and two northern bands, swapped their age-old nomadic life for year-round settlement at the posts. Since then, virtually the entire population had converted to Roman Catholicism, and Western goods replaced all but a few items of aboriginal manufacture in everyday use. Even so, three weeks of interviewing elders at McLeod, and a fourth similarly engaged upriver, exposed a deep vein of traditional culture lying just beneath the surface, one more "typically Mackenzie or N[orthern] Athabaskan" in form and substance than he had found elsewhere, including on the two Nechako River reserves.

---

27. Jenness to Barbeau, 23 October, 1923 (CMH, Barbeau Corres.); Jenness to Sapir, 23 November, 1923 (CMH, Sapir Corres.).

28. Jenness to Barbeau, 23 October, 1923 (CMH, Barbeau Corres.); A.G. Morice, "Are the Carrier Sociology and Mythology Indigenous or Exotic?" *Transactions and Proceedings of the Royal Society of Canada*, 10, section II (1892), 114–15; Richling, *Twilight and Dawn*, 172–73.

Absent an equivalent to Morice's ethnographic accounts of the Dakehl, Jenness's inquiries, aided by unsung interpreters, were broader in scope than was the case at Hagwilget. Material culture figured prominently; so, too, did the history of Sekani relations with neighbours, relations that spawned on-again, off-again trade and marital alliances, blood feuds, and experiments with clan organization and its accoutrements. But as he confessed to Sapir at the time, "medicine practices are their most interesting feature," evident in the numerous first-hand accounts of visionary experiences and sacred knowledge faithfully recorded in all their vivid detail.[29]

Encouraged by what he accomplished in British Columbia, Jenness resolved to continue on with the rebooted Athapaskan project as soon as the division's budget allowed, probably a year down the road. A season with southern Dakehl and their Tsilhqot'in (Chilcotin) near-neighbours was his top priority, followed by another, maybe two, in the area of Great Slave Lake where Mason's preliminary results would provide a starting point for more intensive investigations. But two unforeseen events intervened, both coincidentally, in 1925. The first was purely serendipitous: Jenness's identification of the previously unknown Dorset Eskimo culture in a hodgepodge of artefacts sent to the museum at his own urging, a discovery that, one year on, led him to a second major find, of Old Bering Sea, while digging on Alaska's Little Diomede Island. The second was, if anything, just the opposite: Jenness's Victorian sense of duty—bred in the bone, it would seem, among the scions of New Zealand's respectable middle classes, of which he was one—together with in-house managerial opposition to the alternatives, landing him in the division chief's chair on Sapir's departure for American academia.[30] Through it all, he remained determined to return to Athapaskan research, or failing that, to recruit new blood to carry the work forward. With his Alaskan trip in the offing, he wrote to John Cooper, a specialist on the Algonkian (eastern) subarctic, about picking up where he had left off in British Columbia two years earlier; "… if we can collaborate to clean up the Carrier," as Jenness awkwardly put the case, "practically all the Athapaskan tribes in [the province] will have been studied." No luck. But in 1928, his fortunes improved. He hired one of Sapir's graduate students, Cornelius Osgood, to revive work in that "badly neglected ethnographical province," the Mackenzie valley. Osgood passed the long winter near Great Bear Lake, and in the process launched a career as the first of a new generation of ethnologists to specialize in the study of Athapaskans across the western subarctic. Sadly, he was also the last to do so on behalf of the Anthropological Division until the 1950s when the likes of Catharine McLellan and June Helm, at the start of their own notable careers, were affiliated with its newly revamped research program.[31] By then, Jenness was safely ensconced in retirement.

. . .

---

29. Jenness to Sapir, 2 June, 1924; 12 June, 1924 (CMH, Jenness Corres.).

30. Richling, *Twilight and Dawn*, 136–39; 199–201; 216–17.

31. Jenness to J.M. Cooper, 13 March, 1926; to E. Sapir, 4 May, 1927 (CMH, Jenness Corres.); Richling, *Twilight and Dawn*, 245–46, 298–99.

For those who are familiar with it, the name Diamond Jenness is synonymous with arctic anthropology, and for good reason. As his Arctic Expedition reports—five in all—began to appear in the early twenties, the Copper Inuit, until then practically invisible in the scientific literature, emerged from obscurity to become possibly the most fully examined of indigenous peoples anywhere in the dominion. In a laudatory review of the first and best known of the series, *The Life of the Cooper Eskimos*, Clark Wissler, Sapir's counterpart at the American Museum of Natural History, called special attention to its author's apparent "genius for gathering a large body of data in a short time."[32] By that standard, the product of Jenness's Tsuu T'ina, Wet'suwet'en, and Sekani researches, the yield of eight months' cumulative effort, surely bordered on the miraculous. Remarkable for sure, but what is to be made of the resultant monographs, the first studies of northern Athapaskans based on intensive ethnographic investigations? Above all, they are original works of history and description, as the discipline then prescribed. On the one hand, each is framed by the central idea, current then as it remains to this day, that cultures develop over time through the interaction of internal and external forces. And on the other, they draw heavily on informants' narratives to portray the dimensions of culture as the people themselves know and experience them—"the culture as it appears to the Indian himself," in Boas's memorable phrasing.[33] Not to be forgotten, the material itself speaks to Jenness's well-honed skills as ethnographer, no less his ability to build rapport with the elders and interpreters who were his teachers. The man "must have been a magnificent field worker," Robin Ridington once observed, "for the description he gives us of the Indian worlds he visited are rich in the kind of detail that only a trusted and sympathetic friend would be told." High praise, rightly earned.[34]

Barnett Richling
Bedford, Nova Scotia
April, 2015

---

32. C. Wissler, Review of *The Life of the Copper Eskimos. Canadian Historical Review* 4, no. 1 (1923), 72.

33. Richling. *Twilight and Dawn*, 118–19; J. Berman, "The Culture as it Appears to the Indian Himself: Boas, George Hunt, and the Methods of Ethnography." In G.W. Stocking, Jr., ed. *Volkgeist as Method and Ethic: Essays on Boasian Ethnography and the German Anthropological Tradition* (Madison: University of Wisconsin Press, 1996), 217–19.

34. R. Ridington, "Beaver Dreaming and Singing," In P. and J. Lotz, eds., *Pilot Not Commander: Essays in Memory of Diamond Jenness.* (Ottawa: St. Paul's University, 1971), 115.

The Sekani Indians
of
British Columbia

by
Diamond Jenness

First published by the National Museum of Canada
Bulletin 84, Anthropological Series No. 20
1937

PREFACE

The Sekani Indians of northern British Columbia centre today around two posts of the Hudson's Bay Company, Fort McLeod on McLeod lake and Fort Grahame on Finlay river. The author visited them in those places during the summer of 1924, spending three weeks on McLeod lake and a week at Fort Grahame. The information obtained at that time forms the main subject of this report.

The notes concerning the Long Grass band of the Sekani, whose home lies (or lay in) the Groundhog country at the headwaters of Skeena, Nass, and Stikine rivers, were obtained during the preceding winter at Hazelton from a Gitksan Indian woman who had spent most of her life among them. Her history, as related by herself, seems worth recording.

"I was born at Kispiox about seventy years ago. My father belonged to the wolf phratry in that village, my mother to the owl phratry, so they gave me the name *Luskayok*, which means 'Cry of the baldheaded eagle,' the eagle being a crest in my father's phratry. One of my father's sisters married an Indian of the Long Grass band and went to live in his country. When I was eleven years old, a fight occurred between these Long Grass Indians and the Kispiox people. Several Kispiox men were slain, and five Long Grass Indians, among them my aunt's brother-in-law, who was killed by my mother's brother. The two peoples then settled their quarrel by holding a feast together in the Groundhog country, and my parents, lacking a son, sent me to live with my aunt as a mark of goodwill. The Long Grass people treated me very kindly, and when I was fourteen years old married me to a young chief named Kaiyeish, whose grandmother had been a Kispiox woman also. We were very happy for many years, and had six children, four of whom are buried beside my husband in a big cemetery in the Groundhog country. At first we lived in lodges of cedar-bark chinked with moss, but later we obtained cloth tents from the Hudson's Bay Company. From early spring until nearly Christmas we wandered in and around the Klappan mountains hunting and trapping, then we travelled south to Bear lake, or less often, northward to Telegraph Creek, to trade our furs. Occasionally we visited Bear lake during the summer also, in order to see my people; but we never went to Telegraph Creek during the summer because the Long Grass Indians are not allowed to fish in Stikine river. When my husband died in 1907 his brother wanted to marry me, according to the usual custom; but I refused him, because my husband had told me to return to my people. So the Long Grass people took me down to Bear lake and restored me to my family, who came up from Kispiox to receive me."

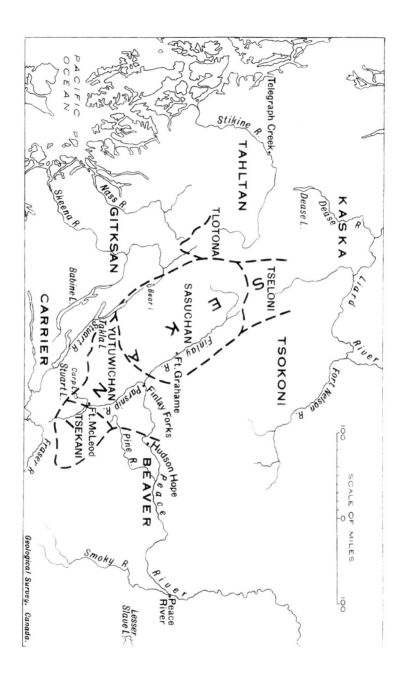

Figure 1. Sketch map showing the territory occupied by Sekani bands in relation to neighbouring tribes

CHAPTER 1
INTRODUCTION

The territory of the Sekani comprises all the valleys within the Rocky mountains between latitude (approximately) 54° 20' and 58° north that combine their waters to make the mighty Peace river, which, flowing east and north, joins the still mightier Slave and Mackenzie rivers to empty at last into the Arctic ocean. On the west the boundary coincides with the line of the Pacific divide except for a spur around Bear lake; and on the east with the line of the Rockies (and the boundary of the province of British Columbia) except for another spur down Peace river to Rocky Mountain canyon.

Within this basin all the valleys converge into two main arteries, the valley of Parsnip river that flows northward, and the valley of the Finlay that flows south. From Finlay Forks, at the 2,000-foot contour, where these two rivers join, their valleys rise swiftly, the Parsnip to the 3,000-foot level, the Finlay to the 4,000. Mountains from 4,000 to 6,000 feet flank them on either side. On the Finlay and its tributaries the valleys become narrower and steeper towards the headwaters; but on the Parsnip they open out towards the south and west, into a more undulating plateau country that is broken by many small lakes.

The whole country is heavily wooded. There is a little cottonwood and birch at the lower levels, but the predominant trees are balsam, spruce, and pine, with a considerable growth of poplar in burnt valleys. The rivers, fed by the snow and glaciers of the mountains, are swift and muddy, with many canyons and rapids. During the flood season of early summer they cut deeply into their banks and produce numerous sloughs that from time to time alter the main channels. Nevertheless they were the Indians' principal highways, because the country was too rugged, the forests too dense, to permit of easy travelling overland. Many rivers had their sources in fair-sized lakes, or in chains of small lakes, which the Sekani frequented for their whitefish and trout.

The climate is rather dry, and most of the moisture falls during the winter months as snow. At McLeod lake the mean temperature in January is around zero, and in July the thermometer sometimes touches 90° F. Spring comes in the first half of March, as a rule, and the ice leaves the lakes some time in April. Potatoes and other vegetables yield excellent crops at the two settlements, Forts McLeod and Grahame, but clouds of mosquitoes plague the outdoor worker unless a strong, cool breeze drives them to cover. Along the river banks and in burnt areas are many blueberries and saskatoon berries which the Sekani ate raw, not dried and mixed with grease after the manner of the Carrier and coast tribes. Bird life is inconspicuous, though the Indians shoot a fair number of grouse, ducks, and geese. Drifting down the rivers in summer one occasionally sights a black or brown bear, a moose, or an otter on the bank, but the animal quickly disappears in the woods.

Since their rivers drained eastward and northward to the Arctic the Sekani lacked the great shoals of salmon that were the mainstay of most of the Indian tribes in British Columbia. Only in one place, around Bear lake, did their territory extend into the salmon area beyond the Pacific divide, and they were excluded from that area in the second half of the nineteenth century. They fished extensively for trout and whitefish both in summer and in winter, but relied for their food supply mainly on the wild animals in which their country abounded. Within the forests there were numerous black and grizzly bears, moose, beaver, porcupine, and rabbits; on the mountain slopes caribou, goats, sheep, and groundhogs. To the cast, beyond the Rocky mountains on the prairie south of Peace river, roamed many herds of buffalo that the Sekani had hunted previous to the nineteenth century, and on which their thoughts lingered long after they were confined within the Rockies by the hostile Beaver and Cree. The grassy plateau to the northwest, around the headwaters of Finlay river, is still one of the finest game areas on the continent. There caribou and groundhogs are particularly abundant, and on the neighbouring mountains sheep and goats; but the moose that are now becoming common reached the district, apparently, not more than half a century ago. The Sekani generally spent the period from about November until mid-summer on the plateaux and mountain slopes, running down the caribou and moose on the snow,[1] and when the snow had melted driving them into snares and trapping groundhogs. About mid-summer they resorted to the lakes to fish, or visited the various tribes beyond their borders.

There were many passes through the mountains that gave them access to their neighbours. In the north they crossed from the valley of Fox river, a tributary of the Finlay, to the Kachika or Muddy, a tributary of the Liard, which brought them into contact with the Kaska branch of the Nahani Indians. Eastward there was a route up Ospika river via Laurier pass to the upper waters of Half-

Plate 1. Fort Mcleod in 1924, showing the Hudson's Bay Company house and store on the right. (Canadian Museum of History 60670)

way river, which led down to the Peace half-way between Hudson Hope and Fort St. John; another, straight down the Peace, which is navigable the whole distance at certain stages of the water except at Rocky Mountain canyon and at Vermilion falls many hundred miles beyond; a third from the Misinchinka valley across Pine pass to Pine river, which joins the Peace nearly opposite Fort St. John; and a fourth from the headwaters of the Parsnip to the Wapiti,

---

1. "They get plenty of animals that is Moose and Red Deer by chasing them with their dogs when the crust." First Journal of Simon Fraser, Series C, No. 16, Bancroft Collection, Pacific Coast MSS., University of California, April 22, 1806.

a tributary of Smoky river that joins the Peace near the modern town of Peace River. Two routes led southward to the Fraser, the route taken by Mackenzie from near the source of Parsnip river across to James creek, McGregor river, and the Fraser, and an easier route from McLeod lake up Crooked river to Summit lake, thence over a short portage to Salmon river and the Fraser; the latter has become still easier today through the construction of a motor road from Prince George to Summit lake. Westward there was a route from McLeod lake via Carp lake to Fort St. James on Stuart lake, used by the Hudson's Bay Company for the freighting of supplies down to as late as 1900; one up Nation river to Nation and Takla lakes; one up Manson river to Manson creek, thence south to Stuart lake or west to Takla lake; one from Fort Grahame up the Mesilinka to Bear lake; one via Ingenika river and another by the Finlay itself to Thutade and Tatlatui lakes, whence there were trails across the divide to the headwaters of Stikine and Skeena rivers.

The routes to the eastward led to the Beaver and Cree Indians, who were not only hostile, but nearly as primitive as the Sekani themselves. Accessibility from this quarter was really a disadvantage to them, except that it brought them the fur traders and, ultimately, relief from the attacks of their enemies. The Kaska to the north contributed nothing to their welfare; those first cousins were even lower than themselves in the scale of civilization. South and west, however, were the Carrier Indians, who had long been in contact with the Shuswap, Bella Coola, and Gitksan; and the Sekani themselves met the Gitksan around Bear lake. Indirectly, then, they came under the influence of the rich cultures on the Pacific coast, and began to orient their lives westward. It was from the south and west, from the Carrier of Fraser river and Stuart lake and from the Gitksan of Bear lake, that they obtained the dentalia shells and the supply of iron observed by Sir Alexander Mackenzie when he passed through their country in 1793 on his way to the Pacific ocean. In these directions the routes are shorter and the trails easier than elsewhere, so that the Sekani have maintained their relations with the west, and today have very little contact with the Indians lower down Peace river.

CHAPTER 2
HISTORY AND SUBDIVISIONS OF THE SEKANI

The Sekani of northern British Columbia comprise a number of bands with no central organization and very little unity. To the neighbouring Carrier they are the *ltat'ten* or "people of the beaver dams," to the Indians on Skeena and Naas rivers the *t'set'sa'ut*, a word that they cannot interpret. The Tahltan call them *tsekini* or *tsenekin*, "people of the contorted rocks," according to some unpublished notes of James Teit, and the same authority states that the Kaska know certain bands as *tseloni*, "mountain top people," and *sastotene* "black bear people." The Sekani themselves have no common name that covers all their subdivisions, but only names for the separate bands.

The term Sekani appears for the first time in Harmon's Journal,[1] where it is applied to natives living on Parsnip, Finlay, and Upper Peace rivers in the same localities as the Sekani of today. Harmon conjectured that "the people who are now called Sicaunies ... at no distant period, belonged to the tribe, called Beaver Indians, who inhabit the lower part of the Peace River; for they differ but little from them in dialect, manners, customs, etc. Some misunderstanding between the Sicaunies and the rest of the tribe to which they formerly belonged probably drove them from place to place, up Peace River, until they were, at length, obliged to cross the Rocky Mountain." In his day many of the Sekani spent the winter months on the east side of the mountains, but withdrew in summer to the Finlay and Parsnip basins from fear of the Beaver and Cree. Concerning their western limits he gives little information. In an early passage of the journal he states that they were often attacked by the Tacullies (Carrier) and Atenas (Shuswap and Gitksan) while they were on the west side of the mountains; in a later passage he describes their constant visits to Stuart lake and their adoption of Carrier manners. On Tachie river, within the territory of the Stuart Lake Indians, there was a village inhabited mainly by Sekani who were rapidly amalgamating with their Carrier neighbours.[2]

Harmon's theory concerning the eastern origin of the Sekani bands is supported by the narratives of still earlier explorers. Sir Alexander Mackenzie, the first white man to explore the upper reaches of Peace river, gives a fairly detailed description of the Sekani under the name "Rocky Mountain Indians." He seems to apply this name to two distinct groups: (1) a western branch of the Beaver as yet uninfluenced by Cree culture, who controlled the river from its junction with the Smoky to Hudson Hope; and (2) another group, the Sekani of modern writers, who had been driven farther up the river from Rocky Mountain canyon to the basins of the Parsnip and the Finlay, although they still crossed the mountains in their hunting and even visited his post near Peace River landing. This second group of "Rocky Mountain Indians," the Sekani proper, still claimed as their territory all Peace River above its junction

---

1. Unless the "Cigne" frequently mentioned in the Journal of the Rocky Mountain Fort, Fall, 1799, means Sekani (*Washington Historical Quarterly*, October, 1928).

2. Harmon, D.W., *A Journal of Voyages and Travels*; Andover, 1820, pp. 190, 193, 215, 308–310.

with the Smoky, and represented the first group as intruders who would short-ly confine them entirely to the western side of the mountains. Mackenzie's narrative suggests, without stating explicitly, that there were two bands at the headwaters of Parsnip river, an eastern band on the Parsnip itself that consort-ed with the Carrier of the upper Fraser, and a western band on McLeod lake that was more intimate with the Carrier of Stuart Lake. He found two Sekani captives in a mixed camp of Carrier and Shuswap near Quesnel, and a Sekani man travelling with the Naskoten River Carrier to Bella Coola.[3]

Mackenzie travelled through this country in 1793. Twelve years later Si-mon Fraser established posts at Hudson Hope and McLeod Lake, and his journal for 1806 contains several references to the Sekani without applying to them that name. At "Rocky Mountain House" (Hudson Hope), he traded with Indians of two bands: (1) Meadow Indians, or Gens du large lands, whose hunting grounds were on the upper reaches of the "Beaver" (South Pine) river, and (2) a closely allied band frequenting Finlay river that traded with "Nakane" (Kaska) Indians to the north and with Carrier and Gitksan at Bear lake and perhaps elsewhere. At Hudson Hope Fraser was visited by more than 200 "Meadow" Indians who told him that their numbers had been greatly reduced by the raids of "Beaver" Indians.[4]

To the Sekani of McLeod lake Fraser gives the name of "Big Men," and he mentions that a branch of them inhabited the upper waters of Nation river. At McLeod lake, Carp lake, and at the divide between the Parsnip and the Fraser he found Carrier visiting the Sekani.

Fraser mentions another tribe, "Says-Thaw-Dennehs or Bawcanne" Indi-ans, who dwelt, apparently, at the headwaters of Smoky river and on the trib-utaries of the Fraser on the other side of the mountains. They were at enmity with the Carrier and "Beaver," but friendly with the Sekani of McLeod lake.[5]

No other information seems to be available concerning the history of the Sekani previous to the nineteenth century. We know, however, that in physi-cal appearance they resembled their eastern neighbours, the Beaver Indians, more than they resembled the Carrier, who adjoined them on the west; also that their dialects are almost the same as the Beaver, but differ considerably from the Carrier. It seems fairly certain, therefore, that not many centuries ago the Sekani and Beaver were one people divided into many bands which differed but little in language and in customs. Their territory stretched from lake Athabaska west to the Rocky mountains, which a few bands had probably crossed before the eighteenth century. About the middle of that century Cree drove the eastern bands around lake Athabaska up Peace river. They in turn drove west their kinsmen, who were further harassed by Cree raiding parties

---

3. Mackenzie, Sir Alexander, *Voyages from Montreal through the Continent of North America to the Frozen and Pacific Oceans in 1789 and 1793*; London, 1801, p. 140 *et al.*

4. "Beaver" in this journal seems to mean Cree, the Beaver Indians proper being called Slaves.

5. For the relevant quotations from this unpublished journal see Appendix.

from Little Slave lake.[6] At the beginning of the nineteenth century we seem to distinguish the following divisions:

(1) A group, named Beaver by Mackenzie, that extended from the junction of Smoky and Peace rivers to the falls below Fort Vermilion. This group had already adopted Cree culture.

(2) A group that controlled Peace river from its junction with the Smoky to Rocky Mountain canyon, Mackenzie's Rocky Mountain Indians, the Beaver of Fraser and Harmon. This and the former group have given rise to the present day Beaver now settled between Hudson Hope and Fort Vermilion.

(3) A group at the headwaters of Smoky river, Fraser's Bawcanne or Says-Thaw-Denneh Indians. Of this group I can find no trace in the later literature. It may have been exterminated, it may be represented by some half-breeds now living around Grande Prairie and Pouce Coupe, or it may have merged with the Beaver on Peace river, especially at Dunvegan.

(4) A group that frequented the headwaters of the South Pine and the adjacent Parsnip river, Fraser's Meadow Indians, or Gens du large lands. They probably survive in the half-breed population around Grande Prairie and Pouce Coupe, for the Sekani of Forts McLeod and Grahame, and the mixed Beaver-Sekani of Hudson Hope, still speak of "Meadow" Indians in that vicinity, naming them variously *t'lokotenne* (Fort McLeod), *t'loketchanne* (Fort Grahame), and *t'lowetchanne* (Hudson Hope). The Fort Grahame Indians state that these Meadow Indians lived west of Dunvegan at the time of the first white explorers, and the Indians of Fort McLeod assert that they used to meet them on Pine river. It is not unlikely, however, that a large part of this group amalgamated with the Parsnip River Indians who traded at Fort McLeod and became merged with the modern Sekani.

(5) A group, the Rocky Mountain Indians of Mackenzie, the Big Men of Fraser, and the Sicaunie of Harmon, that occupied the country around Parsnip and Nation rivers. It was in close contact with the neighbouring Carrier both on Fraser river and at Stuart lake. One band had almost coalesced with the Carrier; it had adopted the same mode of life and established a village just to the north of Stuart lake in Carrier country.

(6) A group on Finlay river that traded with the Skeena River Gitksan and with Carrier at Bear lake, and with Kaska Indians from the Liard River basin. Fraser gives this group no name, but Harmon includes it under Sicaunie.

These six groups were undoubtedly divided into many bands, and neighbouring groups mingled so intimately, and so closely resembled one another, that the distinction into Beaver and Sekani must have been largely arbitrary. On what basis, then, did Harmon make this distinction, and whence did he obtain the name Sicaunie?

When Harmon first visited this country there were only four trading posts west of the fort, near the junction of Smoky and Peace rivers, viz., at Dunveg-

---

6. Mackenzie: Op. cit., pp. 145–46.

an, St. John,[7] Hudson Hope, and McLeod lake. The Indians from the Smoky to Hudson Hope were rapidly adopting Cree culture in the same way as their kinsmen around Fort Vermilion; moreover, they were uniting with the Cree in attacking the Indians farther up the river. The bands west and south of Hudson Hope were alike in two respects; they were all at enmity with the Indians farther down the river, and were all strongly influenced by the Carrier, so that they looked westward for their trade rather than eastward. Harmon, therefore, had some justification for dividing them into two tribes. His predecessors had applied the term Beaver to all the eastern bands, and the name Sicaunie which he gave to the western division was merely an extension, unconscious perhaps, of the name of the band that claimed the country around Fort McLeod to all the bands that hunted west of the Rockies. His classification has prevailed in all the later literature, although even today it is impossible to draw a sharp line between Sekani and Beaver Indians, and the Indians of Hudson Hope, who are usually classed as Beaver, might be included with almost equal justice among the Sekani.

What people, if any, occupied the basins of Finlay and Parsnip rivers previous to the Sekani we do not know. Native tradition and archaeology are alike silent on this point. Very possibly the region was uninhabited, or, if inhabited, only by a few straggling Carrier who wandered farther afield than the rest of their nation. The Carrier themselves may have entered British Columbia by way of Peace river and its headwaters, or they may have come down from Stikine and Liard rivers in the north; but so thoroughly had they assimilated the culture of the older tribes to the west and south that many centuries must have elapsed since they first occupied their present homes. Doubtless they knew the country east of the divide, and occasionally hunted over portions adjacent to their own territory; but, except perhaps on Nation lakes, they seem to have made no permanent settlement there, as they did to the south and west.

Fort McLeod was established in 1805, Fort Connolly, on Bear lake, in 1826. The former post attracted the more southern Sekani, the latter the Sekani of the Finlay River basin, who then ceased to visit the trading posts at Hudson Hope and St. John where they were liable to attack by Beaver and Cree. Thus Sir George Simpson, when approaching Finlay Forks on upper Peace river in 1828, "fell in with two Indians of the Chicanee tribe from which we got a little dried meat. They had beaver, which they mean to trade at Trout Lake (Fort McLeod). This tribe is at variance with the Beaver Indians, and do not like to visit the establishments of Peace River . . . I believe at this moment some of them visit another of the New Caledonian posts in Conolly's or Bear's Lake."[8]

Very little attention was paid to the Sekani during the nineteenth century down to the time of Dawson. M'Lean, in 1833, saw a large encampment at Hudson Hope, and another at McLeod lake;[9] Richardson did not visit the

---

7. This old Fort St. John was at the mouth of South Pine river.

8. Simpson, Sir George, *Peace River. A Canoe Voyage from Hudson's Bay to the Pacific, in 1828.* Ottawa, 1872, p. 20.

9. M'Lean, J., *Notes on Twenty-Five Years Service in the Hudson's Bay Company*, vol. I, p. 238

country, but mentions the "Tsitka-ni, who dwell between the Stikeen and Simpson's rivers, to the north of the Carriers,"[10] and Selwyn, grouping Sekani and Beaver together, states that they did not go below Dunvegan.[11] Dawson alone attempted to define the boundaries of the tribe. He says: "The Siccanies lie to the north and east of the Carriers, occupying the west part of Tacla lake and the region about Bear or Connolly lake. They extend up the North Finlay about 75 miles and down the main stream of the Peace river to Hudson's Hope. North of the Siccanies and toward the coast, are the Nahanies, who are said to speak a different dialect, while the Indians still further north, about Cassiar, are different still."

In a later passage he adds:

> The Sicannie Indians of the vicinity of Fort McLeod, travel eastward up the Misinchinca, but apparently visit it very seldom, as there is no well-marked Indian trail. Near the Summit lake we found traces of an Indian camp a few years old, and we were informed that a trail of some sort leads to this place from the Parsnip west of the Misinchinca valley.[12]

Father Petitot, writing in 1876, says that most of the Sekanais, or The-kka-ne, "The people who dwell on the mountain," were living near the trading posts on Fraser river, but that a small number frequented the upper parts of Peace and Liard rivers, where they had acquired a great reputation for savagery. In a later work he mentions that in 1878 about sixty Sekani visited Great Bear lake.[13] This seems highly improbable; I suspect it was a band of Northern Nahani that descended Gravel river from the western flanks of the Rockies.

The only writer since Dawson who has given any attention to the Sekani is Father Morice. Unlike Harmon, Dawson, and most writers, including the author of the article on the Sekani in the Handbook of American Indians, Morice does not restrict this name to the bands dwelling to the west of the Rockies, but includes the Beaver Indians and even the Sarcee. His classification of the different bands or tribal subdivisions is:[14]

> (1) *Yû-tsû-t'qenne*, "people down over there," from Salmon river (a tributary of the Fraser) to McLeod lake, thence to the Fraser, by 53° 30'.
> (2) *Tsé-kéh-ne-az*, "little-people-on-the-rocks," between McLeod lake and the summit of the Rocky mountains.
> (3) *To-ta-t'qenne*, "people-a-little-down-the-river," on the east-

(London, 1849).

10. Richardson, Sir J., *Arctic Searching Expedition*, vol. II, p. 31 (London, 1851).

11. Selwyn, A.R.C., Geol. Surv., Canada, Rept. of Prog. 1879–1876, p. 60 (Ottawa, 1877).

12. Dawson, G.M., Geol. Surv., Canada, Rept. of Prog. 1879–80, pt. B, pp. 30, 45 (Ottawa, 1881).

13. Petitot, Père, *Monographic des Déné Dindjie*, Paris, 1876, p. 26; *Autour du Grand Lac des Ours*, Paris, 1891, p. 64.

14. Morice, Rev. A.G., *Notes on the Western Dénés*; Trans. Can. Inst., vol. IV, 1892–93, pp. 28–29.

ern slope and adjacent plains of the Rocky mountains within British Columbia.

(4) *Tsa-t'qenne* (who call themselves *Tsa-huh*) or Beaver-people, who roam over the large prairies contiguous to Peace river, on the south side of that stream and east of the Rockies.

(5) *Tsé-ta-ut'qenne*, "people against the rocks," living chiefly at the base of the Rocky mountains on the north side of Peace river.

(6) *Sarcees*, living east of the Rockies by about 51 degrees latitude north.

(7) *Sas-chût-'qenne*, "people of the black bear," from 56 degrees to the north, whose trading post had been Fort Connolly.

(8) *Otzən-ne*, "people between or intermediary," between the territory of the *Saschût'qenne* and that of the *Tselohne* on the west side of the Rocky mountains.

(9) *Tsé-loli-ne*, "people of the end of the rocks," immediately north of the Otzonne; they traded at Fort Grahame.

Morice's classification is frankly based on linguistic, not political or cultural, considerations. Even so it is not altogether satisfactory, for if we include the Sarcee in the Sekani group we should include also the Kaska and other tribes in the north who speak dialects no less closely akin to Sekani. The term would then lose all reference to tribal units. It seems preferable to restrict the name Sekani to its old meaning, as endorsed by the Handbook of American Indians, namely, to the bands of Indians who dwell on the western side of the Rockies around Parsnip and Finlay rivers and their tributaries. They centre at the present time around two posts of the Hudson's Bay Company, one at Fort McLeod and the other at Fort Grahame; but a few of them trade sometimes at other places, such as Takla Lake, Fort Babine on Babine lake, Lower Post on Liard river, McDame Creek on Dease river, and even at Telegraph Creek on the Stikine.

In the early days of the nineteenth century, according to the natives now living around Forts Grahame and McLeod, the Sekani, as defined above, were divided into four bands, each of which possessed its own hunting territory.

(1) *Tsekani* (*tsekani*, Fort McLeod dialect; tsekenna, Fort Grahame dialect): "Rock or Mountain People," who occupied the country from McLeod lake south to the divide, and east to the edge of the prairies.

(2) *Yutuwichan* (Fort McLeod dialect; *yutuchan*, Fort Grahame dialect): the meaning of the name is uncertain, but one conjecture of the natives was "Lake People." This band occupied the country from the north end of McLeod lake down Parsnip and Peace rivers to Rocky Mountain canyon; westward it extended to the headwaters of Manson and Nation rivers, including in its territory Carp lake and the upper reaches of Salmon river.

(3) *Sasuchan* (*sasutten* or *sasuchan*, Fort McLeod dialect; *sasuchan*, Fort Grahame dialect): "People of the Black Bear." The

territory of this band covered all the basin of Finlay river from
the mouth of the Omineca north and west, including Thutade
and Bear lakes.

(4) *Tseloni*: "People of the End of the Rock or Mountain." The
territory of this band comprised the plateau country between
the headwaters of the Finlay and the Liard; the Fox in its upper reaches, and the Kechika or Muddy river, flow through the
centre of the band's domain, but the exact boundaries are uncertain.

Figure 1 (Frontispiece) shows more clearly than any description the boundaries of these four bands, in so far as they can be determined at the present
time; the northern and western limits of the *Tseloni* are still unknown.

At the end of the eighteenth century and the beginning of the nineteenth,
the Sekani, harassed along their eastern boundaries by Beaver and Cree, were
still expanding westward. They had crossed the height of land and occupied
the country around Bear lake and the north end of Takla lake; they had even
established a village on Tachie river, in close proximity to the Carrier of Stuart
lake. Southward they had occupied the country around the junction of Fraser
and Willow rivers until about 1790, when the Shuswap drove them north into
the mountains again.[15] One adventurer encountered by Sir Alexander Mackenzie was journeying with Blackwater River Carrier to Bella Coola, over 200
miles from his home; and as late as 1811 a small war party that left McLeod
lake to raid the Fraser Lake Carrier was stopped by Harmon at Stuart lake.

The establishment of trading posts at Forts McLeod and Connolly checked
their expansion. Fort Connolly became the rendezvous of three tribes, the Sasuchan Sekani, Carrier from lake Babine, and Gitksan from the upper Skeena.
The Sekani and Carrier were generally on friendly terms, but with the Gitksan
the Sekani waged intermittent hostilities, and at last began to retreat eastward.
About 1890, therefore, the Hudson's Bay Company removed the post to Fort
Grahame (then called Bear Lake Outpost or simply B.L.O.) where the Sekani
could trade without molestation. A few of the *Sasuchan*, who had intermarried with Gitksan, moved northward into the Groundhog country at the headwaters of Skeena and Stikine rivers; a few joined the Carrier of Babine; but the
majority settled around the new post on Finlay river and resigned the western
section of their country to the Gitksan and Carrier. So now Gitksan Indians
from Kiskargas and Kuldo claim Bear lake as their territory, and Carrier from
Babine cross Takla lake and hunt on Manson creek and the upper waters of
the Omineca in districts that formerly belonged to the Sekani. On the eastern
side some Beaver Indians from Hudson Hope have at times ascended the
Peace and established trap-lines on Ospika river, and *t'sokoni* Indians from
the Nelson River basin have crossed the mountains to hunt at the head of Akie
river, which flows into the Finlay above Fort Grahame.

---

15. Teit, J., *The Shuswap; The Josup North Pacific Expedition*, Memoirs of the Am Mus. of Nat.
Hist., vol. II, pp. 524, 546ff. [26665-2 ½]

In the south, too, the Sekani have receded. When Harmon was factor at Stuart lake the *Yutuchian* band controlled not only Carp lake, the headwaters of Salmon and Nation rivers, including Nation lakes. Now the Sekani in this region have declined in numbers, and the Carrier have advanced into the Nation Lake district and even to Carp lake, only 4 miles from Fort McLeod. Although there has been much intermarriage between the Stuart Lake Carrier and the combined Tsekani and Yutuwichan bands of Fort McLeod, the latter

Plate 2. Corner of Fort Grahame in 1924, showing a permanent store-
house on posts. (Canadian Museum of History 60673)

still despise the former as "ugly and greasy fish-eaters" and resent their encroachments on Sekani territory. On the other hand, the Carrier immediately south of them, the Fort George group, have declined as much as the Sekani, and no longer frequent the headwaters of the Parsnip as in Mackenzie's day, or visit McLeod lake for trade. Eastward the boundaries remain much the same as formerly, except that the Sekani no longer cross the mountains in their trapping and hunting.

A census made by the Department of Indian Affairs in 1923 gave a total Sekani population of 160, of whom 61 centred around Fort McLeod and 99 around Fort Grahame. The proportion of males to females was 86:74, so that some of the men have to seek wives in other places. Estimates of the population given by earlier writers are unreliable, but without doubt it has greatly declined.

In the summer of 1924 there were 36 adults living around Fort McLeod.

Of this number:

25 were of pure Sekani origin belonging to one or other of the four bands.
3 women were pure Carrier from Stuart lake.
7 were half Sekani, half Carrier.
1 was half Sekani, half Beaver of Hudson Hope.[16]

In the same year, of the 25 adults living at Fort Grahame:

16 were of pure Sekani origin.
1 was a pure Beaver of Hudson Hope.
2 had one parent a Red River native.
3 had one parent a *Tsokoni* Indian from Nelson River area, on the east side of the Rockies.

The intermixture with surrounding tribes is probably greater than appears from this table, which covers only two generations. As the country opens up it will proceed more rapidly, so that within fifty years the Sekani will probably disappear altogether as a separate tribe, unless they are confined on a reservation.

I have mentioned that on the removal of the Hudson's Bay Company's post from Bear lake to Finlay river, a few of the *Sasuchan* Sekani, who had intermarried with Gitksan Indians, drifted north to the Groundhog country. There they have formed a new band known to the *Sasuchan* Indians of Fort Grahame, who meet them around Thutade lake, as the *t'lotona* or "Long Grass" Indians, in allusion to the grassy plateau that forms their hunting ground. Old white residents on Skeena river often name them the "Outlaws," because fugitives from justice in the lower country have taken refuge in this remote band until the hue and cry of pursuit have died away. To the Tahltan of the north they are known as *T'lokotan* or *T'lukotene*, according to the unpublished notes of James Teit. Their territory really belongs to one of the Tahltan clans (*Tlepanoten*), but the usurpation took place without friction, probably because the Tahltan, reduced in numbers by an epidemic, had more or less abandoned this section of the country. The Long Grass Indians generally trade at Telegraph Creek, but do not remain there for the fishing season, as they have no fishing rights in that place. They sometimes visit Bear lake still, and occasionally Takla lake. The number of the band is unknown; in 1923 it appeared to contain about eight families.

The *Tseloni* band amalgamated with the *Sasuchan* or Bear Lake band when Fort Grahame was established, and a new band of breeds, known to the *Tseloni* and *Sasuchan* Indians as Otzane,[17] now occupies its old territory on

---

16. The "Handbook of American Indians North of Mexico", Bull. 30, *Bureau of Am. Ethnology,* appears to be in error when it states (art. Takulli) "An independent band (of Carrier) has settled at Fort McLeod, in the Sekani country."

17. The Gitksan and western Carrier Indians often apply the term *Otzane* to Fort Grahame

Fox and Kechika rivers. The leader and creator of this band was a man named Davie or David, the son of a French-Canadian trapper and a *Sasuchan* mother. Marriage with a Tseloni woman gave him hunting rights in the old *Tseloni* territory, where he raised a family of four daughters. He selected husbands for them with great care; one was a Kaska Indian, the second a *Sasuchan* Sekani, the third a half-breed, with a Scotch father and Kaska mother; the origin of the fourth, now dead, is unknown. Another family of breeds, probably kinsfolk of Davie's wife, joined the band, which in 1924 numbered forty individuals. Davie wielded the authority of a Hebrew patriarch. He kept his party in its hunting grounds aloof from all settlements except for two or three weeks in the early summer when he led them to a trading post, either Lower Post on the Liard or Fort Grahame on Finlay river; and at the posts he camped away from other Indians lest the craving for an idler and more luxurious life should sap the energies of his people and induce some of them to remain. Thus, when he visited Fort Grahame in 1924 he camped on the opposite bank of Finlay river, and departed as soon as he had disposed of his furs. His band was remarkably free of the diseases that have attacked the surrounding Indians; the adults were well clad, the children clean and healthy. As hunters and trappers their reputation was unsurpassed in the whole of British Columbia. But Davie, the leader, was an old man in his seventies, and none of the younger men seemed capable of taking his place. White trappers and prospectors were already invading their hunting grounds, and isolation would soon be impossible. So this attempt to create a new and independent tribe could only prove abortive.

The separation of the Sekani from the Beaver, and the creation of these two new bands within modern times, throws an interesting light on the manner in which new bands and even tribes may have arisen in the distant past. The Beaver, under pressure from the Cree and the early fur traders, adopted a new culture and lost their feeling of kinship with the western members of their group. These western members, the Sekani, had already developed new contacts with Carrier and other tribes, and the formidable barrier of the Rocky mountains assisted a cleavage that was already developing through outside impulses. The levelling power of white civilization has prevented the Beaver and Sekani from becoming markedly distinct, but the parallel case of the Beaver and Sarcee shows what might have happened if the white man had delayed his coming for another century; for the Sarcee, who separated from the Beaver group not much earlier, apparently, than the Sekani, adopted the culture of the Blackfoot in its entirety and retained nothing from their old home except their language.

The rise of the *t'lotona* or Long Grass Indians, and of the *Otzane* of Davie's band, illustrates a second process in the evolution of tribal units. In the case of Davie's band a single family (it makes no difference that one member was a half-breed) became dissatisfied with its old environment and moved away into another territory. In time it developed a spirit of antagonism, or at least of independence, towards its former home and people. The new environment proved favourable, outsiders who married the sons and daughters remained there, and within half a century the one family became the nucleus of a new tribe that claimed a definite territory and possessed a definite name. Davie's band took the name and territory of a kindred band that had recently dissolved; the Long Grass Indians, who probably arose, not from one, but from two or three kindred families, seized part of the territory of an alien tribe and obtained a new name descriptive of their new home. Davie's band is increasing rapidly, but remains in such close contact with the mother group that the two may ultimately unite again, or Davie's band absorb the other. The Long Grass Indians are more remote, and have already taken on the culture of foreign tribes, Gitksan and Tahltan. If conditions favoured their increase, they might easily gain the status of an independent tribe; but their number is small and apparently stationary, so that their neighbours will certainly absorb them, just as the Stuart Lake Carrier have long since absorbed the Sekani whom

Plate 3. Old Davie and other men of the Long Grass band. Photo by Wm. Ware. (Canadian Museum of History, 63435)

Harmon visited on Tachie river.

Still a third process has operated among the Sekani in recent times, the amalgamation of separate bands into a single unit. The *Yutuchan* and *Tsekani* bands, that were often at feud during the first half of the nineteenth century, now occupy a single village at McLeod lake and have almost forgotten their old separation. Similarly the *Tseloni* and *Sasuchan* bands have combined at Fort Grahame. The prime causes of these amalgamations were three: (1) closer contact at the trading posts; (2) the erection of permanent houses of wood around the trading posts instead of temporary lodges of brush or skin; and (3) the partial destruction of the bands through introduced diseases. Two at least of these causes, trading posts and diseases, are directly attributable to Europeans; but parallel forces, for example, destruction through war instead of disease, undoubtedly produced similar amalgamations long before any European made his appearance on the stage of Indian history.

The history of the Sekani bands during the last two hundred years probably repeats, with modifications due to white influence, the history of other Athapaskan-speaking tribes that crossed the Rockies or descended from the north along the western flanks of the mountains many centuries earlier. This will appear still more probable when we examine the social organization and mythology of the present day Sekani, and perceive how they have tried to follow exactly the same road as their Carrier and Tahltan neighbours.

CHAPTER 3
CONFLICTS WITH NEIGHBOURING TRIBES

The preceding section outlines the general history of the Sekani from their discovery to the present day. Down to the middle of the nineteenth century, the Cree and Beaver raided them on the east; on the west the Sekani attacked and were counter attacked by the Gitksan. The Carrier of Babine and Stuart lakes were generally friendly, but the Sekani often raided other divisions of the Carrier tribes to the south, and their neighbours, the Shuswap. Each tribe has its own version of these conflicts, but all blend truth and fiction so inextricably that it is impossible to reconstruct the true course of events. A few Sekani accounts are given here, prefixed with a list of tribal designations, since confusion often arises through a tribe being known under different names to the surrounding peoples.

The Sekani call the Gitksan Indians *ada'*, "labret" people, because they wore labrets in their lips.[1] The Gitksan name the Sekani *t'set'sa'ut*, a term of uncertain meaning that includes also the Tahltan and Kaska tribes to the north, and the Athapaskan tribe, now extinct, that once occupied some territory on Portland canal. The Carrier are named *Agili*[2] by the Sekani, a word that seems to mean "something tied up." The Fort Grahame Sekani interpreted it as "back-pack," because the Carrier who visited them so often carried packs on their backs; but the Sekani of Fort McLeod explained it more plausibly as "the people who are 'tied up' with fixed dwellings, possess permanent homes," in contrast with the Sekani themselves, who lived a migratory life. Different branches of the Carrier are given special names; thus the Fort Grahame Indians call the Babine Lake Carrier *naadotenne*, "fish-hawk people," because, like hawks, they live mainly on fish; and the Carrier of Fort George are known to the Fort McLeod Sekani as *kleglindjenne*, "people at the mouth of the river." The Carrier for their part call the Sekani *t'tatten*, "people of the beaver dams," a term that the Sekani of Fort Grahame apply in turn to the Beaver of Hudson Hope, although fully aware of its application to themselves. To the north the Sekani knew of the *na'ani*, "faraway people" or Tahltan, and the *esbaataotenne*, "goat-people"[3] whose centre is at Lower Post on Liard river. For the Beaver as a whole the Sekani have no general designation, but speak of the *adzikochanne*, "people who live at the mountain that looks like a buffalo head," i.e. the Beaver of Hudson Hope; the *Dodachenne* (Fort McLeod term),

---

1. This is probably the same word as *attah*, the name they applied to the Shuswap. "They (two Meadow Indians) desired us to be on our guard and beware of the At-tah which is the name both them and the big men gives the Atnah tribe whom they represent as more treacherous than really wicked and wood likely if not aware shoot their arrows at us" (First Journal of Simon Fraser, May 28, 1806).

2. Morice (*The Great Déné Race, Anthropos* I, p. 275), says that the Sekani call the Carriers *arelne* ("Carriers"), but I did not hear this term.

3. The "Sheep Indians" of anthropological literature.

or *Dodachanne* (Fort Grahame term) "people of the dead water below the canyon," i.e. the Beaver of Moberly lake; the *t'lokotenne* (Fort McLeod) or *t'lokochanne* (Fort Grahame), "the grass or meadow people," i.e. the Beaver of the Grande Prairie region; and the *t'satene* (Fort McLeod) or *t'satou* (Fort Grahame), "beaver people," i.e. the Beaver of Fort St. John and along Peace river to the eastward. A semi-mythical people called *Dishinni* was commonly identified with the Cree.

The Gitksan encountered only the Sasuchan and Long Grass bands of Sekani, whose territories bordered their own at Bear lake. The Hudson's Bay Company's post established at this lake in 1826 served not only the Sekani, but the Gitksan villages of Kispiox, Kiskargas, and Kuldo. Naturally conflicts arose over hunting rights in the vicinity, and the Sekani finally retreated northward and eastward. Nevertheless, in their own versions of the struggle, they invariably claim the superiority. The Hudson's Bay Company's post, they say, was built on an island. Five Gitksan Indians from Kiskargas once tried to reach it on a raft, but were seen by a Sasuchan Indian on the island, who summoned his two sons by sending up a smoke signal. Before his sons arrived the Gitksan drew near, and he shot four of them with his arrows; the fifth he allowed to return, bidding him warn his people that the Sekani would treat in the same way every other party of Gitksan that ventured near Bear lake.

On another occasion a party from Kispiox fought with the Sasuchan Sekani near the shore of Bear lake. The Sekani wore on their left arms oblong shields of wood (*askwani*) coated on the outside with pitch and sand. One man whose dream-guardian was wind tripped over a stick, and a Kispiox Indian struck at him three times with an ax, but each time the blow was foiled by his dream-guardian. Then a brother-in-law came to the rescue and killed the Kispiox man. The Sekani slew ten of their enemies in this fight. The Gitksan of Kispiox and Kiskargas then requested a Stuart Lake Carrier, Ishal, who had married a Kiskargas woman, to negotiate a peace with the Sasuchan Sekani. The two bands held a great potlatch at Bear lake, and the two leaders of the Sekani exchanged clothes with the two leaders of the Gitksan. Thereafter they lived at peace, and the Kispiox Indians continued to visit Bear lake to exchange for the furs of the Sekani trade goods that had come up Skeena river from the coast.

It was several years before the conclusion of this peace, around 1840, apparently, that a few families of the Sasuchan Sekani broke away from the main band and established themselves as the T'lotona or Long Grass Indians in the Groundhog country. Although they married frequently with the Gitksan, from whom they were separated by Klappan mountains, any member of one tribe who hunted in the territory of the other was killed without pity. Five Long Grass Indians and several Gitksan were killed in a fight about 1865. Then a joint potlatch was held at the headwaters of Nass river, and the Gitksan as a mark of good will presented to a Long Grass family a little girl eleven years of age. The girl married a Long Grass chief, with whom she lived about thirty years; after his death his relatives conducted her to Bear lake and delivered her back to her people.[4]

The Sekani remember no conflicts with the Tahltan or Kaska Indians to the north, or with the Carrier of Babine lake; but they speak of many feuds with the Carrier of Stuart lake, claiming that the latter avoided them and fought from ambush only. There is a tradition, probably fanciful, that a Stuart Lake war party, travelling in seven canoes down Parsnip and Peace rivers, ran into the Rocky Mountain canyon, from which nothing emerged except fragments of their canoes.

John Tod, who was factor at Fort McLeod from 1823 to 1832, witnessed the ill feeling that existed between the Sekani and the Carrier in his day. He writes:

> At Fort McLeod, where Mr. Tod had lived nine years, feuds among the tribes were rife, and consequently hostilities often broke out among them. The Indians used to tell him that the bow and arrow was a good deal more effective in war than the musket. And in case of hunting buffalo, deer, etc., the arrow by penetrating, stuck fast, so that should the animals enter the woods or bush it was found they were unable to proceed far before they fell. Ere the gun, a great many more Indians also were killed by the use of the bow, now almost wholly out of date.
>
> On one occasion a tribe came into the fort. The Indians were called Sycanees and came from the Rocky Mountains. They went in to trade, smoke, etc. I went outside and counted another band of canoes coming up with Indians. They also had tobacco given them for a smoke. These were the Suckalies (Carrier) and were at enmity with the other tribe. They met and there was a row. On each side of the big mess hall, they were drawn up ready to use bows and arrows, guns, etc., on one another. Hearing of this I rushed in bare-armed, commencing to abuse them at an awful rate; swore and kicked; rushed one side, then at the other, seized their arms and banged them about generally. One fellow was about driving a dagger into another. Seizing this I took it from him, and the mark of it remains in my hand to this day. At last I completely cowed them.[5]

The Tlokotenne or Meadow Indians, of Pine and upper Smoky rivers, were always on friendly terms with the Sekani, whom they met frequently along the eastern foothills of the Rocky mountains. Both bands traded at Hudson Hope during the first years of the nineteenth century and both were attacked by the Tsatene lower down the river, so that by 1826, when Sir George Simpson passed through on his way to the coast, the Meadow Indians had apparently

---

4. See Preface

5. *History of New Caledonia and North-West Coast*, by John Tod; Mss. Series C No. 27, Bancroft Collection (from copy in Geological Survey Library, Ottawa).

disappeared from this region as a separate band, and the Sekani of Finlay river were avoiding Peace River trading posts in favour of the post at Bear lake. The Tsatene, like the Cree, sometimes crossed the mountains and raided the Sekani in their own territory. They are said to have wiped out ten families at the head of Parsnip river, carrying away the younger women and the children. This was before the Sekani had obtained many fire-arms. Fort McLeod natives state that the last encounter occurred at Carp lake somewhere around 1850, when the Sekani, discovering a party of Tsatene lurking in their vicinity, shot one of them from ambush. In the morning they heard wailing on a hill-top, and found a corpse that had just been buried. The other Tsatene fled, and never crossed the mountains again.

From Fort McLeod comes also the following story:

A man went out to hunt moose one morning, leaving his wife and mother to move camp. As the women walked along their dog barked at something in the rear, and the younger woman, going back to see what was the matter, found ten Tsatene warriors holding it by the leash. They captured her, but allowed her to return with the dog when she promised not to reveal their presence. Her mother-in-law asked her why the dog had barked, but she merely answered that she had seen nothing, and knew no reason. The two women continued their journey and made camp. When the man returned late in the evening, carrying a moose, his mother drew him aside, saying "Come here. I have some meat for you" and she added in a whisper "Keep watch to-night, for your wife is concealing something." The man and his mother both kept watch. Toward dawn the old woman went down to a creek and waited, listening. She heard men stepping into the water lower down and counted them, breaking pieces from a twig for each one; there were ten. She hastened back to camp to tell her son, but already he had heard the noise and was trying to withdraw his bow from the pack. Now his wife, when arranging the pack the night before, had wound the bow-string so that he could not withdraw the weapon without unfastening the entire pack. Enraged at her treachery, he leaped on her with both feet and killed her. Six Tsatene men sprang out and tried to capture him, but they fell to the ground, one after another, the tendons of their heels cut by the old mother with a small flint knife. The hunter, whose dream-guardian was cariboo, sprang into the bushes crying *sh sh* and so strong was his medicine-power that the Tsatene could neither hold him nor overtake him. The four uninjured Tsatene then went away, leaving their disabled comrades to starve. The old woman remained unharmed, for the Tsatene, instead of killing old people, merely disfigured them by crushing the nasal bones between the fingers. When the hunter returned three nights later, she was lying on the ground awaiting him. He whispered "Come," and she arose and fled with him. The six Tsatene warriors died of starvation.

The fame of the Beaver spread even to the Carrier of Fraser lake and its vicinity, who still threaten their naughty children that the Tsatene will carry them away. But among the Sekani they were less dreaded than than the Cree, *Dishinni*, who had passed the mountains before Mackenzie's day, and who extended their raids, then or later, to Carp lake, between McLeod and Stuart lakes, and to Fort Grahame on Finlay river. The Gitksan and the Tahltan also knew and dreaded them, though they probably never came into direct conflict with them, but merely heard of their depredations from the Sekani. The Cree have, therefore, become a semi-mystical people among these western tribes, though very real to the Sekani. The meaning of the word *Dishinni* is unknown.

The natives of Fort McLeod say that the Cree, armed with guns, often wandered to Carp lake before the first white men appeared, and that the Sekani, having only bows and arrows at that time, could offer no effective resistance. The Cree raided them principally for women, whom they carried off to become their wives. They attacked the Sekani in three places one summer, at the head of Parsnip river, on Pack river, just below Trout lake, and at Finlay Forks, the junction of Finlay and Parsnip rivers. Many Sekani of both the Tsekani and Yutuchan bands were killed in that year.

The Cree once carried away two women of the Tsekani band. Though well treated these women became homesick and seized the first opportunity to escape. They possessed no knives, and had no means of making fire; but they snared grouse with spruce roots and ate them raw; and they built rude rafts to cross the rivers they encountered. After travelling in this way for two weeks they reached their own country.

Two brothers were hunting groundhog one summer in the high mountains near the head of Smoky river. Two Cree, one of whom carried a gun, entered their camp while they were up the mountain, and only their wives remained behind. The Cree did not harm the women, intending to carry them away; but they ascended a short distance above the camp to intercept their husbands. Toward evening the two hunters appeared on the crest of a ridge above them. One Cree shouted "I am going to shoot," and fired his gun; but the bullet passed between the two men. The elder Sekani said to the younger, "Let us throw rocks at them, or they will kill us." The younger brother threw a rock, and missed. Then the elder brother, whose dream-guardian was the groundhog, rubbed a large stone against his chest, breathed on it, and hurling with all his might, struck a Cree on the forehead. The other Cree, seeing his companion dead, fled; but the same hunter threw another stone in the same way, struck him in the nape of the neck, and killed him also.

East of Parsnip river one spring was a family consisting of a hunter and his young wife, the girl's mother, and her younger brother, the last being a mere boy. While the man and boy were hunting some Cree entered their camp, killed the old woman and kept the girl as a captive. They then awaited the return of her husband. The girl heard him crossing a stream near the camp and shouted, "Run. The Cree have captured me." The man dropped his pack and fled, followed by the boy; and the Cree pursued them. As the boy could not run fast enough, his brother-in-law said "Go back and weep as you give yourself up. The Cree never kill small boys like you." The boy returned weeping, and surrendered himself to the leading Cree, who planted a hat on his head to show possession and sent him on to the camp. The hunter escaped, but the Cree carried away his wife and brother-in-law, whom they secured each night with cords, fastening one end to the neck and hair of each captive, and the other to a warrior's waist. After they had travelled three or four days, the girl remembered that her dream-guardian was the beaver, and that she carried a small piece of flint like a beaver's tooth under her belt. That night, when the Cree were sound asleep, she cut the cords with the knife. The two children then fled to the woods, and concealed themselves in the leafy branches of a tall tree. The Cree sent out a bird, one of their dream-guardians, to look for them. It settled on top of the tree and called *ka ka ka;* but the girl, who had greater medicine-power than the Cree, threw a stick and killed it.

All day the Cree searched vainly; one man even gazed right into the tree where the children were hidden without seeing them. When night came, and their enemies had returned to camp, the girl and boy descended from the tree and fled towards Parsnip river. Now when the girl's husband returned to his camp after the departure of the Cree an eagle, his dream-guardian, circled over his head and said to him: "In nine or ten days your wife will pass by here." He, therefore, killed three beaver and built two canoes of spruce bark. One canoe and two of the beaver he left on the river bank for his wife and her brother; in the other canoe, with one beaver, he returned to his home. Within ten days, as the eagle had foretold, the girl and her brother returned, found the canoe and the two beaver, and regained their people.

A Sekani hunter and his aged mother went to Carp lake to fish, and other Sekani intended to follow them. Three families of mixed Cree and Beaver came to the same lake. The eldest Cree, named Usdjenta, had three wives, one of them a Sekani woman named Chiwan who had been taken prisoner many years before; the second Cree had two wives, the third one; and all three men had many children. They pitched their camp at a distance from the Sekani, and never moved away from it after dark. Consequently the hunter, instead of fleeing and abandoning his aged mother, left his camp before daylight every morning, travelled far out into the woods in different directions, marking the snow to indicate to approaching Sekani that there were Cree in the neighbourhood, and returned long after sunset. His mother, whom the Cree did not molest by day, sat up and kept watch while he slept. At last eight Sekani families came and joined him. Usdjenta, the eldest Cree, decided to attack them, although his two companions shrank from the unequal contest; but Chiwan his Sekani wife, secretly warned her people, who attacked first, killing men, women and children, even a young girl who fled on to the ice and begged for mercy. Chiwan alone they spared, although they killed her children, lest when they grew up they would try to avenge their father's death.

In another year some thirty Cree paddling in three canoes down Parsnip river discovered three Sekani families camped on the bank. While the children fled, their parents loaded their guns; but the Cree shouted "Friends, friends," making signs of peace, and disembarked close to their camp. The Sekani believed them, brought back the children from the woods and joined in a common meal. One of the Cree, taking a fancy to a little Sekani girl, said to her, "Run away and hide. In a few minutes we are going to attack your people"; but the child, too young to understand the meaning of his words, neither ran away nor told her people. As soon as they had eaten the Cree went down to their canoes; but when the Sekani followed to see them depart the Cree seized their rifles and shot down the whole party. Then they plundered the tents and continued their way down the river, toward Finlay Forks.

Now it happened that a large band of Sekani was hunting elk near Finlay Forks; three men, with dogs, were pursuing a wounded elk that had fled up the mountain, while the other hunters ranged themselves along the bank at intervals of about half a mile to intercept the animal when it was driven into the water. The oldest and most experienced hunter, who was stationed at the southern end of the line, saw a man examining the river from a promontory farther up, and, suspecting that he might be a Cree, launched his canoe into the water and watched.[6] As soon as the Cree rounded the point in their three canoes, he pushed out from under the bank and fled downstream, shouting to each hunter as he passed, "The Crees are coming. Follow quickly to protect our families." One after another the hunters shot out from the bank and followed him to the camp. The Cree approached, shouting "Friends, friends," and,

Plate 4. Sekani women and children at Fort Grahame. (Canadian Museum of History 60707.)

meeting with no hostility, stopped close to the camp, dragged their spruce-bark canoes on to the bank for sleeping-shelters and prepared to dry their meat. The Sekani recognized some of their kinsmen's possessions in the hands of the Cree, and an old woman named Kloazi, Mouse, brandishing a spear, urged her people to take vengeance; but they were afraid of a battle, because the two parties were almost equal in numbers. So the Cree and Sekani remained

---

6. Indians travelling on a river in hostile country stopped at every curve and landed one of their number on the point to search the route ahead.

side by side for two days, neither party daring to attack the other, and neither willing to leave first lest it should be trapped on the march. So they sat in their camps and feasted, the Sekani supplying most of the meat. On the second day the Cree had an argument among themselves, and one man said "I am going to embark. Who will come with me?" Three men paddled away down the river. The other Cree then said to the Sekani, "Tomorrow we are going to hunt elk. Let some of your warriors accompany us." The Sekani selected four young men, whom they warned to keep watch and to sleep at a distance from their companions. The Cree and the four Sekani travelled fast all day without halting; when night came they built their fires some distance apart and kept watch, both sides fearing an attack. The Sekani said to each other in the morning "Let us pretend to hunt squirrels, and when the Cree go on ahead we will run away." Soon they came to a grove of jackpine where a squirrel was racing among the branches. The Sekani chased it laughing, and when the Cree called to them they answered "Go ahead. We will overtake you presently." But as soon as the Cree were out of sight the Sekani fled over a low hill. The Cree fired a few shots at them without result, then, fearful of returning to their canoes, continued down the river on foot to their own country.

On another occasion a party of Cree armed with guns ascended Finlay river and pursued two Sekani men of the Sasuchan band into a mountain a little north of Fort Grahame. One of the Sekani hurled down a large rock, which struck a Cree on the forehead and killed him. Hence the mountain is now named "Man struck by a rock."

Two families of the Sasuchan band who were descending Finlay river to the Forks to hunt moose were massacred by some *Nadowa* Cree who wore their hair short, whereas the other Cree who were raiding the Sekani at this time wore their hair long. The Beaver of Hudson Hope now apply the name *Nadowa* to the Cree of Moberly lake, a few miles to the south.

To the T'lotona band of Sekani, as to the Tahltan and Gitksan, the Cree, *Dishinni*, have become a semi-mythical people. They are always dressed in buckskin adorned with beads, and travel four or six in a band, without women. If observed they disappear, changing into burned trees or vanishing into thin air without leaving a trace. Sometimes they stand four in a row on a hill-top and watch runners being dispatched to discover who they are; but when the runners draw near they disappear. To shoot at them is useless, for they can catch a bullet in the air. They hover around camps to steal the women, making mysterious noises; the T'lotona have often seen their footprints or the marks they have made on trees. Berry season is their favourite time for raids. They expectorate on their hands and wave them in the air when they sight a woman, and the woman, unable to scream, falls into their hands; or they transform themselves into logs when the men pass by, only to resume their human form and seize any women who may be following behind. One party of *Dishinni* penetrated as far as Kispiox, the Gitksan village on the upper Skeena; but when it saw the women carrying baby cradles it turned back, mistaking the cradles for coffins. Many years ago Dishinni stole a four-year-old T'lotona boy and taught him to perform the same feats as themselves; but when he grew up they sent him back to his people to tell of their power. The boy's name was Migina, "Singing," because he never ate, but lived by singing only; he could vanish into the air under the eyes of the onlookers. He did not remain with the T'lotona, but returned to the *Dishinni* as soon as he had displayed his powers. The raids of the Cree seem to have continued down to about the middle of the nineteenth century, fifty years after the establishment of the post at McLeod lake. The Sekani, like the Blackfoot and other tribes, dreaded their medicine power almost as much as their raids. They relate the following story.

An early factor at Fort McLeod named McIntosh had two wives, one a Cree woman, the other a Carrier from Stuart lake. His Cree wife bore him one son. When the boy was eight years old McIntosh hired a Sekani Indian to perform some work at the post during the spring. The Indian was lazy, and instead of working went down to Trout lake to fish with his brother Kłezuye, but fell sick there and died. Kłezuye went back to McLeod lake, and asked the factor for some blankets so that he might bury his .brother in proper state; but McIntosh refused, stating, very imprudently, that the man had been such a worthless fellow, that he himself had caused, his death through evil medicine. Kłezuye returned to Trout lake brooding over McIntosh's remarks. Three days later he secretly re-ascended Crooked river to McLeod lake and awaited an opportunity to take vengeance.

Now every morning McIntosh's wives used to go out in a canoe to set a fish-net. As Kłezuye watched them he prayed his dream-guardian, the beaver, to fill the factor with its own restless and sleepless nature in springtime. His prayer was answered. One morning McIntosh went out of his store and told his wives that he himself would set the net and take his boy with him. They set the net at the mouth of Carp Lake creek and paddled back toward the fort. As they were passing the rancherie the boy saw Kłezuye aiming his gun at them and shouted a warning to his father. The Indian fired immediately, and the two bullets with which he had loaded his gun struck McIntosh under the arm. The factor leaped forward, fell overboard, and was drowned, while his murderer fled around the back of the rancherie to ːhe mouth of Pack river, where he had left his canoe, and paddled up to the factor's store as though he had just returned from Trout lake. As he loitered around the store the boy recognized him and pointed him out to his father's wives. They did not dare to shoot him, but two days later, when he left with other Sekani for the hunting grounds, the Cree woman bent two sticks into the shape of halfmoons, cut four human figures in a blanket, and arranged the six objects in a line; then, with her son and fellow-wife, she hurried away to Stuart lake. On the trail she met a friend, and warned him not to go near the trading post on McLeod lake; but he disregarded the warning, stayed a few hours at the post and continued down Pack river to his fellow countrymen. Soon his legs swelled so greatly that he died within a few hours, and more than half the Sekani perished in the same way. Thus the Cree woman avenged her husband.

After the middle of the nineteenth century peace reigned in the Sekani country. The surrounding tribes, greatly reduced in numbers, had become outwardly Europeanized, and were more concerned in protecting their own territories from the encroachments of white settlers, traders, and prospectors, than in raiding their neighbours. The Sekani too changed. They adopted European clothing and weapons, abandoned their temporary lodges of brush or skins in favour of permanent cabins, and took on the externals of the new civilization that approached them from every quarter. The laws of the white man extended everywhere and the tribes could wander freely into the territories of their former enemies. The Sekani did wander, some down Peace river to the settlements of the Beaver, others west to the Carrier of Stuart and Babine lakes and to the Gitksan of Skeena river. A few settled in those places, others returned with alien wives; but the majority of the Sekani kept themselves isolated in their old haunts, losing more and more their ancient customs and beliefs under the influence of the missionaries and traders.

CHAPTER 4
PHYSICAL APPEARANCE AND MATERIAL CULTURE

Mackenzie has left the following description of the Sekani whom he met at the headwaters of Parsnip river:[1]

They are low in stature, not exceeding five feet six or seven inches; and they are of that meagre appearance which might be expected of a people whose life is one succession of difficulties, in procuring subsistence. Their faces are round, with high cheek bones; and their eyes, which are small, are of a dark brown colour; the cartilage of their nose is perforated, but without any ornaments suspended from it; their hair is of a dingy black, hanging loose and in disorder over their shoulders, but irregularly cut in the front, so as not to obstruct the sight; their beards are eradicated, with the exception of a few straggling hairs, and their complexion is a swarthy yellow. . . . (The women) are in general of a more lusty make than the other sex, and taller in proportion, but infinitely their inferiors in cleanliness. A black artificial stripe crosses the face beneath the eye, from ear to ear, which I first took for scabs, from the accumulation of dirt on it. Their hair, which is longer than that of the men, is divided from the forehead to the crown, and drawn back in long plaits behind the cars.

The Sekani of the present day resemble in height the nearest Carriers, males averaging 169.3 cm., females 157.8 cm. Both tribes are slightly taller than the coastal tribes of British Columbia, from whom the Sekani differ also by their narrowness of head and sparseness of build, the latter a consequence, probably, of their more active life, and greater privations.[2] The narrowness of the head causes a lower cephalic index, bringing the Sekani into the sub-brachycephalic group; the figures are males 79–3, females 79–2. The combination of narrow head and lean features makes the cheek-bones appear unusually outstanding, although actually both the breadth and length of the face seem to differ little from those of tribes to the westward. The nasal indices were, males 70–7, females 71-6, figures slightly lower than those given for coast tribes, through a reduction, apparently, in the breadth of the nose; but in this case a comparison with the measurements of another observer is unsatisfactory because of differences in technique and the difficulty of determining the nasion in living subjects.[3]

---

1. Mackenzie, Sir Alexander, *Voyages from Montreal through the Continent of North America to the Frozen and Pacific Oceans in 1789 and 1793*; London, 1801, pp. 204ff.

2. Many of the Fort Grahame Sekani in 1924 were distinctly undernourished, and suffering from skin and eye diseases.

3. Detailed figures of Sekani measurements and a comparison with the Beaver, Chipewyan, and Cree Indians, are given by Professor J.C. Boileau Grant, in Bulletin 81 of the National Museum

The eyes vary from dark brown to medium brown, and occasionally show the epicanthic fold. The hair is black, and either straight or with low waves. Formerly men as well as women often parted it in the middle and sometimes plaited it into two braids. The southern Sekani state that after the establish ment of the trading posts on McLeod lake some of the men shaved the crown of the head and painted it with red ochre;[4] but the Sekani of the Finlay River basin claim that this practice was restricted to old women. The Tahltan paint ed only the parting of the hair with red ochre, according to some notes by the late James Teit, and the Carrier seem not to have painted the head at all. At the present time the men trim their hair with scissors. and either eradicate their beards, as in Mackenzie's day, or shave with European razors; in any case their beards are scanty. The women still part the hair in the middle, but usu ally leave it unbraided, except the women of the Long Grass band, who, being in close contact with the Gitksan and Tahltan Indians, pay more attention to its dressing and braid it with multi-coloured ribbons. Short hair being consid ered a disgrace except in widows, the girls of this band rub their heads with a preparation of roasted wild celery or parsnip (*Heracleum lanatum*) mixed with fat taken from the head of the mountain sheep. The Gitksan Indians of upper Skeena river, and the neighbouring Carrier, use the same preparation. but with bear fat substituted for mountain sheep fat; they claim it not only foments the growth of the hair, but lightens its colour.

DRESS

Both sexes have long since adopted European clothing, and retain of their old dress only the moccasins and mittens. Mackenzie describes the ancient costume as follows:

> Their dress consists of robes made of the skins of the beaver, the ground hog, and the reindeer, dressed in the hair, and of the mooseskin without it. All of them are ornamented with a fringe, while some of them have tassels hanging down the seams; those of the ground hog are decorated on the fur side with the tails of the animals, which they do not separate from them. Their gar ments they tie over the shoulders, and fasten them around the middle with a belt of green skin, which is as stiff as horn. Their leggings are long, and, if they were topped with a waistband, might be called trowsers; they, as well as their shoes, are made of dressed moose, elk, or reindeer skin. The organs of genera tion they leave uncovered.
>
> The women differ little in their dress from the men. except

of Canada. For the statements in this paragraph I have compared my own measurements (in Grant's report just mentioned) with those given by Dr. Franz Boas for the coast tribes in "The North-Western Tribes of Canada," *Report of the British Association for the Advancement of Science*, 1898, pp. 628–83.

4. The Carrier report the same practice among the Beaver Indians.

in the addition of an apron, which is fastened round the waist, and hangs down to the knees.

They have a brown kind of earth in great abundance, with which they rub their clothes, not only for ornament but utility, as it prevents the leather from becoming hard after it has been wetted.

This description probably applies to the summer costume only. Mackenzie's robe was perhaps the sleeveless shirt (*gassue'*), laced together at the shoulder and fastened around the waist with a belt. Sleeves were added later, and some of the natives attached two strings to the bottom which they passed between the legs and tied around the waist; but at an early date they adopted the moose-skin breechclout (*tson or entsat*) of the eastern tribes. The women seem to have lengthened the shirt, first to the knees, then to the ankles; and they replaced the short skirt (*chaka*) with a European petticoat. The commonest material for shirts was moose or caribou hide, though other skins were employed on occasion, such as lynx, beaver, and mountain goat. Fort McLeod natives speak of loon-skin shirts among the neighbouring Carrier Indians of Stuart lake, but deny their use by any Sekani band.

In cold weather both sexes threw over the shirt a rectangular robe (*tsede'*) of groundhog or woven rabbit skins, fastening it over one shoulder and drawing it in at the waist with a belt. Some of the best hunters had robes of marten fur, but

Plate 5. A Sekani robe of groundhog skins.
(Canadian Museum of History 75944)

they disappeared as soon as marten fur became commercially valuable. The groundhog robe, though no longer worn on the person, survives as a sleeping robe or covering for a bed. An average specimen 5 feet by 6 feet, such as that shown in Plate 5, contains about twenty-four skins arranged in parallel rows, trimmed to fit and sometimes roughly matched for colour.

Leggings (*esle*) were generally of caribou hide. Those of the men reached to the thighs, and the narrowed upper ends tucked into the belt; but women's leggings barely reached the knees.

Moccasins (*ke*) were generally made of moose or caribou hide, but sometimes of the more lasting beaver skin. The Sekani of the Parsnip and Finlay River basins wore inside them socks of groundhog or rabbit fur, but the Long Grass people are said to have made the feet of double thickness and dispensed with socks. Five pairs of moose-hide moccasins collected at McLeod lake and at Fort Grahame in 1924 all conform to exactly the same pattern (Plate 6). They are of three pieces, a bottom or foot, a tongue, and an ankle flap. A T-shaped seam runs up the back from below the heel, and a straight seam from the bottom of the tongue to a little under the toes. The rounded tongue extends down to about the base of the toes, and its visible edge is outlined with two rather fine strands of coloured horse-hair, substituted for the older moose-hair or porcupine quills. Overlying the tongue is a false tongue, in two specimens of smoked moose-hide, in the other three of coloured cloth; on this are floral designs worked in beads or silk. A band of coloured cloth conceals the seam uniting the flap with the bottom piece. This flap, which extends about half-way up the leg, is kept in position by two rawhide laces whose ends are sewn (in one case knotted through a hole) on each side of the moccasin about the junction of flap, tongue, and bottom piece. Most of the sewing has been done with sinew, but the cloth is attached with cotton thread.

In winter both sexes wore round caps (*tsa'*) of various furs, beaver, marten, fisher, groundhog, etc. Among the Long Grass Indians half a century ago the caps of the women were shaped like bonnets, fitting around the neck, whereas men's caps, made of beaver skin or from the paws of the lynx, merely covered the top of the head; whether this applied also to the main Sekani bands I do not know. A man who had acquired "medicine power" through some animal often wore a cap made from its fur, especially when going to war; or he would attach to his cap the tail of the animal, or a tail feather from his bird "medicine," to ensure good luck.

Mittens (*bat*), like other parts of the costume, were of various skins, that of the moose being preferred. The majority are now stitched with European thread on a sewing machine, and ornamented with beaded designs that are predominantly floral (Plate 6). Some natives even prefer gloves, which they make themselves or purchase from the Hudson's Bay Company.

The Sekani never practised tattooing, apparently, nor could any of the living natives recall the black stripe painted across the face beneath the eyes that Mackenzie noticed in the women. They remembered, however, that both men and women daubed red ochre mixed with fat over the cheeks, and often

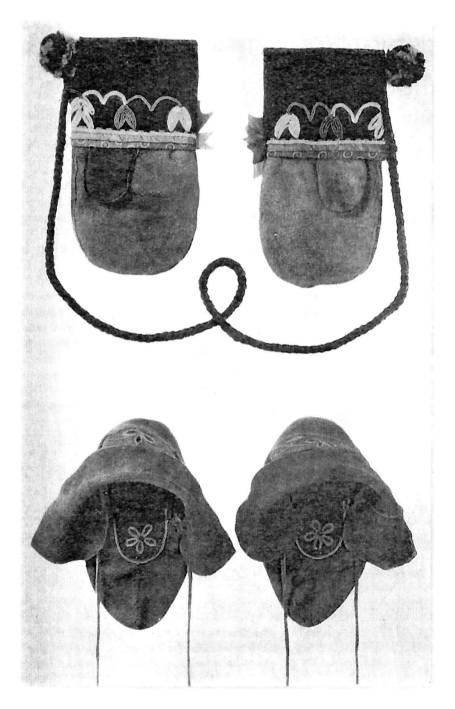

Plate 6. Sekani mittens and moccasins, beaded.
(Canadian Museum of History 75945)

rubbed off portions of the ochre to leave some fantastic design, of no set pattern, but pleasing to the whim of the wearer.

Of their ornaments Mackenzie says:

> They have also a few white beads, which they get where they procure their iron: they are from a line to an inch in length and are worn in their ears, but are not of European manufacture. These, with bracelets made of horn and bone, compose all the ornaments which decorate their persons. Necklaces of the grizzly or white bear's claws, are worn exclusively by the men.

The white beads, of course, were dentalia shells, obtained through Carrier and Gitksan natives from the coast; they were worn both in the ears and noses. Other ornaments worn by western tribes, such as anklets and cedar-bark necklaces, were not adopted by the Sekani; nor did they sprinkle their heads with eagle-down at dances, though both sexes planted the white plumes of the eagle in their hair.

DWELLINGS

Both in the Parsnip and Finlay River basins the Sekani lived originally in conical lodges covered with spruce bark, for which in post-European times they often substituted moose-skins. Morice has described their dwellings thus:

> The habitations of the Tse'kehne, whether in winter or in summer are built after the eastern or conical model. Four long poles with forking extremities are set up one against another, the lower ends of which form on the ground a square on the dimensions of which will depend the size of the lodge. A score or so of other poles are then set up in a circle, the top of each resting on the point of intersection of the first four. In winter small fascines of spruce are laid horizontally all around the lower perimeter of this frame, so as to leave as few points of access as possible for the cold air from underneath the outer covering, which is then wrapped around the cone resulting from the converging poles. This covering consists of dressed moose skins sewn together, and its perpendicular edges correspond to the entrance of the lodge. They are either buttoned or clasped together from four to five feet above the ground up to the top. On one side of the opening thereby produced is sewn a smaller skin, which forms the door. Two sticks attached transversely thereto on the inside give it the requisite consistency, while the upper one, which slightly projects beyond the edge of the skin door, serves as a latch, its projecting end being, when necessary, fastened with a string to the adjoining part of the lodge covering. The smoke escapes through the interstices between the converging poles left uncovered at the top. To guard against snow, rain, or adverse winds, an additional piece of skin is sewn on the outside

from the apex of the conical covering down to some distance, while its free side is secured to a long pole planted in the ground close by. This appendage is utilized as a shutter wherewith the top opening of the lodge is partially, or entirely covered, as the state of the weather may suggest . . . Summer and winter, the fire is started right in the centre, and, instead of the wooden tripod used among the Blackfeet to suspend their kettles, the Tse'kehne prefer a stick reaching horizontally at the proper distance above the fire to two opposite poles of the frame to which it is fastened.[5]

This was the typical winter dwelling, though it was used in summer also. At that season, however, the Sekani often contented themselves with crude wind-breaks of the same conical shape, but covered with spruce bark, hides, or boughs to a height of only 4 or 5 feet, leaving the top quite open. Most, if

Plate 7. Rude dwelling of poles and spruce bark, Fort McLeod. Between the two Sekani women is the wife of a Kentucky trapper who spent the winter of 1923–24 on Misinchinka river. (Canadian Museum of History 60678)

not all, the Indians now have cloth tents, but similar shelters may still be seen among the neighbouring Beaver of Hudson Hope. Quite as common, perhaps, as the conical summer wind-break was the simple lean-to, constructed by planting three or four sticks in line at an angle of about 50 degrees and covering them with spruce bark, boughs, or hides.

In 1924 there were several wooden houses, frame or log, at both McLeod lake and Fort Grahame. At the former place there was also a rectangular lodge

---

5. Morice, Rev. A.G., *Notes on the Western Dénés*; Trans. Can. Inst., vol. IV, 1892-93, p. 192f.

of poles whose walls and roof were covered with spruce bark. The sheathing extended over the lower half of the walls only, the upper parts being left open (Plate 7).

The furniture inside these dwellings was naturally meagre. Mackenzie sums it up thus:

> Their kettles are also made of watape (woven spruce roots), which is so closely woven that they never leak, and they heat water in them, by putting red-hot stones into it. There is one kind of them, made of spruce-bark, which they hang over the fire, but at such a distance as to receive the heat without being within reach of the blaze; a very tedious operation. They have various dishes of wood and bark; spoons of horn and wood, and buckets; bags of leather and net-work, and baskets of bark, some of which hold their fishing-tackle, while others are contrived to be carried on the back.[6]

In post-European times the Sekani substituted birch bark for spruce bark in their cooking vessels and baskets, although, unlike the Beaver Indians, they never replaced their spruce-bark canoes with birch-bark ones. For torches they used bundles of jackpine twigs instead of rolls of birch bark, lighting their fires, like all the northern Indians, with pyrites. They had four ways of cooking meat and fish: boiling in spruce-bark (later birch-bark) baskets over a slow fire; boiling in similar baskets, or in baskets woven from spruce roots, by means of hot stones; roasting on spits; and drying in the smoke of a fire.

None of the old spruce-bark or spruce-root baskets survive today, but the Sekani still make a few birch-bark baskets like the one shown in Plate 13.

Plate 8. Wooden spoon and a skin scraper made from the shoulder-bone of a moose. (Canadian Museum of History 75941)

6. Mackenzie: Op. cit., pp. 206–7.

This is a well-made specimen, neatly stitched up the sides and around the reinforced rim with spruce roots. The only decorations are two narrow lines of black horse-hair beaded under the stitching of the rim, and at intervals a false over-stitching with bands of dyed horse-hair.

The spoons of horn have disappeared likewise, but one occasionally sees wooden spoons, like the specimen in Plate 8, some of whose handles are rudely serrated or decorated with hatched lines. Bags of moose-hide are common still; there are rough bags closed with draw-strings (Plate 9), used for carrying berries and meat; net bags of babiche (Plate 10) and beaded moose-hide bags with flaps that button or tie over (Plate 9), used for all sorts of miscellaneous objects. For cleaning these moose-hides the Sekani employ either a caribou antler, chisel-ended and with serrated edge,[7] or the shoulder-bone of a moose sharpened like a draw-knife (Plate 8).

Game was scarce during the winter months, so the Sekani gathered in summer a large stock of dried meat and stored it under spruce bark on a platform raised on four posts that had been carefully smoothed to prevent wolverines and other animals from climbing up. For still greater security they sometimes erected these caches, not on posts, but in trees, as described by Morice:

> They erect sorts of scaffoldings immediately against the trunk of a tall tree. ... These consist of two long, heavy sticks crossed and firmly bound to the trunk of the tree at their point of intersection, while their ends are secured to some stout overhanging branch by means of strong ropes. Rough boards or split sticks are then laid across this frame which form a floor over which the meat or any other eatable is deposited, carefully wrapped over with skins or spruce bark. Even the bear cannot get at those caches without previously demolishing their floor, which is practically impossible.[8]

At McLeod lake and at Fort Grahame the Sekani have now erected miniature storehouses on posts (Plate 2). These are apparently modified forms of their earlier caches, which may still persist away from the settlements.

The Long Grass Indians cooked their food in the same manner as the rest of the Sekani, but also practised other methods which they learned, apparently, from the Gitksan and Tahltan. Thus they sometimes boiled their meat in wooden boxes with hot stones, like the coast tribes; and at other times they heated some stones in a small trench, laid fireweed leaves above them, the meat on the leaves, a covering of bark above the meat, and finally hot ashes. Hunters away from camp occasionally boiled their meat in the stomach of a mountain goat by encompassing its upper edge with a green twig and filling this novel bag with water.

In their caches, too, the Long Grass people displayed more variety than their fellow tribesmen. Although they preferred to store their meat on wooden

---

7. Morice: Op. cit., p. 70.
8. Op. cit., p. 197.

platforms raised on posts or fastened in trees, the absence of trees throughout much of the Groundhog country often forced them to build high platforms of stones. Hunters who intended to return for their meat within a few days piled it on the ground and covered it with a blanket; placed it in crude hampers made of interlaced willow boughs concealed under a layer of brush; or merely set a burning log beside it and set a few traps.

Plate 9. Sekani bags of moose-hide, the upper beaded.
(Canadian Museum of History 75946)

TOOLS AND WEAPONS

The old tools and weapons have long since passed out of use. Even in Mackenzie's day they had been modified through the infiltration of iron from the
Pacific coast.

> Their arms consist of bows made of cedar, six feet in length,
> with a short iron spike at one end, and serve occasionally as a
> spear. Their arrows are well made, barbed, and pointed with
> iron, flint, stone, or bone; they are feathered, and from two to
> two feet and a half in length. They have two kinds of spears, but
> both are double edged, and of well polished iron; one of them is
> about twelve inches long, and two wide; the other about half the
> width, and two-thirds of the length; the shafts of the first are
> eight feet in length, and the latter six. They have also spears
> made of bone. Their knives consist of pieces of iron, shaped
> and handled by themselves. Their adzes are something like our
> adze, and they use them in the same manner as we employ that
> instrument. They were, indeed, furnished with iron in a man-
> ner that I could not have supposed, and plainly proved to me
> that their communication with those, who communicate with
> the inhabitants of the sea coast, cannot be very difficult.[9]

The Carrier, Tahltan, Slave, and perhaps other Athapaskan tribes tipped
their bows with stone points, and the Sekani did likewise until they obtained
iron from the coast. McLeod Lake natives said that although they preferred cedar for their bows, it was so difficult to obtain that they generally used willow or
balsam; and that in shooting they used the Mediterranean grip. Arrows, they
added, were made of saskatoon or birch, those for children being winged with
two feathers laid flat, whereas hunters' arrows had three half-feathers set on
edge and fastened down with spruce gum and sinew. The same natives have a
tradition that in war they used a moose-jaw club, and an oblong wooden shield
coated on the outside with pitch and pebbles. Morice figures a curious kind of
"war or hunting bow" made of mountain maple, with a wrapping of sinew and
a coating of dyed porcupine quills. This was probably a reconstructed weapon
specially ornamented, for the Sekani had ceased to use the bow for war, or
for large game, fully half a century before his time, although boys retained it
for shooting grouse. He illustrates also three types of arrows, a "cut" arrow, a
triple-headed arrow, and a blunt arrow all with triple feathering.[10]
    Mackenzie mentions two kinds of spears that differed only in size; both had
iron blades McLeod Lake natives say that bear hunters used a stoneheaded
lance, whereas beaver hunters used a toggled spear with a triplebarbed head

9. Mackenzie: Op. cit., p. 206.
10. Morice: Op. cit., pp. 56–59.

of bone antler, or simply hard wood.
A sketch of the latter weapon, drawn
from their description, is shown in
Figure 2.

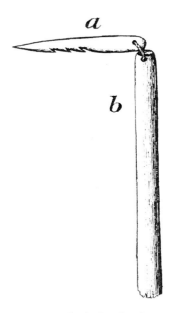

Fishermen had three-pronged
leisters with bone points for spear-
ing fish at night from their canoes
by the light of jackpine torches. In
winter they dug holes through the
ice with chisels of moose or caribou
antler mounted on long wooden handles, cleared away the snow from the
holes to leave only transparent ice,
and, lying under brush shelters, used
these same leisters to stab the fish
that approached their lures; or else
they hooked the fish with long gaffs.
During the months of February and
March the Gitksan Indians still use
a gaff in this way to catch the steel-
head salmon in the shallow upper

Figure 2. Sketch of a Sekani beaver spear.

waters of Kispiox river; for bait they often use only a piece of red flannel, but
the Sekani, who caught not salmon but Dolly Varden trout, used bunches of
fine sinew. There were also fish-hooks, as mentioned by Mackenzie, "small
bones, fixed in pieces of wood split for that purpose, and tied round with fine
watape," which were jigged or occasionally set overnight concealed in a wrapping of sinew. The modern Sekani state that their fishing-lines were made of
sinew, but Mackenzie speaks of "nets and fishing-lines made of willow-bark
and nettles; those made of the latter are finer and smoother than if made with
hempen thread."[11]

DEADFALLS, SNARES, NETS, AND WEIRS

In fishing and hunting, however, the Sekani relied less on their weapons than
on deadfalls, snares, and nets. Deadfalls they still employ occasionally for
groundhog, fisher, and marten, in earlier times probably for other animals
also. But they procured most of their game, whether groundhogs or moose,
with snares. "They have snares made of green skin [babiche]," says Mackenzie," which they cut to the size of sturgeon twine, and twist a certain number
of them together, and though when completed they do not exceed the thickness of a cod-line, their strength is sufficient to hold a moose-deer: these are
from one and a half to two fathoms in length." A few years after Mackenzie's
day Simon Fraser saw the Indians snaring mountain sheep:

---

11. Mackenzie: Op. cit., p. 206.

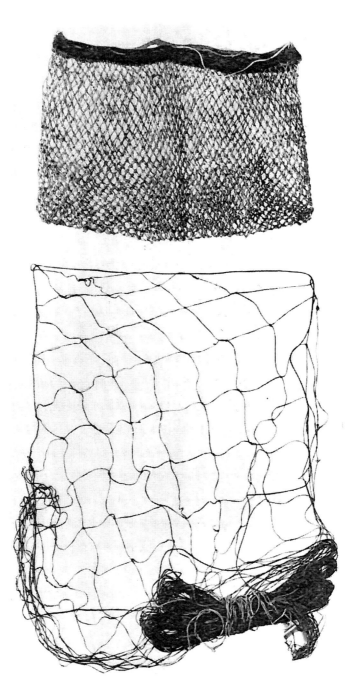

Plate 10. A babiche hunting bag, and a babiche net for catching beaver. (National Museum of Canada 75943)

We were greatly amused looking at some of the [Meadow] Indians running after the wild sheep which they call As-pah. They are really expert, indeed running full speed among the perpendicular rocks which had I not ocular demonstration I could never believe to have been trained by any creature either of the human or brute creation for the rocks appeared to us which perhaps might be exaggerated a little from the distance to be as steep as a wall and yet while in pursuit of the sheep they bounded from one to another with the swiftness of a Roe, and at last killed two in their snares.[12]

The bear and the moose, of course, required much stronger snares than the rabbit and grouse, and the Sekani probably set their nooses in two or three different ways. By constructing long fences of brush, and setting snares at intervals of a few feet or yards, the Indians captured whole flocks of grouse, and whole herds of caribou, as explained by Morice:

The Sékanais ... previously set in a continuous line 40 or 50 moose hide snares in suitable defiles or passes in the mountains frequented by the animals. Two of the most active hunters are then deputed to watch at either end of the line, after which the hunters, who usually number fifteen or more, drive the band of

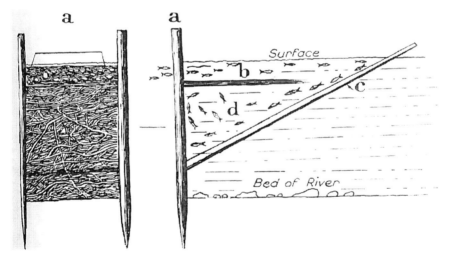

Figure 3. Sketch of a fish-weir.
(a) Fence of brush across a stream with gaps in the top.
(b) Horizontal platform of small saskatoon branches, closely laced together just below the surface of the water with the sharp points facing downstream.
(c) Sloping floor of poles, one end of which is above water.
(d) The sluice-box in which the fish are trapped.

---

12. *First Journal of Simon Fraser*, Op. cit., May 26, 1806.

deer or cariboo to where the snares are set and, by loud shouting and firing of guns, they scare and thereby force the reluctant game to pass through the noose which at once contracts around their necks. The deer immediately scamper away with the movable sticks, to which the snares are attached, and which, being soon caught among fallen or standing trees or other obstacles, cause the caught animal to stop suddenly with the result of being strangled to death in a short time."[13]

The Sekani caught large numbers of groundhogs during the summer months, most of them with snares. Mackenzie saw a "kind of wooden trap, in which, as our guide informed me, the groundhog is taken";[14] but the present day natives seem to have forgotten it. They did, however, kill many of these animals with sticks, after smoking them out of their holes or flooding them out by diverting a stream; and if the groundhogs retreated into crannies among the rocks they twisted long sticks in their fur and pulled them out into the open. Beaver they generally caught, and still catch, in nets of babiche, for they only used the spears described a page or two earlier when they broke down the animals' houses. Plate 10 shows an ordinary beaver net; its dimensions are given by Morice:

Both hands outstretched with the thumbs tip to tip are the standard measure for the width of the beaver net. Large nets require twelve such units, while the smaller ones have only nine or thereabouts. Such nets never exceed twenty-five feet in length.[15]

The Sekani had also fishing-nets, which they made of nettle fibres or willow roots and used both summer and winter, setting them in winter under the ice. In recent years they have learned from their Carrier neighbours to make fish-traps, which they did not use in earlier times, although in small streams they were accustomed to set up weirs of brush that intercepted the fish, and constructed also the sluice-box shown diagrammatically in Figure 3.

TRANSPORTATION

Toboggans came into use, apparently, only in modern times; previously the Sekani carried all their possessions on their backs during the winter months. They did, however, possess snow-shoes, which were rare or unknown among their Carrier neighbours. Plate 13 shows a specimen that came from the Long Grass band, though it was obtained at Hazelton; but whether it correctly reproduces the ancient type is not certain, for today snow-shoes are freely traded throughout northern British Columbia and the Indians often imitate

13. Morice: Op. cit., p. 132.
14. Mackenzie: Op. cit., p. 217.
15. Morice: Op. cit., p. 159.

foreign models.

For summer travelling the Sekani had canoes of spruce bark which have been described by Mackenzie:

> The bark is taken off the tree the whole length of the intended canoe, which is commonly about eighteen feet, and is sewed with watape at both ends; two laths are then laid, and fixed along the edge of the bark which forms the gunwale; in these are fixed the bars, and against them bear the ribs or timbers, that are cut to the length to which the bark can be stretched; and, to give additional strength, strips of wood arc laid between them; to make the whole watertight, gum is abundantly employed. These vessels carry from two to five people. Canoes of a similar construction were used by the Beaver Indians within these few years, but they now very generally employ those made of the bark of the birch tree, which are by far more durable. Their paddles are about six feet long, and about one foot is occupied by the blade, which is in the shape of a heart.[16]

There is no record of the Sekani substituting birch bark for spruce bark in their canoes, nor any memory of birch-bark boats among the present inhabitants.[17] Today they use either Peterborough canoes, or crude dugouts of cottonwood like those of the Carrier and Gitksan. After trimming the log to shape they hollow it out with fire and adzes, then spread the gunwales with wedges of graduated length, first softening the wood by filling the canoe with water. The final wedges become the thwarts, which number from four to six according to the length of the boat (Plate 11). The paddles are crudely shaped, and seldom used on the swiftly flowing rivers, where more progress can be made by poling.

The Long Grass Indians used both spruce-bark canoes and dugouts. In emergencies, also, they used a covering of moose hides instead of spruce bark, like the Tahltan Indians, or built a crude raft.

---

16. Mackenzie: Op. cit., p. 207.
17. *First Journal of Simon Fraser*: Op. cit., May 26, 1806.

Plate 11. A dugout canoe at Fort McLeod.
(Canadian Museum of History 60664)

CHAPTER 5
SOCIAL ORGANIZATION

In the earliest times of which we have record the Sekani were divided into bands, each of which possessed its own hunting territory. Sometimes the individual families scattered and hunted separately, sometimes they wandered in groups of two or three; yet just as frequently, perhaps, they held together for mutual support and moved as a unit from one place to another within their domain. There were no family hunting grounds, no districts of which a family or small group of families claimed exclusive possession. Family rights to special hunting grounds have come only in recent times, after the fur trade induced the Indian to return year after year to the same trapping district and to conserve its supply of beaver. Even today the change from band to family ownership of districts is not complete; the entire band claims the final possession of every district within its area, and if for any reason one family fails to occupy its usual trapping ground another does not hesitate to take its place.

Each band had a leader, who was neither hereditary nor elected, but acquired his position through force of character, skill in hunting, and sane judgment. His authority, therefore, was merely nominal; he was a leader, not a chief, and if he presumed to issue orders, he had no means of enforcing them. When the hunters discussed their affairs over the evening fires and laid their plans for the morrow, the voice of the leader carried more weight, but no more actual authority, than that of the youth who had just entered the ranks of manhood. At any time a new leader might arise to supersede him, and his influence inevitably waned with advancing years. Parties that separated off from the band to fish, to hunt, or to raid neighbouring tribes selected their own leaders.

The only laws, therefore, were the regulations prescribed by custom. Since every family was coequal with every other, and often depended on its neighbours for support, it was necessary to consider all food as common property whenever two or more families lived side by side. The hunter who killed an animal useful for food would not even retain its hide, but presented it to some other man in the camp, lest he should be accused of unsociability and niggardliness. The only exception was the skin of the groundhog, because it had little or no value. He might retain the skins of animals whose meat was useless, such as the marten, fisher, and fox, though even these he often gave away to relatives. After the establishment of the fur trade, with its totally different estimate on the value of skins, the Sekani ceased to give away the furs of the beaver and lynx, and many of them now retain also the hides of the caribou and moose. The old regulations, however, prevented a family from amassing any of the necessities of life at the expense of other families, preserved their social equality, and provided for those who were unfortunate, in so far as they could be provided for under the harsh conditions of a wandering life.

Lacking definite chiefs, or a council, to maintain law and order and to regulate the actions of the individual families, the Sekani had no recourse but the blood-feud to check murder and other serious crimes. Each band was small and its members closely related, so that feuds within a band seem to have been much rarer than feuds with neighbouring bands or with the Carrier and other tribes on their borders. The Sekani ascribed most deaths to sorcery, and often sought vengeance on the supposed murderer and his kindred, sometimes even on a totally innocent group. Thus Harmon relates from Stuart lake that:

> A Sicauny has just arrived, who states, that a little this side of McLeod's Lake, where he was encamped with his family, an Indian of the same tribe, rushed out of the wood, and fired upon them, and killed his wife. Her corpse he immediately burned upon the spot; and then, with his son and two daughters, he proceeded directly to this place. ... All the savages, who have had a near relation killed, are never quiet until they have revenged the death, either by killing the murderer, or some person nearly related to him. This spirit of revenge has occasioned the death of the old woman, above mentioned, and she, undoubtedly deserved to die; for, the last summer, she persuaded her husband to go and kill the cousin of the murderer, and that, merely because her own son had been drowned.[1]

In another passage the same writer mentions that:

> Yesterday, five Sicaunies came here, from McLeod's Lake, who form a small war party. Their leader, or war chief, desired me to allow them to go where they might think proper; upon which I enquired of them, whither they wished to direct their course, and what their business was. The speaker replied, that, when they left their lands, their intention was to go and try to take a scalp or two from the Indians of Frazer's Lake, "who," he added, "have done us no injury. But we have lost a relation; and we must try to avenge his death, on some one."[2]

A Fort McLeod native related the following incident which occurred in the time of his grandfather:

> The mother of a Yutuwichan Indian named Gwatcha had a grudge against some Indians of the Tsekani band, and urged her son to shoot them. Gwatcha shot and killed one man, after which his band moved away to fish at Carp lake. A Tsekani man named Nasawaya decided to fish there also and was advised before he left McLeod lake to shoot Gwatcha's mother if any one attacked him, because she was the cause of all the trouble between the two bands. Nasawaya was leaping over a small creek just outside the Yutuwichan camp when some one shot him in

---

1. Harmon, D.W., *A Journal of Voyages and Travels*, Andover, 1820, p. 229f.

2. Harmon; Op. cit., p. 203f., Cf. Morice, A. G., *History of the Northern Interior of British Columbia*, p. 133 (Toronto, 1904).

the elbow and knocked his gun from his hands. He picked it up and ran into the woods, but presently circled round the camp and shot Gwatcha's mother dead. Some Yutuwichan hunters pursued and captured him, but let him go when they discovered who he was, merely saying, "You did right, but you had better avoid our people." So Nasawaya fled to another district.

Gwatcha's father had been sitting beside his wife when she was shot, but could not pursue the murderer because he had taken his gun apart to clean it. By the time he had put it together and followed his companions Nasawaya was far away. Four years later the two men met at McLeod lake, where some of the Yutuwichan Indians were gambling with the Tsekani. His daughter said to him, "There is Nasawaya, who shot our mother. Are you not going to kill him?" Her father tore his clothes at the knees, took up his gun and knife, and, stealing behind the circular wind-break of spruce-bark within which the people were gambling, stabbed Nasawaya between the shoulders. Then he ran toward the woods, while the gamblers scattered to their lodges. But Nasawaya snatched up his gun, knocked down a woman who tried to hinder him, and shot his assailant dead. Then he applied to his wound some medicine bought at the Hudson's Bay Company's store and in a short time was well again.

Feuds of this character were not confined to the Sekani, but common among all the tribes of the Mackenzie River basin. There was no chief or council to suppress them, and the spiritual dangers that the Indians associated with manslaughter were too slight to be an effective deterrent. The Sekani believed, for example, that if a man failed to tear his clothes at the knees before slaying an enemy he would fall sick afterwards and die. After the slaying he should arch a stick in front of a fire and, kneeling before it, let the heat strike his body under the arch; otherwise he would fall sick, have bad luck in his hunting, or meet with some other misfortune. For the same reason, before crossing a stream or a river, he should break off the top of a spruce tree and carefully step over it; and he should smoke, not a European pipe, which would cause his throat to swell and make him short of breath, but a pipe whose stem was fashioned from a twig of saskatoon or red willow, split, hollowed out, and bound together again. The pipe or cup of a man who had slain a woman seemed to the Sekani so tainted that no one else dared to touch it. Nevertheless, all these penalties were evidently too trifling to carry any weight, and even the fear of a blood-feud has seldom checked murder in regions, such as northern Canada, where the population was sparse and weakly organized.

When the Sekani were confined to the western side of the Rockies through the hostility of the Beaver and Cree they impinged continuously against the Gitksan and Carrier Indians, who were organized in the complex manner so characteristic of the Pacific coast. The Sekani not only fought, traded, and intermarried with them, but assimilated many of their customs and tried to adopt their divisions into exogamous matrilinear phratries. The two bands that centred around McLeod lake, the Tsekani and the Yutuwichan, naturally copied the Carrier of Stuart lake who were their nearest neighbours; the Sasuchan band that frequented Bear lake and the Finlay River basin imitated the Carrier of Babine lake and the Gitksan whom they met at Fort Connolly. Thus certain divergencies in organization between the Carrier and Gitksan became reflected in the Sekani also, so that the system adopted at McLeod lake was not identical with that of their kinsmen on Finlay river.

Actually the McLeod Lake Indians remember very little about the phratries they adopted, because in the general decline of native customs that followed the advent of the fur trade and the subsequent colonization they abandoned the system before it had time to establish itself. They say that the Carrier of Stuart lake had five phratries: *tsayu*, "beaver"; *Uɬtsamashu*, *yisilyu*, *kwanpahotenne*, and *eske*, the last four names being untranslatable.[3] The Sekani of McLeod lake tried to arrange themselves into similar phratries under chiefs whom they called *Daiyi* (probably the Chinook word *taiyi:* chief), and they even held one or two potlatches to establish the system; but they quickly abandoned the attempt when they discovered that it did not help them under the new conditions of life, and merely provoked the scorn of Europeans. Yet if a McLeod Lake native today visits Stuart lake to take part in any ceremony, the Stuart Lake Carrier consider him to belong to the Tsayu phratry, and would forbid his marriage to a woman of that phratry if their own system had not also broken down during the last fifty years.

The Finlay River Sekani, on the other hand, seem to have been intriguing with the phratric system for nearly a century. They call a phratry *tsinadjinni*, and bestow the title of *teneza'* (a Carrier word for the chief of a phratry, or the chief of a clan within the phratry) on any man who gives a potlatch. *Daiyi* they consider an old word that has no reference to the phratric system but means the leader of a band. They first attempted to establish phratries about 1850, apparently, for an elderly man whom the Hudson's Bay Company now

---

3. This list corresponds closely with that given by Morice except that he omits the fifth phratry *eske, and* translates *kwanpahotenne* as "inhabitants of the fire-side." (Morice, A.G., *Notes on the Western Déné*; Trans. Can. Inst., vol. IV, 1892–93, pp. 203f.) He seems to be mistaken, however, when he states that four phratries (or, as he calls them, gentes) obtained among the Carrier. There were five in several districts, and in one, apparently, only two. The following list covers those Carrier groups from which I have specific information:

Hwittsowittenne group (around Bulldey river): *tsayu, lachsamshu, lakselytu, gitamtanyu, and gilserhyu.*

Uanwittenne group (Babine lake): *tsayu, lachsamshu, kivanpe' hwotenne, gitamtanyu, and gilserhyu.*

Nattlewittenne group (at the east end of Frasor lake): *tsayu, ɬtsamashu, laksilyu, tamtanyu, and gilserhyu.*

Nu'tsenni group (main part of Fraser lake): *tsayu, ɬtsamashu, yiselyu, tamtanyu, and tsoyeztottenne.*

Tattcatotenne group (around Cheslatta lake): *tsayu, ɬtsamashu, yisilyu, tamtanyu, tsuyezhottenne.*

Yuta' hwotenne group (Stony Creek Indians, just south of Vanderhoof): *yisilyu and gilserhyu* only.

(1924) dignify with the title of "Chief of Fort Grahame" heard from his mother that sixty or seventy years ago some Gitksan Indians from the village of Kispiox visited Bear lake and asked the Sasuchan Sekani to join them in holding a potlatch. At that time the Sekani recognized no phratries, but each man assigned himself for the occasion to the phratry of a Gitksan relative or friend. They then retained these affiliations for a period, but lost them as soon as the Hudson's Bay Company removed its post from Bear lake to Fort Grahame.

The last twenty-five years have seen their revival, for now many of the Finlay River Sekani are wandering westward again and visiting both the Carrier and the Gitksan Indians around Babine lake and river. They recognize today three phratries, which they call *laksel, lachsibu,* and *lachsamshu. Laksel* is in Gitksan[4] *lakse'l,* the name of the Raven phratry; *laksamshu* (*shit* or *yu* means *"people"*) is the Gitksan *lachsamillich* ("on beaver"), the name of a clan in the Eagle phratry. Their phratric system, therefore, comes from the Gitksan, but owing to Carrier influence is not identical with it; for they have only three phratries against the Gitksan four. But neither is it identical with the Carrier system (itself derived mainly from the Gitksan), for the Carrier have, or had until recently, five phratries. To reconcile these different systems when celebrating a potlatch together the three peoples adopted the following equation:

Sekani	Babine Carrier	Gitksan
laksel	*gilserhyu* and *kwanpahotenne*	*lachsel*: the Raven phratry
lachsibu	*Gitamtanyu*	*lachgibu*: the Wolf phratry
lachsamshu	*Lachsamshu* and	*giskahast*: the Fireweed phratry
	tsayu	*lachskik*: the Eagle phratry

These equations, of course, are not arbitrary, but correlate with the principal crests in each phratry. The most important crest in the *lachsel* phratry of the Gitksan is the raven, which is a crest in the *laksilyu* (called *kwanpahotenne* at Babine) phratry of a Carrier group at the eastern end of Fraser lake, but appears nowhere else, apparently, in Carrier territory and was not adopted by the Sekani. However, the next ranking crest in the *lachsel* phratry is the frog or toad, which appears in both the *gilserhyu* and *laksilyu* phratries in many Carrier districts, and is the principal crest of the Sekani *laksel.* Similarly the principal crests of the Gitksan *lachgibu* or Wolf phratry are the wolf and the grizzly bear, and one or other (sometimes both) of these animals is the crest of the *Gitamtanyu* phratry of the Carrier and of the *lachsibu* phratry of the

---

4. Hazelton dialect.

the Gitksan and Carrier. They, too, had[5] three phratries, Raven, Wolf, and Fireweed, as opposed to the Gitksan four, Raven, Wolf, Fireweed, and Eagle, and
two, Raven and Wolf, among the Tahltan. Each phratry had its crests which
were represented at potlatches by appropriate emblems. The crests of the Raven phratry were, raven, eagle, and frog or toad;[6] those of the Wolf phratry,
wolf, black bear, and a small owl;[7] and those of the Fireweed phratry, fireweed,
sun or moon, grouse, and the big horned owl.[8]

At potlatches, particularly at the potlatch to appoint a new chief, members
of the Raven phratry attached the beak of a raven to their hats, painted a raven or a toad on their skin robes (or represented it in applique on a woollen
blanket), and sang:

Why are you so long in coming?
You must be crazy.
Don't you know the feast is ready?
You have enough to feast on.
Why delay your coming?
Come on in.
You act as if you were insane.
You have so much to feast on.
You act as if you were insane.

Similarly the Wolf people, dressed in wolf or black bear skins, planted owl
feathers in their hair, and sang:

Where is the wolf?
Let him come in.
Come in quickly.

The Fireweed people covered their heads with fireweed, and, instead of
singing, hooted like the big horned owl. Hence a stranger wishing to know the
phratric affiliations of a Long Grass Indian would ask "What does he wear on
his blanket, a raven, a wolf or fireweed?"

How widely the matrilinear system of society once prevailed throughout the
world is much disputed, but today it has entirely disappeared except among a
few primitive peoples in out-of-the-way corners. It is, therefore, very instruc-
tive to find one of our Canadian Indian tribes deliberately attempting to adopt
it, under the influence of neighbouring tribes. Their earlier kinsmen in the

---

5. About 1900. The condition of the band today is unknown.

6. The Raven phratry of the Tahltan recognized as its crests raven, eagle, toad, and otter. Raven
and frog are the principal crests in the Raven phratry of the Gitksan, and the eagle appears in a
modified form, though it is the principal crest in the eagle phratry.

7. The Wolf phratry of the Tahltan had only one crest, wolf. Wolf and black bear, but apparently
not owl, are crests in the Gitksan Wolf phratry.

8. Fireweed, moon, grouse, and owl are all crests in the Gitksan Fireweed phratry.

Sekani. The *laksamshu* phratry of the Sekani recognizes as its principal crest the *beaver*, which is a leading crest in the Carrier *tsayu* and in the Gitksan *lachskīk* or Eagle phratries. But when the *tsayu* phratry of the western Carriers was decimated by an epidemic about fifty years ago its survivors were absorbed into the *laksamshu* phratry, whose principal crests, sun and moon, are the same as those of the Gitksan *giskahast* or Fireweed phratry. Hence the Sekani *lachsamshu* phratry equates with two phratries of the Carrier that are now amalgamated, and with two phratries of the Gitksan that still remain distinct.

Among the Finlay River Sekani the *laksel* phratry, which surpasses the other two in numbers, has adopted the following crests (*nattsi*, which is also the Carrier word for crest): frog or toad, marten, caribou, and beads. At a potlatch any member of the phratry has the right to use one or all of these crests, if he wishes. The crests of the *lachsibu* phratry are wolf, grizzly bear, and black bear; and of the *lachsamshu* phratry beaver and owl.

Potlatches, which occur only in June and July when the families gather at Fort Grahame after the winter's trapping, are simple feasts in which the members of the phratry that issues the invitation range themselves at the back of the house and wait on the representatives of the other two phratries, who sit on the floor along the sides. The Sekani do not dramatize their crests, as do the Carrier and Gitksan, no one wears a mask, and no one sings or dances; but they have attempted to introduce some principle into their seating arrangements inasmuch as the leading *teneza'* in each phratry occupies the central place and the other members group near him in the supposed order of their importance. A few men have assumed potlatch names or titles, generally, if not always, during real potlatches at Babine in which Carrier or Gitksan Indians participated. Thus the *laksel* phratry has the titles *daiya*, "he goes towards the moose," and *asbazudi*, "tongue of a mountain goat"; the *lachsamshu* phratry *dzak*, "a beaver-house"; and the *lachsibu datchinkadiye*, "a conspicuous tree." The individual who acquired the title "He goes towards the moose" purchased for his potlatch five cases of eggs, and large quantities of tobacco, canned salmon, milk, and other foods. Since the expense was greater than he could bear alone, his fellow phratrymen shared it with him.

Children belong to the phratries of their mothers, marriage within a phratry is discountenanced, and the phratry of a man (or woman) who dies at Fort Grahame arranges and pays for his burial by one of the other two phratries. During the greater part of the year, however, the families are scattered over a wide range of territory and the phratric system lapses completely. It really functions, in fact, only during the months of June and July when the people gather at Fort Grahame, though it can be revived at any season of the year by individuals visiting the Carrier and Gitksan. Some of the older people who do not roam outside Sekani territory hardly know to what phratries they belong, and depend for guidance on their kindred.

The T'lotona or Long Grass Indians also adopted a phratric organization, but they derived their system from the Tahltan and Gitksan rather than from

Cordillera, the Carriers and the Tahltan, had made the same attempt and succeeded; but we were never able to see the beginnings of the process, or to follow it through all its stages. The McLeod Lake Sekani entered the road sixty or seventy years ago, but turned back. The Long Grass band completed the process, apparently, but the history of this band is obscure and it is fast disintegrating, if it has not already disappeared. The Finlay River Sekani have travelled half the distance. They have set up a phratric system in which descent rigidly follows the female line. But their system now functions for a few weeks only, and the advancing tide of Europeans will surely prevent it from rooting, even if the band maintains its place for another century, as seems most unlikely, and does not melt away as other tribes are melting around them.

CHAPTER 6
MARRIAGE, CHILDHOOD, AND BURIAL

The simplicity of Sekani society reveals itself in the kinship system, which is totally unlike the Carrier and Gitksan systems where exogamy and matrilinear descent prevailed. The terms of relationship at Fort Grahame are:[1]

Term	Used by both sexes	Man speaking	Woman speaking
settane	my older or younger brother my male cousin		
hotige	my older brother my older male cousin		
asidle	my younger brother my younger male cousin		my brother's son
se'tise'	my older or younger sister my female cousin		
sāde	my older sister my older cousin		
esdje'	my younger sister my younger female cousin		my brother's daughter
abba	my father		
ane	my mother		
esta	my paternal uncle my step-father		
sase	my maternal uncle		
abedze	my paternal aunt		
songwe	my step-mother		
seskege	my children		
setchwạ'	my son, step-son	brother's son	sister's son
setchwe'	my daughter, step-daughter	my brother's daughter	my sister's daughter
sazi		my sister's son, my sister's daughter	
ase	my grandfather		

1. At Fort McLeod there are only minute phonetic differences; every syllable in these words is. I believe, high-toned.

asụ	my grandmother
asa	my grandchild
esụ	my father-in-law
senaze	my son-in-law
setcha	my daughter-in-law
klaze'	my brother-in-law, my sister-in-law

In this system the inclusion of cousins on both the maternal and paternal sides with the siblings, even without other evidence, shows that exogamy with patrilinear or matrilinear descent had no place in Sekani social organization. That a man should call his brother's children his own, and that the same term should mean both paternal uncle and step-father, proves the existence of the levirate, which indeed is attested by the natives themselves. It is only natural, therefore, that a man should have different terms for his sister's children and his brother's children. Marriage with two sisters, or with a deceased's wife's sister, is indicated by the use of the same term for maternal aunt and step-mother, and by a woman calling her sister's children her own. I cannot understand, however, why a woman should apply the same term to her brother's children as to her own brothers and sister.

Marriage among the Sekani was regulated by the degree of consanguinity. First cousins of all kinds, uncles, aunts, nephews, nieces, grandparents, and grandchildren were debarred from intermarriage, but there were no restrictions beyond these relationships. Polygamy was not uncommon, often taking the form of a man marrying two sisters. If a wife died, the husband frequently, though not always, married her sister, should there be one unmarried; and if the husband died, his brother married the widow. Morice says that "polyandry was in honour conjointly with polygamy,"[2] but the Sekani themselves state that it occurred only rarely. Wrestling for wives, common among some Athapaskan tribes of the Mackenzie River valley, was unknown.

From Morice, also, comes the following account of a Sekani marriage: "Among the Sekanais nothing was simpler or more expeditious than the contraction of marriage. Whenever a young hunter had made up his mind on mating a fair child of the forest, with scarcely any previous courting, he would in the day time simply ask the girl of his choice:

'Will you pack my beaver snares for me?' To which, if she refused him, she would make answer: 'No, there are plenty of women, ask another one.' But if agreeable to the maid, she would at once answer without any conventional blushes: 'Perhaps, ask my mother.' Upon which the lad would not ask her mother, but the girl would immediately tell her about it. Then, following her parent's advice, she would hasten to erect a branch lodge alongside their own

---

2. Morice, A.G., *The Western Dénés*, Proc. Can. Inst., Third Series, vol. VII, 1888–89, p. 123.

Plate 12. Sekani family at Fort McLeod. (Canadian Museum of History 60673)

primitive habitation, and in the evening, the affianced youth (such he was after the proposée's answer) would on entering it hand her his 'Beaver snares.'
Without further ceremony, they were man and wife. Supposing the woman
proposed to was the former wife of the man's deceased brother, there was no
declining his offer, she was bound to accept his 'beaver snares'"[3]

The ceremony was really more complicated than would appear from this
account. The bridegroom had to serve the bride's parents for a considerable
period before he could take his wife away, and he generally obtained his father's approval before approaching the girl. If his father and the girl's mother
gave their consent the youth was invited to hunt with the family, and became
the girl's husband immediately, erecting a separate lodge for himself and his
bride close to her parents' lodge. For a year or even longer the two families
continued together, and the youth handed over to her parents everything he
secured in his hunting except the bare necessities of his bride and himself.
The bride-price, however, was never fixed, depending on the youth's success
in the chase. If the girl's parents were dissatisfied they could take the bride
away; but if all parties were content the fathers of both bride and bridegroom
helped out the young couple with liberal presents. The youth was freed from
his bondage after the birth of the first child, or, if no child was born, after a
year or a little over. He could then take his wife wherever he wished. Generally
he returned to his father and kinsmen, but occasionally he remained with his
wife's parents for a year or two longer, though on a more equal basis.

A newly married couple never lived under the same roof as their parents,
for this would have been contrary to the dignity of both families. If the girl's

---

3. Morice: Op. cit., p. 122.

father died, however, her mother, in the absence of adult sons, found a home with the son-in-law, who was obliged to supply all her needs.

Divorce look place at the will of either party. The husband merely abandoned his wife, or the wife her husband, without preliminary notice. The offspring went with either parent according to mutual agreement, but divorce seldom occurred after a child was born. The woman remarried immediately, or returned to her kinsmen, who provided for her until she died or found another husband. As the Sekani lived a migratory life they had no property except what they carried or wore on their persons. It would seem that the woman retained any ornaments she had received from her husband, although on this point my information is rather indefinite.

The accepted penalty for the unfaithful wife was death or a severe beating; for her paramour, death. But since society was organized but loosely, and the task of exacting the penalty devolved on the aggrieved husband and his kin, misconduct sometimes passed unheeded. The lending of wives to guests was not a Sekani custom; only their awe at the presence of the first white men made them complaisant in this respect towards the crew of Sir Alexander Mackenzie's canoe. Mothers kept careful watch over their unmarried daughters and shielded them from abduction by never allowing them to go out for wood or water alone. On the whole the standard of morality seems to have been high, and the marriage tie faithfully observed.

A woman in labour encamped apart from her husband, who would have bad luck in his hunting if he approached her. She knelt on the ground, supporting herself with a stick,[4] and when the baby issued, cut the cord with a sharp stone and hung the placenta in a tree out of sight. She then sat on a pile of brush above a pit filled with hot stones over which she or a kinswoman (if any was at hand to help), poured water that the rising steam might check the hemorrhage. Bathing with warm water concluded the operation. The baby, wrapped in a bag of groundhog or rabbit fur, was carried on its mother's back wherever she went, and nursed for about three years until it could digest a diet of meat and fish. The mother drank large quantities of moose broth whenever it was procurable, to ensure a plentiful supply of milk.

Neither infanticide nor abortion was practised, if we may believe the modern Sekani. Even twins were preserved, although often it must have been impossible to rear them, and the weaker succumbed. The child received its first clothes when it began to walk—a coat of caribou fur that reached to the ankles, leggings of the same fur, and moccasins with an inner lining of rabbit fur. At the age of about five it assumed clothes corresponding to its sex, patterned exactly like those of its elders.

The name was given soon after birth, either by the father, or by a man known to have many dream-guardians. Usually it was simply a modification of the dream-guardian's name, as "moose-antler" when the dream-guardian was "moose"; but it might also be a name revealed in the dream that gave medicine-power. Dogs were often named in the same manner. Today dream-guard-

---

4. Sekani women today follow the same procedure, but rest their arms on a box.

ians are disappearing, and children frequently receive high-sounding titles of little significance, or adhere to names bestowed by the missionaries. Nicknames have always been common, and at Fort Grahame, where the Indians are attempting to establish a phratric system, a few men have taken titles in potlatches; but the name given soon after birth, which in olden times was always associated with the dream-guardian idea, is still regarded as the individual's true name through life.

The life of the average child was uneventful until the age of puberty. As the first set of teeth dropped out they were thrown towards the rising sun to make the new set grow more rapidly.[5] At puberty boys and girls underwent special rituals. The ritual for boys was positive in its aim, seeking to make them successful hunters in after life. The girls' ritual, which was repeated periodically through life, had a negative purpose, the protection of the community from the mysterious danger that attached, it was thought, to all women at regular intervals. It is needless to add, perhaps, that similar rituals for both sexes prevailed over the larger part of North America, so that their functions among the Sekani do not necessarily explain their origin.

Let us consider first the ritual for boys. Each boy underwent a period of probation that lasted from one to two years, its exact length being determined by the duration of a hard lump at the base of the nipple which appears at puberty and disappears at its close.[6] At its first appearance the boy was sent into the woods to seek his hunting medicine, as described in the chapter on Religion. Thereafter, he hunted with his father and kinsmen, but was adorned with special ornaments and subject to special taboos. On his wrists and ankles, and around his neck, he wore twisted cords of birds' down (from birds of any species) which would give his limbs a feathery lightness in the chase. He was forbidden to eat the liver, leg-meat embedded in sinew, marrow, and blood of all animals, for they would make him heavy and slow of foot. Forbidden, too, were the heads of animals, for they would dim his sight. He might eat and drink very little until evening, and then barely enough to satisfy his needs. At the close of his probation, when the hard lumps disappeared from his breast, he removed his ornaments, observed only such food taboos as were enjoined upon him by his dream-guardian, and married as soon as he wished.

The ritual for a girl and for a married woman was the same. Each month she camped apart for several days in a small brush hut, drinking from a special birch-bark cup and supplied by her mother or female relatives with dried meat and dried fish. If she ate fresh meat or fresh fish at this season she would spoil the hunters' luck. Since even to look at a hunter would impair his success in the chase, she covered her eyes whenever she left her shelter. She might not walk in a hunter's trail, or touch his beaver net, though she could handle his knife, ax, or snow-shoes. If she looked inside the den of a black bear that a hunter had slain he would kill no others; and if she walked through running

---

5. Tahltan Indians for the same reason buried them under the roots of a young jackpine, according to a note by James Teit.

6. This, at least, is the Sekani belief. I do not know whether it has any physiological foundation.

water no more fish would be caught in that stream. Several foods were forbidden to women who were able to bear children. They might not eat eggs for then labour would be accompanied by much pain; or a beaver that had drowned, for they would choke in their chests (become consumptive); or young beaver, which would make them blind; or the head of any animal, which would have the same effect as young beaver. Only when a woman became old and unable to bear more children were these taboos lifted from her.[7]

Practically all the camp labour fell on the women, in order that the men might devote their whole time to hunting, which sometimes kept them away two or three days. It was the women, therefore, who carried the water and collected the firewood, cooked the meals, cleaned the hides, and made the clothing. Often, when the men returned worn out but successful, the women followed their trail and brought the meat to the camp; and on the march they carried all the camp paraphernalia so that the men could search ahead for game. There were several signals or signs for conveying information to people travelling behind:

(a) If the children made too much noise, the hunter stopped and whistled two or three times in succession.

(b) A zig-zag mark on the snow meant that the hunter had sighted game and that his family should remain quiet and wait for another signal. A blanket or coat left on the ground meant "stop and camp."

(c) A column of smoke on a hill-top meant that something had happened, usually that the hunter had killed game, and that the party behind should hasten to join him.

(d) Spruce boughs 3 or 4 feet long thrown on the ice meant "Make haste, something is wrong."

(e) Three sticks planted in line close together meant that the party in front had gone ahead a few miles. If the sticks were planted far apart, a foot or more, that the party was at least a day's journey ahead.

(f) A bundle of grass, or a rag, tied to a stick meant "starving."

(g) Hair tied to a stick (today a little cross) meant "some one has died."

---

7. The Long Grass people, through their association with the Carrier and Gitksan, acquired the belief that any marital association between husband and wife produced a taint that was displeasing to animals. Hence hunters slept for long periods apart from their wives, who accompanied them merely to take care of the hides and meat.

Life in a Sekani camp, however, was not all hardship. The people had dances and amusements similar to those of other Indians. None of the early explorers has described the ancient manner of dancing, which has long since been
forgotten. We know, however, that the only musical instrument was the tambourine, a parchment of caribou skin stretched tautly over a circular wooden
hoop and beaten with a thin stick, usually split at one end. It differed from the
Carrier and Gitksan instrument in having under its membrane two snares or
vibrant cords that the drummer could tighten or slacken with his thumb by
means of a noose (Plate 13), Whether the Sekani used this drum in dancing
is not certain, but it was indispensable for the gambling games to which they
were passionately addicted. McLeod Lake natives remember three varieties,

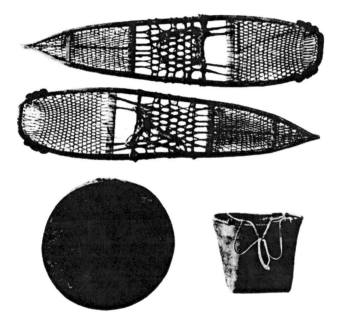

Plate 13. Sekani drum, birch-bark basket, and snow-shoes. (Canadian Museum of History 75942)

two played with sticks, the third with crudely made dice.

(a) The *nāt'a* game: there were generally eight players, four on
each side facing one another. Between them lay twelve sticks for
use as counters, and a drummer sat close by beating a tambourine. Side A began, each man hiding in one hand a stick of wood
or bone, and a selected player on side B guessed which hand
concealed it. If he guessed right for Nos. 1 and 4, but wrong for
2 and 3, 1 and 4 dropped out and 2 and 3 each won a counter.
He guessed again to eliminate 2 and 3, after which his own side
hid the sticks.

(b) The *atched* game: played like the preceding, but one of the four sticks was marked. As the drummer beat his tambourine side A hid the sticks beneath four mittens, "I hope you miss it"; and the guesser of the opposing side tried to knock off the mitten that concealed the marked stick. If he guessed rightly he took a counter; but whether he guessed rightly or wrongly it was his side's turn to hide the sticks.

(c) Dice (*tsaiili*: "throwing up"): a bone dice marked differently on four faces was tossed into the air. The count depended, of course, on the face which turned up.

The last of these games, dice, was also an ancient Carrier game, Morice says,[8] that had fallen into disuse long before his time. The other two games were probably of equal antiquity, for Simon Fraser saw the Shuswap play a game of hazard that "resembled that of the Rocky Mountain Meadow Indians by means of a small stick, bone, stone or anything else of a small size which under their robe they hide in one of their hands and afterwards place them in kimboo while they continue humming a song which is the only one I observed among them and either win or lose as their antagonist point out the hand that contain the mark or not."[9]

Still another game, snow-snake (*didzazi*), which was very popular with the younger men and also lent itself to gambling, seems to date from pre-European times. For this, the Sekani, unlike the Gitksan and some of the Carrier, did not make an artificial mound of snow, but bounced their darts off the natural surface.

The Sekani, constantly on the move from one hunting or fishing ground to another, could make little provision for those who were unable to keep pace with their wanderings. The aged and infirm dropped out and died of starvation. Their kinsmen built them good shelters, laid beside them whatever goods they could spare and some wood to replenish their fires, and departed hastily to soften the grief of farewell. If they killed game in the vicinity, they occasionally rescued an abandoned relative before death intervened; but often this would have been useless and even cruel, for the never-ending quest for food was certain to drive them away again sooner or later, this time never to return. So, generally, they made their victim as comfortable as they could and vanished quickly behind his brush shelter, that no look of reproach might follow their departing forms and bring misfortune upon them later.

Harmon states that in the early years of the nineteenth century the Sekani of Fort McLeod burned their dead; whereas, while they resided on the other side of the mountain, they were accustomed to bury them in the ground. Elsewhere in his journal he mentions that a Sekani burned the body of his murdered wife near McLeod lake, and describes from his own observations the cremation of a Sekani hunter in the half-Carrier, half-Sekani village between

8. Morice: Op. cit., p. 81.

9. *Second Journal of Simon Fraser*; Bancroft Collection, June 3, 1808 (copy in Library of Geological Survey).

Stuart and Trembleur lakes.[10] The present inhabitants of Fort McLeod seem not to recollect the earlier practice of burial in the ground, but have a clear remembrance of cremation.[11] The corpse, clothed in the garments of everyday life, rested on four large logs, over which four other logs were then laid. The ankles of women were bound together with red willow roots twisted into rope; those of men were unbound. After the fire had burned down the calcined bones were wrapped in spruce bark and buried in sandy ground. Often the wife carried them on her back to a good burial place near an old campsite or on familiar hunting territory; and sometimes, to display her grief, she crushed them to powder and carried them suspended from her neck inside a moose-skin bag, which she embroidered on both sides with porcupine quills. These practices, borrowed by the Sekani from the Carriers during the first quarter of the nineteenth century or a little earlier and continued until the end of its second quarter, illustrate how rapidly, in a tribe of low social organization and simple culture, even the burial customs can be assimilated to the customs of neighbours more advanced.

After cremation was discontinued, the Sekani revived an old custom, probably never entirely abandoned, of covering the dead man with the brush hut that had sheltered him during his last days and then deserting the locality for a period. Persons of influence were buried in coffins raised on platforms or trees. Thus Morice says "Supposing the deceased was an influential person dear to the band, they would hollow a kind of coffin out of a large spruce tree and suspend his remains therein on the forks formed by the branches of two contiguous trees. Some instances are also recounted in which the remains of such persons were closed up in a standing position in the hollow trunk of a large tree while in its natural state. The lid or door of these primitive coffins was usually formed of a split piece of wood which, when strongly laced with long switches of red willow, held it to the trunk of the tree in its original shape."[12] Fort McLeod natives told me that the hollow log or coffin was often closed with groundhog robes instead of with a board, and that it sometimes was set on two posts carefully smoothed so that no mice or other animals could climb up and desecrate the corpse. The custom was abandoned half a century ago, when the natives adopted the ordinary Christian method of burial in the ground.

Neither food nor property was burned or buried with the corpse, but whatever the dead man left behind him was divided among his family or kin. Widows and widowers underwent no bondage, and could remarry whenever they wished. The eldest son or nearest male relative gave a feast to all the band six months, a year, or two years after the funeral, according to his success in hunting; but whether this was an ancient custom, or derived from the Carrier, is uncertain. In any case it was purely commemorative, and involved

10. Harmon, D., Op. cit., p. 310; 215–16.
11. *Pace* Morice, A.G., *American Anthropologist*, vol. 27, No. 4, pp. 576–77.
12. Morice, A.G., *The Western Dénés*; Proc. Can. Inst., 3rd ser. vol. VII, 1888–89, p. 146.

no change in the name or rank of the giver of the feast, as usually happened among the Carrier.

The modern Sekani, especially the older people, still continue to mourn months and even years after their relatives have been taken from them. A man (or woman) will sit on the shore of McLeod lake in the morning, or at dusk, and lament his dead wife in a loud piercing wail, that echoes far over the water, rising and falling through the scale of an octave. After it dies away, one may see the melancholy mourner returning to his cabin to take up again the burden of his daily life.

The above description of the burial customs deals only with the McLeod Lake Indians. The early customs of the Fort Grahame natives are unknown to me, but they were probably very similar, since the two branches of the Sekani were in frequent contact throughout the nineteenth century. The marriage and puberty customs in both groups were the same.

The T'lotona or Long Grass band of the Sekani, who separated from their kinsmen and moved into the Groundhog country about 1850, developed very different social customs through their contact and intermarriage with the Gitksan and Tahltan. These I shall discuss in the same order as before, beginning with the marriage customs.

The youth who wished to marry consulted his parents, and, after gaining their consent, announced his desire, not to the girl he had chosen for his wife, but to her parents and kinsmen. If they approved they invited him to accompany them to their hunting grounds, where he presented all the furs he obtained to his future father-in-law. Not until the kinsmen were satisfied with the number of bales he had supplied would the girl's father hold the marriage feast, so that sometimes the youth was in bondage for several years. At this marriage feast, with the clans sitting on opposite sides of the lodge, her father distributed among his kin all the furs the youth had collected, and the youth's own parents added further gifts from their own stock. Then at last the youth might take his bride to his father's home or hunting grounds. Yet although she was now his wife, fully bought and paid for, custom still required him to make small presents to her people at irregular intervals.

Divorce occurred frequently, provided there were no children, but after children were born it was rare or unknown. The usual cause was infidelity, but a husband might cast off an idle and useless wife, and a woman might leave her husband if he failed to provide for her. Kinsmen generally tried to patch up an estrangement. If the husband was at fault but wished his wife back, his sister or aunt carried a peace offering to her kinsfolk, and, if successful, brought the wife back with similar offerings. A man rarely took upon himself the initiative of sending his wife away, but laid the burden on his father or nearest kinsmen.

Instances of polygamy were said to be unknown, but in one or two cases a woman had simultaneously taken two husbands who had previously served her parents for a term and agreed to share her between them.

A baby had no name until it was about a year old, but was called simply "boy child" or "little woman." After about twelve months it received the name of its father's crest, slightly modified, at a feast in which the father, the mother, or the mother's brother called on the principal men to pronounce and sanction it. The mother's kinsmen acknowledged their courtesy by giving them presents, and at the same time distributed presents among the father's kin. This first name lapsed at adolescence, when the child received a permanent or "feast" name, also derived from its father's crest. The permanent name indicated his rank, and the relative position he should occupy at feasts.

At adolescence boys fasted to obtain "medicine" for hunting, as described later. Every girl was isolated in a special lodge for about a year, and thereafter remained as close as possible to her mother until she married. During her isolation her parents announced her approaching maturity by giving a feast at which the father's kinsmen distributed small presents to the kinsmen of the mother. When her people were travelling the girl blackened her face, covered her head with a deep bonnet that prevented her from seeing the mountains or the sky, and followed their trail half a mile behind, guided, whenever necessary, by marks that her mother set up. No man was allowed near her, nor might she touch any of their possessions, but at streams her mother or sisters lingered behind to carry her across. She entered the camp after night-fall and made her way to a rude shelter her parents had erected for her in the vicinity, wherever possible behind some bushes. Throughout her probation she might eat the fresh insides of animals, the heart or the liver, but not the outside flesh and fat unless it was dried.

In their movements from place to place the Long Grass Indians seem to have set up signs that were slightly different from those of the McLeod Lake and Finlay River Sekani.

(a) A burning tree was an urgent call, meaning that a party was hurrying to catch up, that it had too much meat, or that someone had fallen dangerously ill.

(b) A slanting stick left in an empty camp indicated that the camp had been moved in the direction to which the stick pointed. Lines were drawn in charcoal round the stick corresponding in number to the hunters who happened to be absent when the camp was moved.

(c) An upright stick with a black ring around it meant that some one was dead. If the ring lacked completeness by the width of three fingers the person was dying. The number of survivors was indicated by a circle of sticks around the dead man's stick, long ones for adults and shorter ones for children.

(d) A stick pointing to the sky, marked with a rayed circle to represent the sun, indicated the time of day a person had passed that place.

The gambling games were also slightly different from those of the other Sekani. One was played with from two to four sticks, but my informant had forgotten the details. In another a man on one side juggled in his hands two bear's teeth or bones, one of them specially marked, and the guesser on the other side had to choose the hand which concealed the marked bone. Other games were:

(a) Snow-snake, played with a long heavy stick and no snow-bank.

(b) Hoop and spear. A man stood at one end of a level patch of ground and bowled a hoop towards another man at the other end. Fast runners pursued it and tried to catch it on long sticks before it reached the mark.

(c) Two men interlocked their middle fingers and tugged against each other; or, alternately, they tugged on the bone of an animal.

(d) Men tested their strength by trying to break in their hands the hind leg bone of the beaver.

(e) Men inflated the bladders of different animals, dried them and tried to burst them with their fists. A moderately strong man could burst the bladders of the caribou, moose, and bear, but no one, it is said, could burst the bladder of the mountain goat.

(f) Tug of war with a rawhide line, or with a slippery pole. In this game the sexes often took sides against one another.

(g) Boys played with bull-roarers, thin, flat laths of wood, wider at the bottom than at the top, attached by caribou sinew' to a stick and swung through the air. They also made buzzers from the knuckle bones of the caribou.

(h) Girls played hide and seek to train themselves to be quick of eye.

When a man died women relatives belonging to his own phratry washed the corpse and consigned it to the care of the other two phratries, whose members gathered to weep and burn it. They wrapped it in skins proportionate in number to the dead man's dignity and burned it within twenty-four hours, hastening the death-rites through fear of the ghost. In more recent times the Long Grass Indians have substituted Christian burial for cremation; they lay out the corpse for at least two days, and carry it for interment to a large grave-yard at the southern end of Hotlesklwa lake (about latitude 57° 20', longitude 127° 55'), the lake "where fish are as numerous as grains of earth."[13]

At a convenient time after the cremation the dead man's phratry feasted the other two phratries, and paid the people who had performed the obse-quies. At the same time it bestowed on the dead man's successor, usually his sister's son, the crest ornaments and rank of the deceased. If the man had belonged to the Wolf phratry, for example, his successor donned a wolf skin and entered the lodge with drooping mien to the accompaniment of a mourn-ful song. Presently the singers changed to a lively tune and he danced more cheerfully, finally taking his seat in the new place to which he had fallen heir. A brother or sister of the deceased then entered the lodge, clad in a robe of

---

13. According to Angus Beaton, a white trapper and prospector who had travelled extensively in the Groundhog country, there is a large graveyard at "Spruce island," an isolated forest of spruce trees close to Buckington lake.

tanned caribou hide decorated with the phratric crest either painted in red or worked in porcupine quills; and after them other kinsmen entered garbed in much the same fashion.

About the end of the nineteenth century the old style of costume disappeared, and the Long Grass people substituted for this decorated robe of caribou hide a robe of marten, lynx, or beaver, or else a coat of European style on which the crest was patterned in coloured cloth or pearl buttons.

Relatives cut off the widow's hair immediately after the funeral, for if she failed to show proper respect for her dead husband and kept her hair long one of her own brothers would shortly die. She remained with her father-in-law, or the nearest kinsmen of her husband, for two and sometimes three years, being regarded as a mere servant and treated accordingly. A chief's widow, however, was generally respected, and not forced, like other widows, to keep her face blackened so that it would reveal her tears. After about two years, when her hair was long again, a widow might remarry or return to her people.

An unmarried brother of a dead man normally married the widow in order to retain the use of her property; otherwise the widow and her children turned for support to her nearest kinsman. When a wife died the husband married any sister that was still unwed. Since husband and wife belonged to different phratries neither could inherit the other's property. The property of a woman normally went to her mother, sister, or aunt, not to her own children, although they belonged to her phratry, because her mother's brothers or her own brothers were bound to support them, and whatever valuables a man possessed went to his brother or sister's child, who belonged to his own phratry.

CHAPTER 7
RELIGION

The Sekani are today faithful adherents of the Roman Catholic Church, and at Fort McLeod have built a church where they hold services of song each Sunday, though the missionary may visit them only once a year. There is no church at Fort Grahame, but there also the natives meet frequently to chant Christian hymns. Monotheism, however, is a new doctrine to them. The idea was first implanted, apparently, by the white factors and by Iroquois and other Indians in the service of the two great trading companies during the first years of the nineteenth century. The Sekani then began to talk about *Hat,* God, just as the Carriers spoke of *Yagastā,* "he who sits on top of the sky," and the Tahltan of *Yekaside,* the kindly chief of the sky. The term *Hatā* is said to have been applied previously to any outstanding medicine man who claimed to have received his power from the thunder-bird; but it is open to question whether the notion of the thunder-bird also was not borrowed within the last two centuries, perhaps from the Cree. Certainly it does not appear prominently in the mythology of the Sekani.

The new doctrine of monotheism received a powerful impetus from Oregon, where the teachings of the first missionaries, perverted apparently by two natives educated on Red river near Winnipeg, produced an amazing Messianistic craze that spread northward up Fraser river through the Shuswap to the Carrier, whom it reached about 1830. One of the early writers, John M'Lean, thus describes it:

> Two young men, natives of Oregon, who had received a little education at Red River, had, on their return to their own country, introduced a sort of religion, whose groundwork seemed to be Christianity accompanied with some of the heathen ceremonies of the natives. It reached Fort Alexandria, the lower post of the district, in the autumn; and was now embraced by all the Nekaslayans (Carriers of Stuart lake). The ceremonial consisted chiefly in singing and dancing. As to the doctrines of our holy religion, their minds were too gross to comprehend, and their manner too corrupt to be influenced by them. They applied to us for instruction, and our worthy chief spared no pains to give it. But, alas! it is for the most part labour in vain. Yet, an impression seemed to have been made on a few; and had there been missionaries there at the time, their efforts might have proved successful. But the influence of the "men of Medicine," who strenuously withstand a religion which exposes their delusive tricks, and consequently deprives them of their gains—together with the dreadful depravity everywhere prevalent—renders the

conversion of the Tekallies an object most difficult to accomplish.[1]

Several branches of the Carrier nation were affected by this craze, none more than the western branch on Bulklev river, who carried it to the neighbouring Gitksan. They carried it also to Babine lake, whence it spread to the Sekani of Bear lake who later moved to Fort Grahame. From this source, apparently, or from the Gitksan of upper Skeena river, it reached the Tahltan, on Stikine river. The Carrier of Stuart lake conveyed the same doctrine to the Sekani of McLeod lake, among whom it remains today but a memory. But at Fort Grahame its repercussions still echo, despite the faithful labours of Roman Catholic missionaries.

The craze took much the same form among all three Athapaskan tribes, Carrier, Tahltan, and Sekani, though the first-mentioned developed it more than the other two. The new "Messiah fell into a trance or died," as the natives say, for an hour, a day, or two days; his soul mounted to the sky, whence God sent it back with a message. The signal for its return was a low song breathed through the lips of the apparently lifeless body. The bystanders took up the new song, the "Messiah" rose to his feet, and the people danced and sang around him. Preaching, prophecy, confession of sins, healing of the sick, baptism, renaming, frequently but not invariably accompanied the manifestations; and these rites were repeated at intervals of a few days until the craze wore off.[2] Sekani Messiahs, unlike the Carrier, adopted no peculiarities of dress and received no "paraphernalia from the sky."

The following accounts come from Fort McLeod, and refer to manifestations that occurred between 1870 and 1880. It is probable that many occurred earlier, since the craze reached the Stuart Lake Indians around 1835; but on this point I have no information. After 1880 it subsided in this region permanently.

Six McLeod Lake Sekani, five men and one woman, have "died," ascended to heaven, and returned to life, receiving from God these new names: Loud Singer (*adji*), He Flew up to the Sky (*yatassa*), He passed on top of the Sky (*yagina-tał*), *Dizasf-cun*, a name of unknown meaning, and Good Singer (*uzadjin*); the last-mentioned was a woman.

Adji was not ill. He lay quietly in his tent, surrounded by onlookers. With eyes closed, and breathing still, he lay for twenty minutes, dead. Once before he had visited heaven and returned to earth, so that the people knew what was about to happen. The murmured syllables of a song issued from his lips. He sat up, and gazing with a far-off look at the audience, described

1. M'Lean, John, *Notes on Twenty Five Years Service in the Hudson's Bay Company*; vol. 1, London, 1849, pp. 263–64.

2. For a literary description of the cult among the western Carrier. See Barbeau, C.M., "Indian Days in the Canadian Rockies," Toronto, 1923, Ch. 1.

what he had seen in the sky. "God has named me Adji, the Loud Singer," he said. "Hereafter you must do no evil." He issued other injunctions similar to those the priest now gives. Then the people sang his song, but they did not dance.

Uzadjin, Good Singer, who died at a great age about 1914, visited the sky more than a score of times, securing a new song on each occasion. Each time she lay as if dead for a period varying from half an hour to an hour, and on recovery announced what she had seen or heard. She reported on one occasion that she had heard a bell ringing in heaven, and warned the people that some one would shortly die. Uzadjin sometimes healed the sick by dancing round them and singing her heavenly songs.

Dizaskun was the last native of Fort McLeod to visit the sky. Besides acquiring a new name for himself, he gave a new name to his mother.

Fort Grahame natives gave similar accounts:

Before the Bear Lake band of the Sekani moved to Fort Grahame a man named Matoteha died and returned to life. Before his death he asked the people not to burn his body, but to keep watch. He lay in his tent all night, motionless. At dawn he began to sing, repeating always the same song. As it gained in volume his eyes opened, his body moved, and at last he sat up. "I have been to a far country," he said. "I have seen God. God bade me warn you not to kill, or steal, or do anything that is evil. In that country live all the good Indians who have died heretofore." Matoteha then rose, took up his drum and danced; and the people danced with him, singing his song.

Matoteha was a very great medicine-man. His other name was *Hatā*, a name given only to medicine men who far surpassed their fellows. Once he visited the thunder-bird and its young high up on a mountain, and plucked a feather from the tail of the young bird, despite the terrible heat. Because no one believed him when he returned, he asked his son-in-law to draw near, but the man was unable to approach him because the red feather scorched him like lightning. Matoteha, for a heavy payment, restored the dead to life by placing his feather under the head of the corpse. At last, when he was an old man, he died again at Bear Lake, and warned his people as usual not to burn or bury his corpse. They watched over him for ten days; but when his body began to waste away and the spirit failed to return, they placed him in a burial house on top of a platform.

Another Indian named Satche died at Bear Lake and returned to life. He told the Sekani that he had visited God's home in a beautiful country, but was ordered to return and teach people the true way of life; then, after two hours, he might go back to the sky. Two hours later Satche died and never rose again.

The daughter of William Bear, an old man living at Fort Grahame in 1924, had a similar experience about 1905. She was dead for two hours, and on returning to life declared that she had seen a beautiful land wherein lay a wonderful house with nothing but good things inside and around it. It was God's home, but God taught her no song.

Old Davie, the leader of the new *tseloni* band, is the only man still living who has visited the sky. He has died on several occasions, seen God, and received new songs that, issuing through his half-closed lips, announce his return to life.

This Messianistic craze developed not illogically from the earlier beliefs of the Sekani. The Christian doctrine of a single God who dwells in a far-away heaven has merely replaced the older but still surviving notion of "supernatural power" residing in birds and animals. Instead of dying and mounting to the sky to receive *nadetche*, medicine power, direct from God, the Sekani received it from an animal by fasting and dreaming in solitude. The new songs, and the new names, obtained by the modern Messiahs, closely resemble those obtained by the seeker of medicine power before them. Baptism and confession of sins have been added from Christian rituals, but in the main the new Messianistic practices are but a modification of the ancient rites.

Plate 14. Old Davie and some of the women of the Long Grass band. (Photo by Wm Ware. Canadian Museum of History 63134)

In the old Sekani religion there seem to have been no deities. Animals were like human beings in ancient times, and there were many strange monsters that preyed upon mankind. All these monsters were destroyed long since; they lived only in *witchetsa*, "olden times." The legends tell of great heroes, of a trickster who wandered over the earth making things as they are today, and of a great flood; but many of these stories have been derived from the Carrier, the

Cree, and other neighbouring tribes, and the ideas they embody seem hardly to have touched the native life. There may have been local spirits, supernatural beings that haunted special localities such as rapids, lakes, or mountains, but if so they have been practically forgotten. More deep-seated and lasting was the belief that man and the animal world are linked together in some mysterious way and that the animals possess special powers which they may grant to man if he seeks them in the proper manner.

It is difficult, perhaps impossible, to obtain from a Sekani a clear notion of this mystic bond that binds the animal world to man. It is not in the individual animal that the power resides—not in the moose or lynx that falls a victim to the hunter's rifle—but in the species as a whole. Two men may acquire different powers from the same animal, and it is conceivable that different animals may impart the same power. Moreover these powers seem to be separate units, not portions of a greater power diffused through the universe, part in one animal and part in another. The Sekani, apparently, felt no necessity to seek a single source for it, like an all-powerful sky-god, or a vague, mysterious, all-pervading force; he had no yearning towards abstractions. In the old days, tradition said, animals and man had been alike. Animals still resemble man in certain ways, and even surpass him; the animal thinks like man, excels him in strength, speed, or cunning. So man logically turned to the animal world to secure help for the crises of life, and established a certain relationship with it. The animals might withhold their help and grant a man no "medicine"; but, generally speaking, he who sought it by the proper methods seldom went home empty handed.

Certain animals were more closely associated with man than others, and it was from these, not unnaturally, that the Sekani obtained their "medicine." One native expressed their attitude thus: "The Carrier, who are fish-eaters, may obtain medicine from fish and water-animals; but we live by the chase, and our medicines came from the bear, the moose, the caribou, animals and birds essential to our life." This was the Sekani "hunting medicine," *nadetche*, obtainable only before marriage when man was free from taint; it differed slightly from another kind of "medicine," the "medicine" used for sickness, which might be gained at any time. To reveal the details of the "hunting medicine," or to use it often, destroyed its force. An old man whom it could serve no longer might tell of the medicine he had received in youth, and sometimes people discovered each other's medicines through beholding their operation. But the vision was almost never revealed. It was the heart of the medicine, as it were, and the medicine was a secret gift, for use in emergencies only, often just once in a lifetime.

Every youth, then, when he reached the age of puberty, was sent forth alone to seek a "hunting medicine" that he could summon to his aid in after-life. This was part of his puberty ritual. He left in the early morning, fasting, and wandered all day in the woods, beside a lake, or up the mountain side. He might return in the evening, eat a scanty meal, and go out again the next morning; or he might remain away two or three nights. Some youths were fortunate and gained their medicines in a single day; others sought for three or four weeks. Few failed, or, if they failed, did not confess their failure, since no one would ask them what they had seen or heard.

A youth unable to obtain medicine in the ordinary way might even bring influence to bear on the animal world. He would enclose a number of frogs inside a circular wall of birch bark from which they could not escape, and sleep inside the enclosure. During the night the frogs would disappear into his sleeping body and medicine of some kind would quickly come to him.

The following descriptions given by Fort McLeod natives illustrate the manner in which a boy might gain his medicine:

> A boy at puberty may be out on the mountains, seeking his medicine. He hears singing, though no one is in sight; wondering, he continues on his way. A caribou approaches him, and he falls to the ground, apparently dead. The caribou walks around him all night. At last the boy wakens, and after remaining in the same place for two days, returns to his home. Before entering the camp he smokes his body over a fire of balsam brush, lest his people smell the taint of the caribou that visited him. Thereafter, when hunting, he may wear a cap of caribou fur, if so instructed by his animal visitor.

> A boy may sleep the first night on a caribou trail, the next night on a bear trail, and the third beside a lake. On the third night he may see a big fish like a canoe swallow a moose, a caribou, or a bear. He will probably remain there two more nights before returning home. After he becomes a man, and is known to possess medicine power, no one may rise and walk about when he eats; for then he will have difficulty in swallowing his food and angrily snap his teeth, causing the offender's death.

> Another youth may go out to the woods for five days and five nights, sleeping on the ground beside a fire under the open sky. At night a grizzly bear cub lies on one of his shoulders, a black bear cub on the other. The youth awakens and says to himself "Now I have good medicine." He clasps the cubs tightly in his arms, and they disappear into his body. Presently he hears a song, the song of the black bear cub, succeeded by the song of the grizzly cub. When he awakes he is still lying on the ground beside the embers of his fire; but the song remains in his memory. Thus he has medicine for black and grizzly bears. It may happen that five or ten years later he and his people are starving. Then he will sleep apart from his wife and sing the songs that the bear taught him. When day dawns he goes out hunting, finds black and grizzly bears and kills them without difficulty. If a youth sees a bear for several nights and hears the bear's song then he will have strong medicine, but it will avail him only for killing bears, not for moose or other game. Similarly moose medicine is useless except for moose.

> Still another youth may be wandering in the woods, seeking his medicine, when he comes upon a moose labouring in deep

snow. He approaches it, intending to shoot, but the moose says to him "Do not shoot me. You will be starving some time or other in the years to come and then I will help you." The youth allows the moose to-escape, receiving medicine in return. A few years later, perhaps, when his people are starving, a moose will plant itself in his tracks and allow him to kill it.

Or he may obtain medicine from a black bear in the same way, by sparing a black bear in its hole. In time of need, remembering the bear's promise of aid, he will go out alone and easily kill one or two bears.

An old man at Fort Grahame thus described his acquisition of hunting medicine:

When I was a boy my mother sent me out into the woods to seek my medicine. I climbed the slope of a mountain and at sunset reached the nest of an eagle. It contained only one eaglet, the second having been shot by an Indian; but the mother bird returned before dark. I slept under the nest that night, and the mother eagle spoke to me, saying "I fly all around until I find game; then I pursue and kill it. You go and do likewise." The next day I went home. My brother met me near the camp and said "We were afraid that a grizzly bear or something had killed you" and I answered "No. I merely stayed out all night because I saw something." No one asked me what I had seen, for the people knew that a man must not reveal his medicine. Now in my dreams I often see where there is game, and never fail to find it the next morning. That is my medicine. But since the priests have come to us the Indians at Fort Grahame no longer seek the old medicines. They carry rosaries when they go to the woods, and count half the beads as a prayer each morning, and the other half each night. But I am not sure whether the rosaries arc as effective as the old medicines.

Even a girl may acquire hunting medicine. A Fort McLeod native narrated the following episode that occurred, he said, when he was a young man:

A party that was hunting in the mountains lost an axe, and sent a young girl back along the trail to search for it. She wandered back several miles and met a wolverene carrying the axe. It spoke to her, and gave her the axe, for which she thanked it. Thereafter she possessed medicine for wolverenes.

Songs and amulets often accompanied medicine, but not invariably. A man who had medicine for caribou might wear a caribou horn attached to his belt, or a cap from the fur of a caribou head; he might have seen a caribou in his vision, and been told to wear one of these things. Or he might wear a necklace of swan's neck with the feathers turned in, and when driving caribou against a fence set with snares attach the feathers to the end of the fence that the animals might not break away in the wrong direction. Another man who had also obtained medicine for caribou might receive no song, and be told to wear no amulet; or the same amulet might be worn for another purpose. Certain hunters wore caps made of grizzly bear skin, or carried arrows blackened in the fire and painted red or green, arrows that never missed the mark. Others again were subject to taboos. One man at Fort Grahame will not eat fat from the belly of the moose; another will not eat any meat from a bull moose; a third will not eat the tail of a beaver. All medicine was obtained through dreams, and dreams are infinitely varied in pattern. Whatever a youth saw in his dreams, whatever he was told to do or wear, that was his medicine, that he obeyed.

The Sekani tell many stories of the uses of hunting medicine. If moose were escaping across the top of a snow-slide a man who had medicine for moose might cry aloud and cause a fresh snow-slide to overwhelm and kill them; if he had medicine for wolf he might howl like a wolf and rob their legs of strength so that they could not travel. A man who had medicine for caribou would dream of them at night and whistle; the caribou, hitherto unseen, would draw in towards the camp and be killed the next morning. Likewise a man who had beaver medicine would walk across a creek above a beaver house, thus preventing the animals from escaping up-stream. A man who died at Fort McLeod not long ago had medicine that would cause snow. When his people were starving, unable to kill moose, be burned the feathers of a swan in the fire, and sang his medicine song all night. Snow fell for two days, and the moose, floundering in its depths, were killed without difficulty by hunters mounted on snow-shoes.

An old man at Fort Grahame narrated this story:

> My grandfather had loon as his medicine. When his people were starving near Thutade Lake he said to them, "Don't go out on the ice. I shall get fish alone." In the morning he went out alone, wearing a hat of loon skin, dug a hole in the ice and speared many fish. He left them on the ice, and, returning to camp, sent his people out to bring them in. For more than a month he supplied the camp with fish. The people then wandered away to hunt caribou. They discovered a large herd, and built two fences with inset snares. One of the hunters then said "Let every one remain in camp while I go after the caribou alone, for I have medicine." He went out alone and said to the caribou, "Go down yonder and be caught in the snares." Later the people went out to see what had happened; every ₅nare had caught a caribou. In spite of their medicines, however, four Sekani and many Carrier at Babine and Stuart Lakes died of starvation that winter; for the moose had disappeared from the entire country.

How does this "hunting medicine" work? It works through a kind of mental telepathy. Caribou, moose, beaver, and other animals know the thoughts of men who have received medicine from them; they have spoken to them, given them songs perhaps, or told them to wear certain amulets. There is a mystic bond between them, and provided the men observe the rules the animals will obey their wishes. But always a man must beware of wearing out his "hunting-medicine." It is for emergencies only; used even three times it loses much of its strength.

Medicine for sickness bears the same name, *nadetche*, as hunting medicine, which it resembled in many ways. Both were obtained through dreams, both were secret and lost if the dream was revealed, both often involved taboos, and both might be associated with certain tokens or amulets worn or carried on the person. The Sekani attach much significance to dreams in everyday life; a hunter who dreamed that game was lacking in a place would certainly avoid that locality. Hence when a man dreamed repeatedly about anything a mysterious bond was forged between him and the object of his dream, and he acquired medicine power through the association. The object might be an animal; more often, apparently, it was inanimate, like water or a gun. Whatever it might be the medicine power resided not in the object, but in the man himself, who acquired the power through the dream-association. Its ultimate source the native seemed unable to explain, nor indeed was he interested in its metaphysical basis. But he firmly believed that it supplied a vital need in his life, helping him on those occasions when his hunting medicine was of no avail. For the hunting medicine assisted him only in time of starvation, not in sickness, or when enemies were near at hand; and it could be used only once or twice in a life-time. This other medicine never wore out, and though it served as a rule for sickness only, it might apply to other purposes. Few men acquired it, a fortunate few, and they not by searching for it at puberty, as for the hunting medicine. It came to them fortuitously, usually after marriage, since it involved no close association with the animal world and the taint of marriage made no difference. A man who obtained one medicine often obtained several, for he was blessed with peculiarly receptive powers. He was, therefore, a man of importance in his band, a true medicine-man, whose services were requisitioned in all cases of sickness. He was also a source of danger. His power was like a magic ray that can not only cure but cause sickness and death. It might even be dangerous to himself. Thus a medicine-man might be forbidden in his dream to eat food when people were walking near him. If he disobeyed the taboo, he would become insane, and the person walking near would die. Such a man, therefore, would always warn the people to sit down before he ate, and if some one chanced to rise to his feet, he would strike him with a hat, or stick, to recall the taboo to his remembrance.

Sickness, to the minds of the Sekani, was produced by one of four causes. It might arise from some physical cause, as a knife; from the patient's soul leaving his body and wandering away; through the machinations of a medicine-man; or, finally, from some cause unknown. Practically, these could be reduced to two, for the physical cause, the knife or the arrow, might be only the instrument of medicine power, and any sickness that seemed inexplicable could be ascribed to the evil machinations of a medicine-man. He might work his evil in at least two ways, probably in many; he might point his medicine token at his victim and pray that its counterpart might enter his body unseen; or he might enter a sweat-house, seize the wandering soul of his sleeping enemy in his hands and beat it so that it could not return. Cases might occur, the Sekani thought, where a malady was caused by wrong-doing, eating forbidden food, for example; and a medicine-man might even reproach the patient with his sin. But confession in no way aided recovery, as was believed by so many tribes; and the sin was always a disobedience to one of the regular puberty regulations, or to a taboo imposed during the reception of medicine power.

Nearly all sickness, therefore, arose from medicine power. Logically, it could be countered most effectively with similar power. The Sekani did not neglect their simple remedies, nearly all herbal; but in the main they relied on the fortunate owners of sickness medicine, who used their talents to gain both wealth and influence.

An Indian, we will suppose, is sick. His relatives send for a medicine-man, or a medicine-man offers his services of his own accord. In his sleep, he may say, he has discovered the cause of the malady, and will undertake a cure for suitable payment. The relatives accept his services. What follows depends in part on the nature of the man's medicine power. If he possesses no tangible token of his power he may enter a sweat-house, where the cause of the sickness, if still unknown, is revealed to him; there he can catch the wandering soul and restore it to its owner; there he can extract from the patient's body the bone or other baneful object implanted magically by some unfriendly medicine-man. All this he can do even without visiting his patient. 'But if, like most medicine-men, he carries with him some token of his power, such as a knife, he will probably visit the patient in his tent, or join him in the sweat-house, sing his medicine song, and rub the sick man with the token, or bring it into physical contact with him in some other way. He will then breathe on the sufferer, and pretend to extract by suction the bone, or piece of metal, which he can hold up as the cause of the malady. Every man had his own individual methods, but discovery through dreaming, especially in a sweat-house, massage, and the apparent extraction of some object, were common to almost all.

An elderly Sekani of Fort McLeod thus described the medicine powers of himself and his grandfather:

> When I was a youth I received medicine for water. Others have possessed this medicine before me, and some have borne tokens of it in the shape of large lumps on their arms or bodies; but I had no token or visible sign of medicine. When the influenza epidemic swept the country in 1918 and many of my people were stricken by the disease, I called for cold water, my medicine, and drank two or three cupfuls. The water caused me to vomit, voiding all my sickness, and in two days I was well again. That is how my medicine has helped me, although it may never help me again.
>
> My grandfather, *Intsidene*, "Wind Man," had four medicines, beaver, knife, crane and a black powder (some men, greater than their fellows, have owned 50 medicines). Beaver

was hunting medicine; he received it in the woods when he was a young boy; crane, knife and black powder were sickness medicines that came to him later in life. I do not know how he received his medicine for black powder, but when he was a very old man, and had no further use for his powers, he told me about crane and knife. This was how he gained his crane medicine.

He had many dreams about the crane after he was married. At the end of a year he divorced his first wife and went to hunt on the Parsnip river. It was the end of winter, when the cranes return from the south. As he crossed the summit of a mountain, alone, a crane flew close to his head and called "Loud noise close to sky, let us play for the people over yonder." My grandfather, realizing that he was to receive a new name and medicine power, lay down and slept; as he slept the crane came and sang to him all through the night, leaving him at daybreak. Thus he received medicine for crane, and with it a new name and a song.

Knife medicine he received in another way. He dreamed so frequently of a knife that at last he felt sure that he would receive medicine from it. He was hunting once on the mountains, all alone, when he heard a voice say "Marten. I am lonely. I have been here a long time and wish to go back to mankind. Help me." My grandfather could see no one, but as he walked along, searching, he saw a knife lying on the ground beside a hole from which it had just appeared. He picked it up, saying to himself, "Now I have medicine for knife," continued his hunting, and at night returned to his home. On this occasion, and also when he received medicine for black powder, he obtained neither a song nor a new name.

To cure the sick he used one or other of these three medicines, knife, crane and powder. He sat down beside the patient, closed his eyes, and sang his crane song. When he was using the powder medicine, he laid his black powder beside him, and as he sang his medicine power issued from his lips like a hiccough. Then he mixed some of the powder with water and rubbed it on his patient. He shaped his hand into a funnel, blew the medicine from the powder into the man's body and once more sang his medicine song. Now he left him, and, going into the sweathouse for an hour or two, discovered whether his patient would live or die. A patient who was to live would begin to recover immediately.

I never saw him use his crane medicine, only the crane song. The knife that he found served him for every purpose, not for healing alone. The medicine power was not in the knife, but in himself; it was but a symbol or token of his power, and for healing he often used some other knife. He hardened its blade in the fire and rubbed it over the place where the patient felt pain, saying *ha ha ha ha ha ha*. Then, as when using the powder, he blew the medicine into the man's body and retired to the sweat-house to learn whether he would recover.

My grandfather could kill people with the knife medicine. He could take a piece of iron, rub it between his hands, point it in the direction of his victim, praying that it would enter his body, and cause the man immediate pain. Another medicine man, discovering the cause of the pain in the sweat-house, would suck a piece of iron from the patient's body.

The knife medicine preserved my grandfather from sickness all his life. When he was very old he obtained for the first time a steel knife that would keep a sharp edge. He said to his people, "My knife keeps sharp. I shall die soon." Soon afterwards he died.

The notion of sickness medicine was capable of great expansion in the hands of an imaginative or ambitious Indian. Early explorers among the Athapaskan tribes of the Mackenzie River basin tell of strange practices by the medicine-men, such as the swallowing of knives and long boards. These tricks were rare but not unknown among the Sekani, where certain possessors of sickness medicine claimed to be able to swallow bunches of porcupine quills. Some of the neighbouring Carrier tribes practised walking over red-hot coals, and employed the drum and rattle in their medicine ritual. They had also an elaborate ritual for acquiring hunting medicine, and prayed over offerings of burning caribou fat when game was scarce. None of these customs, however, were adopted by the Sekani.

Nevertheless, the Sekani did acquire, either from the Carrier or from the Gitksan (since it prevailed among both), the belief in a very strange "medicine power" that seems wholly alien to their mode of thought, but is in harmony with the beliefs and practices of the tribes along the Pacific coast. It was a belief in what one man called "air medicine," though its name at Fort McLeod is *anatak*, at Fort Grahame *senidje*, words that the natives seem unable to translate. It was an intangible thing, like air, or wind, pregnant with medicine power like an animal, but infinitely more potent. It would squeeze a man between its "hands" and place him in a big kettle strewn with feathers to keep his body warm; and it filled him with such explosive force that he shot through the air like a bullet from a gun. One man at Fort McLeod who had acquired this medicine chanted the formula he had learned (it consisted of meaningless syllables only) and was immediately shot across the lake into the woods on the far side. Some hunters sought him the next day, and found him lying on the ground, half dead. Another man was carried out of sight and did not return until two years later, when his brother, who was hunting groundhogs, found him on a mountain side, strong and well. Five years afterwards the two men ascended another mountain to hunt goats; but when the medicine man approached the summit he sang his *anatak* formula and flew far away. He was seen again only once, when a hunter sighted him from a distance. *Anatak* gave the gift of foresight; its possessor knew several days beforehand what game he would kill. Another medicine, called *ixwasi*, that closely resembled it, caused its possessor to fly through the air like a bird, or like, a tiny transparent man.

Fort Grahame natives, who called the same medicine *senidje,* gave a slightly different account. *Senidje,* they said, struck a man between the shoulders like a gust of wind, or caught him by the hair, and flung him many yards over the ground. He lost his wits, and in that condition received instruction and medicine power from *senidje.* Their description closely parallels the accounts given by the western Carrier of an intangible, invisible force called *kyan,* which strikes a man senseless and then renders him crazy for a period. Such an experience qualifies him for membership in a secret society, the "cannibal" society found under various forms all along the British Columbia coast.

The T'lotona or Long Grass band, hybridized by intermarriage and close contact with Tahltan and Gitksan Indians, had a different conception of medicine power. Dreams still remained its basis, but the distinction between hunting and sickness medicine was drawn along other lines. Both were obtained at the same time, and by the same procedure, but few men obtained more than the hunting medicine; and the sickness medicine had two grades, the lower giving only the power of diagnosis, not of cure.

Every youth at the age of puberty was sent to climb a mountain, either alone or with a companion of the same age. He carried with him, or found on the mountain, a flake of obsidian, with which he cut out the tongue of a ptarmigan, an ermine, or an owl. He threw the tongue into the fire, and as it burned he prayed, "May I become a swift runner, an accurate shot, a powerful medicine-man able to cure all diseases." For four days and four nights he fasted, neither eating nor drinking. The higher he ascended the mountain the more certainly his prayer would be answered. On the fifth day he rejoined his people camped below and built a hut beyond the range of their hearing. There he remained from spring until autumn, supplied by a boy with food from his parent's home. He might eat meat of any kind, but only the minimum necessary for life, and the heads and hearts of all animals were forbidden him.[3] Herbs were permitted, and an occasional draught or pill of devil's club, which induces stupor and is favourable for dreaming. No woman might pass near his lodge, and if he visited his parents he but lengthened the term of his isolation. He stayed alone in his lodge, seeking the dream that would give him medicine power.

Not every youth obtained a significant dream that gave him medicine power; but if he performed the ritual faithfully he was sure to receive one of the three blessings for which he had prayed, swiftness of foot, accuracy of aim, or medicine power. Power came through dreaming of some animal, a caribou, or a grizzly bear; and it would be the greater the nearer the animal approached him, the more familiarly it allowed him to handle it. If he could touch it, if he could place his hand in its mouth, he was certain of great power. It would be greater still if he dreamed of three animals, and obtained medicine from each

---

3. No Long Grass hunter would eat the head of any animal lest his tongue should hang out while he was pursuing game and make him short of wind.

one. With each medicine went a song, a song sung by the animal about itself. Two caribou medicine songs ran as follows:

(a) O mother caribou bring your young.
Bring them slowly and feed on the grounds where you will find plenty.
When you come come carefully.
The spirit of my patient hovers near.
Don't crowd your young, lest they trample on my patient's spirit.
(i.e. as you slowly come so will the health of my patient return)

(b) I need your help, O caribou.
Come swiftly to me.
You see I have laid my hands on the sufferer.
Come and lay your hoofs where I have laid my hands.
I need your help.
Without your help there is no healing in my hands today.
Come so quickly that your tail stands erect.

The songs and dreams did not originate with each new medicine-man, but were inherited mystically from some ancestor. A great medicine-man who had received power from many animals might even impart some of it to his son; but only if the latter were sickly, since the father was bestowing breath from his own life. Father and son then slept together under one blanket inside the family lodge, and when the father dreamed of his medicine song the son dreamed the same song with him, and could sing it without prompting when he awakened; the medicine power accompanied the song.

Every medicine-man had his own charms or amulets, things that his dream animal told him to use when effecting a cure. He might wear the velvet of a caribou horn attached to his clothing or carry it in a bag by his side wrapped in white swans-down; or his charm might be a strip of fur from a mountain goat or a grizzly bear. Sometimes he painted it on his drum, for the Long Grass medicine-men, although rejecting the rattle of the coast tribes, adopted the use of the drum. When he was called in to heal a patient the door was shut, and no one allowed to enter or go out. Little children who might be present had to remain quiet and take no part in the performance. The medicine-man sat beside the patient and sang his song, and the audience joined in the singing. At a certain stage he laid his charm on the sick man, and his medicine power, working through the charm, effected a cure. The patient was not healed at one sitting; but the ceremony had to be performed repeatedly, night after night, until the cure was complete.

This was the true medicine-man, the only man who had medicine for healing. He charged so high a price for his services that he was summoned for serious cases only. For lesser cases the natives would call in a dreamer, a lower order of medicine-man, who underwent the same training, but received power from his dream only to determine the cause of a malady, not to cure it. Often the mere knowledge of the cause sufficed to dispel the ailment; if it failed the dreamer advised the relatives to call in a fully qualified medicine-man to co-operate in the cure.

The procedure of dreamers differed slightly, but one woman treated her patient in the following manner. She sat down beside him and asked her heart whether he would live or die. Her heart suddenly leaped into her mouth, rendering her half unconscious. Bystanders placed swans-down on her head and vermilion on her cheeks to allay its throbbing. Gradually she recovered her poise, and gave her diagnosis. If the case were serious she might say "I saw the spirit of an animal resting on his chest; if it reaches his throat he will die. Summon a real medicine-man who has cut a tongue and received the power of healing." The relatives sent for the best medicine-man in the neighbourhood, who, in co-operation with the dreamer, sang over the patient, laid his charm upon him, and effected cure.

The most powerful medicine came from a rare bird, named *mis'kaiya*, a fish-eater, pure white, about the size of a duck. The youth who caught it and burned its tongue became one of the greatest medicine-men in the community. Next to this bird ranked medicine from the caribou, because the caribou, being a swift runner, effects the speediest cure. Below caribou ranked mountain sheep, and below that again grizzly bear and other animals.

Women underwent a different training in girlhood and could not qualify as professional healers. They could, however, become dreamers. A father might make his daughter a dreamer as he made his son a medicine-man by sleeping under the same blanket with her, and inducing the same dream and song. When a girl was about two years old the mother sometimes inserted in her ears the two sharp bones that lie under the tongue of the raven. Gradually the skin grew over them, the girl became keen of hearing, and as she grew to womanhood was very susceptible to dreams. In her dreams she could understand the raven that visited and spoke to her. She could even foretell what would happen in the near future, the death of a neighbour, or the number of caribou he would kill on his next hunt

A violent form of hysteria, which sometimes developed into total dementia, was very common among the Sekani and surrounding tribes. The Indians of Fort McLeod attributed it to the breaking of a food taboo, especially a taboo imposed when receiving medicine power. But the Sekani of Fort Grahame, the Long Grass band, and some of the Carrier tribes attributed it to the land-otter. The simpler and probably older form of the belief was found at Fort Grahame. The natives of that place asserted that the otter assumed the form of a youth or maiden and seduced its victim, who forthwith became insane. One method of cure was to lash the man to a tree near the edge of a lake and await the otter's appearance The animal approached at the insane man's call, and was shot by hunters concealed in the bushes. Its victim recovered his senses after drinking some fluid from its body. No cautious man or woman was ever deceived by the otter, for its teeth always remained those of an animal when the rest of its form became human, and it hid its mouth when it smiled.

A recent case of otter-sickness, or hysteria, was treated at Fort Grahame, the natives say, by a Kaska medicine-man from McDame on Dease river. Beating a drum, he danced and sang over his patient and extracted from the young man's chest the otter spirit that provoked the malady. The youth was cured, but the medicine-man warned him to avoid otters thereafter. Four years later the youth met another otter and died.

The T'lotona or Long Grass Indians, under the influence of the Gitksan, reinterpreted the otter belief so that it explained not only hysteria, but tuberculosis. They held that the otter stole the breath of its victim, who might become subject to paroxysms of hysteria, but more frequently languished in a kind of trance, dreaming of the otter night and day. Unmarried individuals alone were susceptible, and girls more than youths, especially girls who were disappointed in love. Medicine-men sometimes effected a cure, restoring the patient's breath by singing and drumming; the patient then acquired the lower grade of medicine power, the gift of prophecy and of diagnosing the cause of sickness through dreams. But often the medicine-man failed and the patient died. So susceptible were unmarried girls that their contact with any part of the otter was liable to induce the disease. Hence a man who had been rejected by a girl would secretly mix with her food the tip of the otter's tail, or one of its whiskers. Sometimes she became so crazy that she followed him everywhere. At other times the "medicine" appeared to have no effect, and the girl might marry and even bear children. But after two or three years she became languid and comatose. A medicine-man might cure her, but no one could discover who had "poisoned" her food.

APPENDIX
EXTRACTS FROM THE FIRST JOURNAL OF SIMON FRASER, 1806

(Series C. No. 16, Bancroft Collection, Pacific Coast MSS., University of California, Berkeley. Copy in Library of Geological Survey, Canada, Ottawa)

"Wednesday 16th April. About 9 A.M. Mr. John McKinver arrived[1] from the Meadow Indians, after an absence of seventy odd days, he informs us of his having starved much at different times. He accompanied the Indians far off in search of Beaver but though they saw many Beaver Lodges they killed but few on account of the depth of snow which is from five to six feet deep in the Beaver country. They saw no large animals of any kind no not even a track during their long and intricate route until within two days march of the upper end of the Portage at the place they returned the Indians showed him the place where Trout Lake[2] was and told him it was only three encampments distant from there but he could get no one to accompany him the place where Trout Lake[2] was and told him it was only three and the misery they endure to go there and from there to come here proves this plan to be of little use. Could it be done it would certainly be more proper to send them all to Trout Lake where Beaver is near the Fort and it is certain they will never work well until they have an establishment formed in the Beaver country."

"Wednesday 23rd April. Menard arrived with four young men from the chiefs band they brought 22 Beaver skins, 2 carcasause and six Pechause belonging to the chief which are well dressed, traded the value of two skins. These Indians are not Meadow Indians but of another tribe and the relations of the chief who always sides with the Meadow Indians and who has much authority over them. We attempted to get some information concerning their country but they seemed rather stupid and not much inclined to satisfy our desires which perhaps is not a little owing to the little knowledge we have of their language for our interpreters are none of the best, however we understood that Finlays branch does not terminate in chutes and Rapids as reported but with the intervening of some Portages that it is navigable to its source and from thence there is a Portage about half the length of this, a large Lake called Bear Lake where the Salmon comes up, and from there is a River that falls into another much larger (according to their Report than over the Peace River) that glides in northwest direction. In that Lake they say there are plenty of fish and that the salmon are unnumerable with plenty of Bears and animals of the fur kind there about, but no large animals of any kind. It is from that quarter they get their Iron works and ornaments but they represent the navigation beyond that Lake as unpracticable and say there are no other Indians excepting a few of their relations that never saw white people there about and to get Iron

---

1. At Rocky Mountain Portage, i.e., Hudson Hope.
2. Now called McLeod lake.

works they must go far beyond it, which they perform in long journeys on foot. We cannot imagine what River this is by their description and the course it runs it cannot be the Columbia, and I know of no other excepting Cooks, but whatever River it is and wherever they get these, their Iron works and ornaments are such as I have seen with the Cassuss.[3]

Tuesday 6th May. By what we could learn from the Indians at different times an establishment would be well placed on the big River that falls into the main branch of the Peace River, about half way between this and the Beaver River. This River at its confluence with the Peace River is large an appears to contain a large quantity of water and the Indians say it is navigable a considerable way up, and that Beaver, Bears, and large animals of all kinds are amazing numerous, it is thereabout is what may be properly called the Meadow Indians or as they call themselves *Les Gens du large* lands. But it is then likewise they are most subject to be killed by the Beaver Indians of both forks and Fort Vermillion and on that account they seldom now remain there but nine tenths of the year. But out in the mountains where there is neither Beaver nor anything else but Badgers and where they undergo great misery, according to their reports there is but a very short distance from that River to a branch of McKenzies River that the *Nakanés* inhabit with whom they have often intercourse. Most every one of them told us if there was a Fort on the Banks of that Big River and if the Beaver Indians could be prevented from killing them that they would make excellent hunts and that it was the only good place they knew."

"Friday, May 9th. Menard and the Indians arrived. They had a few skins Beaver Credit and traded 30 with the value of 80 skins dried provisions and twenty on Aryenal skins. This is the band of Indians that were attacked last summer by the Fort Vermillion Indians and they did not see the Fort since they were at the Beaver River two years ago consequently they never saw this place before. Last winter they went down within two or three days march of Beaver River but were not at the Fort. I repremanded them severely for not coming here last Fall and asked them the cause of not making a better, to which they replied that they had made a few furs but that they lost all when attacked by the Beaver Indians and that ever since they generally kept in their lurking holes in the mountains and that they wished to come and see white people in the Fall but did not know where to find them, their being none at Beaver and being told that this place was abandoned in the Spring and transferred to Tinlays branch they went there but found no one in consequence of which they thought the white People had abandoned the country and then returned to their lands where they were found in the month of March by Indians that had

---

3. Carriers.

been out on purpose to look for them in the month of February who informed them of there being a Fort here."

"Wednesday May 28th. In the morning Pauce Coupe's comrade came to us[4] with a couple of Indians that never saw white people before, they are exceedingly well clothed in leather and though they never were at the Fort, they have guns which they got from their relations. They are the relations of the Meadow chief but of a different family. They gave us some information about their lands. What information we got from these Indians is chiefly about Finlay's branch and the country beyond it, which is conformable to what we have heard from the other Indians at the Portage. The only additional information we got from them is that there is an immense number of Beaver all along Finlay's branch and the River that falls into it and that there are a few camibance about what they call the Bear Lake. They seem to be well acquainted with the Carriers with whom they live in amity and from whom I imagine they got the most part of their Iron works and ornaments at least they are of the same kind. They desired us to be on our guard and beware of the At-Tah which is the name both them and the big men gives the Atnah tribe whom they represent as more treacherous than really wicked and wood likely if not aware shoot their arrows at us."

"Thursday 10th July. This[5] is a fine River and not unlike the Athabasca but not so large and the Indian we left at the height or point of land informed us that the upper end of it was the most ordinary residence of the *Says-Thaw Dennehs* (Bawcanne Indians) which corroberates with what the Carriers tell us of these Indians, they being enemies, when they go a hunting in that quarter, I have seen one that was wounded last summer and his brother was killed, which is likely the same that was mentioned by one of the Bancanne Indians last winter at Dunvegan as being killed there. All accounts agree that large animals as well as those of the fur kind are in great abundance particularly towards the upper end, could this be relied upon and that the Bancanne Indians are really there-abouts an establishment is my opinion would be well placed at the point of land.[6] There is excellent fish in the three Lakes and in two of them Salmon abounds in its season and by all accounts animals are not far off, indeed of this we had ocular demonstration ourselves so that people would live well there a no immaterial object in this quarter and the Baucanne Indians would be much more easily got to come there than to any part of the Peace River on account of their being afraid of the Beaver Indians, and the Big men, though they seldom meet they live in amity."

---

4. At Finlay Forks.
5. McGregor river.
6. The divide between Parsnip and Fraser rivers.

Plate 1. The buffalo tent, from painting by L.G. Russell.
(Canadian Museum of History 81437)

The Sarcee Indians
of
Alberta

by
Diamond Jenness

First published by the National Museum of Canada
Bulletin 90, Anthropological Series No. 23
1938

Rock's
Mills
Press

PREFACE

Very little has been recorded about the Sarcee Indians of Alberta apart from the accounts of their Dancing Societies and Sun Dance published by Dr. P.E. Goddard in the series of Anthropological Papers of the American Museum of Natural History. In the summer of 1921, therefore, the National Museum of Canada sent Mr. Jenness to their reserve near Calgary to discover what he could concerning their earlier customs and beliefs. The field-notes he gathered on that occasion provide the material for this report.

CHAPTER 1
HISTORY AND NUMBERS

European explorers of the late eighteenth century frequently mention the Sarcee Indians, although it was only during the last 10 years of that century that the tribe became regular visitors at any trading-post. Our earliest reference comes from Matthew Cocking, who speaks of five tribes of "Equestrian Indians," the Powestic-Athinuewuck or Water-fall Indians (Gros Ventres), the Mithco-Athinuwuck or Bloody Indians (Blood), the Koskitow-Wathesitock or Blackfooted Indians (Blackfoot proper), the Pegonow or Muddy-water Indians (Piegan), and the Sassewuck or Woody Country Indians (Sarcee).[1]

The erection of a trading fort at Cumberland House in 1774, followed soon afterwards by the establishment of other posts farther up North Saskatchewan River, quickly made the Sarcee well known. Thus, Umfreville wrote in 1790:

Though this nation [the "Susee"] have a language entirely to themselves, and which no others can learn, they are very few in number, being no more than a small tribe which was separated from the main body, and now harbour in some country about the Stony Mountain, where they keep to themselves, for not many have as yet appeared at any of the trading-houses. Those who occasionally visit us are a crafty deceiving set, much given to theft and intoxication. Though their tribe is small, they cannot live in amity with their neighbours; for the last summer, a number of them fell upon an encampment of Blood Indians, whom they were at peace with, and most of the men absent, they inhumanly butchered several women and children, which it was expected would be severely revenged the first opportunity.

These Indians are lazy and improvident; they bring us very few peltries, and those ill drest. Wolves skins are their chief commodity. Their women are the most ordinary of any I have seen, but they are all liberal of their favours, when a person has wherewithal to pay for them. They retain a close alliance with the Nehethawas [Cree], rather to profit by their protection, than for any mutual esteem subsisting between them. Their language is equally disagreeable and difficult to learn; it rather resembles the confused cackling of hens, than the expression of human ideas; yet one of our interpreters has attained a sufficiency of it to answer the purpose of trading with them.[2]

---

1. Burpee, L.J., *An Adventurer from Hudson Bay; Journal of Matthew Cocking, from York Factory to the Blackfoot country 1772–73*, edited by L.J. Burpee; Proc. and Trans. Roy. Soc., Canada, Third ser., vol. 11, sec. 11, pp. 110–11 (Toronto, 1908).

2. Umfreville, E., *The Present State of Hudson's Bay*, pp 198–200 (London. 1790).

It is not likely that Sir Alexander Mackenzie ever encountered the tribe, although he remarks in his "Voyages" that

> At the Southern Headwaters of the North branch dwells a tribe called Sarsees, consisting of about thirty-five tents, or one hundred and twenty men ....
>
> The Sarsees, who are but few in number, appear from their language, to come on the contrary from the North-Westward, and are of the same people as the Rocky Mountain Indians described in my second journal, who are a tribe of the Chepewyans.[3]

Duncan McGillivray, in 1794, casually mentions visits by Sarcee Indians to his trading post at Fort George, on the North Saskatchewan,[4] but his contemporary Alexander Henry the younger describes them in some detail:

> The Sarcees are a distinct nation, and have an entirely different language from any other of the plains; it is difficult to acquire, from the many gutteral sounds it contains. Their land was formerly on the N. side of the Saskatchewan, but they removed to the S. side, and now dwell commonly S. of the Beaver hills, near the Slaves [Blackfoot], with whom they are at peace. They have the name of being a brave and warlike people, with whom neighbouring nations always appear desirous of being upon amicable terms. Their customs and manners seem to be nearly the same as those of the Crees, and their dress is the same. Their language greatly resembles that of the Chepewyans, many words being exactly the same; from this, and their apparent emigration from the X., we have reason to suppose them of that nation. They effect to despise the Slaves for their brutish and dastardly manners, and, though comparatively few in numbers, frequently set them at defiance. Formerly they killed many beavers; but, from the proximity of tribes who were indolent, they have become nearly as idle as the others. Of late years their numbers have much augmented, in the summer of 1809, when they were all in one camp, they formed 90 tents, containing about 150 men bearing arms."
>
> The Sarcees, who all traded at this post in the winter of 1810–11, were excellent beaver hunters while on the N. side of the Saskatchewan, but from intercourse with the Slaves have become fully as lazy and indolent. A quarrel which they had last summer with the Assiniboines has caused them to remain near the mountains for the present; the environs of the Beaver Hills are generally their station. These people have the reputation

---

3. Mackenzie, Sir Alexander, *Voyages from Montreal on the River St. Lawrence through the Continent of North America in 1789 and 1793*, pp. LXX–LXXII (London, 1801).

4. *The Journal of Duncan McGillivray*, edited by A.S. Morton (Toronto, 1929).

of being the bravest tribe in all the plains, who dare face ten times their own numbers; and of this I have had convincing proof during my residence in this country. They are more civilized and more closely attached to us than the Slaves, and have on several occasions offered to fight the others in our defence. None of their neighbours can injure them with impunity; death is instantly the consequence. I have already mentioned their (Athapascan) origin. Their manners and customs are nearly the same as those of all the other Meadow [Plains] Indians. They are a hard people to deal with; the most arrant beggars known. A refusal makes them sullen and stubborn; for being as they term themselves, our real friends, they imagine we should refuse them nothing. Most of them have a smattering of the Cree language, which they display in clamorous and discordant strains, without rule or reason. Their own language is so difficult to acquire that none of our people have ever learned it.[5]

McGillvray's and Henry's greater contemporary, David Thompson, contributes some further information:

The Sussees are about ninety tents and may number about 650 souls. They are brave and manly, tall and well-limbed, but their faces somewhat flat, and cannot be called handsome. Trey speak a very guttural tongue which no one attempts to learn.

The country of the Stone Indians and Sussees are full from four to six hundred miles in the plains eastward of the Mountains, and too far to look for horses; the Sarcees content themselves with rearing horses, but the Stone Indians are always in want of horses which appears to be occasioned by hard usage. They are most noted horse stealers.[6]

From these passages it appears evident that in the eighteenth century the Sarcee controlled much the same area around the upper waters of Saskatchewan and Athabaska Rivers as they occupied in the nineteenth. Directly north of them were their kinsmen the Beaver Indians, directly south the Blackfoot proper, beyond whom lay the two other Blackfoot tribes, the Blood and the Piegan. To the east and northeast were the Cree, who seem to have spread up Saskatchewan River during the first half of the eighteenth century, to be followed a few years later by some of the Assiniboine. To the westward, on the other side of the Rockies, dwelt the seldom-encountered Shuswap; and

5. Goues, E., *New Light on the Early History of the Greater Northwest*, vol. II, pp. 531–32, 727.

6. David Thompson's Narrative, edited bv J.B. Tyrrell; The Champlain Society, Toronto, 1916, pp. 327 and 367.

southeast of the Blackfoot hunted the Fall Indians or Gros Ventres, whom the Sarcee frequently met at the trading-posts.

There can be no doubt that the Sarcee drifted to the Saskatchewan from the northward, possibly towards the end of the seventeenth century, certainly at a period that did not long precede the penetration of the prairies by European fur-traders. Their speech still differs very little from that of the Beaver Indians who once occupied the basin of Peace River, and both tribes retain the memory of their common origin. The Sarcee offer two different reasons for the separation. According to one account

> Once when faction broke out between two chiefs, all the Indians rallied behind them, thus forming two bands that separated and developed into distinct tribes, the Beaver and the Sarcee.

The other relates that

> In the course of a certain winter the whole body of Indians set out to cross a river on the ice. Half of them crossed in safety, but just as the other half was about to attempt the passage the ice mysteriously broke. The two bands were afraid to rejoin later and parted company, one becoming the Sarcee, the other the Beaver.

The early nineteenth century saw the trading-posts on the prairies increase in number, and every Indian tribe obtain an abundant supply of horses as well as a considerable number of firearms. The intermittent warfare of the previous century became intensified, and the Assiniboine and Cree Indians definitely joined forces in unceasing attacks on the three tribes of the Blackfoot, who in self-defence now formed a loose confederacy. The Gros Ventres soon retreated south of the Canada-United States boundary, but the weaker Sarcee, encompassed by enemies on all sides and no longer able to stand alone or avoid taking sides in the conflict, alined themselves whole-heartedly with the Blackfoot and ranked as the fourth tribe in that confederacy. Yet we can see traces of their earlier independence not only in the statements of Umfreville and Henry just quoted, but in their still surviving traditions, which preserve the memory of several conflicts with the Blackfoot. Naturally, they attached themselves most closely to the nearest tribe of the Blackfoot, the Blackfoot proper; with the Blood and Piegan they seldom came into contact, though they still recall one fight with Blood Indians on the site of the present city of Calgary.

Several nineteenth century writers have given us glimpses of these ceaseless conflicts among the plains' tribes, in which the Sarcee played their part. Sir James Douglas records in 1835 that

> A month or two ago a war party consisting of 300 Strong-wood and Beaver Hill Crees made a hostile incursion into the Blackfoot county, and accidentally fell in with a straggling party of 20 Circus warriors who on perceiving the enemy threw themselves into a thicket of trees, and after hastily constructing a tempo-

rary barricade, boldly opened a spirited fire on the Crees who not relishing the idea of a rapid advance on their determined enemy contented themselves with maintaining a weak and desultory fire during the day. In the night the Circus, who were not very strictly guarded, escaped from their fortification, leaving 11 of their number on the field of battle; of Crees, 3 killed and 10 wounded. The Circus who escaped reached their main camp and a strong party of their friends gave pursuit to the Crees, who took up a strong position in the woods where they could not be attacked but at a manifest disadvantage; and the two parties finally separated, without any further attempt on either side.[7]

Raids of one kind or another occurred almost yearly down to about 1875, so that in 1921 it was still possible to find on the Sarcee reserve men and women who had taken part in them. Three old men dictated the following reminiscences.[8]

When I was ten years of age I accompanied two warriors to Montana in order to steal horses from our enemies. We came upon an encampment of Dakota Indians, and by the light of the moon I stole among their tents and drove off four horses. The three of us then started out for home, but had travelled only half a day when we fell into a trap laid for us by a large band of Sioux. My companions escaped, but the Sioux surrounded me and one of them counted a coup by striking my head with a stick ornamented with an eagle feather. When they saw that I was only a boy, however, they let me proceed. A few hours later I met a little Sioux boy who also was riding all alone; and because his people had been merciful to me I let him go too, merely taking his tobacco pouch from him. Afterwards I caught up with my companions and we brought our stolen horses safely home.

On the other side of Red Deer River four Crees once rode into camp and were immediately killed. I myself struck one of them while he was still alive. Not long afterward another small party of Crees likewise rode into our camp by mistake and met with the same fate. The Sarcee children shot arrows into their dead bodies.

About 1860 the Sarcee made a truce with the Cree and established a common camp at a buffalo pound that the Cree had built. As soon as the buffalo drive ended, however, they moved away, taking with them a certain Blackfoot Indian who had temporarily joined his fortunes to theirs. Before they departed some Cree who were friendly with my father advised him to camp

---

7. Private Papers of Sir James Douglas, 1st ser., ser. C, No. 12, Bancroft Collection, University of California.

8. See also pp. 2, *et seq.*

apart, because their people were planning to attack the Sarcee; and as we moved away some one in the Cree camp did fire a shot that wounded the Blackfoot Indian in the leg. My father, with two or three kinsmen, therefore detached himself from the rest of our people, and set up his camp a few miles away.

The following morning the main body of the Sarcee again moved camp. The warriors and the women rode ahead; behind them travelled a score of children in the charge of an old man and in the rear of the train another band of about ten children conducted by a second old man. Suddenly the Cree rode down on them from behind, killed the two old men, carried off the children, and attacked the warriors and the women as they were pitching their tents. Both sides suffered many casualties, the Sarcee far more than the Cree. Finally night put an end to the battle and the Sarcee escaped in the darkness.

About 1862, when the Sarcee were travelling near Fort Vermilion, a dense fog arrested their progress and caused them to pitch their tents under a hill not far from a lake. An old man then left the camp to pursue a buffalo, which he overtook after many miles and killed. The Sarcee noticed his absence at their dance that evening, and as soon as it was daylight they sent out a few warriors and women to look for him. I wanted to accompany the party, but my father said that I was too young and ordered me back to the camp.

A few hours later we heard the sound of firing, and thought that our search party had discovered a herd of buffalo. What really happened was that one of that party, riding ahead of the rest, approached a man on the slope of a hill under the impression that he was the missing hunter. When he discovered that it was a Cree Indian, he turned his horse and galloped back to warn his companions, but the horse caught its foot in a badger hole and fell. Before the man had time to flee two Cree rode down on him, and, though he shot one of them, he himself was shot and killed by the other. Then a large force of Cree suddenly appeared on the hill top and galloped down on the Sarcee, whose horses were already tired from the day's journey. As they fled the horse my uncle was riding became utterly exhausted, and my father offered to take him on his own horse. At first my uncle refused, saying that my father had a large family to support and should try to save himself; but in the end, he mounted behind him and let his own horse go. The Cree overtook them, nevertheless, and though my father killed one man and wounded another, both he and my uncle were killed, along with five other Sarcee who fought beside them. The remainder reached within sight of our camp before they were surrounded. A hand-to-hand mêlée ensued, in which the women fought as desperately as the men; but hardly one of the party succeeded in reaching the tents.

Meanwhile some of us were piling poles, travois, bags and other things around the tents to form a barricade, while others dug holes in the ground for cover. I was hurried away with a party that carried two large tents to the shore of the lake where we should be protected in the rear. There our enemies soon surrounded us, not only Crees, but Indians of three other tribes allied with them, some armed with guns, the majority with bows and arrows. The noise of their guns was deafening, and their arrows pattered on the water like rain. Our women and children huddled inside the tents, holding dried skins over their heads to ward off the arrows; and behind the tents stood the men, led by three distinguished warriors, one on each flank and one in the middle. Whenever the enemy approached too near one or more men would charge them. Several times a man failed to return, and a relative would then rush out to look for him; but generally the relative too was shot the moment he left his cover.

One young man was particularly heroic. He drove back the enemy repeatedly until at last an arrow struck him in the throat. He jerked it out and rushed forward again, but fell to the ground dead. Then his father rushed forward, shot two Cree who were trying to despoil his son, seized their guns and ran back toward the tents again. A bullet struck his leg and he fell; but as he lay on the ground betwixt friends and foes, both of whom were striving to reach him, he calmly reloaded his gun and shot a Cree who was charging down. Two of his relatives succeeded at last in dragging him back to shelter, still clasping the two guns that he had captured. Ever afterwards this man bore the honorable title Two Guns.

I was lying inside one of the tents, which kept shaking and blowing up at the bottom so that I could see what was happening. At one time I saw two of our men lying outside, both shot in the legs; at another a Cree and a Sarcee grappling with each other's guns. An old woman who was lying near me, shielding her grandchild, leaped up to stretch a skin, over their heads when a bullet suddenly struck her brass bracelet, pierced her wrist, and tore, out her grandchild's eye. In the height of one assault the wife of Bull-Head, one of our leaders, peered out of our tent and, seeing three Cree trying to enter the other tent, caught up an axe, cleft the skulls of all three from behind, and carried back one of their guns.

Throughout most of the battle I did not see our three leaders, but near the end, when many of the enemy had exhausted their bullets and some of them were loading their guns with pieces of steel wire, I heard them singing their medicine songs and challenging each other to feats of bravery. Suddenly all three of them charged out and drove the Cree back. As they were racing in again, the man who had been guarding the middle of the camp stopped to pick up a wounded friend. A bullet struck his leg, but he hobbled on until a second bullet struck his other leg and he fell just outside our tent. His two co-leaders kept up their charges until the second one was wounded and only the third, Bull-Head, remained to organize the defense. This warrior called to the survivors, just before sunset, "Don't skulk there round the tents. Charge the enemy with me." Every man who could still fight rushed to the attack and drove the Cree back. The enemy then retreated, being afraid, apparently, of Bull-Head's great medicine-power, because he had killed more men with his tomahawk and Hudson Bay sword than all the rest of the Sarcee combined.

The Cree and their allies suffered heavily in this battle, but the Sarcee lost at least twenty families, including women and children. Never again did they recover their earlier strength."

My grandfather and my mother belonged to the Sioux[9] nation, but my father was a Sarcee and I myself was born among the Sarcee. One day my father went out to hunt buffalo and did not return to our camp for two days, for he had discovered that the Cree were lying in wait to intercept him. Not knowing this, however, our people sent out a search party, which ran into our enemies and was driven back to our camp. As often as the Cree overtook a man woman or child the pulled their victim off his horse and killed him. In their first charge they reached the middle of our camp and drove us into and behind our tents. Every one of our horses was killed, and a pond in the centre of the camp became red with blood, for the arrows pattered on the water like rain and the smoke of the guns almost blotted out the view. One Cree leaped into a tent filled with women and was felled with an axe. The battle raged all day, but toward evening some Blackfoot came to our aid and we drove our enemies off. During their retreat I followed four of our warriors, and when they surrounded and killed one of the foe, I shot all his arrows into his corpse. The Cree and their allies suffered heavily, not only during the battle, but afterward on their retreat, when they had to leave many of their wounded to die on the trail. Our own losses were even heavier, for we filled two tents with the bodies of our dead.

In the winter of 1869 a kinsman of mine, Crow-chief, with his wife, another man, and a boy, left our camp to hunt for buffalo, and had just killed an animal when they were attacked by a party of Cree. The other man fled precipitately and was never heard of again, probably because he froze to death; but Crow-chief, his wife and the boy tried to regain our camp. His wife's pony was so slow, however, and the Cree were gaining on them so rapidly, that Crow-chief turned aside and hid in some brush, leaving his wife and the boy to be captured. The Cree killed

---

9. The Sarcee commonly applied the name Sioux to the Gros Ventre.

the boy and surrounded the brush in which he was hiding, but, doubling on his tracks, he galloped past them and reached our camp. That night the enemy stole all our horses; and they way-laid and killed an old man whom we sent out the next morning to procure others. Then, late in the afternoon, they attacked us in our camp but with the help of some Blackfoot Indians we killed two of them and drove the rest off. Two years later some missionary sisters at Lake St. Anne rescued Mrs. Crow-chief from the Cree and restored her to her husband.[10]

Always a small tribe, apparently, the Sarcee suffered throughout their history not only from these intertribal wars, but from all the epidemics of smallpox and other diseases that ravaged the other plains' Indians. Estimates of their earlier population vary. Mackenzie gave them "about 35 tents or one hundred and twenty men,"[11] whereas Thompson and Henry, as we have just seen, estimated ninety tents, 150 warriors, and about 650 souls. A quarter of a century later Sir John Franklin raised the number of tents to one hundred,[12] and the same figure appears in the Private Papers of Sir James Douglas which date from the same period.[13] A smallpox epidemic in 1836, and an epidemic of scarlet fever in 1856, both decimated them; and when their strength had been still further reduced by at least one crushing defeat at the hands of the Cree, and by the starvation that attended the diminution of the buffalo herds, they were afflicted by a second epidemic of smallpox that crippled them completely. In his brief account of the tribe in 1885 Hale states

> The adopted tribe, the Sarcees, have greatly diminished in numbers through the ravages of the smallpox. In 1870 this disease raged among them with great virulence. They were then residing on the American side in Montana. Mr. McLean writes "An eye-witness told me that at the Maria's River, in Montana, there stood fully 100 lodges, and not one containing less than ten bodies." His estimate of dead Sarcees was 1,500. This tribe, now numbering less than 500 souls, have their Reserve near Calgary.[14]

Although in this passage Hale's informant has probably confounded the Sarcee with some other tribe, his description of the desolation the epidemic produced is in no way exaggerated, being fully confirmed by contemporary missionaries.

---

10. What probably was the same incident is recorded in Hughes, Katherine, *Father Lacombe, the Black-Robe Voyageur*, pp. 139, 157–60 (New York, 1911). The date given there, however, is 1867.

11. Mackenzie, op. cit., p. LXX.

12. Franklin, J., *Journey to the Shores of the Polar Sea*, vol. 1, p. 170 (London, 1824).

13. "Private Papers of Sir James Douglas," 1st ser., ser. C, No. 12, Bancroft Collection of Pacific Coast MSS., University of California (copy in the Dominion Archives, Ottawa).

14. Hale, Horatio, *Report on the Blackfoot Tribes*; Rept. British Association for the Advancement of Science, 1885, pp. 698–89.

Plate 2. Old Knife inside his tipi. (Canadian Museum of History 53312).

Even in 1921 the Sarcee were still dating events from 1870, and an old man named Many Wounds retained a vivid memory of their sufferings in that year.

When I was ten years old I killed my first buffalo, a young calf, with a bow and arrow, and a few weeks later I killed a full-grown animal in a pound. In the late summer of this year, when the berries had begun to ripen and we had encamped near the Blackfoot just north of the Red Deer River, smallpox broke out among us. It attacked the Indians in different ways. Some became red all over, but their skin did not break out into open sores; others were covered with red sores oozing pus. Some were attacked in the throat; their tongues swelled and they suffocated. Others felt pain in the spine and died in one night. Father Lacombe visited us for a time and vaccinated a few individuals; but there were no medicines that could cure us. We broke up camp and moved south, abandoning the dead and the dying in their tents or dropping them beside the trail. Gradually the plague mitigated, but not until it had wiped out nearly 200 families. My father, my mother, two brothers and a sister all died, so that I had to live in the tent of a married sister.

In 1877, along with the Blackfoot and the Alberta Assiniboine, the Sarcee signed a treaty resigning their hunting-grounds to the Dominion Government on certain conditions, one being that each member of the tribe should receive an annual gratuity of $5. Two years later pay-sheets record the payment of this annuity to 672 persons, organized in five bands, as follows: Big Plume's band 287; Bull-Head's 134; Painted Otter's 43; Little Drum's 145; and Many Horses' 63. These bands, however, probably included Indians of other tribes, for the pay-sheet of the following year records only 396 persons, the pay-sheet for 1881 (the first year in which the annuity was distributed on the present Sarcee reserve near Calgary) 485 or 458,[15] and the pay-sheets for succeeding years numbers that are still smaller. *The Handbook of American Indians North of Mexico* (art. Sarcee) states, without giving its authority, that "in 1897 two divisions [of the Sarcee] were reported, one at Calgary and the other near Battleford"; but since nothing further seems to be known of the Battleford Sarcee, they perhaps comprised merely two or three families that merged with the local Assiniboine and Cree, just as by 1921 some Blackfoot and Cree families had merged with the main body of the Sarcee on the reserve near Calgary. We may safely presume that at the time they resigned their territory and submitted to confinement, i.e. in 1880, the Sarcee numbered between 400 and 450. From 1880 until 1920 (and perhaps later), they declined steadily, not because certain families wandered away from the reserve (for others moved in to counterbalance the loss[16]), but because of an exceedingly high death-rate occasioned by tuberculosis and other causes.[17] The statistics of the births and deaths on the reserve from 1891 to 1901 are as follows:

Year	Births	Deaths
1891	14	16 (7 consumption)
1892	10	14 (8 grippe, 2 consumption)
1893	14	15 (4 consumption)
1894	10	11 (2 lung disease, 3 consumption)
1895	8	18 (6 consumption)
1896	13	15 (1 consumption)
1897	12	18 (14 consumption)
1898	9	12 (7 consumption)
1899	8	19 (12 consumption)
1900	5	10 (4 consumption)
1901	4	6 (3 consumption)

In 1924 the reserve sheltered 160 Indians, all commonly considered Sarcee, though an uncertain proportion were originally Cree and Blackfoot. Even Assiniboine and other elements have been present, seeing that the Pax Britannica and the reservation system established after 1880 seem to have produced no greater fusion of the plains' tribes than had been going on for centuries. We know from the narratives of the early explorers that women taken

---

15. Papers on the Sarcee reserve contained two records for this year that gave different totals.

16. Between 1897 and 1910, 46 Indians moved into the reserve and 21 moved out of it.

17. Thus Many Wounds, whose description of the smallpox has just been quoted, had six children, only one of whom reached maturity.

in inter-tribal raids commonly married their captors, and that even warriors frequently changed their allegiance.[18] The tribes have, therefore, intermingled their blood from time immemorial, and it is not surprising that in physical appearance the Sarcee present no features that would distinguish them from other plains' Indians. One can place little confidence in such statements as that the Sarcee "are not so fine or tall a race as the Blackfeet," or that "they are of a lower order and inferior mentality."[19] On the contrary, in physique, mentality, dress, and customs they seem hardly distinguishable from the Blackfoot, although they have preserved their Athapaskan tongue almost unchanged.

---

18. Thompson met a family of Cree origin that had gained a high place among the Blackfoot.

19. Wilson, E.F.: *Report on the Sarcee Indians*; Rept. British Association for the Advancement of Science, 1888, pp. 248, 243.

CHAPTER 2
SOCIAL ORGANIZATION

Like other plains' Indians, the Sarcee were a democratic people who did not countenance hereditary distinctions of caste or rank. They were divided into several bands, each containing a number of closely related families that usually hunted in company, and always camped together as a unit when the tribe united, unless it happened to be holding a special celebration such as a Sun Dance. Girls belonged to their mothers' bands, boys above the age of nine or ten to their fathers', though they still retained close contact with their mothers' kin; for since the bands were very small and freely intermarried there was no outward distinction between their members: a family could temporarily hunt or travel with another band at will, and even change its allegiance permanently. Alien families who joined the tribe attached themselves, by permission, to one or other band and were soon completely absorbed by intermarriage; at least, such was the custom in the late nineteenth century, probably also in earlier times. The bands, indeed, seem to have been very fluid, constant neither in number nor composition; they could arise quite naturally whenever a man had several sons, and by his success in hunting or warfare drew into his orbit one or more other families. Probably several such bands were destroyed during the hostilities and epidemics of the nineteenth century, and new ones arose to take their places. In 1921, long after they had lost their significance, the Sarcee still grouped themselves into five bands, which they generally named after the outstanding family in each.

1. Blood, *Klowanga* or Big Plume's band.
This comprised the families of Yellow-Lodge. Dick
Knight, Bull Collar, Peter Big Plume, Joe Big Plume,
Jack Big Plume, and a few women who had married into
the Cree and Blackfoot tribes and were living on other reserves. Most of the families were of mixed Sarcee
and Blood descent, whence the name of the band.

2. Broad Grass, Tents Cut Down, or Crow-Child's band.
It comprised the families of Crow-Child, Bertie Crow-
Child, Sleigh, Many Wounds, and Peter Many Wounds.
Most of them were of mixed Cree and Sarcee descent,
and the name Broad Grass recalls that the Cree element
came from the north where the grass is thick and long.

3. People who hold aloof (*natsistina*) or Crow-Chief's band.
It comprised the families of Charlie Crow-Chief, Tony, Wolf,
Otter, Oscar Otter, Pat Grasshopper (senior and junior), and
Bob Left Hand. Most of the members were pure Sarcee.

4. Uterus or Old Sarcee's band.
It comprised the families of Old Sarcee, One-Spotted,

103

David One-Spotted, Fox Tail, Two Young Men, Tom
Heaven-Fire, Two Guns, Crow-Collar, George, Big-Crow,
Dick Starlight, Jim Starlight, Sarcee Woman, Young
Bull-Head, Dodging a Horse, and Anthony Dodging a
Horse. Many of them were mixed Sarcee and Blackfoot.

5. Young Buffalo Robe or Many Horses' band, occasionally
called also "Those who keep together."
It comprised the families of Tom Many Horses, Big Knife,
Running in the Middle, Dog, and John Waters. Most
of the members cosidered themselves pure Sarcee.

Each band had its leader, who was not elected, but recognized by common consent because of his prestige. Although he possessed no formal authority, and had no means of enforcing his wishes except by popular support, his advice and instructions were rarely disobeyed. Similarly, there was no elected chief for the entire tribe, but always one or more band leaders who through their greater influence could generally sway the people to their views and, therefore, tacitly ranked as chiefs. The Indians discussed all matters of importance at informal councils composed of the band-leaders, the older and more experienced men, and noted warriors. At such councils each man's opinion weighed theoretically as much as any other's, but the views of the more influential naturally prevailed. The rank and file then accepted without question the decisions of the council, any men who dissented were free to move away, and, if they wished, to dissociate themselves altogether from the tribe.

Quite separate from the bands, and indeed cutting right across them, were five societies or clubs, to one or more of which every male Sarcee belonged at some time or other in his career. Each society held an annual 4-day dance attended by every member of the tribe, and during those 4 days the leader of the society enjoyed complete control of the camp and all its activities. One society, the Painted Red or tasyilna, served also as a police force at every Sun Dance festival. Throughout all the rest of the year, however, the societies were dormant, and their members scattered among the bands. Although their leaders naturally participated in every informal council called by the tribal and band leaders, their authority was then no greater than that of other influential men within the tribe.

Because the Sarcee lived entirely by hunting, their movements conformed very closely to those of their principal game animal, the buffalo. Comparatively few herds of buffalo remained about the headwaters of Saskatchewan River during the winter months; most of them migrated south in the autumn, and did not return until the spring. During the greater part of the year, therefore, the Sarcee moved about in small groups, generally subdivisions of their bands consisting of from one to a dozen families. These groups rarely travelled more than a day's journey apart through fear of the Cree and other enemies; and they frequently united, either in summer or in winter, to organize a buffalo drive for their common benefit. Toward the end of summer, when the berries were ripe, they always amalgamated that they might celebrate together the dances of their "societies" (see page 44), and in certain years the festival of the Sun Dance.

One other factor influenced their movements, the necessity for abundant fuel and shelter during the winter months. In summer they could gather on the open prairies all the low brush and buffalo dung they required to cook their food, but in winter these were covered beneath the snow. At that season, therefore, they retreated to the edge of the woods, and made only such forays out into the open plains as were necessary to replenish their supply of meat.

During the early nineteenth century, then, their movements in a normal year followed this general pattern:

Winter: groups of several families camped along the edge of the woods at distances of 1 or 2 days' journey apart.

Early spring (when buffalo began to come north): these groups moved out on to the open prairies.

Summer (when many buffalo herds roamed.the plains): numerous small parties of Indians, even single families, hunted separately a few miles apart. Once or occasionally twice in the season the entire tribe united to drive the herds of buffalo into a pound or to force them over a cliff. This was the usual season for visiting the trading-posts, though in some years visits were made in winter.

August: the tribe united for the society dances and the Sun Dance.

September: the tribe dispersed again into groups, which gradually retreated to the edge of the woods. This was the favourite season, also, for raids on neighbouring tribes.

An important member of the tribe, the owner of the Beaver Bundle (see page 83), kept an official tally of the months with sticks. How he reconciled his lunar calendar with the solar year the present-day Indians could not remember; and their list of " moons," *tca'taya,* contains only eleven names, not twelve.

January–February: *halit·ca*: "old man moon."

February–March: *mitsi di·kaiye*: "moon white," i.e., white-headed eagle mean.

March–April: *tci·z*: "ducks."

April–May: *tacγatci*: "frogs."

May–June: *i·γasa'*: "hatching time."

June–July: *itca·γana dat·i*: "birds come out of next."

July–August: *am·wa* or *am·wa acícasyat·i*: "the mid-year without snow."

August–September: *tcitçatinittas*: "ripening berries."

September–October: *itk'as·i natcinittla*: "leaves falling."

October–November: *tak'otitc*: "ice forming," or *tcaz·i tayanit·a*: elk sits down in the creek."

November–December: *saska acícasyati·* "midyear with snow."[1]

The united tribe camped on the open prairies presented a very picturesque sight. The large, conical tipis of buffalo hide, erected on four pole foundations and many decorated with pictures of their owners' visions, stood in a great circle from whose centre rose the tipi of the leading chief (or two tipis, if there were two chiefs of equal standing).[2] Sometimes the circle was complete, sometimes a gap was left towards the east. In and out of the tipis moved the women, busily engaged in preparing meat, tanning hides, and in other occupations that fell to the lot of their sex. The warriors, for the most part, lolled in their tents or on the grass outside, ready to spring into action at the slightest warning from the two or three mounted men who guarded the horses grazing peacefully on the outskirts, or kept a lookout from the neighbouring hill-tops.

In the arrangement of such a camp the Indians followed certain definite rules. The man who first reached the site chose a suitable location for his tent; later arrivals then adopted his tent as the starting point for their circle and followed its circumference sunwise. The women erected the tents unaided, for no man would demean himself by lending his aid;[3] and they generally turned the doorways toward the east, because the prevailing winds were north and south. The bands kept together, each occupying a certain section of the circle, irrespective of what band occupied the next; and within each section the individual families camped in any order, except that a man on no account occupied a site next to his mother-in-law. Medicine-men enjoyed the privilege of camping at any place around the circumference, but remained as a rule with their bands.

The exact date at which the Sarcee adopted this circular arrangement for their summer camp we do not know, but almost certainly about the same time as the Black foot. Now in 1755, when Hendry visited the prairies, the Blackfoot still pitched their tents in two parallel lines,[4] an arrangement that

---

1. This term is now used for Christmas.

2. Except during the Sun Dance, when the woman whose vow occasioned the festival set up her own tent in the centre (see p. 52).

3. Today, on the reserve, men frequently help their wives to set up the poles, and to draw around them the canvas that has replaced the old cover of buffalo hide.

4. Hendry, Anthony, *The Journal of York Factory to the Blackfoot Country, 1754–1755*, edited by L.J. Burpee; Proc. and Trans. Roy. Soc., Canada, Third ser., vol. T, sec. IT, Toronto, 1907, p. 337.

was very satisfactory for repelling slow infantry attacks, but not the sudden raids of mobile horsemen. In Hendry's time, however, horses were still scarce on the Canadian prairies, and they did not become common until the first quarter of the nineteenth century. That, presumably, was the period when the institution of the camp circle took root, although it had existed long before on the prairies of the United States. Among the Sarcee it functioned only in summer; in winter, when they lived on the edge of the forests, they pitched their tents in any order.

If the Sarcee ever erected lodges of brush like their kinsmen in the Mackenzie River basin, their descendants today retain no memory of them; and it was not until after their confinement to a reserve that they built log houses for the winter months. Their one and only home was the familiar tipi, the conical tent made by wrapping from 12 to 16 tanned buffalo hides, stitched together, around a framework of from 14 to 24 poles. When the herds of buffalo disappeared their hides were replaced by canvas, but the shape remained essentially the same. The overlapping edges of the cover were laced together below the peak, leaving a small entrance slit at the bottom that could be closed with a rectangular curtain of hide or cloth. The inside diameter measured generally about 14 feet; and the furniture was meagre, as befitted a people constantly on the move. In the centre was an open fireplace from which the smoke curled upward to the two adjustable cowls near the peak; around the sides the sleeping places, each with the roll of blankets or skins, and back-rest of willow-twigs supported against a tripod, that one may still see on most of the prairie reserves. Honoured guests slept at the back opposite the door—a place reserved also for any unmarried son old enough to go on the war-path—while the owner and his wife slept on one side or the other, usually on the south. The least honourable position was among the storage near the door, where the mother and her daughters usually sat whenever distinguished male visitors entered the tent. Here lay the meat and the leather water-buckets, the woman's stone ax with which she broke dead limbs for fuel, scrapers and fleshers for dressing hides,[5] stone mauls, horn ladles, perhaps, too, the clay pot that preceded cooking vessels of iron.[6] The hide bags or "parflèches" with spare clothing, on

---

5. An old Sarcee woman thus described her method of dressing buffalo hides After scraping off the meat and fatty tissue with an adze-shaped tool bladed with a section of an old gun-barrel (her mother had used a stone) she punched holes around the edges of the skin and pegged it out to dry. Then she removed the hair with a fleshing-tool of elk's leg-bone serrated along its chisel-shaped edge, and scraped the whole hide perfectly smooth. Next she rubbed it with the fat, liver or brains of the buffalo, and after exposing it to the sun or a fire for a day or two to let the fat soak in, steeped the hide in water for another day. Finally she rinsed it, and pulled it vigorously backwards and forwards over a cord of sinew. This final treatment left the skin dry and soft.

6. The Sarcee state that they abandoned their clay pots about the time they obtained horses. This seems very probable, for we know from Cocking's Journal that the Blackfoot were still making and using pots in 1772 ("An Adventurer from Hudson Bay. Journal of Matthew Cocking from York Factory to the Blackfoot country, 1772–73," edited by L.J. Burpee; Proc. And Trans. of the Royal Society, Canada, vol II, 1908, pp. 109, 111). No one seems to have described the actual process of manufacture. An old Sarcee said that the women kneaded and hollowed out the pot by hand, dried it in the sun, then laid it with its mouth to a fire where the smoke baked it and prevented it

Plate 3a. Woman drying meat.
(Canadian Museum of History 52787)

Plate 3b. Woman scraping a skin.
(Canadian Museum of History 52835)

the other hand, and the women's sewing equipment, generally lay between the bed-rolls and the wall of the tent; while the man's bow and arrows, his shield,

---

from cracking. In the nineteenth century all the plains' tribes, and even some of the Chipewyan Indians, often boiled their meat in a hide, or in the paunch of the buffalo, propped into the shape of a bag by a peg under each corner. Naturally, they could not place this vessel over a fire, but heated the water with hot stones.

club, and knife, and the bags containing his paints and medicines, hung from the tripod at the head of his bed.

The scouts guarding these tipis from the hill-tops scanned the horizon for two objects, human enemies and buffalo; for to the Sarcee, as to other plains Indians, the buffalo was the staff of life. From its flesh came nearly all their food; from its hide they obtained covers for their tents, shields, and saddles, bags to hold their pemmican and clothing, buckets for carrying and vessels for boiling water, bedding, even certain parts of their clothing; and from its bones they fashioned various tools and weapons. The pursuit of the buffalo, therefore, was the principal occupation of every man and youth in the community; and as failure in the hunt spelled starvation and death, it was generally conducted as a co-operative

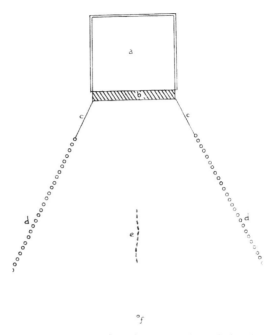

Figure 1. Sketch plan of a buffalo pound: (a) corral of notched rails, built as high as possible; the logs were often lashed together with rawhide; (b) an embankment consisting of a railed fence with earth heaped against the outside, giving an easy incline to the approaching buffaloes, but leaving a sheer drop into the corral; (c, c) lines of logs resting on the ground at one end, at the other in the fork of a post; (d, d) men and women behind willows or blankets to guide the buffaloes; (e) buffaloes; (f) man on foot or horseback driving them.

enterprise, particularly in the days before the Indians obtained abundant horses and firearms. On a few occasions during the year (mainly in midsummer, when the herds were very numerous) an individual hunter might conceal his head beneath a coyote skin, creep up within range, and shoot down a single animal with his arrow; but the percentage of buffalo killed in this way was extremely low. The great majority were destroyed by the united efforts of a number, of men, and often of the entire tribe.

On the present-day Sarcee reserve near Calgary is a narrow, 40-foot deep gulch with precipitous sides, one side indeed so precipitous as to be almost perpendicular. A man approaching it on horseback receives no warning of its presence, even in broad daylight, until he has almost ridden over the edge. This was only one of several places where the Sarcee united to surround the buffalo and stampede them over the cliffs, thereby destroying a whole herd within a few minutes; yet from this gulch alone they collected in 1918 and 1919 several tons of bones, which they sold for fertilizer.

Where nature had provided no suitable cliff the Indians erected corrals or pounds into which they drove the buffalo, there to be shot down from the barriers. The shape of the early Sarcee pound is not known. The present-day Indians remember only those they built in the latter half of the nineteenth century, which were rectangular enclosures of logs lashed together with rawhide and raised to as great a height as possible. One long side of the rectangle was banked with earth on its outer face, so that it presented a gentle slope to approaching buffalo but terminated at the pound in a sheer drop. To prevent the herd from breaking away to either side a fence of logs extended outward for a short distance from each of the two front corners, and these fences were prolonged for half a mile or more by two gradually diverging lines of men, women, and children, stationed behind willows or blankets. Down this laneway one or two horsemen guided the buffalo; the sentinels then closed in behind them, and all united with wild veils to drive the terrified animals pell-mell into the trap.

The Sarcee retained a clear recollection of the erection of these pounds during the summer months, but not during the winter. At that season, they said, they hunted in small groups, each consisting, until horses became plentiful, of several footmen under a leader on horseback. The leader generally selected one man, mounted, if possible, on a spare horse, to search out the buffalo. He himself then pursued and shot down the animals; and his followers butchered the meat, carried it back to camp, and divided it equally among the different families. Theoretically the leader could retain all the hides, though in practice he nearly always shared them also. If, however, he needed a new tent for himself, he could call on the wives of his followers to tan the necessary hides in payment for the meat they had received.

CHAPTER 3
THE CYCLE OF SARCEE LIFE

Nameless, but generally not without honour, the Sarcee child entered the world of the living. To usher it in, the parents chose some honest, warm-hearted woman who would carefully take hold of its right hand when it emerged from its mother's womb—not the left hand, lest it be left-handed ever after—and pray with sincerity, "May the kindliness and charity I feel toward others animate you also." Then when she had severed the cord, bound the stump with sinew, washed the babe and wrapped it in soft furs, an attendant equally warm-hearted laid it in its moss bag and repeated the same prayer, confident that in some mystic manner it would work out its fulfilment. For at least a day, while the mother regained her strength, this attendant watched over the sleeping infant, keeping it near the warm fire and turning it over at intervals from one side to the other.

If the new-born child was a girl, and the midwife or her assistant a medicine-woman, the father might ask her to select and confer a name immediately. More often (always, apparently, if the child were male) he delayed a week or two, then approached some old medicine-man or successful warrior, offering in payment a horse or its equivalent. The old man generally pondered for a night in his tent,[1] seeking a name from some brave deed in his career, from some vision in earlier life, or, most prized of all, one suggested by a new vision specially vouchsafed to him for this occasion. Whatever the name, it should be new, or at least not borne by any living person, though it might have belonged to one long dead. As soon as the old man was ready he notified the father, and, in the presence of the parents, took the infant in his arms, announced its name and invoked the "Maker's" (Great Spirit's) blessing.

The child, whether boy or girl, remained inseparable from its mother until it attained the age of 9 or 10. She attended to its needs in the camp, and, whenever the camp was moved, carried it on her back, in her travois, or on her own horse before or behind her, if it was unable to walk or ride alone. Its ears were pierced by an old woman during this period, but without the ceremony that marked the similar operation among the Blackfoot.[2] Girls younger than 5 or 6, and boys up to the age of 9 or 10, went freely naked, but older children wore clothes patterned after those of their parents. Their exact shapes in earlier times we do not know; in the second half of the nineteenth century they consisted of moccasins and leggings for both sexes (girls' leggings came only to the knees, boys' to the thighs), a sleeved dress for girls that overlapped the leggings, and for boys a breech-cloth and a short shirt, also sleeved. As a rule, all these garments were made of elk or deer skin except the moccasins, for which the heavier buffalo hide was more suitable. In winter children and

---

1. There was no sweat-house ceremony, as among the Blackfoot (see Wissler, C, *The Social Life of the Blackfoot Indians*, Anth. Papers, Am. Mus of Nat. Hist., vol VII, p. 16 (1912)).
2. Cf. Wissler, C., *Blackfoot Social Life*, Anth. Papers, Am. Mus Nat. Hist., vol III, p. 30.

111

adults alike added robes of buffalo hide, and often wore caps made from the furs of smaller mammals such as the wolf and the antelope.

At the age of 9 or 10 the boy's life changed. Hitherto he had remained at his mother's side, and counted as a member of her band. Now his father undertook his education, and he was enrolled in his father's band. In later life he could revert, if he wished, to his mother's band, or attach himself to any other, but during the years of his adolescence his status was determined for him.

The training imposed on him was fairly rigorous. His father taught him to ride and drive horses, made him a bow and arrows, and even provided him with a set of gambling sticks, though not without admonishing him never to lapse into an inveterate gambler. On a horse of his own he accompanied his father to the buffalo-hunt, and helped to carry home the meat. His father supervised his dress, sometimes even to the extent of himself making or purchasing the lad's clothes; and other men in the community took an active interest in his upbringing. Every camp selected one old man, often the leader of a society, to supervise the young boys and to impress on them the tribal ethics—strict honesty within the tribe, obedience to parents, respect for the aged and blind, and reverence for the medicine-bundles and for everything pertaining to religion. It was he who mustered the boys each morning to bathe in the river, summer and winter alike—unless the ice was too thick to break—in which case he made them roll naked in the snow; any youth who was slow or recalcitrant he might chastise with thorns. Occasionally, when the tribe moved camp, the same old man held the boys back for 3 or 4 hours, then, himself mounted on a horse, made them race on foot to the new camp 10 or 15 miles away, that they might be untiring and swift-footed on the warpath: the youths who excelled in these races generally became scouts a year or two later.

Few taboos restricted their liberty, and such as there were related mainly to food. Both boys and girls had to abstain from eating certain parts of the buffalo. On no account might they touch any part of an unborn buffalo calf.

Only the exceptional lad accompanied a war-party before he reached the age of 14 or 15. Its leader then bestowed on him temporarily the name of his grandmother (father's mother), but urged him to attempt some brave deed that would justify his receiving a name previously borne by an uncle or other near relative. When the party returned from the raid a crowd immediately gathered around the boy and asked him his name. Should he still bear his grandmother's name they laughed at him; but the old woman herself would comfort him, saying "So they have given you my name. Well, you need not be ashamed of it, for I was a capable woman in my day." Naturally, however, the lad lost no opportunity of distinguishing himself on the next war-party. The horse or other trophy he then captured he presented to some male relative who had taken special interest in his welfare; and often this relative took the place of the father in enrolling the lad, at his own expense, into the "Mosquito" society (See page 45).

Success on the war-path, a new and honourable name, and membership in the Mosquito society, gave the lad a new status. His father procured him finely ornamented clothes made from the furs of the mountain lion, the lynx, or the otter, gave him his best horses, and decorated the special horse that he rode whenever the tribe moved camp. A beaded collar encircled this horse's neck, a beaded stick and strips of weasel fur dangled from its halter, the saddle and the buffalo-hide "saddle-cloth" both carried beadwork, and the whip that the lad brandished fitted into a highly polished handle of elk horn adorned with strips of otter or weasel fur. Some youths carried bright-coloured fans, others war-clubs, or gleaming two-edged daggers slung from the arm in beaded leather sheaths. Some again wore fur bonnets with two upstanding buffalo horns, which for ostentation they often tied to their horses heads. Thus arrayed[3] they pranced to one side of the cortege as it moved over the prairies, jesting with one another under the ogling eyes of the marriageable girls and the whispered remarks "See how well-dressed that boy is. His father must be very fond of him." When at last the tribe reached its new camping place and the women set about erecting the tents, these young dandies sat in state on a neighbouring hill-top and only descended when the meal was cooked.

Not only on the march but around the camp the youth dressed well and maintained a fine appearance, that his name might spread from tribe to tribe. His father secured his passage from the Mosquito into some other society, where he could play a more prominent role in the affairs of the community; and on all ceremonial occasions he now painted his face with the special emblems of this society in place of the haphazard markings of earlier years.[4] At night, too, he no longer slept at the side of the tent, like the women and children, and the married men "whose legs had grown heavy," but at the back opposite the door, a place commonly reserved for honoured guests.

Plate 4a. the four-pole foundation of a tent.
(Canadian Museum of History 52842)

Thus did the young Sarcee gallant make his debut. The tribe, regarding celibacy in either sex as monstrous, expected him now to seek a wife. Before he

---

3. Such was the mode of adornment in the middle of the nineteenth century, after the trading-posts had flooded the plains with European gewgaws.

4. The Sarcee remember the following native paints:

a. Several tints of red, brown, and yellow obtained from ochre, the colour of which vanes naturally, also changes with heat;

b. white from clay;

c. yellow from buffalo gall-stones;

d. black from charcoal, and also from a certain kind of earth, which, however, was never used for body decoration.

In painting bags these substances were mixed with buffalo fat, but in decorating the body with water only.

married, however, he selected another lad as his "comrade," and established with him a kind of brotherhood relation that endured through life. Thenceforward the two friends became well-nigh inseparable. At evening they often mounted a horse, one behind the other, and circled the camp singing love songs, or playing simple melodies on a flageolet. Then toward midnight they dismounted, appointed a trysting-place, and stole away to their sweethearts' tents, hoping that when they scratched against the outer walls the girls would creep out and join them. Sometimes the girls did steal out, despite the certainty of a thrashing if their mothers detected them; and the youths, catching two horses (regardless of who owned them) mounted each with his own sweetheart and, singing, rode around the camp until nearly dawn.

Plate 4b. The tent cover removed, showing interior arrangement.

Plate 4c. The door of the bee tent.

Many a youth courted two or three girls at the same time, and even made overtures to the married women, for, with strange inconsistency, public opinion encouraged libertinism among single or married men while enjoining the strictest virtue on the women. The youth who succeeded in seducing a married woman generally fled with her to another band or tribe where they might escape detection for several months. Occasionally the husband pursued them, recovered his wife, and either killed her or cut off her nose; but

Plate 4d. The wolf tent.

since any punishment of this nature was liable to excite ill-will among her relatives he more often exacted one or two horses from her seducer and let the matter drop. Many husbands considered it beneath their dignity to pursue eloping wives; they merely recovered the equivalent of the marriage price from the relatives and purchased other wives. Secret infidelity aroused more resentment than open elopement. Parents sometimes disowned a girl who went astray before marriage, letting her become the common property of the camp; and a husband, after degrading his unfaithful wife by sharing her with his "comrade," divorced her, often to meet the same fate. By our standards, therefore, the moral code was extremely lax for the one sex, and unduly severe for the other. It is not surprising that Sarcee mothers kept the strictest watch over their unmarried daughters, and never allowed them to sleep or to wander away alone. The marriageable girl never mingled openly with any youths except her own brothers, so that it was difficult for an admirer to discover whether or not she would welcome his attentions. One method was to flash at her the light from a looking-glass: if nothing happened she would probably accept him; but if she disliked him she would tell the other girls and make him their laughing-stock.

If the winning of his spurs on the war-path was the first "crisis" in a boy's life, the second—and the first in a girl's—was marriage. A youth generally chose his own wife and informed his parents, who then carried out the necessary negotiations with the parents of the girl. A girl had less freedom, for she was usually affianced as soon as she was marriageable; but she, too, could make "her preference known to her mother and expect to receive a certain measure of consideration. The formal betrothal brought into play definite rules of conduct. Not only did the youth publicly avoid his fiancée, but their parents also avoided one another; furthermore, the youth might not even speak to his future father- or mother-in-law, and if either should happen to enter a tent in which he was present, he was obliged to slip away at the first opportunity. Yet at the same time he was expected to exchange coarse jests with his fiancée's sister or girl-chum, a prerogative he would possess after marriage, when either might become his second wife; and similarly his fiancée jested with his brother or comrade. Secretly, too, they met as often as they wished; and quite often he openly sent her a necklace, or his personal bracelet in return for her own; she for her part nearly always furnished him with a pair of moccasins specially made with her own hands.

Formal betrothals were naturally irksome, and seldom prolonged more than 2 or 3 weeks unless the youth made it known that he was going on the war-path and preferred not to marry until his return. The fixing of the actual wedding day rested with the girl's father. Choosing a convenient occasion, he dressed his daughter in her finest clothes, equipped her with horses, travois, bedding, and other household effects, and bade her erect her tent beside her future parents-in-law. There the bridegroom immediately settled down with her while his parents and kinsmen collected the bride-price.

Many marriages were contracted at short notice without a formal betrothal, particularly when the tribe was on the march. A crier would walk round the tents in the evening and announce that the chief and council had decided to move camp early the next morning. As the train marched away the gaily dressed youths pranced on their horses over to one flank, while the maidens lingered near their mothers. A youth might then ride up to some girl who had taken his fancy and ask her to marry him. Not daring to consent immediately, however well-disposed she might be, she would answer, "I will speak to my parents when we make camp." The youth retired as quickly as he had approached, but in the evening, when the Indians were pitching their tents, the mother would find out from her daughter what he had said and tell the father. Then, if both approved of the marriage, they informed their relatives, gathered together everything their daughter needed and sent her on the following day to pitch her tent beside her new parents-in-law. The youth generally observed that his suit had been accepted and kept away from the camp until evening, when his people directed his returning footsteps to the tent of his waiting bride.

During the first few' days of their marriage the newly wed couple visited each of the bridegroom's kinsmen to present a pair of moccasins that the bride had made; and, after a brief meal, they carried back to their tent some trifling gift in recompense. In this same period, too, the young husband, either with his own hands or through his father, delivered the bride-price—horses, clothing, a gun perhaps, and other articles that the bride's father could apportion among those who had contributed to the dowry. If this initial payment seemed inadequate (and there was no fixed amount, except that it should exceed the dowry) he joined his wife's band for a time to work off the debt in labour; he took over the care of his father-in-law's horses, and surrendered all the meat (sometimes also the hides) he secured in hunting, being supported himself each day by the cooked food his mother-in-law sent over to his tent. Should one of his brothers-in-law admire any article in his possession he was expected to give it up cheerfully, unless it happened to be a society emblem that might never be surrendered without payment. His wife, however, might voice a protest where he might not, and very often she checked her brothers from carrying off anything they wished. Occasionally a man took to the war-path soon after his marriage. If he then succeeded in capturing a horse he invariably presented it to his wife's parents, who prized the animal very highly and lauded their daughter and son-in-law throughout the entire tribe.

A man called his wife *is'θaiya* and she called him *sik·ala*. Some men had two wives, often sisters; and when a man's wife died, he commonly married her sister. Similarly, when a woman's husband died, she sometimes passed into his brother's household. Hence there was a special term, *sindatli*, for a man's sister-in-law or a woman's brother-in-law, and they were allowed great liberty in conversation, whether actually married to one another or not. Two wives of the same man, even if not sisters, commonly called each other older and younger sister if their ages differed considerably; otherwise the second wife was simply the "second woman" *sexti*. Marriage between first cousins was prohibited because they ranked as brothers and sisters. Aunts and uncles on either side (except a mother's sister, who was simply another "mother") ranked with older brothers and older sisters; and nephews and nieces with younger brothers and sisters unless they were so much younger that they could merge with sons and daughters. There were special terms for older and younger brothers and sisters, and women used a different word from men for "my son" and "my grandchild": yet even with these additions the terms used to express relationships were rather few, as will appear from the following table:

icitɬa: my younger brother or male cousin; also, if only a little younger, my nephew.

yin·iya: my older brother or male cousin; also, my uncle.

isdatsa: my younger sister or female cousin; also, if only a little younger, my niece.

sid·a: my older sister or female cousin; also, my father's sister.

sindaɬli: my wife's sister or husband's brother (older or younger).

it·aya: my father.

in·aɣa: my mother; my mother's sister.

si·ya: (man speaking) my son; my nephew, if much younger.

si·za: (woman speaking) my son; my nephew, if much younger.

si'tsa: my daughter; my niece, if much younger.

is·aya: my grandfather, on either side.

is·o: my grandmother, on either side; also, my husband's sister.

masdjone: my wife's brother.

is·uvea:(man speaking) my grandchild, of either sex.

ic·iya: (woman speaking) my grandchild, of either sex.

is'θaiya: my wife.

sik·ala: my husband.

The Sarcee, like other plains' tribes, sharply differentiated the duties and status of a wife from those of her husband. She was obliged to carry wood and water, to attend to the food, the cleaning and dressing of hides, and the making of the family clothing; these things a man might do on the war-path, but not at home, except that a father might decorate the clothing of his unmarried son. Unaided, she erected and dismantled the tipi, or, if she needed help, called in another woman—but not her husband until recent times, when the reserve life broke down many of the old customs. During the day her place was near the door; even if she were lying down when a man entered the tent she had to rise and sit near the entrance. Grumbling, or interference in her husband's conversation with an outsider, earned her a severe thrashing. A brave, energetic man sometimes had two, three, and even four wives, of whom the first or head one occupied the place at his side; but she, too, had to move near the door at the entrance of visitors, and if ever the wives quarrelled the husband generally thrashed them all alike. His duties were both simple and precise: hunting, attending to the horses, and war. From his wife he demanded implicit obedience and respect; to be struck by a woman was a serious disgrace. If he owned fine clothes he expected her to display them outside his tent, just as she would display the fine clothes of her bachelor son, because by so doing she enhanced his prestige in the tribe.

Though he was absolute master in his own home, a man could not always abuse his wife with impunity, lest her parents take her away from him and marry her to some one else. This they might do if he were simply lazy, and failed to provide for her by hunting; if he proved a coward in war his wife would certainly scorn to live with him. Yet unless she had kinsmen ready to protect her she was largely at his mercy, for a woman could never divorce her husband, though she might run away from him. A man, on the other hand, could divorce his wife for infidelity, laziness, jealousy, in fact for any reason at all; and generally he not only retained her property to compensate him for the price he had paid for her but expected her people to make up the deficit. Little children always accompanied the mother, but boys in their teens could attach themselves to whichever parent they chose. Powerful checks on divorce were the woman's dependence on the man for the prime necessities of life, and the man's need of a woman's services in making his home comfortable. The Sarcee, moreover, deprecated marital infelicity, and always advised young couples to behave very sedately toward one another for several months after marriage, lest joking and playing should lead to quarrels, and the quarrels become never-ending.

Even in 1921, when all the younger Sarcee demanded church weddings, some of the older people still married after the manner of their forefathers. The man paid his bride's family one or two horses and sundry other things, and the bride received many presents from both her own people and her husband's kin. She then lived with him without further ado; but if he tired of her he sent her back without ceremony and both parties returned all gifts.

In July of that year a man 68 years of age, who had lost his first wife by death and divorced two subsequent wives, was preparing to visit a Cree reserve many miles away to inspect another prospective mate. He planned to visit her in company with a friend, and, if she measured up to his expectations, to retire to his friend's tent and send for her, offering in payment a horse and rig. Should she hesitate, however, and suggest a delay of a week or two, he intended to take the first train home and seek out some one more amenable.

Unscrupulous fathers sometimes used these old marriage customs, in modern times at least, as a means of acquiring wealth. Thus in 1919 a Sarcee youth paid liberally for the privilege of marrying a Cree girl, whom he took home to his people. The young people seemed very happy, and at several dances during the subsequent weeks the youth's kinsmen bestowed shawls and other presents on the bride. But one day, when the husband happened to be absent, the girl's father suddenly appeared and carried off not only his daughter, but all the presents she had received. To add to the insult, he refused to return what her husband had paid for her. The Sarcee then discovered that he had played the same trick on two or three other unsuspecting youths.

After marriage a man and his father-in-law no longer kept aloof, but his mother-in-law continued to avoid his presence, being forbidden either to speak to him or to look straight into his face. Though he might support her after her husband's death she could not share his tipi unless she was blind (when her infirmity made it compulsory) or unless he removed the taboo by giving her a substantial present such as a gun or a horse. In 1921 the Sarcee still adhered very strictly to their mother- in-law taboo, though some of the younger generation seemed to regard it rather lightly.

As soon as she conceived the young wife became the object of special care. Heavy work was forbidden her, but she collected firewood and performed other light duties around the camp, gathered a supply of dried berries to feed the old women who would be summoned in case of sickness, and again when her delivery drew near, and prepared a moss-bag for the reception of her baby. No ugly man might approach her, nor might any one grimace in her presence, lest he mar the face of her unborn child. If she struck a dog, a horse, or a child, her own child might develop a birthmark, for the Indians believed that birthmarks arose from some thoughtless action of the mother during pregnancy. Neither she nor her husband might step over a dog lest she suffer a miscarriage; consequently, the family dogs were driven outside the tipi. Neither might her husband choke a dog, a buffalo calf, or a horse, lest his child be stillborn. He slept on a separate couch after the third month, and after the seventh the woman's own mother often remained constantly at her side. Many an expectant mother tried to determine the sex of her child by its movements in the womb, believing that a boy was more active than a girl and often she attached to her dress one of the curious "buffalo-stones"[5] in the hope that it would facilitate her delivery. The Sarcee generally desired large families, but a woman who for any reason wished to avoid conception bought an amulet from some medicine-man or woman who would guarantee its efficacy.

The first pangs of labour drove the mother into a separate tent, and brought to her aid three or four old women, one of them a medicine-woman. They warned away all men and unmarried girls, laid the mother on worn-out robes, dressed her (if not already so dressed) in her oldest clothes (which were afterwards hung up in a tree to rot[6]), and removed all bracelets and other ornaments. The medicine-woman then gave her a decoction of boiled herbs or other specific for easy delivery, and encouraged her to walk to and fro inside the tent as long as she could. If parturition was long and difficult word passed outside, and the anxious husband or a near relative vowed to the Maker that he would buy a medicine-bundle, join a society, or perform some other meritorious action if mother and child both survived. When at last the moment for delivery arrived the woman dropped to her knees, and one attendant, standing at her back, held her shoulders while another tightly clasped her round the waist.[7] They buried the afterbirth in the ground, bound a broad belt of hide round the mother's waist, and, laying her on her bed, counselled her not to rise before the next day. As soon as the tent was in order again women relatives appeared bringing them berry soup, and tobacco for the attendants to smoke. Unmarried girls, too, might enter now, and the father often glanced inside to see his new-born babe; but he generally departed just as quickly, fearing that his legs might become "heavy" if they touched any object in the tent and there-

---

5. See pp. 83, 84.
6. In recent times they were burnt.
7. If the mother were alone, as happened not infrequently, she grasped a pole of the tipi.

by render him incompetent in war.[8] Each attendant, however, he rewarded with a gift, such as a dress, a blanket, or a beaded belt.

In so far as it was possible for a hunting people constantly on the move, the Sarcee seem to have enjoined on the mother a certain amount of post-natal as well as pre-natal care. She lay down as soon as she was delivered, not sharing the Blackfoot belief that crawling around the tent hastened recovery. Only after 1 or 2 days of complete rest in her tipi did she return to her husband's tent; and for some time afterwards she refrained from all heavy work and concerned herself mainly with the care of her child. As the diet of the Indians consisted principally of meat, she could not wean it until it reached the age of about 3. When that time came she left it in charge of a relative for a few days, or made her breasts distasteful by smearing them with nicotine.

Twins occasioned no special concern. The Sarcee generally attributed them to the mother's error in eating the meat of a buffalo cow that had borne twin calves, but sometimes also to intercourse after she had become pregnant and received from a medicine-woman a belt or other object to facilitate delivery.

It was quite common for a man to adopt a boy, particularly if he had recently lost one of his own sons; but the adoption of girls was rare. No payment was necessary, since the boy did not give up his own parents, but merely acquired another home.

---

8. Stepping upon the clothing of the mother or of her new-born child was believed to bring men ill-luck, but not necessarily, as the Blackfoot thought, lameness.

CHAPTER 4
THE CYCLE OF SARCEE LIFE (CONTINUED)

In a Sarcee camp hardly a day passed unmarked by same interesting or exciting event. The buffalo hunt, of course, never lacked its thrills, nor did enthusiasm ever wane at the summer Sun Dance, or the festivals of the organized societies. Even on non-festival days something was generally stirring in and around the tents. At dawn one or more of the old people always wandered away to pray on a hill-top, and the boys to take their morning bath in the river. Young warriors rounded up the horses to make sure that none were missing, and women huddled over their cooking-vessels, or laboured at the dressing of hides and the making of moccasins. Throughout the hours of daylight two or three men checked the horses from straying too far away, and kept a lookout for buffalo and human enemies. Listen to the singing from within that tent; old P— is selling his medicine-bundle, and each time he unwraps one of the articles inside it he teaches the purchaser its appropriate song. This man is decorating his blanket with his war deeds, that one the outside of his tent with scenes from a vision. Yon string of horses moving among the tipis indicates a wedding; the gaily dressed girl who leads them must be the bride herself. Here are the boys lined up for a sling-fight; did you see that lad charge his foe and capture a trophy? Away in that far tent where the drum is throbbing some of the men have turned to gambling, and are staking their horses, their weapons, and even their clothes on their skill and luck in the "hand" game. Several of the young fellows plot a party tonight; they intend to sing and drum outside old D's tipi until he rises from his bed, allays their ardour with a pipe or a pot of berry soup, and speeds them on their way to molest some other involuntary host.

All these incidents never happened, it may be, at one place on one day. Yet camp life was always full of variety, for young and old knew many distractions and pastimes for hours not occupied by more serious pursuits. The favourite pastimes of adults were two gambling games, "hidden sticks" or the "hand game," and "four-sticks" or "dice."

In the hand-game a number of players divided into two groups that took their places on opposite sides of a tent. At the back of the ten sat the chief as arbiter, with ten painted sticks for tallies. The gaming outfit was produced— two pairs of wood or bone pencils, known technically as a "long" pair and a "short" pair, though they were generally of about the same length, 4 or 5 inches, and distinguished only by marks or cords. The group that first received the sticks handed them to its two most skilful players, who sat or knelt down side by side, while opposite them sat or knelt the guesser of the other group. Then the play began. Some one furiously pounded a drum, each hider juggled his pair of sticks from one hand to the other while the rest of the company sang, shouted, imitated the cries of birds and animals, and tried in every way to distract and confuse the leading players. Suddenly the guesser jerked forward his finger and pointed successively to whichever hand of each opponent he imagined to hold a pair of sticks. If he guessed both pairs aright his party received two tallies, if only one each party received a tally, whereas if both guesses were wrong the hiders received two tallies. After discovering which hands concealed the sticks the guesser had next to find out which held the long pair and which the short, the prize for this further guess being one tally. The game ended as soon as one party or the other succeeded in winning all ten tallies, and the losers then handed over the stakes.

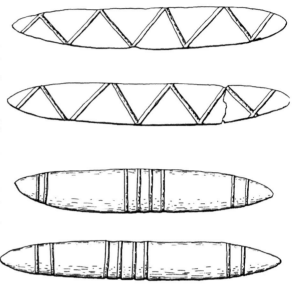

Figure 2. A set of gambling sticks.

Women sometimes played a simplified hand-game with only one pair of sticks. Their favourite game, however, was dice, for which they used two pairs of flat bone sticks, pointed at each end and decorated by incising and painting, on one face, the one pair with a zigzag design, the other with a banded or other pattern. The player threw the dice onto the ground or a blanket, and read the count as follows:

	Points
One zigzag or one band up and three blanks	6
Two zigzags and two bands up	4
Two zigzags or two bands up	2
One zigzag and one band up	2

No other throws counted. Two women, or occasionally four, matched each other and kept the tally with twelve long sticks.

Outdoors men gambled at still another game, which called for a small hoop with beaded spokes and two arrows. The hoop or wheel was bowled against an obstacle, and, as it fell, one man from one side and one from the other thrust his arrow under it and read the score according to its direction in relation to the spokes.[1]

Much gambling accompanied two other games, shinny and lacrosse, the former more popular with men, the latter with women. Children, as usual, had many more pastimes than adults. They indulged in wrestling and kicking contests, fought with mud balls slung from the ends of sticks, coasted on strips of hide or make-shift toboggans, competed with darts and with bows and ar-

---

1. For a fuller description of this game, see Wissler, op cit, vol VII, p. 60.

rows, lined up in opposing ranks for the wheel and the ball games, and played with toys such as buzzers, bull-roarers, and tops. Since Wissler has described exactly the same games among the neighbouring Blackfoot Indians,[2] it is unnecessary to discuss them in detail here. Two minor pastimes not included in his account were fighting with clubs made from hard bulrushes woven at the ends into balls, and a girls' game like pick-a-back. In the latter the girls sat in a row facing a girl at a base. This child then closed her eyes, and, chanting *sitsigotiga* straight to me," groped for each girl in turn and "pick-a-backed" her to the base.

Pastimes such as these served to while away idle days in camp, but for the adult Indian they paled before the excitement of hunting and of war. No one might interfere if a man wished to go on the war-path. Indeed, during the nineteenth century, youths received every encouragement to go, and if they had the luck to capture guns or horses quickly became leaders of new raiding parties. Even women sometimes accompanied their husbands, though a man who had two or more wives would never take the first wife. The widow of a warrior remained with his people for a time before returning to her relatives; and the parents of the slain man kept as a memento his buffalo horse or some other object that had belonged to him.

Sometimes a man went out to raid the enemy single-handed; more often he announced that he was prepared to lead a war-party and *invited* others to accompany him. Because enlistment was purely voluntary, only a man distinguished by his courage and previous successes could hope to lead a party. The raiders marched rapidly but cautiously, nearly always sending a scout ahead to spy out the country. Whenever they sighted this scout returning, and while he was still a mile or more away, they chanted their "scouting song"; and at night, after they had camped, they chanted another song, or group of songs, commonly known as the "wolf song," because it ended in a howl like a wolf's. Every large party included a medicine-man who could perform the ceremony called "looking for enemies." He designated an appropriate evening, and while their buffalo meat was roasting over a fire, instructed the warriors to build him a small shelter and to bring offerings of cloth and other things over which he might pray for the success of the givers. From inside the shelter he intoned the "looking for enemies" song, and the circle outside joined in with him. Four times they repeated the song, and each time, at its close, he offered up a prayer. Then, unseen by the watchers outside, but plainly audible, his familiar spirit visited him; and after the visit had ended, the medicine-man came out to share the silent meal. All then lay down to sleep, the medicine-man merely lingering to paint his face with the pattern prescribed by his medicine-dream. Very early the next morning he wakened the warriors and gave them his message: "In such and such a place horses and men have been delivered into my

---

2. Wissler, op cit. vol VII, pp. 53 *et seq.*

hands," or "Such and such a place I was told to avoid." Whatever the message might be the warriors responded *a-i* and faithfully carried out his instructions.

Occasionally the warriors scried out their fortunes with a badger skin after the manner described by Old Sarcee, an old and highly respected Indian who had witnessed the ceremony during his youth. A certain man in his war-party killed a badger and removed all its inside organs, leaving only a little blood. He poured on this blood a little water, and sprinkled over it first some gunpowder, next red ochre, and finally tiny shreds of sage-grass. Then he laid the skin on its back for the night, facing the head toward the east and resting it on a pillow of sage-grass that covered two lumps of buffalo dung. In the morning the leader ordered all his followers to dress in full war-costume and scry out their fortunes. The man who had prepared the skin went first. One glance inside revealed the fate that was awaiting him: if doomed to be scalped by the enemy he saw his scalpless head; if to die of sickness he gazed on his emaciated and discoloured body; but if he was destined to attain a ripe old age he beheld his grey-haired form carrying a walking-stick. One after another the warriors advanced to learn their fate. When it came to Old Sarcee's turn his leader said to him "Go and look at yourself. We must all die some day, and if you are destined to reach old age you will be able to tell your grandchildren about this skin." Old Sarcee saw himself greyhaired, blind in one eye, and wearing two shell necklaces that symbolized he would become the owner of two medicine-bundles. When he reported what he had seen, the leader told him that he would attain great honour in his old age, but not in his youth. The oracle proved true in every detail.

Many a man on the war-path solemnly vowed that if he returned in safety he would perform some meritorious action—he would join, for example, a certain society, or purchase a medicine-bundle or a painted tent. Sometimes, too, the Sarcee followed the Blackfoot custom of confessing to one another the names of their sweethearts; but whereas the Blackfoot believed that this narration of their conquests in the field of love contributed in some way to their success in war, the Sarcee attached no significance to it and in fact converted the episode into a jest. Some man conspicuous for his energy and courage cleaned the intestine of a buffalo and filled it with meat as far as one end, where he concealed a tough cord of rawhide. He then cooked his "sausage," cut it into sections, and distributed it among the warriors, secretly bestowing the part containing the rawhide on the laziest and most worthless member of the party. As each man bit off a mouthful from his portion he exclaimed "I'll bite this off with so-and-so," mentioning the name of his sweetheart; but the victim, vainly clinching his teeth on the rawhide, became the laughingstock of all his comrades.

All the plains' tribes dressed and looked so much alike that an Indian who met a stranger on the open prairies could not tell whether he were friend or foe except by speech or signals. Every tribe, therefore, had its sign language or set of signals whereby its members communicated with one another from a distance. The Sarcee signs were:

Sarcee: flick the right index in the corner of the mouth and click.

Blackfoot: close the last three fingers and pass the thumb and extended fore-finger down the side of the leg.

Blood: draw the half-closed hand across the teeth.

Piegan: draw the closed fist down the cheek.

Cree: make the motion of cutting the throat.

Dakota Sioux: flip the thumb and forefinger together.

Other Sioux: make the movement of parting the hair.

White man: pass the hand across the forehead, indicating the wearing of a peaked cap.

Going to war: hold the right hand up, palm out, and move it forward; turn it down and at the palm toward the ground; finally sweep the hand under and forward as for "advance."

Scalp taken: make the motion of cutting and removing a scalp.

Horse stolen: hold the hand up, palm out, then drop the arm, pointing the forefinger toward the ground.

Gun taken: shake the uplifted hand, palm out, then make the motion of pull-ing back the hammer of a gun.

Wounded: hold the palm up and point to the wound.

Victorious: hold the palm up, then close the fist and shake it toward the ground.

All the enemy killed: rub the palms together.

One or more of own party killed: hold up a blanket and let it drop once for each man killed.

Number of horses or scalps taken: hold up the hand and swing it in the direc-tion of the enemy's camp the corresponding number of times.

Fight in progress: close the fists and pretend to rub them together while keep-ing them, however, an inch or two apart.

Cease fighting: set the fists together, then move them wide apart.

Peace: raise a blanket or a white flag.

Enemy or buffalo in sight: hold up the hand and draw in inwards signifying "come in close."

Go back: hold up the hand and push it away.

Keep quiet: lower the hand toward the ground.

Come quick: draw the hand quickly inwards.

No: wave the hands apart.

Yes: hold the right arm out, index pointing outward, then quickly close the index and sweep the arm inwards.

What is it? shake the right hand, palm out, in front of the face.

Good: hold the hand out in front, palm down, fingers pointing out, and wave it sideways, sometimes a little upward.

Many, much: with both hands make the gesture of scooping something up, e.g., a handful of beads from a dish.

Finished: put the hands together and wave them apart.

I am poor: point the left index out and run the back of the right index along it from the tip in.

Although certain raids originated in a lust for vengeance that could be appeased only by blood, the majority were more in the nature of sporting events played for the highest stakes, seeing that their primary aim was not so much to annihilate the enemy as to secure scalps, horses, guns, and other trophies that brought a man honour and renown. There was no more merit in killing a man and taking his scalp than in stealing his gun or driving away his horses. Whenever he could, naturally, a warrior took all three, scalp, gun, and horses; but a small party of half a dozen men could not successfully attack a large camp, and the Sarcee, though brave often to recklessness, avoided pitched battles unless the weight of numbers leaned heavily on their side. Hence, nearly all their raids were tip-and-run affairs. Here they drove off a band of horses, there they massacred three or four isolated foes and bore off their scalps and women, after which, elated by their success, they retreated as quickly as they could and approached their main camp singing "praising songs." Immediately their people gathered inside or outside a tent, and, to the beating of drums, chanted songs of victory while the women danced joyfully in front of the conquerors.

Tribal etiquette permitted a warrior to paint his exploits, once in his lifetime, on his blanket, on the inside lining of his tent, or on a special suit of clothing decorated with the tails of weasels;[3] and these paintings, interpreted

---

3. He could repaint them on a second blanket, tent-lining, or suit of clothes if the first became worn out, but not if he sold it.

by their owners, give us vivid glimpses of certain raids that occurred in the third quarter of the nineteenth century.[4] Plate 5 shows the blanket of Old Sarcee, painted by a relative with red and blue figures from patterns the old man himself had cut out in paper. He was 79 years old when he thus revived his war memories, rather reluctantly, because he could no longer depict them on a buffalo hide, but only on the worthless hide of a steer. The scenes are not in consecutive order, but arranged to suit his fancy and to conform with the shape of the blanket.

Scene 1 (in centre): four figures in blue represent Cree Indians, four in red, across the three guns and the tomahawk, Sarcee, the figure on the right grasping a knife being Old Sarcee himself.

"When my brother exhausted his horse during a certain buffalo-hunt he abandoned it to graze all night in the open prairie. Early the next morning I was sent to bring it in, and discovered it picketed beside a river by four Cree Indians, who had removed its saddle and lain down to sleep, one of them using the saddle as a pillow. Three of the men possessed guns, the fourth only a tomahawk. I stealthily hid their guns in some brush and summoned three of my kinsmen, to whom I handed over the stolen weapons. We then awakened the four men and mocked them. Suddenly a band of our Blackfoot allies rode up. They immediately massacred three of our prisoners; the fourth, grasping his tomahawk, tried to swim across the river, but we shot him before he reached half-way."

Scene 2 (left centre): a blue tomahawk.

"I was once travelling with a party north of Calgary, near a place called "Picking Berries," when some Cree stole into our camp and drove off a few of our horses. We pursued and overtook them, but they took refuge in a trench, held us at bay during the day with rapid fire from their guns, and escaped during the night, without a casualty on either side. Afterwards I gathered a blanket, a set of bow and arrows, and this tomahawk from their trench; and one of my companions, One-Spotted, picked

Plate 5. Old Sarcee's blanket.
(Canadian Museum of History 77013)

---

4. See also the war-narratives in Ch. 1.

up a blanket. We presented these trophies to some of our old men in accordance with our tribal custom."

Scene 3 (left side towards bottom): two blue horses, and a man standing between them holding their bridles, inside a red square; a line of blue tracks leading from the man to four red spade-like figures outside the square.

"Shortly before the great smallpox epidemic ravaged our tribe (1870 A.D.) thirteen of us discovered a camp of Cree near Big River, and I with four other men was sent forward to steal some of their horses. I crept inside their corral before daylight and led out two horses, as you can see in the picture. One I gave to my compaions, the other I kept for myself."

Scene 4 (half-way up left side): eight red figures inside a red circle surrounded by a dozen red figures outside; blue dots leading outward from the circle.

"Twelve of us (only eight are shown on the blanket) went on the warpath to Montana, where some Sioux sighted us through telescopes and pursued us. We took refuge in a trench where their bullets would strike the ground above us, and in the darkness we watched the fires that they had lit all around. Our leader then suggested that some one gifted with medicine power should scout out a route of escape. I volunteered, and, finding one exit unguarded, returned and led our whole party to safety."

Scene 5 (top and bottom): two rows each of four horses, two red and two blue.

"Eight of us went on the warpath against the Sioux, and I was sent ahead to spy out the enemy's camp, which was close to the bank of a river. All night I lay concealed in a cutbank. At dawn I saw a Sioux warrior wearing only one moccasin drive their horses out of the corral and hobble two of them near a tent. With my gun cocked and ready I boldly walked past him, cut the hobbles of his two horses and drove off the entire herd, which numbered many more than are shown on the blanket. The Sioux evidently mistook me for a fellow-member of his band, because he quietly re-entered his tent without raising an alarm. We rode hard all that day, and at evening, when we were safe from pursuit, divided up the horses among us."

Scene 6 (top left-hand corner): two lines of six figures each, one red and the other blue, joined by tracks; two blue figures lying prostrate between them.

"I joined a party of Blackfoot, Blood and Sarcee Indians that started from Blackfoot Crossing to raid the Sioux. One noon, however, our enemies discovered and attacked us. Two of our men (the two blue figures lying prostrate) were killed before an eclipse of the sun put an end to the fighting."

Scene 7 (half-way up right side): tobacco pouch, pipe, tomahawk, and bow and bowcase with quiver full of arrows.

"Eight different bands of Indians attacked us near Fort Vermilion, and in the fighting fifty of our tribe were killed, including our chief Bull-Head. The enemy then retired, and we who survived searched the battle-field to pick up anything they had left behind. I found the bow and arrows, tomahawk, pipe and tobacco pouch."

Scene 8 (right side towards middle): seven red figures inside a red circle, surrounded by a dozen figures outside it; two men close together, one grasping the other.

"Once when we were travelling north of Red Deer River we encountered some Cree Indians, who fled for cover to a hole in the ground. We surrounded them and killed two men before the rest escaped during the night. One of our own warriors had been shot in an attempt to rush their position. To prevent the enemy from stripping the corpse and taking the scalp I crept forward and dragged the body back to our line."

Scene 9 (right side towards bottom) : two red horses and a man standing between them holding their bridles, inside a red square; blue tracks leading to a figure outside the square.

36

"A number of us joined with a party of Blackfoot, Blood and Piegan warriors to raid the Sioux, and after travelling several days we sighted one of the enemy's camps. I and six other men were sent forward to raid it. We crept into the corral shortly before dawn and each led away one horse. Mine I presented to the leader of the party."

The picture writings on this blanket are so palpably realistic that even without their author's interpretations their meanings could hardly remain in doubt. Yet the Sarcee had also a few more conventionalized symbols, four of which are shown in Figure 4, where *a* represents a war party, *b* a scout's movements, *c* a scalp, and *d* a captured horse.

The successful warrior had other ways of making known his exploits besides painting them on his blanket or his tent. During the festival of the Sun Dance, and at certain other ceremonies, he could recite them in public, when he faced the risk of correction or ridicule if he dared to exaggerate or embroider. For special occasions, too, he generally wore some trophy that he had captured in battle, or

Figure 3. Head-plume worn as a war memorial (1/4 natural size).

made to recall some deed. Figure 3 shows the head-plume that was worn by one old warrior to commemorate the following encounter with some Sioux.

> About 30 of us set out to raid the Sioux. As we lay in hiding near their camp a solitary man walked unsuspectingly towards us. We shot him, stripped him of his clothes and tore off his scalp. I was the last to reach his body and secured only a fragment of his scalp, but even that entitled me to count a coup. Most of us then returned home, but four men remained behind to steal some horses. One enemy was killed, one brought back a few horses and the other two returned empty-handed. Afterwards, to commemorate my part in the raid, I made this head-plume, using horse-hair instead of the original scalp because my fragment was too small.

Sport combined with danger in most of these raids, and in some was uppermost, so that now and then one had an unexpectedly happy confusion. In the early part of the nineteenth century, apparently, seven Sarcee warriors who had travelled far to the southward discovered a camp of "Utah" Indians, and while six of them remained in hiding during the night one youth crept forward to reconnoitre. Right in the centre of camp he came upon two tents and cautiously peered through their doorways. In the first slept an Indian and his wife, in the second, all alone, their daughter, whose clothes were hanging all around the wall. The scout returned to his comrades, told them what he had seen, and said "Wait for me here one day, and if I don't come back, go home, for you will know that something has happened to me." He then re-entered the camp and crept in under the girl's blanket. Recognizing from his clothes that he was a stranger, she pulled the communication line that connected her

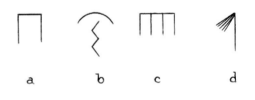

Figure 4. Conventional war signs.

tent with her father's and began to stir up the fire; but when the fire-light fell upon the youth and she saw how handsome he was, she begged her father to spare his life and let her marry him. The father consented, and, calling in all the chiefs and leading men, asked them to treat the young man courteously, because he was making him his son-in-law.

The youth lived with his wife's people for some time; he even accompanied them on the war-path and brought in many horses to pay for his bride. But when he began to pine for his own home his father-in-law consented that he should return and take his wife with him. Four of her brothers accompanied them, carrying for his kinsmen many blankets and other things to indicate that he had married into a wealthy family. He remarked their nervousness as they drew near the main Sarcee camp and went forward alone to ensure their friendly reception. Entering first the tent of his father, he asked him to summon all the chiefs, to whom he related his story. The Sarcee joyfully welcomed the Utah Indians and entertained them for several weeks; then, when the time came for the visitors to return home, every man and woman in the camp brought them a horse or some clothing to repay them for their earlier presents. Peace reigned between the two peoples for many years thereafter, but in the end war broke out again.

The Indian overtaken by sickness turned for help to those medicine-men who were reputed to have gained through personal visions the power of healing. They chanted their dream-songs over him, gave him perhaps an amulet to wear, and thenceforth watched his progress from day to day, not without receiving substantial payments. Occasionally a medicine-man sucked out blood and pus through a bird-bone tube, or he prescribed a herbal remedy, learned in most cases from the neighbouring Cree;[5] but genuinely efficacious remedies there were few or none, the Indian placing his chief reliance m incantations and prayers. Old men visited the tipi to pray over the patient, and relatives sought to bring about his recovery with fervent vows. The Sarcee seem never to have run amok when afflicted with incurable diseases, as sometimes happened, apparently, among the Blackfoot.

When the end of life drew near relatives painted the dying man either with red ochre, or with the marks peculiar to the society of which he had been a member, dressed him in his finest clothes, and wrapped his other garments in a bundle behind him. Often a young man stepped forward and threw a fine blanket over the corpse, thereby expressing a sympathy that was none the less genuine because it did not escape subsequent reward. Parents and wife put on their oldest garments, the father unbraided his hair, and the mother and the wife cut their hair short. The women also gashed their legs with flints or arrow-points, and frequently cut off a finger at the joint, so that even though the depth of their sorrow found no outlet in weeping, the pain of the mutilated fingers would release their tears. Neighbours always stood ready to perform the operation, one woman holding the patient's wrist while another laid a knife to the joint and severed it with a blow from an axe. Refusal to undergo the mutilation indicated heartlessness; even men at times submitted to it voluntarily, especially fathers stricken with grief by the loss of favourite sons.[6]

After a short delay to enable all the people to join the funeral train the relatives placed the dead man, his clothes, weapons, and occasionally certain other possessions on a travois, lashed it to one of his horses, and dragged it to a tree on a neighbouring hill-top. There, wrapping the corpse and its clothes into a bundle, they deposited it on a high branch, abandoned the weapons and other goods, killed the horse at the foot of the tree, and returned to camp, leaving

---

5. One old medicine-man, Many Wounds, claimed to know through a vision herbal remedies for seven different complaints. In each case he prescribed a potion made by crushing a herb and boiling it in water. One herb, he stated, made the water red; that he gave for chest troubles. Another, which turned the water yellow, he used for cramps in the stomach.

6. Of the women living on the Sarcee reserve in 1921 one had lost three joints on one hand and one on the other; a second woman the first joints of both her little fingers; and a third a joint on each thumb and little finger.

the parents and the wife to weep under the grave, even to sleep there a night or two until some kinsmen led them home. In camp they clipped the mane and tail of one of the deceased's best horses and distributed his property according to his wishes, if he had expressed any, and if not, by mutual agreement among the nearest kin, including generally the widow. After their confinement to a reserve the destruction of horses was prohibited, but as late as 1919, when they buried an old warrior named Wolf-Carrier, the Sarcee secretly killed his favourite horse, and threw into a crevice between two rocks all his property except his horses and his medicine-bundles.

Men of distinction received special burial. Fellow-tribesmen laid out their corpses in their tents, hung up their spare clothing around the walls, killed their favourite horses outside, and forthwith abandoned the camp.

When a man was killed in war the father, if still alive, clipped the mane and tail of one of his son's horses, and, after piercing with a friend's aid both his shoulder-blades, passed through the holes a cord whose ends were attached to a buffalo-skull. He then drove one arrow into his breast, and others into his arms and legs; and, leading the horse by the halter, paraded around the camp, pitifully dragging the buffalo-skull behind him. At once some warrior leaped forward, snatched away the halter, and, mounting the horse, rode around the tents singing war songs and calling for volunteers to follow his banner in seeking revenge. Then the old father, released by some one else from the buffalo-skull and the arrows, marched proudly to and fro, chanting the praises of his son and of the warrior who had undertaken to avenge him. That same evening volunteers gathered in the leader's tent to learn the time of their departure. Often the father joined them when they set forth, their leader riding one of the dead man's horses.

With few exceptions, men who lost their wives or sons either joined war-parties, or paid prolonged visits to other bands or tribes in order to forget their grief. A bereaved father sometimes wandered off alone and attempted some desperate deed against his enemies, careless whether or not it cost him his life; generally, however, his "comrade" (if still alive) accompanied him and endeavoured to shield him from harm. Parents, husbands, and wives mourned for an indefinite period, wearing their oldest clothes. As a rule the tribe considered about 6 months sufficient. At the close of that term, therefore, a friend called them into his tent, painted their faces, and dressed them in good clothes, for which service they or their kinsfolk paid him later.

The average Sarcee stoically accepted death without fear, even though he cherished no hope of a happy Elysium. The soul or the shadow, he fancied (regarding the two as identical), wandered away to a cold sandy region far to the eastward, there to dwell with its fellows in ragged tents, and to gnaw around its camp-fire the dry bones of buffaloes that had perished ages ago. Many wept as they sat, longing for the bright world that had been taken from them; and at night they sometimes wandered around the camps of the living Indians, making shrill noises like the wind. Often during the hours of darkness the Sarcee have seen a long flame shoot up and down in the sky, and recognized the fire of the shades. Yet happily, even into that world of gloom and misery hope could send a tiny gleam. In every child that began to stir in its mother's womb the Maker implanted the soul or shadow of some one who had gone before; and whenever a baby died, and a new one was born soon after, its mother knew that the soul of her earlier child had come back to her in the later.

My mother was examining an old battle-field when she felt a wind blow under her dress, and discovered a day or two afterwards that she had conceived. Later, when I was born, she was not surprised to find a birthmark on my chest, for she knew that I was the reincarnation of some warrior who had been killed in the battle.

CHAPTER 5
SOCIETIES

An earlier chapter mentioned the five societies or clubs, to one or other of which every male Sarcee belonged at some time or other in his career. Dr. Pliny Goddard has described them in considerable detail,[1] but since my information, derived from three elderly men, differs from his on certain points, and supplements it in others, an independent description of the societies will not be out of place, even though it may entail considerable repetition.

The names of the societies were:

tsi: "mosquitoes."

łikuwa: "dogs."

tasyiłna: called by Goddard "police," but translated by my informants as "those painted red."

nakołtcujna: called by Goddard "preventers," but translated by my informants as "those who make others their associates."

da wa': a small yellow bird found in swampy places, species not determined.

The number of members in each of these societies varied from year to year, but seldom rose above fifty or fell below twenty. Every male Indian had to join the Mosquito society before he was eligible for any other; hence nearly all the members of this society were young men. From the Mosquitoes he could pass into any other society he wished, and might, if wealthy, belong to three or four at the same time. Generally he sold his membership in one and joined another at intervals of a few years, then dropped out from them all when he became old. Middle-aged men tended to congregate in the Dogs and Painted Red societies, letting the younger men predominate in the other three; but the latter always required one elderly man to make the proclamations for the annual dances, and usually contained three or four. Although the societies, therefore, possessed the germs of an age-grading system, they never developed it, or established any precise order of rank.

Throughout the greater part of the year the societies were in abeyance, and their members scattered among the different bands. Only during one short period did each in turn become prominent, during its four-day summer dance, celebrated at a time determined by its leaders, but always before the celebration of the Sun Dance. It then erected a very large tent (or joined together two ordinary tents) in the centre of the camp-circle alongside the tent of the tribal chief; and its leaders assumed complete control of the camp in place of that

---

1. Goddard, P.E., *Dancing Societies of the Sarsi Indians*, Anth. Papers, Am. Mus. Nat. Hist., vol. II, New York, 1916.

chief, even to the extent of forbidding any one to leave without their consent. They directed any buffalo-hunting that occurred during the four-day period,[2] and under their direction the hunters carried all the buffalo meat to camp for the society to distribute, if its proper officials were not themselves present at the hunt to distribute the meat on the ground. One society, and one alone, the "Painted Red," functioned also at another season; it acted as a police force during the celebration of the Sun Dance.[3]

The "Painted Red" society was peculiar in another respect, for it had only one leader, whereas all the others had two. These officials were not elected, but obtained their rank by the purchase of the necessary insignia. The "Dogs" had in addition two special officials, "lariat owners," who were virtually co-ordinate with the leaders and always consulted on matters of moment.[4] Each society counted furthermore four (or in one case two) quasi-officials called "workers", who did not participate in the dancing but sat near the door; their duties were to erect the tent, to tend the smudge fire, to distribute all the food, and to perform such other labours as were necessary.

New members were inducted at any period preceding the annual dance, generally all at one time. The workers erected a special tent for the occasion, and those who were selling their membership called in the equivalent number of purchasers, whom the old men (the drummers and singers) painted with the appropriate markings and instructed in the songs and dances. The new members compensated these old men with clothes and other goods, in addition to paying the ex-members who had resigned to them their seats.

Every society dance began and ended in the same way. After the tent was erected and the members gathered inside it, the workers kindled a smudge of sweet-grass, over which the leaders held their insignia and silently prayed. The other members followed them; each stood over the smudge with a blanket drawn over his head and offered a silent prayer. At night again, just before the members lay down to sleep,[5] the same ceremony was repeated. Evening prayer was indeed not an uncommon feature in the every-day life of the Sarcee, for they believed that it protected them from evil spirits and ensured them good dreams; but in their society dances they at no time omitted either the closing or the opening prayer.

MOSQUITOES

This society had two leaders and two workers. Every member stripped to his breech-clout, painted a red streak across his face from one cheekbone to the other, daubed his body white, planted a white eagle feather with pendant

---

2. At all other periods individual hunters could ride freely outside the came and even run down the buffalo.

3. Goddard assigns this function to three societies, the "Dogs," the "Painted Red," and "Those who make others their associates."

4. Goddard gives the "Mosquitoes" one leader, the "Dogs" four, and the rest two each.

5. Those for whom there was no room in the tent slept in their homes.

string on the right side of his head, and bound the claws of the same bird to his right wrist. The two leaders wore bandoliers of buffalo hide trimmed along the edges with buffalo-calf hoofs (later bandoliers of buckskin trimmed with deer toes); and they daubed their bodies, not white, but yellow. Four old men took their places in the centre of the tent, beat four drums and sang, with intervals between their songs for smoking. The members, seated in a circle around them, rose and danced without moving from their places during the first three songs, then, at the opening of the fourth, rushed outside and scratched with their bird-claws every one who ran away. Women and children, however, they spared, generally also men who stood their ground and held out the backs of their wrists. If for any reason the camp was moved during the four-day period the Mosquitoes, mounted on horseback in full regalia, pursued and scratched every youth who was not a member of their society.

Although the Sarcee did not actually invent either this or their other so-cieties, but borrowed it from some neighbour, almost certainly the Blackfoot, they themselves ascribed a local origin to it and bolstered up their belief with the following legend.

"A small Sarcee war-party was discovered by its enemies and forced to scat-ter. One man threw off his clothes to aid his escape. A swarm of mosquitoes began to attack him but their leader rebuked them, saying. "Do not touch my son. He then taught him the Mosquito society ritual and bade him fearlessly sting all nonmembers, whether man, woman or child."

DOGS

In this society were two leaders, two lariat owners, and four workers. The lead-ers wore a kind of poncho made from a red Hudson's Bay Company's blanket, which was lined with skin on the inside, with beads and weasel skins on the outside, and fringed at the bottom with eagle feathers. It almost touched the ground behind, but in front barely covered the waist. This was the only gar-ment they wore, apart from a breech-clout and moccasins; but they brought to the festival the two society pipes which were their chief badges of office.

The insignia of each lariat owner was a lariat made from the mane of the buffalo, and worn like a bandolier over the left shoulder with one long end trailing on the ground. That no one might step on this end they always danced behind the other members, who merely wore their finest clothes. Each man planted a bunch of owl feathers in his hair, painted with red his face, forearms, and legs, then encircled his face with a streak of blue and added two bands of the same colour around each wrist and ankle.

In the middle of the tent sat four old men holding four rattles that had been borrowed from the beaver bundle (see page 83); sometimes also four other old men to help in the singing. Beside them were dishes of meat or berry soup contributed to the society by women related to the members. At the opening of each song, the two leaders led the Dogs in a dance around the old men, single file, while non-members looked in through the door; behind any mem-ber danced his wife, if she wished, holding the tail of his blanket. At the end of each dance they resumed their seats and smoked in turn from one of the large society pipes. The workers distributed the food at the close of the fourth dance, thus concluding the day's performance.

At the last two or three festivals of the Dog Society some of the members wore bonnets of buffalo hide that supported two upstanding buffalo horns and trailed a strip of skin decorated with three horizontal rows of feathers. This head-dress really belonged to a Blackfoot society, the Horn, which was well known to the Sarcee, but never adopted by them.

PAINTED RED

This society had four workers, but only one leader, whose insignia, carried in every dance, was the *misdo'ti dis·oli*, "woolly pipe," wrapped in red flannel and eagle feathers. It had a stone bowl about 2 inches wide, decorated where it joined the wide wooden stem with red plumes, ribbons, and strips of weasel skin. Each member encircled his head, wrists, and ankles with strips of wolf skin, planted a goose feather on each side of his head, and painted a black band across his nose and cheeks and another around each wrist. The leader blackened, in addition, his lower jaw, and extended the patch upwards into two curling mustachios.

Four old men, with four drums, sat close to the four workers near the door of the tent. Each planted in the ground before him a stick to which was fastened bells, goose feathers, and a cluster of human hair. A few members too old to dance sat at the back of the tent, and the remainder lined the side walls.

As soon as the drummers began a song the members rose from their seats and danced toward the fire in the centre of the tent, then faced about and danced toward the walls. If any one kept his seat through shyness or other cause, one of the old men pulled out his stake and point it at him; then, if the man was still sitting at the end of the dance, he walked over and tore his blanket. They danced four times, with intervals for smoking; but toward the end of the fourth song they rushed outdoors and tore the blanket of any man they captured outside his tent. The victim who lost his temper received no compensation, but whoever shove no annoyance was given better clothes at the conclusion of the festival.

The police duties performed by the Painted Red society during ie the Sun Dance festival will be described in a later chapter. As usual, there was a legend to account for the society's origin; it ran as follows:

"Once when the Sarcee were moving their camp they left far behind them an orphan girl. In following their trail she passed close to a blackbird, which called to her 'My daughter, come here.' It then gave her this society, which she sold to a man for a very high price."

THOSE WHO MAKE OTHERS THEIR ASSOCIATES

This society closely resembled the preceding, Painted Red. Its members wore the same wolf-skin bands around the head, wrists, and ankles, and its leader (or leaders)[6] carried a black stone pipe wrapped in cloth. Faces and bodies were painted red, but each man bore two black streaks across his face, one on a level with the eyebrows and the other across the mouth. The leader wore (over the left shoulder, as always) a bandolier of tanned buffalo hide decorated with diagonal rows of beads, a fringe of elk toes along one edge, and four bells and four buffalo-tail pendants at the bottom.

The four old drummers, and the four workers, sat near the door, and the members danced inwards towards the fire, but did not turn around and dance toward the wall. Like the members of the Painted Red society, they ran outdoors after the fourth dance and tore the clothes of any man they found outside his tent.

The Sarcee offered two different legends in explanation of this society. The first ran:

> Long before the coming of the white man our people were ravaged by smallpox. After many of them had died the survivors moved their camp, leaving behind by accident a small orphan boy. No sooner were they out of sight than the dead appeared to this boy, gave him a bundle containing a black pipe, and bade him organize a society among his people when he grew up.

The second legend was much fuller:

> A man whose wife had just died asked his father to make him a bow and arrows. The father summoned together all the men in the camp and instructed each one to make four or five arrows, reserving for his own hands the making of the bow. When they were finished the widower departed, telling his parents that he was lonely and intended to journey to the country whither his wife had gone. Travelling eastward, he came to a sand-mound marked with the emblems of various societies, and, on a flat spot near its centre, a ring of little stones surrounded with sand. The man laid his bow and arrows and his blanket on the south side of the ring, sat down facing the east, and filled his pipe; but before lie could it he saw, approaching from the east, a hunter driving a buffalo. Presently the stranger shot the buffalo with an arrow and laid out the animal ready for skinning; but in place of skinning it he mounted his horse and rode back over a hill. The traveller went over to look at the buffalo, but found only a little mouse pierced by an arrow. He left it there and, returning, sat down again beside the ring of stones. Soon the stranger reappeared and began to ride round the mound, for it was really a camp, and the circle of stones within it a chief's tent. In a loud voice he called "Prepare yourselves, for a human being has come to visit us, then he disappeared over the hill again." The traveller sat waiting, and as he waited he heard the rattle of

---

6. Two informants said there were two leaders, two others claimed there was only one.

dishes, although his eyes saw nothing; but looking behind him, he noticed a dish containing four white puff-balls, a white ball of grass seed, a prairie onion, and a peculiar piece of coloured meat. An invisible host then addressed him saying, "My son, if you eat all this food you will obtain your desire." The man ate everything; it tasted to him like buffalo meat. Immediately the camp was visible to his eyes. His host then asked him "My son, why have you come?" and he answered, "Father, I was lonely for my wife, and I came to find her. She was dressed as I shall describe." After he had described her dress his host said "After four days and four nights, my son, you shall find her. Those four days and four nights we shall dance." And his hostess added "If you are asked, what you would like to take back with you choose that black pipe hanging on the door. It belongs to the *nakoɫtcujna* society. With it are two other things that give the people much joy, a beaded wheel and two arrows; they are for the young people. If you ask for anything else you will never re-cover your wife." The woman then showed him how to play the beaded-wheel game, and the proper painting for the *nakoɫtcu-jna* society.

Half the men in the camp danced that night, while the trav-eller watched them. He looked for his wife, but could not see her among the dancers. The next night the rest of the men danced; and still his wife was absent. On the third night half the women danced, and even yet his wife was not among them, but on the fourth night, when the rest of the women were dancing, his wife entered the tent, recognized her husband, and sat down beside him. His host then said "you may take your wife home now, but you must not look back."

The man started out for his home, but after sleeping three or four nights he looked behind him and immediately found him-self back at his starting-point. The chief warned him "If you look back four times you will have to go home alone. Moreover, never tell your wife that you wish she were a ghost again, for if you do she will come right back here." The two started out again and reached their home in safety: but for the rest of her life the woman neither blinked her eyelids nor closed them during sleep.

Now it happened one day that the man's people said to him, "What is that you have brought back?" "This is a black medi-cine-pipe," he answered, "that I received with my wife. I was told not to sell it for more or less than seven horses. I was giv-en also a wheel and two arrows to use as a game. You have no games, so I will show them to you. That is how the wheel game originated, and the *nakoɫtcujna* society, whose leader is the owner of the black medicine-pipe."

The couple had seven children after their return. One night, however, a hunter came in from the chase and entered their tent. It filled with smoke, and the woman went outside to adjust its ears. She remained outside a long time without effecting any improvement, while her husband became more and more angry. He burst out as she re-entered, "Why didn't you stay out all night? I wish you were a ghost." That night the woman did become a ghost and left him.

BIRDS

There were two leaders and four workers in this society. Its members stripped to their breech-clouts and moccasins, keeping the latter untied, painted their faces and bodies red, and drew two black lines vertically across each eye and each corner of the mouth. On his back every man carried a water-bag made from a buffalo's bladder, and the leaders wore bear-skin belts and anklets. Thus arrayed, but covered with their blankets, they gathered in the tent set up by the four workers and prayed. Conducted then by their leaders outside the tent they arranged themselves in a circle on their blankets, their leaders on the west side facing east and the workers on the east side facing west. In the centre sat four old men, each beating a rattle borrowed from the beaver bundle on a dry buffalo hide stretched out in front of him. These old men then began to chant one of the society songs, and the "Birds" danced around them, while the people gathered near to watch. Disfigured persons were expected to keep aloof, because the *Dawu'* was a timid bird and its impersonators would flee in terror to their tent if such a person approached.

Because the society did not share its food with the rest of the tribe, its members generally had to hunt during the festival to supply their personal needs. In that case, as soon as this first dance ended, its leaders led them on foot to the hunting field, leaving the old men in camp. If they failed to kill a buffalo they returned in silence to their tent; but if they succeeded, their leaders assigned to every man a back-load of meat, and, blowing whistles in the van, led them back triumphantly. The old men welcomed them by beating their rattles on the buffalo hides and chanting one of the society songs, while the "Birds" danced around them, each man carrying his pack. Because their burdens were heavy they danced around only once, after which they threw their packs inside the tent, filled their water-bags at the river, and returned to dance four times again, with intervals between each dance. Two men carried in their bags instead of water the blood of the buffalo. They now carried this inside the tent and handed it over to the workers, who set about preparing their meat; and after all had eaten, they again danced outside. So they continued during the four days of the festival.

Since the "Birds" might not ride on horseback during their festival they had to entrust their horses to relatives and march on foot if for any reason the tribe moved camp during that period.

To explain the society's origin the Sarcee relate a legend of the usual type:

A woman who had been thrashed by her husband fled to a small lake and fell asleep at the water's edge. There the bird *Dawu'* visited her and taught her the song and ritual for a new society. When she grew old she taught them to her eldest son, who established them in the tribe.

CHAPTER 6
THE SUN DANCE[1]

Though the annual dances of the five societies offered a welcome break in the routine of Sarcee life, they paled into insignificance before the great festival of the Sun Dance, celebrated by the united tribe in August when the saskatoon and other berries ripened. Like so many other of their customs, the Sarcee seem to have derived this festival from the Blackfoot, but at a period so remote that, having forgotten its real origin, they ascribed its introduction to the following myth:

A young man who had an ugly scar on the side of his face fell in love with a certain woman, who promised to many him if he succeeded in removing it. Accordingly he travelled away toward the sun and came to a camp, whose chief asked him what he wanted. "I merely came on a visit," he replied, and went on to another camp. There too he was asked what he wanted, and replied "I am looking for some one who can remove this scar from my face." "We can do nothing with it," the people answered. He received the same answer at the third camp. At the fourth Morning Star in the form of a boy came to him and asked him what he wanted; and again he replied, "I want some one to remove this scar from my face," Morning Star stayed with him for a while, then went back and said to his father, the Maker. "I have found a friend." His father answered "We do not want any human beings here"; but when the boy insisted, he consented to let him bring the young man to his home.

So the young Indian came to the lodge of the Maker. The Maker asked him what he wanted, and when the youth told him, he said "Stay with us for a while." He ordered the Indian to make four sweat-baths, and as soon as they were ready joined him inside them. When the youth emerged from the fourth bath his form was perfect. The Maker then seated him on one side, Morning Star on the other, and asked his wife which was her son. The woman hesitated for a long time and finally pointed to the Indian. "How foolish you are," replied the Maker. "The other is our son."

The Maker now adopted the youth as his second son and detained him with them. He warned the two youths not to wander far away, because the family was at war with the geese and the swans. One day the two youths wandered away to a slough, where the geese and swans attacked them. Morning Star shouted, "Our enemies are pursuing us"; but the young man caught

---

1. Dr. P.E. Goddard has published an incomplete and rather confused account of the Sarcee Sun Dance in Anth. Papers, Am. Mus. Nat. Hist., vol. 16, 1915–1921, pp. 273–82.

up a stick and killed so many of the birds that the remainder fled. In recognition of his courage the Maker made him a scalp-lock shirt, painted his face as the owners of such shirts paint their faces to-day, and taught him certain songs. Meanwhile his wife piled in the middle of the tent everything she owned except a white buffalo-calf skin. The Maker observed this omission and sang "I want only the white calf-skin"; and when his wife laid down the white calf-skin he placed the scalp-lock shirt on top of it. The old woman then chanted a song of praise over her adopted son. At its conclusion the Maker laid a row of white sage out to the door of the tent for the youth to step on, and bade him do likewise whenever he transferred the scalp-lock shirt to another Indian.

Now they sent the youth home to his people. Just as he was leaving Morning Star said to him "My friend, give me the woman who refused you. I shall watch over you and hear every word you say." The youth returned to the grandmother with whom he had lived before his journey, but the old woman did not recognize him. "It is I, your grandson," he said to her. "Why do you stare at me so much?"

As he stood outside his tent that evening he saw the woman who had refused him standing outside her tent, whereupon he turned round and went indoors. She came to his lodge soon afterwards, and he told her to accompany him out to the prairie. They climbed a high hill together, and, standing on its summit, the youth called "My friend here is the woman you wanted." Immediately Morning Star came down and stood beside them. "Close your eyes," he ordered, and they all ascended into the sky.

The youth is now the Evening Star. It was he who brought to mankind the scalp-lock shirt and the Sun Dance.

Strictly speaking, the Sun Dance was not an annual festival, because it could only be held in fulfilment of a woman's voluntary vow. Nevertheless, the Sarcee seem to have celebrated one every year from at least the middle of the nineteenth century until some time after they occupied their present reserve near Calgary. The entire festival covered a period of 9 days: during the first four the tribe moved in easy stages to the chosen site; on the fifth it built the Sun Dance lodge; and during the 4 succeeding days it "danced." Occasionally it lingered at the site a day or two longer to indulge in further entertainments, but the festival proper ended on the ninth day. Its leading actors were:

(1) The Sun Dance woman, i.e., the woman who had vowed to hold the festival, and her husband.

(2) The "mother" and "father" of this couple, i.e., the woman who had held the last Sun Dance, and her husband.

(3) Two young men who had vowed to "take the buffalo's head," i.e., to use the sweat-houses, keep the fires, drive off the dogs, and perform certain other necessary labours; also their instructors, the two men who had performed same duties at the preceding Sun Dance.

(4) An old man chosen as "confessor" by the husband of the Sun Dance woman, on account of his knowledge of the ritual.

(5) A man who had vowed to fast, and his instructor, the man who had fasted at the previous festival.

(6) Braves who had vowed to undergo torture.

(7) Women who had vowed to eat of the sacred buffalo tongues.

(8) The members of the Painted Red Society, who policed the camp during the festival.

Only a married woman, free from all taint of infidelity, might vow to give a Sun Dance, and then only during her first marriage, or, if her husband had died after she had given already one or more Sun Dances, during her second marriage. Occasionally a woman gave three or four during her lifetime, receiving greater honour from each one. She could make her vow on any occasion that gave rise to anxiety or danger, and at any season of the year before midsummer. The illness of a kinsman, or his absence on the war-path, offered the most usual pretext. She rose up before the crowd gathered in the sick man's tent and said "Pray for me, I beseech you, for I intend to give a Sun Dance in the summer if my kinsman recovers." The news spread quickly from camp to camp, and other Indians publicly vowed to undertake certain roles at the forthcoming festival, on grounds similar to those of its giver. The whole tribe palpitated with an air of expectancy, and every family examined and overhauled its wardrobe.

Within a few hours of her declaration the husband of the Sun Dance woman called an old man into his tipi, handed him a pipe, and invited him to become the confessor. The old man held the pipe over a smudge of white sage, pointed it north, east, south, and west, and finally lit it. Both men then smoked, after which they carried or led the sick man outside his tent to face the east, and the old man called out "So and so (naming the woman) has promised to give a Sun Dance next summer if this her kinsman recovers. If she has lived purely all her days may he recover quickly, but if she is not pure may he die."[2] Leading the patient inside again he advised the woman to call in

---

2. If the man died the woman's vow ceased to be binding, and the Indians suspected her of secret

the giver of the last Sun Dance, the owner of the ceremonial head-dress that she would purchase and wear during the festival.[3]

Summoned by a messenger the previous Sun Dance woman now entered the tipi and received a pipe filled with tobacco, but not lit. After praying over it she handed it to the patient, who puffed it four times and handed it to the new Sun Dance woman and her husband. When they in turn had prayed over it they passed it to some man to light. He took it by the bowl, held it twice over the smudge and pointed it northward and eastward; then, taking it by the mouthpiece, he held it twice again over the smudge and pointed it southward and westward. Finally he lit it, and every one smoked. Just before the gathering dispersed kinsmen smeared the patient's face and body with dark red paint, which they renewed from time to time until he recovered. From this date onward a smudge of white sage burned continually in the Sun Dance woman's lodge, no dogs were allowed within, and no loud noise in the vicinity, but at frequent intervals the old Sun Dance woman visited her to teach her what she had to do.

With the coming of summer the scattered camps reunited, pitched their tents in a circle around the lodge of the chief, and directed all their energies to the buffalo hunt. To the tipi of the Sun Dance woman, advanced a little in front of the rest, the hunters brought all the buffalo tongues, which her husband heaped together on a clean robe preliminary to drying. To cut them open he hired two old women who had partaken of the sacred tongues at a previous Sun Dance. They slit each tongue down to its base, taking care not to puncture a hole in either half, since this would be regarded as a sign of unchastity; a pure woman, the Indians believed, could be quite careless, but the Maker himself caused the hand of the impure woman to slip, however cautiously she worked. Two tongues, with the hair still clinging to their bases, they set on one side for ritual eating by the women who had vowed to partake of them; the remainder they stored in parflèches for general consumption during the festival.

As soon as he had stored one hundred dried tongues in his tent, sometimes even before he had obtained that number, the Sun Dance woman's husband presented some tobacco to the chief, who cut it up, called in the old men to share its smoking, and in open council fixed a date for the festival. At the same time the woman's husband distributed tobacco throughout the camp and for-

---

infidelity.

3. This head-dress, which could only be worn at a Sun Dance, has now disappeared. Its last Sarcee owner, Nancy, who died in 1911, believed that none of her tribeswomen were strictly chaste, and, therefore, bequeathed it to a Miss Hodgson (later Mrs. Hill), whose mother was half Sarcee and half French-Canadian, and whose father was the white stockman on the reserve. What became of it later is not known. Except at the Sun Dance it was always wrapped in a deer skin, and a digging-stick that had originally belonged to the beaver medicine bundle (See p. 83) was fastened to the outside. Evidently the Sun Dance head-dress was closely connected with the beaver bundle, for if its owner happened to be absent in another tribe, the wife of the beaver bundle owner could take her place at the Sun Dance and substitute the head-dress she wore in the beaver ritual.

mally requested the Indians not to scatter, because the hour of the Sun Dance was drawing near.

At last the day came when the chief issued the proclamation "Prepare to move to the Sun Dance site." Early the next morning the Indians broke camp; the two workers (the young men who had vowed to perform all the chores) saddled and attached the travois to the horses of the Sun Dance woman and her family, placing all the tongues in one travois, the chief temporarily abdicated his place, and the woman's husband led the cavalcade, followed by his wife and the rest of the tribe. About mid-afternoon the procession halted, and the workers erected a sweat-lodge of willows, facing the east as usual, and with a square hole for its twenty-four stones; behind this hole they kindled a smudge of white sage, and at the back of the lodge, on the piled-up earth, laid a large pipe filled with tobacco. When the stones were hot an old man called out "Come, all who wish to enter the sweat-lodge." Slowly a small procession drew near. In front were the old and the new Sun Dance women, "mother" and "daughter," their heads covered by their blankets. Beside them walked the confessor, and, behind, their husbands, the husband of the new Sun Dance woman wearing a blanket that carried in the middle of the back a painted disk representing the sun. These five took their places at the back of the sweat-lodge, and as many old men as could crowd within sat around the sides.

Now the Sun Dance woman took up the pipe from the back of the lodge, and, followed by her "mother," walked around the north side and handed it to one of the old men. He held it up and prayed over it, then handed it back. She made a gesture as if he were conferring a blessing on her, and passed it on to one of the workers, who lit it and returned it, through her, to the old man. The two women then resumed their places alongside their husbands, and the pipe circulated from hand to hand.

The workers lowered the curtain when every one had smoked and passed in water to pour on the hot stones. Amid the dense cloud of steam that filled the lodge an old man beseeched the Maker to bestow long life, health, and prosperity on the Sun Dance woman and her husband, on each old man inside the lodge, and on every person in the camp. During his prayer the other men intoned a special song, and at its conclusion ejaculated with one voice *e-i.* Some one then poured more water on the stones and a second man prayed in much the same manner. After four or five had prayed, first the front then the back curtain was raised to lower the temperature and let in fresh air. Four times it was raised and lowered before the last man had offered up his prayer. The gathering then dispersed, but as the five principal actors retired to their tents the confessor led the Sun Dance woman to one side to receive her confession. She attested her fidelity to her husband, revealed any overtures she had rejected before or after her marriage, and even recalled to memory any occasion when she had exposed her body, while bathing, to the gaze of another woman. Confession brought immediate absolution; actually there was no question of her purity, since fear of the Maker effectively deterred every unchaste woman from vowing to celebrate a Sun Dance.

From this day until the festival ended the chief withdrew his tent from the centre of the circle toward its circumference and yielded the place of honour to the Sun Dance woman and her husband. They now slept on opposite sides of their tent, and the woman fasted, neither eating nor drinking during the day, and at night taking only four mouthfuls of food and four of water. If, overcome with thirst, she drank more than this quantity, the Indians believed that heavy rain would fall for 4 days and 4 nights, thereby delaying the festival and compelling her to fast all the longer.

The Painted Red society, detailed to police the camp during the festival, now pitched its tent near the tent of the chief. Somewhere in the circumference the Indians joined two tents together so that the old men and some of the women could practise special Sun Dance songs.

On the second and third days the tribe again moved camp and repeated the first day's ceremony; but on the fourth, when it finally reached the appointed site, it erected the sweat-lodge with more ceremony. The workers now called for one hundred sticks to build its frame, one hundred stones for its fireplace, and a buffalo skull, painted half red, half black, with white sage in the eye-sockets, to place on the pile of earth at the back. A score or more young men, therefore, went out to gather the sticks, and each rode around the camp, singing, before he laid his contribution on the lodge site. At evening the chief marched out in front of his tent and cried "Let us hasten on with the Sun Dance, for the woman is still fasting."

On the fifth day, at sunrise, the men began to erect the great Sun Dance lodge. Some dug the post-holes, others brought in the ten or twelve posts,[4] each forked at its upper end. No sooner were these stamped into place than two or three scouts went out to find a suitable centre-pole, which had to be "captured" and brought in with all the formality attending the capture of a prisoner. While they were absent a number of old warriors, each carrying a drum, piled a heap of manure outside the camp and arranged themselves in line behind it. The scouts located a tree, marked it by breaking off a branch and fastening it to the trunk, and rode homeward, zigzagging, and shouting a war-whoop every time they crossed their trail. The moment they came into view the warriors beat their drums and sang; and when at last the scouts halted near them, one old man stepped forward, recounted four brave deeds, and scattered the manure with his feet.[5] Immediately the others scrambled to seize a flying piece, believing that the successful man would surely capture a horse the next time he went out on the war-path. The scouts and warriors then reentered the camp, and gathered together young and old, men and

---

4. The Sarcee held their last Sun Dance about 1890, and my informants had forgotten the exact number of posts.
5. Kicking manure signified that the speaker had told nothing but the truth.

women, to bring in the centre-pole. Half a dozen men only remained behind to dig for it a hole.

The "capture" of the centre-pole was the most joyous and colourful event in the Sarcee year. Dressed in their finest clothes, the Indians marched out from the camp, some on horseback, some on foot. Girls mounted behind their sweethearts, or on horses of their own; and two young braves occasionally bestrode the same horse. Two men carried axes to chop down the tree, others firearms to shoot at it when it fell; but before the first stroke was applied an old warrior stepped forward and related his four brave deeds, while the axmen pointed their weapons at the trunk. After they had trimmed the limbs from the fallen tree and adjusted ropes around its trunk horsemen and footmen crowded around, lifted it from the ground and carried it through the air for a few yards. Then they dragged it to the camp, women vying with men in hauling on the ropes. In front, and on each side, pranced the mounted girls and men, one of whom galloped behind the pole from time to time and fired a gun at it. Not until they had brought it to rest beside its hole did the shouting and yelling die away.

Amid all this excitement the Sun Dance woman and her husband rested quietly in the camp; but now, while others prepared to erect the centre-pole and complete the lodge, her relatives drove all her horses to her tent that her confessor might pray over them, and her "parents," the former Sun Dance woman and her husband, brought over the headdress that they were transferring. The mother covered her daughter's face with red paint; the father painted the face and body of his son, daubing him all over with red paint, then drawing black streaks across his forehead, around his chin, around his shoulders, and across his chest and back, and finally planting a single black daub squarely in the middle of his nose, all the while chanting two songs, one for the red paint and the other for the black. The mother then taught her daughter certain everyday duties, such as how to erect a tipi and to fasten a travois on a horse; and the father similarly instructed his son. Not until all these rituals were ended did the father plant a crow's feather over his son's forehead, and the mother place on her daughter's head the sacred Sun Dance head-dress, and give into her hands the digging-stick that symbolized the walking-stick she might hope to use in her old age, and which she actually used as a walking-stick throughout the festival. Before its 4 days ended the new Sun Dance woman and her husband paid a heavy price for these sacred objects, which henceforth passed into their possession.

Simultaneous with this ceremony in the Sun Dance woman's tent, was a ceremony in the tent of the two workers, who received instruction from their predecessors in exactly the same way, and for a corresponding price. Each had his blanket tied around his waist, a crow's feather planted over his forehead, and his face and body smeared with the same patterns in red and black paint as the husband of the Sun Dance woman.

After the transfer of the head-dress came the ritual eating of the buffalo tongues, carried out a few yards away within a conical enclosure of branches interrupted by a wide entrance. The two workers carried the parflèches of buffalo tongues inside this enclosure, around which soon gathered a crowd of Indians. Then from the tent of the Sun Dance woman came a solemn procession; in front marched the husbands, behind them the women, father preceding son and mother daughter. Beside the daughter walked the confessor, who halted the train four times to hear her confession. As soon as they entered the enclosure the Sun Dance woman lay down, rested her head on the bags of buffalo tongues, and prayed "I have given this Sun Dance for my kinsmen, for my children, and for my grandchildren. I have always been faithful to my husband. If my confession is not true may the Maker punish me, but if it is true may he bless me and my kinsmen, and grant that I reach old age." At the close of her prayer she sat up, the confessor opened the bags, and the women who had vowed to partake of the sacred tongues stepped forward. Each swallowed a small portion of her tongue[6] and distributed the remainder among her kinsfolk in order that they also might share her blessing. Thus she publicly attested her purity and obtained the favour of the Maker; but if she lied, so the Indians believed, either she or a relative was sure to die soon afterwards.

One parflèche contained a fresh buffalo hide, which the confessor now spread out on the ground in front of him so that an old warrior might recount four war deeds over it. The workers then cut it into lashings for fastening the "nest" to the centre-pole. This led to another procession; the father and mother took their places in front, the daughter and son behind, each carrying a whistle made from the wing bone of an eagle; and all four, closely followed by the confessor, marched over to the hole where the centre-pole lay. The Sun Dance woman lifted her foot toward it four times, not touching it until the fourth movement; then her husband sat on its upper end, his three companions shook it, all four blew their whistles, and the people round about raised the war-whoop. After four shakings the man sprang off, leaving his blanket in the fork or nest at its top. Immediately a number of Indians pressed forward to pray at this nest, and to leave in it offerings of moccasins, cloth, and other articles. Some of the men then hoisted the pole into place, while others raised the war-whoop again.

The two women and their husbands now withdrew to the back of the sweat-lodge, where the Sun Dance woman for the last time repeated her confession. All five then entered, carrying bunches of white sage to wipe away the perspiration, and the three men sang and prayed in turn. This sweat-bath marked the end of the Sun Dance woman's role. She might break her fast immediately; and though she wore her head-dress throughout the remainder of the festival, she played no prominent part in the proceedings but mingled freely with the crowd. The painted buffalo skull that had rested at the back of each successive sweat-lodge remained undisturbed behind the last one and was never employed again.

The withdrawal of the Sun Dance woman and her husband did not interfere with the completion of the lodge. The men put in place the rafters,

---

6. Only two tongues were used in the ritual. If there were only two women, each received a whole tongue; if more than two (as was usual) each received a portion of a tongue.

long poles that stretched from the nest of the centre-pole to the forks of the peripheral posts. Half a dozen or so then remained in camp while the rest of the tribe rode out over the plain to gather branches. Singly or in pairs they returned, singing, and lined up at a distance from the lodge, with the men in front and the women and girls behind. Then, chanting the special "raising of the Sun Dance wall song," they slowly marched to the lodge and deposited their branches, which the men who had remained behind quickly draped between the posts and over the rafters. With the building of this wall the fifth day's proceedings came to an end.

The sixth morning saw the construction of two roofless shelters within the Sun Dance lodge, one, just to the right of the entrance, for the braves who had vowed to undergo torture, the other, at the back of the lodge, for the man who had vowed to fast. Before the latter were placed two buffalo skulls, one on each side of the door. Here the faster was decorated—for a price—by his "father," the man who had fasted at the preceding festival. His face and body were plastered with yellow ochre, and each shoulder, elbow, and wrist, and the middles of the forehead, breast, and back, bore a half-circle in dark red paint to represent the new moon. From his hair rose two eagle feathers, a fillet of twisted juniper encircled his forehead, a whistle was suspended from his neck, and a short string dangling at its end an eagle feather hung from each little finger. His only garment was a blanket, tightly wrapped around his waist.

About four o'clock in the afternoon four old men, each carrying a drum, mustered all the children east of the camp-circle, where they formed a procession, the old men in front symbolizing courage, the children purity. Beating their drums and chanting the opening song they marched towards the lodge, but on the way they halted and raised the war-whoop four times, the last time at the entrance. The whole tribe then streamed in behind them, the faster came out of his tent and entered his shelter, and the braves who had elected to undergo torture made their way to their appointed hut.[7] At the back, to the right of the faster's shelter, sat the chiefs and old men smoking; on the other side of the shelter were a number of old men with drums; and between these old men and the braves' hut gathered the women and children. The warriors of the tribe grouped themselves on the opposite side of the lodge, and from time to time performed grass dances about some singers who squatted before a large drum; but many of the younger men leaned on poles near the entrance, or, mounted on horseback, watched the proceedings from without (See Figure 5).

The festivities lasted from late afternoon until daylight the next morning. Throughout all these hours chief interest centred on the braves voluntarily undergoing torture in fulfilment of vows they had made in times of stress or danger. Unless they numbered more than four, each submitted to the ordeal on a separate night. While a youth fastened to the top of the centre-pole two long thongs whose ends trailed on the ground below,[8] the victim stripped to his breech-clout

_____

7. Sometimes the braves postponed their exhibition until the following day.

8. One-spotted, an old man who had fasted at the last Sun Dance the Sarcee held, said that

inside his shelter, tied white sage around his head, wrists, and ankles, and lay on his back in front of the entrance. There two old warriors who themselves had submitted to the torture on some previous occasion covered his face, body, and limbs with white clay, and after one of them had kneaded the flesh over each lung and drawn it up with his fingers, the other pressed a stick against it and punctured it with a steel arrowhead, working the instrument backwards and forwards to enlarge the hole. Sometimes the surgeon would ask of his victim, or of kinsmen who stood near, whether the incision should be deep or shallow; but he was in no way bound by their wishes, and, indeed, if they said "Make a shallow incision' he might scorn their weakness and cut deeply. Into each hole he insert-ed a wooden peg, over which he looped the end of one of the two thongs. The brave then rose to his feet, gripped the thongs in his hands, and jerked heavily against them, twice to each side, yelling loudly to evince his courage. If a thong broke, or tore out the flesh, the sur-geon immediate-ly cut away the

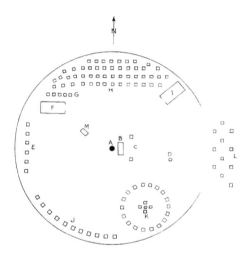

Figure 5. Sketch plan of the Sun Dance (A) centre-pole; (B) fireplace; (C) two warriors proclaiming their war deeds; (D) warrior dramatiz-ing his war deeds; (E) chiefs; (F) hut of faster; (G) old men with drums; (H) women and children; (I) hut of braves; (J) men; (K) men dancing around drummers; (L) youths on horseback; (M) smudge.

other thong and released him from further torture; but this rarely happened. In most cases, after he had tested his thongs, he advanced to the centre-pole, flung his arms around it, and silently prayed for courage; then he walked back until the thongs drew taut again, and, straining backward, danced up and down while the old men beat their drums and the people sang. As soon as he tore one thong loose he lay down on his face to be released from the other, and, with a prayer to the Maker, buried the shreds of torn flesh at the base of the centre-pole. Should neither thong have broken away at the end of several songs a kinsman came to his aid and jerked him sharply backward by the

during his youth had climbed the pole and attached the thongs. Four braves had submitted to torture that evening, and he had been forced to cling to the top of the pole all night, and part of the next day, until their dances ended and he received orders to cast off the thongs.

shoulders; but even this sometimes failed, and he continued to suffer torment, while a cold stream of perspiration drenched his body. Finally an old warrior would take pity on him, and, advancing with uplifted knife to the centre of the lodge, cry aloud "With this knife I slew my enemy. Now I demand the release of this brave." The men who had bound him were then obliged to cut him free and let him withdraw to his hut to recuperate.[9]

The man who had vowed to fast underwent a far milder ordeal, for the sole object of his fasting was to obtain a vision from the supernatural world. He was, therefore, confined to his shelter during the 4 days of the festival, and forbidden all food and drink except a very small amount each morning after the people had retired to rest.[10] No one might enter the shelter, and no one speak to him, except the faster of the previous Sun Dance, who acted as his instructor and visited him every morning. To dispel the taint of human beings so displeasing to the animal world from which he expected to receive his vision a smudge of juniper bushes burned continually in a shallow, rectangular pit between his lodge and the centre-pole, and the instructor wrapped a blanket over his head, and over the food and water he carried, whenever he visited the hut. This food and water the faster had to be offered four times before he might accept. From the vision that came to him he acquired a new Sun Dance song, which he revealed to his instructor, and through him, to the old men who drummed and sang at the side of the shelter. Then, in the evening, when the festivities recommenced, these old men listened while the faster sang it; and as soon as they could repeat it correctly they took up the tune so that the faster might dance. Thus he carried out his part until the conclusion of the festivities, when he emerged from his shelter and resumed his ordinary life.

The incidents thus far described constituted the fixed program, as it were, of every Sun Dance, inasmuch as all the principal actors—the Sun Dance woman and her entourage, the workers, the eaters of the sacred buffalo tongues, the tortured braves, and the fasters—had publicly vowed several weeks or months before to perform their respective roles. Over and above these, however, numerous unheralded episodes lent colour to the scene. Now a warrior bearing a bundle of sticks would march to the central fireplace and proclaim his four brave deeds, emphasizing each one by hurling a few brands into the flames: to enhance his glory relatives then distributed blankets and other gifts among the poorer members of the tribe. Another warrior in full battle attire might take up his station between the entrance and the fireplace, line up his friends with levelled guns to represent his foes, and dramatically enact his victories. At some pause in the dancing, again, an old man would lead out a

---

9. An old man, Running-in-the-Middle, stated that during his ordeal a stout, heavily built woman tried in vain to release him by pulling on his shoulders with her full weight. Just as he was fainting the man who had bound him cut his thongs and assisted him back to his hut.

10. At the last Sarcee Sun Dance the instructor brought food and water to the faster, One-Spotted, in the evening instead of in the morning. Why he thus reversed the usual procedure One-Spotted did not know.

youth who had distinguished himself in battle, confer on him a new name,[11] and exhort him to strive after greater glory. So incident followed incident in constant succession, and the only uneventful hours were those when the Indians were resting. We cannot wonder, therefore, that the Sarcee looked forward to their Sun Dance as the brightest episode in their year, and that volunteers were seldom lacking to undertake the principal roles.

---

11. Generally the name of some relative who had recently died, or who had discarded the name some years earlier. The old man received no payment for his goodwill.

CHAPTER 7
GRASS DANCES

Younger than the Sun Dance just described was an organization, mainly social, but in one of its aspects religious, which the Sarcee sometimes called the "Sioux Dance," because they believed it reached them through the Blackfoot from the Sioux, and sometimes by its Blackfoot name *Kaspa*. Actually it was a form of the Grass Dance that spread so widely among the tribes of the North American plains. It reached the Sarcee, apparently, about 1800. Eight years later some visiting Blackfoot Indians brought about its modification, and in 1900 it was combined with the women's Circle Dance that had just been introduced from the same quarter. It thus passed through three stages of development, an early, a middle, and a late.

EARLY PERIOD

In its early form the Grass Dance generally occurred during the Sun Dance, though it could be held in or out of doors at any time of the year. It began late in the afternoon, either inside a tent, or outdoors within a circular compound made of branches. The chiefs and principal warriors sat in the place of honour at the back of the tent or compound, the men who were to participate in the dance lined the two sides, and a pot of berry soup occupied the centre. To the right of the entrance (looking in) six men sat around a big drum whose membrane was made at first of buffalo hide, later of deerskin; and on the opposite side of the entrance were four owners of wooden swords, the principal dancers. A crowd of women and children peered through the opening, but were not permitted inside the enclosure.

Whenever the six drummers beat their drum and sang, one or more of the sword men rose to dance. Immediately all the others in the compound except the chiefs and old warriors joined the dance, which was a kind of caper round and round, one man following another. Youths making their debut for the first time sometimes held back, fearing that the crowd of onlookers might laugh at them; but they too had to join in when one of the sword men vigorously beat their legs. It happened on one or two occasions that the son of some wealthy man stayed away altogether from the dance; but even that was of no avail, for the four sword men went out and arrested him, haled him in to the dance, and fined his father a blanket or clothes.

Normally the drummers chanted one long song four times and ceased, when the dancers could sit down and rest; but often in their excitement they chanted one song after another until the dancers almost fell from exhaustion. At intervals between the songs the sword men distributed the berry soup, and some old warrior carrying a stick strung with four horse-tails narrated four of his war deeds. An old man, or a drummer, sometimes arrested the progress of a dance by calling out "You people, inside and outside, keep quiet and listen to the woman's voice in the drum." The drummers then sang a special song four

154

times, and at the fourth rendition lowered their voices, when the Indians believed they heard the echo of a woman's voice a note or two behind the men's.

The drum itself resembled a European kettle-drum; it was about 2 1/2 feet in diameter and 1 foot deep, with a membrane on both faces. A broad yellow band divided the upper membrane into two parts, one of which was covered with dark blue, the other with dark red, flannel. Similar flannel muffled the sticks. In use the drum was suspended 3 or 4 inches above the ground by loops that fitted over the forked ends of four pickets strung with brass bells, bunches of horse-tail, feathers, and weasel skins.

The principal functionaries in the dance were clearly the sword owners. They could sell their swords as readily as other paraphernalia, but only during the Grass Dance. The purchaser occupied a seat in the tent or compound beside the seller, and at a pause between two songs changed clothes with him. The two men then danced four times around the enclosure, one behind the other, to the beat of a special song, the seller preceding and carrying the sword during the two first circuits, the purchaser during the two last. Meanwhile kinsmen of the purchaser piled clothes to the conventional value of the sword in the centre of the compound, and any man who contributed to the pile from his own stock was entitled to dance behind the two principals. As soon as the dance ended the seller led out an old man from the back, stationed him beside the purchaser in front of the drummers, and called on him to narrate four of his war deeds; at the close of each narrative the people shouted and the drummers smote their drum. The new owner then occupied the seat of his predecessor, who found a place somewhere or other among the dancers.

MIDDLE PERIOD

About 1888 some Blackfoot visitors brought much new paraphernalia for the Grass Dance, including porcupine-quill head-dresses, never before worn by the Sarcee; and the latter paid many horses for them, even when there were two or more objects of the same kind. They were then obliged to modify their dance in order that the owners of these new objects might display them and dance to the special songs that accompanied their use. Accordingly, the ceremony now opened with songs to which the entire company danced, proceeded in regular order through the list of individual songs and dances, and closed with general ones again. Below is the list of the new articles that were introduced, arranged in the order in which their owners danced:

Article	Number of owners	Number of Songs
Feather Belts	4	4
Big drum	1	1
Mirror and wooden gun[1]	1	1

1. These two objects went together, the mirror being worn on the chest.

Article	Number of owners	Number of Songs
Swords	3 or 4	1
Crow-collars	2	1
Whistles	2	1
Eagle-feather belts	2 or 3	1
Tomahawk pipe	2	1
Feathers on beaded belt	2	1
Calf-skin leggings, hair head-dress, and stick	2[1]	1
Dog-feast stick	1	1
Pipe-stem	1	1

The four owners of feather belts, who had four songs in common, danced together in one place during their first two songs; at the third they ceremoniously removed their belts from the wall of the hall or tent and fastened them around their waists; and at the fourth they danced around the room, two in one direction and two in the other. All other performers merely danced around four times. There was an interlude after the performance by the owner of the mirror and wooden gun during which the sword men distributed food.

When the owners of these various articles had completed their dances special songs were chanted for certain other individuals, who rose and danced in the following order:

> Giving away a horse. In the course of this dance the performer threw a stick out of doors to represent the horse he was "throwing away."

> Wounded warrior.

> Warrior who had been surrounded by his enemies, but had escaped.

> Warrior who had captured a scalp.

> "Cut-rope song," for a man who had stolen a horse.

Such, in general outline, was the Grass Dance during the middle period of its development, though the performances were often interrupted by the sale of one or more of the ceremonial articles. The procedure at such transfers scarcely varied, so that the sale of a whistle will serve as an example. The drummers started up a special "transfer" song, during which the four belt-owners, followed by the sword men, danced four times around the inside

---

2. This was the special paraphernalia for the leader of the Grass Dance.

of the hall or tent, marched once around its outside, then approached the purchaser, whom a sword man led by the hand to the seller of the whistle that the
two might exchange clothes. The drummers now chanted the whistle song,
whereupon the seller and purchaser danced four circuits, the former leading
throughout. Whenever they reached the east side of the tent they blew the
whistle, the seller twice, then the purchaser twice; after which they resumed
their seats, the purchaser retaining the whistle.

Once a year, on the average, there occurred in connection with a Grass
Dance a special ritual called the Dog Feast, never held except in fulfilment
of a vow for some one's recovery from sickness. Yet it was not the vower who
conducted the ritual, but the owner of the ceremonial dog-feast stick, the stick
adorned with beads and feathers that has been listed already. Whether the
feast was once independent of the Grass Dance or had always been an integral
part of it, the Sarcee did not know, but they believed that it came to them from
the Blood Indians about the end of the nineteenth century.

> A certain Blood medicine-man named "He who goes in front"
> fell ill and died. Before he expired he told his people to leave his
> body unburied for four days. While he lay dead in his tent a dog
> visited him and said "You shall come to life again; and hereaf-
> ter every Indian who is at the point of death shall recover if he
> promises to perform the ritual I shall now show you." The dog
> then taught him how to hold a dog feast, and the medicine-man
> came to life again.

The last dog feast took place in 1913. The man who
conducted the ritual on that occasion, John Whitney,
gave the following account of the ceremony.

The vower of the feast killed the smallest pup he
could find, threw away the skin, and boiled the meat in
a pot which he carried inside the dance-hall and placed
on the floor behind the central sweet-grass fire. All the
men (and, in later days, the women also) took their
usual places for the Grass Dance, but the owner of the
dog-feast stick (Plate 6) occupied a seat immediately
to the left of the door next to the drummers. The performance that he normally presented at a Grass Dance
was now expanded into six movements. The first was
his usual dance four times around the hall, imitating
a prairie chicken or other creature; but the five succeeding ones, each of which called for a special song,
constituted the real dog feast.

He began by dancing for a time beside the door, then,
when the drummers quickened the time of their song,
moved in a sunwise direction toward the pot, brandishing the stick like a spear. Three feints he made with it;
at the fourth, he dipped it into the vessel and pointed

Plate 6. The beaded stick
carried by the leader of
the dog-feast society.
(Canadian Museum
of History 81441)

it toward the north, the east, the south, and the west. Turning to one of the four old men who sat at the back of the hall he made three passes, and at the fourth placed the tip of the stick on the old man's tongue. He then returned to his seat for a minute, and, when the drummers revived the song, repeated the performance with the three other old men in turn. Thus closed his second movement, the first of the dog feast proper.

The drummers opened the third movement with another song, whereupon the dog-stick owner dragged some man or other towards the pot, held a piece of the dog-meat above his head, and made him jump for it four times like a dog. At the fourth leap he dropped the meat into the man's mouth.

During the fourth song he distributed the rest of the meat among the entire company, when each man before eating uttered a silent prayer of this general type: "Maker, I ask for myself, my family and my tribe long life, more clothing, more money and more horses. Keep me out of danger and grant me your help." All the bones were then thrown back into the pot except the skull, which was laid on the ground between the pot and the fire.

At the termination of this ritual meal the drummers commenced another song during which every man stood with uplifted hands. As the last notes died away he howled *ho ho* like a dog, dropped his hands, and sat down.

Now the drummers began the sixth and final song. The old man who had first tasted the stick danced around to the leader, took from him his ceremonial stick, and, imitating the capture of a horse, or the taking of a scalp, made four circuits of the hall, touching the skull with the stick at each circuit. When he had retired to his place the other three old men performed similar dances; then each in turn brandished the stick in the direction to which his narrative referred and proclaimed his four brave deeds. With this ending of the dog feast the Grass Dance pursued its normal course; but after the gathering had dispersed the man who had vowed to give the feast removed the pot of bones and the skull and hung them in a tree as a thankoffering to the Maker.

In the first decade of the twentieth century the Sarcee developed an aversion to the eating of dog's flesh. At their last three dog feasts, therefore, they omitted the third movement (when the leader dropped a piece of meat into a man's mouth), and modified the fourth by hiding their portions of meat behind them.

LATE PERIOD

About 1900 the Blackfoot introduced the Sarcee to the movements and paraphernalia of the "Circle" dance, *klatsinata*, a dance exclusively for women, which the Sarcee immediately combined with their Grass Dance to produce what they called the Sioux-Circle Dance. They held this in winter within a regular dance-hall, but in summer out of doors within an enclosure made by their wagons, or by planting trees in a circle and lining them with canvas. A visit from Indians of another tribe always provided a suitable pretext; but the dance could not occur except on the invitation of the husband of a woman who possessed an eagle-feather head-dress, and ranked, accordingly, as a leader in the Circle Dance. The Sarcee have owned in some years four of these head-dresses, in other years only two. Each was a half-moon of eagle tail-feathers, stained red at their tips, rising up from a beaded head-band from which dangled over each ear a train of similar feathers and the skin of a weasel. The husband of one of these head-dress owners announced the date of the celebration, and a day or two beforehand purchased a supply of bread, fruit, tea, and other goods from the stores in Calgary. With the help of friends and kinsmen on the morning of the appointed day he prepared the dance-hall or enclosure while his wife and other women cooked the necessary food. Then, toward sunset, the owner of the big drum entered the hall with his instrument, which two or three men pounded for a few minutes as a signal to dress.

The first to march in were the head-dress owners, who hung up their insignia on the back wall; behind them trooped the whole crowd of performers. Two, three, or four old men (their number corresponded with the number of women, owning head-dresses) occupied places about the middle of the back wall, dividing the women on one side from the men on the other. Immediately to their left sat the head-dress owners, to their right the leader of the Grass Dance, the proud possessor of a horn bonnet. At the right of the entrance sat the owner of a painted stick decorated with five eagle feathers, a woman who acted as a kind of marshal; and opposite her, to the left of the entrance, were the sword and whip owners, next to them the drummers, and from the drummers around to the leader of the Grass Dance all the other men who were taking part in the performance. One man, however, the owner of the tomahawk pipe, occupied a special place; he sat on the woman's side of the hall, slightly in front of them.

The proceedings opened with four or five Grass Dances. As soon as the drummers began a song the owner of a whip or a sword rose to his feet. This was the signal for the other men to dance; accordingly, they circled around the hall, capering, shouting, crowing like roosters, and exercising their talents in a thousand other ridiculous actions. Thus they continued through four or five dances while the women quietly watched them from their places. The drummers then changed to a Circle song, using in addition to the big drum a number of smaller ones, and changing the beat from a sequence of four quavers to an iambic rhythm. At once the head-dress owners lined up near the door, the rest of the women formed a semicircle behind them, and the whole troop shuffled in a clockwise direction around the hall while the men stood up in their places. Alone, in the opposite direction, danced the woman marshal, to strike with her eagle-feather stick any man who was slow in rising to his feet. After the last woman had passed the men fell in behind them and shuffled around also, when any man who saw two of his sisters-in-law, or a sister-in-law and a "comrade's" wife, dancing one behind the other squeezed in between them. A number of beats in quick succession terminated this dance, when the men and women retired to their seats.

Thus the entertainment alternated between four or five Grass Dances and four or five Circle ones. When this began to pall the drummers chanted

songs for various individual performances. First danced the leader of the Grass Dance, the owner of the horn bonnet; next the
tribal councillors, and after them
the members of two very modern clubs, the Tall Hats and the
Shells. The Tall Hats were young
men who wore on their shoulders
badges (made in Calgary) bearing the inscription Two Hats , the
Shells a group of married men
each of whom wore a shell at his
throat. A whip or a sword owner
then laid down a blanket before
the old men at the back of the
hall, who moved forward and sat
on it. Throughout four successive
songs everyone remained still; at
the fifth the old men danced four
times clockwise around the hall
and sat down again. The whip
or sword owner again advanced,
placed on their heads the wom-
en's head-dresses, and handed
to one of them the eagle-feather
stick, whereupon they repeated
their dance, and at its conclusion
each in turn narrated his four war
deeds, receiving a cheer (shout)
and a drum beat for each one.

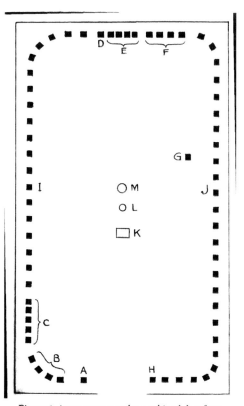

Figure 6. Arrangement at the combined dog-feast
and Grass Circle Dance about 1913. (A) leader of
the dog-feast; (B) whip and sword men; (C) drummers; (D) leader of the Grass Dance; (E) the four
old men; (F) the four women with head-dresses;
(G) the tomahawk-pipe owner; (H) the woman
marshal; (I) row of men; (J) row of women; (K) a
smudge of sweet-grass; (L) dog skull; (M) pot containing the meat, and later the bones of the dog.

As soon as the old men returned the head-dresses to their
owners another Circle Dance en-
sued in which the leaders for the first time wore these head-dresses. Then
came a series of individual dances, performed successively by the owners of
the following articles:[3] big drum; belt; wooden gun; cow-hide shield; whistle;
crow-collar; tomahawk-pipe; whips;[4] swords; horn bonnet.

This series led to another for various war exploits. There was a song for the
old men at the back of the hall; for the man who had captured a scalp; for the

3. It is hardly necessary to mention that all these articles were decorated, the majority with
eagle plumes, coloured ribbons, strips of fur or beaded skin, and small brass bells. The cow-
hide shield bore locks of hair to represent war deeds.

4. If two or four whip or sword men were present they danced simultaneously in opposite
directions.

man who had escaped, after being surrounded by his enemies; for the man who had been wounded in battle; for the man who had stolen a horse; and for the man who had captured a gun. In recent years many of these songs have been omitted because no one present was qualified to dance to them. Finally, the drummers chanted a song for "throwing away a horse," a song that always aroused much expectation in the audience, but no response unless some one present was willing to donate a horse. In that case the donor, after dancing once or twice around the hall, threw a stick outside as far as he could. The crowd of men and women scrambled for it, and the winner redeemed it later for the prize.

In any of these individual performances a kinsman could share the dance of a principal provided he deposited a blanket in the middle of the hall. Some entertainments evoked quite a pile of blankets, which a whip or a sword man distributed to the poorer members of the audience before the final series of Grass and Circle Dances that concluded the festivities.

Various other by-plays enlivened the Grass Circle Dance, so that no two performances were ever exactly alike. Sometimes during an interval between the dances one of the drummers rattled a cluster of bells while his companions pounded the drum and sang a special invitation song. Then some man or other arose and swayed up and down with his knees to the rhythm, looking expectantly across the hall at his sister-in-law or "comrade's" wife. If she was too shy to rise and sway with him he crossed over and slapped her lightly on the back, when etiquette compelled her to join him at the repetition of the song. He generally presented her afterwards with some slight gift as a mark of his esteem, and her husband made an appropriate return.

If no one volunteered to dance when the drummers started up a song they sometimes changed, out of pique, to another that obligated all the men to rise and dance continuously for as often as the song was repeated, since otherwise the drummers would strike and leave the hall. If, however, the drummers were too exacting, and kept on singing when the dancers were exhausted, an old man made them stop by striking their drum with a stick decorated with locks of hair and proclaiming his four war deeds. The same old man, carried away by excitement, sometimes joined in a Grass Dance, brandishing his hair-lock stick in the direction in which he had performed his war deeds. Then at the close of the song he stationed himself in front of the drummers and cried "Listen to me, my children. You saw me pointing my stick over yonder. I shall tell you the story of that deed. Over yonder I captured the scalp which you see represented on this stick. B— there knows all about it, for he was with me." So he recounted his four war deeds, and received an ovation for each one.

The dropping of a shield or other ceremonial object during a dance evoked a similar by-play. The owner of a whip or a sword picked up the article and deposited it in the centre of the hall. As soon as the dance had ended one of the old warriors held it aloft, and, followed by all the men, danced around four times to the accompaniment of a special song. He then narrated his four war deeds and returned the object to its owner.

Much the same procedure attended the sale of one of the ceremonial articles. Its owner, after instructing the drummers to strike up the "transfer" song, turned to the whip and sword men and named a purchaser, who, though frequently taken unawares, would have been utterly disgraced if he declined. The owner of the ceremonial belt then led the whip and sword men in a dance four times around the hall, and at its conclusion seated the purchaser beside the seller, who changed clothes with him and painted his face, if there was any paint on hand. The drummers then sang the song appropriate to the article, and with the seller leading the two men capered around four times, while kinsmen who wished to contribute to the purchase price threw each a blanket into the middle and danced behind. After the fourth circuit the two men halted beside the drummers, an old man, standing beside them, narrated his four deeds, and the purchaser whispered to him how many horses he would pay. Seller and purchaser then exchanged seats while the old man publicly announced the price.

The owner of the tomahawk-pipe, who sat in front of the women, played an easy but very important role. At intervals between the dances he filled his pipe from a stock of tobacco in front of him and handed it to the nearest of the four old men at the back of the hall, each of whom smoked it in turn. The pipe-man then puffed it himself once or twice and handed it to the last performer. If the drummers also wanted to smoke they sang a special song and the pipe-man refilled his pipe for them. The rest of the people brought their own pipes, but the pipe-man had to supply them with tobacco.

With dances and interludes of one kind or another a Grass Circle Dance lasted from early evening until 3 or 4 o'clock in the morning, when it terminated with a closing song learned from the Cree. In recent years, however, this song has been generally omitted, and the Indians have drifted away without ceremony whenever they wished.

CHAPTER 8
RELIGION

In early days the Sarcee, like other plains' tribes, were an intensely religious people, although a century and a half of European contact has now modified their old beliefs. Whether they once predicted a dualism in nature, like the Plains' Cree—a good spirit and an evil one, of whom the latter was the more active—we do not know; but after the middle of the nineteenth century they were true monotheists, placing their hope and trust in an all-powerful deity they called the Maker. They conceived of him generally as an old man, but believed that he might assume any shape he wished and could appear and disappear in the twinkling of an eye. His home they placed vaguely in the sky, anywhere between the four quarters of the compass, though they usually thought of him in the east.

To the Maker the Indians directed their morning and evening prayers, and addressed their oaths. "If I lie may the Maker take my children," a man would say, "but if I tell the truth may they live long." Trees around Sarcee camps carried offerings to him, pieces of cloth, moccasins, and other objects;[1] for even though nothing but a bad dream had troubled a man, he frequently set out some offering, after praying and singing in the sweat-lodge. Old men commonly ascended a hill-top at sunrise and prayed that the Maker would bless the camp below; and old men and old women gathered around the sick, praying the Maker to heal them. Many a mother carried her child to some old man to gain his prayers; or she begged a grey hair from his head, and, placing it on the head of her child, prayed that the Maker would extend its life until its hair too became grey. On solemn occasions they made a temple of the sweat-lodge, believing that prayers uttered under its roof were more likely of fulfilment than prayers made elsewhere. For special rituals[2] they varied the shape of the sweat-lodge fireplace and the number of stones to be heated. Even the dirt moved to make room for these stones they did not throw idly outside, but carefully piled at the back of the lodge.

Though the Maker was supreme in the Indians' thoughts, and the object of their constant prayers, they could not disregard all the other forces that seemed to affect their lives for good or ill. Nature to them was not divisible into animate and inanimate; but just as man possessed an incorporeal mind imprisoned in a corporeal body, so did every rock, every tree, and every animal

---

1. No Indian would touch such an offering, however valuable it might be. The Sarcee say that once, during the celebration of a Sun Dance, a woman did carry off a piece of red cloth that had been hung up as an offering to the Maker, and a man followed her example by taking a bow and arrows. But the Maker saw them and said I do not approve of human beings carrying away their offerings in this fashion."

2. The ritual with the beaver medicine-bundle called for a round fireplace; that with the pipe medicine-bundle a triangular one; and the rituals for painted tents and the Sun Dance a square one. The sweat-lodge ceremony during the Sun Dance required twenty-four stones in the fireplace; on other occasions the Indians used either twelve or eighteen

likewise conceal an invisible mind or soul within its visible form. And just as in dreams or visions man's soul had power to separate itself from its body and wander abroad, so could the souls of external objects. Man, therefore, was not a special creation largely divorced from the rest of nature, but an integral part of it.

Nature, again, the Sarcee saw, was infinitely varied. From some source or other, perhaps from the Maker, he himself had been gifted with certain power, the animals, the rocks, and the trees being gifted with others. Through contact with these objects in dreams and visions he believed that he could derive either an increment to his own powers, or protection from some of the ills of life. They could give him prosperity and long life, power to heal sickness, or immunity from death or capture in war. A man who saw in his vision a weasel, an eagle, a buffalo, or a bear was fully assured of his safety in the next war (not, however, in succeeding wars, since this greater immunity would render him too powerful). Consequently, his dreams and visions assumed the utmost significance, even though he realized that many of them were illusory, especially those that came to him in the darkness of night.

Significant visions always conformed to a definite pattern. The "visitor"—generally a bird or an animal—appeared to the sleeping Indian either in its own or in human form, conferred on him some blessing, and, in token thereof, showed him some object, outlined its ritual use, and taught him one or more songs that should accompany the ritual. The Indian remembered his vision, and a few months or a few years later he made a similar object which he kept as his "medicine. Not that he believed that any special virtue or power resided in this objective "medicine." That virtue or power lay only in the vision, or rather in the contact he had then gained with what we may call, from lack of a more suitable term, the supernatural world, a world that to the Indian himself seemed only a part of the natural. The medicine-object was only the symbol of this contact, helping him to revive it whenever he sang the proper songs and performed the proper ritual. By itself, therefore, it was valueless. Theoretically he might lose it or sell it, and as long as he retained for himself the songs and the ritual he could make another like it that would answer the same purpose. In actual practice, however, this was not the case. The Sarcee regarded man as but a pawn on the chessboard of life. The powers placed in his hands were very slight; and if through the supernatural world he gained some increment to them, he should accept his blessing with due humility, and refrain from offending his benefactor in word or in deed, lest he lose the increment and meet with disaster. Hence, he should keep his vision more or less secret, not impart it lightly to others as a matter of little account. Any loss of his medicine-object implied the loss also of the favour of his supernatural benefactor; and once he had been deprived of this favour, once he had lost the blessing, it was useless to make a duplicate of the medicine- object that symbolized it. So even when an Indian lost his medicine- object by accident, and did not sell it along with its ritual and songs, he rarely replaced it;[3] and medicine-objects taken from

---

3. In 1912 an Indian named Crowcollar sold a highly prized medicine object—the bear-knife

fallen enemies had no value except as ornaments, not merely because the visions they symbolized were lost and the rituals and songs that went with them unknown, but because they had proved their worthlessness by failing to protect their wearers in battle.

Like other plains tribes, however, the Sarcee could not reconcile themselves to the idea that a power and blessing once conferred on an Indian by the supernatural world inevitably perished with him and could not be preserved for future generations. They subscribed to the doctrine that this power and blessing might persist endlessly provided the original beneficiary's experience could be kept alive and another individual place himself in exactly the same rapport with the supernatural benefactor. The original beneficiary had to transfer his experience—to reveal his vision, teach the ritual and the songs, which the recipient then made his own; he sold his experience, that is to say, just as he sold a horse or a dagger. The price he exacted varied in proportion to the accredited value of the experience and blessing. In no case, however, might he give it away for nothing, because that would belittle its value and offend the supernatural benefactor.

Every Sarcee youth, therefore, hoped for a vision that would increase his natural powers or grant him some protection during life's journey. He even went out of his way to seek such a vision, by sleeping alone on a hill-top, near a thicket, or on the margin of a lake or river. How he distinguished between an ordinary dream that possessed no significance, and a vision of deep religious import, is not quite clear. The vision, of course, had to conform to the general pattern outlined above; but so might an ordinary dream. Possibly the former was more intense than the dream, and left a clearer after-impression. However that may be most Indians obtained visions at one time or another, and every one without exception possessed some medicine-object or charm, either procured by himself or purchased from another. Each child received one for its protection when it received its name, each hunter carried one to give him success in the chase, and every ailing person sought a new one that would set his feet on the path to recovery.

As we would expect, therefore, these medicine-objects or charms varied greatly in character. Many were not only charms but ornaments of feather in a man's hair, beads attached to his clothing, or a bracelet of bird's or animal's claws that he wore around his wrist. Naturally, the majority of them interested only their owners and ranked as purely personal possessions. A few, however, which had been handed down for generations, figured in public ceremonies and deeply concerned the whole tribe; they were lodged in private hands, and bought and sold like other goods, although their owners were really only custodians of what was virtually public property. Between these two extremes

---

bundle to Dr. Pliny Goddard, of the American Museum of Natural History. Whether he revealed the ritual and the songs to Dr. Goddard at the same time the Sarcee could not say, but in any case Crowcollar took it upon himself to make a duplicate of the bundle. In the eyes of his tribesmen, however, this duplicate possessed no value whatever, they fully believed that he made it merely to sell to some unsuspecting white man.

were other medicine-objects, each the property of some individual, but at the same time held in high esteem by others.

Generally speaking, the older a medicine-object, the greater was the esteem with which the Indians regarded it. An object that had passed from hand to hand through several generations tended to draw to itself other medicine-objects, until it finally evolved into a complex bundle, each article in which possessed some definite significance. Such bundles were opened on special occasions only, and then only with great ceremony and to the accompaniment of complex rituals. Yet these rituals were not peculiar to the bundles, but attended in greater or less degree every medicine-object that concerned more than a single individual, and were even extended to certain objects, mostly connected with war (e.g., weasel-tail coats, horn bonnets, tents and blankets decorated with war paintings), that were not primarily religious at all, though they gained a tinge of religiosity from the ritualism that enveloped them. For every ceremony connected with any of these objects, the owner painted his face (sometimes also his body) with a special design that differed for each medicine-object; at the opening of the ceremony he prayed over a smudge of sweet-grass or white sage in the centre of his tent; when passing a pipe, dancing, or merely walking around the tent, he moved in the direction the sun travels, i.e., from west through north to east, and from east through south to west; and most of his actions he repeated four times, or rather made three preliminary feints before he actually completed the action. Even his songs he chanted four times, though Sarcee songs were wordless, consisting of meaningless syllables only; at least none of the eighty or so songs that were recorded on a phonograph, many of them medicine songs, contained any significant words. Finally, in every ceremony connected with the transfer or sale of a medicine-object, the seller and the purchaser adopted the fiction that they were parent and child, respectively, and the "child" had to receive the most detailed instruction.

Some concrete examples of visions and of the medicine-objects to which they gave rise will make the subject clearer:

> My uncle sent me out, one mid-winter evening, to bring his horses into our camp, which we had pitched beside the Bow River. In passing a grove I noticed a woodpecker hammering on a tree, and I watched it extract two worms. The bird then put me to sleep, and as I lay on the ground it said to me, "I pity you because you are a very poor youth. One dayyou shall be rich. I give you this eagles' wing bone to cure your people's ailments. I give you also this pendant to heal any wounds that you may receive; even though a bullet passes right through your body it will make you well again." It then taught me two songs, and disappeared. I awoke, rounded up the horses, and returned to camp. Some years later I made a replica of the wing-bone (Plate 7a) and used it to heal people. I made, too, a replica of the pendant, which protected me on several occasions when I helped to steal horses from the Sioux.

> Many years ago, when I was a young man, I camped alone

in some brush at the bottom of a deep valley just south of the Red Deer River, and climbed a neighbouring hill to see if any enemies were lurking in the vicinity. On top of the hill was a picket, marking, as I thought, an old tent-site until suddenly a bird settled on it and disappeared. When I walked over to examine it the picket too disappeared, and in its place wriggled a snake and its young. They fled down a hole, but presently the mother snake issued forth again and began to sing. At the close or her song she said to me, "I have seven children, so I shall give you seven sons. Take care of them. For if one dies the others will die too. In years to come make a hat and line it with snake-skin. That shall be your medicine-charm." It disappeared and I awoke. In after years I made the hat and used it to cure Indians who had become crazy; I placed it on their heads and sang my snake-song. In my lifetime I have had seven sons four of whom were full-grown when the eldest died. Since then five others have died and now only one remains. I burned the hat when my eldest son died.

Once when my parents were camped close to a buffalo-pound, my mother left her tent to look at a half-skinned buffalo. That night the buffalo changed to a human being, entered her tent and asked her to be his sweetheart. She made a noise

Plate 7. "Medicine" objects.
(Canadian Museum of History 81442)

that wakened her husband, who roused her and asked her what was the matter.

After she had told him her dream and they had settled down to sleep again the buffalo appeared to her a second time and said "You have informed on me. Now you shall bear twins three times in succession." Her first twins were a boy and a girl, her second two boys, and her last two girls. She bore no other children.

When I was about eight years of age, travelling on foot far behind my people, I lay down in the shade of a rock, placed my blanket under my head and fell fast asleep. Presently some one kicked my feet and said to me "My father invites you to his tent." Looking up, I found myself inside a strange tent, seated beside a strange man whose hair hung loose and unplaited, and whose only garment was a breech-clout. He said to me "I am the Man Who Does Not Invite Others. This shall be your tent, my son. Look well at it." Two other men then entered; their bodies were painted white, on their foreheads were arcs of yellow paint, and in their hands they carried drawn bows. The tent-owner grasped an eagle-tail feather in each hand and held out his blanket as a target, but when they sped their shafts against it the arrows, instead of penetrating, fell to the floor. The archers vanished, and the tent-owner said to me "That rock where you fell asleep is my tent. I give it to you on one condition, that you never eat fish. You will become violently ill if you ever taste fish, and the only thing that will cure you is smoke from a smudge made with the fur of a yellow dog like that one lying near the door. Moreover, you must never smoke during the hours of daylight." I closed my eyes, and when I opened them again I was lying beside the rock.

More than thirty years later I visited some neighbours and was offered something that looked like ordinary pemmican. On tasting it, however, I discovered that the meat was mixed with fish. Almost immediately I began to choke, and only with difficulty made my way home. There his wife made a smudge with the hair of a yellow dog and supported me while I inhaled the smoke. Suddenly I coughed, and a fish about 3 inches long fell from my mouth into the fire. The smudge cured me, but my transgression had destroyed my blessing and medicine-power. Since there was no need afterwards to observe the taboos enjoined on me, I may eat fish freely and smoke by day as well as by night. I may even paint my tent, if I wish, like the tent I saw in my vision, but the blessing that should accompany it is gone and it would be of no value.

A few years ago, while gathering wood. I saw a little hawk chasing something which I think was a ghost. That night I dreamed that I should make a charm of hawk feathers and bells, and either fasten it to my hat or wear it in my hair. It would heal any one who was dying. (Plate 7b.)

Once, after it had been raining for several days, I saw a bad-ger running along the road towards me, and I dismounted from my horse to kill it. The badger, however, disappeared, and that night, as I slept, Thunder told me that I had done right not to kill it. because it was his wife. He directed me to make these two bracelets from the skin and claws of a badger. (Plate 7c.)

I bought this whistle and bandolier (Plate 7d, 7e) from an old woman named Bird-Hat, who derived them from a vision. She daubed my body yellow, painted three black stripes around each wrist and ankle, laid the bandolier over my right shoulder and said "Now you need never fear a gun. If an enemy tries to shoot you he will either miss his aim or his weapon will not go off. Henceforward one must never eat the dried guts of any animal." Afterwards I slept out on the prairies for three nights, and in a vision on the third night saw some maggots. The bandolier has protected me in war, and the whistle I use in doctoring the sick.

Chief Big Belly, when a boy, found a high bank in which there were many snakes, some of which he killed. He climbed on top of the bank to snare another one, but the serpents put him to sleep. In his vision the father snake appeared to him and said, "My son, come over to my tent." Big Belly then saw a camp of four tipis, and was invited to enter one on which a snake was painted. Its owner, the father snake, said to him, "Although you have been killing my children I shall give you these four painted tents and a medicine charm. Kill a hawk, and tie to its feathers some copper and brass arrowheads. Then when any one is ill tie the charm to his hair and do what I do now." As it spoke it took some charcoal from the fire, chewed it in its mouth and spat it on to its hands, when the charcoal changed to yellow paint. "If you sell your charm you may make a second one," it continued, "but no more. For killing my children your only punishment shall be that you shall die without warning in the prime of life."

Through his possession of the snake's charm (Plate 7e), which he made when he grew up, Big Belly became a very success-ful medicine-man. He used to paint his patients with charcoal transformed into yellow ochre as the snake had transformed it. But he died suddenly when he was in the prime of life, accord-ing to some Indians because he drank too much Florida water. Before he died he sold his snake-painted tent to Many-Horses.

The Sarcee, who possessed as scanty a knowledge of herbal remedies as other plains' Indians, entertained from early times a profound awe of the Cree, who seemed to know the mysterious virtues of every plant and shrub. When hostilities between the two tribes ceased, and their confinement to neigh-bouring reserves fostered peaceful intercourse and occasional intermarriage, Cree medicines, especially love and horse medicines, became credited with a wide circulation. The individual Indian, of course, disavowed all knowledge of them, because the Sarcee dreaded them exceedingly and looked askance at any one who admitted their use; but nearly every one suspected some neighbour. Typical of many cases, they say, was the experience of Sleigh, an old man still living on the reserve in 1921. He asked a Cree woman to become his wife without going through the ceremony of marriage before a priest. After they had lived together for a time she became afraid that he would desert her sooner or later, so she mixed a love medicine with some tobacco and gave him a pipeful to smoke. It aroused so mad an infatuation in Sleigh that he readily consented to a proper wedding before a priest. This allayed her fears of desertion; but his infatuation lasted so long, and he embarrassed her so much by perpetually hovering at her heels, that she finally gave him another smoking mixture as a "sedative."

All or nearly all the love medicines of the Sarcee seem to have been herbal, and none had any repute that did not come from the Cree. The Sarcee never dreamed that he could ever acquire one through a vision, as he might acquire the power of healing. Similarly horse medicines were nearly always herbs or roots to be rubbed as liniments over the animal's face or body, or mixed with water and poured down its throat, and they, too, came mainly from the Cree. But because the horse belonged to the same realm of nature as the Sarcee's familiar supernatural visitants, the buffalo, the badger, the eagle, and the snake, he conceived that it also might appear to him in a vision, confer on him a horse medicine, and teach him the appropriate songs. This was most likely to happen when an Indian was especially fond of a certain horse, treated it kindly, and never consented to part with it. It might then reveal to him in a vision the herb or root that would give it surpassing speed, or cure the diseases of itself and other horses. His fellow tribesmen might know the plant he used, might even learn his songs, but their knowledge would be valueless to them because they lacked his vision. The profession of a horse medicine-man was, therefore, very profitable once he had established a reputation for himself. Yet he had to be very careful not to offend his benefactor, under penalty of losing his power. He had to reserve for himself alone not only the horse, but the whip and rope he used for it; and he might not use that whip and rope on any other animal.

The Messianic Ghost Dance religion that created so great a turmoil among the Indians of the United States throughout the nineteenth century passed the Sarcee by until the twentieth, when a slight echo of it reached them through the Assiniboine or Stony Indians of Morley. Somewhere around 1910 a native of that place named Cough Child claimed that God had revealed himself to him in a vision, instructed him to sleep for four nights on a certain mountain, and to rub white paint on his cheeks whenever the thunder clapped. Afterwards he should return to his people and restore their pure religion, because Christianity had destroyed all the power with which the Maker had endowed them through prayer and the medicine-pipe. To Cough Child himself God gave the power of healing diseases; the sick man on whom he breathed would rise up well, and the woman in labour on whose womb he breathed would give birth to her child immediately.

After proclaiming his mission Cough Child held a dance, for which he painted a thunderbird on his blanket and covered his body and clothes with white paint. He found several men who would drum for him and sing his songs, and soon gathered large congregations. Gradually his fame spread far and wide. Cree Indians living to the northward sent for him to heal them, and from distant Utah a man brought his child so that he might restore its sight. Every patient who was cured received from Cough Child, for a price, a white feather and was told to whiten his cheeks for protection whenever it thundered.

The Sarcee near Calgary were familiar with Cough Child's mission from its inception, yet they placed little credence in it, and the movement soon died out. As late as 1921, however, at least one woman on the reserve publicly wore a white feather.

CHAPTER 9
MEDICINE-BUNDLES

The outstanding charms or medicine-objects among the Sarcee were the medicine-bundles, of which mention has been made already. They, too, the Indians say, resulted from visions, but from visions of long ago when man was perhaps in closer touch with nature than he is today. The long passage of years enhanced their reputation and value until at last they ranked among the tribe's most precious possessions, though they continued to rest in individual hands. Ambitious men, indeed, tried to buy as many as possible, not merely to win the favour of the supernatural world, but to increase their prestige and spread their fame throughout their own and surrounding tribes; but so highly priced were the bundles that only exceptionally could a man succeed in owning two at the same time.

Of the half dozen bundles in their possession the Sarcee prized especially two, the beaver and the medicine-pipe. The latter reflected the Indians' awe and reverence of the thunder; the former was associated not only with the Sun Dance, as already noted (footnote, page 55), but with the cultivation of tobacco, which the Sarcee discontinued only when they were confined to their reserve. A second medicine-pipe bundle, held in much less esteem, was purchased from the Cree in the latter half of the nineteenth century; it is now in the National Museum of Canada. The Sarcee possessed in addition a bear knife bundle, which was sold to the American Museum of Natural History in 1912, and two black pipe bundles, one of which was destroyed when its owner died, the other sold to the Blackfoot Indians.

There was one other object that we should logically include among the medicine-bundles, viz., the ceremonial head-dress purchased and worn by the woman who gave a Sun Dance. The ritual connected with it, however, has been described in an earlier chapter, so that here we need only insert the legend of its origin.

A man who had gone into the mountains to hunt buffaloes came upon a moose lying with its head toward the south. He was on the point of shooting it when he heard some one singing on the top of a neighbouring peak, and, looking up, saw a second moose, husband of the one that was lying down. The male moose put the hunter to sleep. The female then rose, and her husband circled her jealously; but she said to him,

> You always treat me in this way. I told you that I had no oth-
> er husband. Look at my head-dress. If I took another husband
> while I wore this head-dress I should die."

When the hunter awakened both animals had vanished. Some years later he made a head-dress corresponding to the one he had seen in his vision and presented it to a woman who was giving a Sun Dance. That is how this head-dress became associated with the Sun Dance, and why the woman who gives the Sun Dance must be pure.

BEAVER BUNDLES

The beaver bundle contained, inside a wrapping of elk hide, a small bag of buffalo scrotum filled with dried saskatoon berries, eight rattles, a digging-stick, one beaver skin, one skin of a white muskrat, and the tail of a buffalo. These, however, were only the most significant articles.

It concealed also the stem of a pipe, two buffalo stones, two elk ribs, the skins of a prairie dog and of young deer, antelope, and sheep, several bird skins, and a pair of wristlets made from wildcat claws that the wife of the bundle-owner wore at rituals.

The man who owned the bundle in 1921, Two Guns, explained its origin by the following myth:[1]

A hunter once sighted a herd of buffaloes close to a big lake. He left his horse, concealed himself in a hollow, and, when they drew near, shot one very fat animal. After rolling the carcass on to its back he removed the insides and piled up a portion of the meat; then, rolling the carcass back again, he made another pile of the meat, severed the legs, and knocked off the ribs. While he was thus butchering it a whale (a big fish with a horn on its head) came out of the lake and circled round him, saying "Do not be afraid of me, my son. You see that little cloud in the sky yonder. Those are the thunderbirds; they are trying to seize me, but they are afraid of human beings and you will protect me." Then the thunders came down and said "My son, stand aside. We want to eat that whale. Why did he go to you for protection?" But the hunter answer "Do not kill him, my father. He came to me for protection. Spare him." The thunders said again "My son, he has not as much power as I have." "That is not true, my son," the whale responded. "We who live on the earth have more power than those in the sky. The thunders come only once a year; they have not the power to stay with you. If you surrender me to them you will step over a little water one day; but if you save me I will give you this bundle." To this the thunders replied "My son, if you give us this whale nothing you wish for on this earth will ever escape you."

The man listened to both, and finally said to the thunders "I pity this whale, but I will also have mercy on you. Spare the whale, and take that fat buffalo instead." The thunders answered him "We regret it, my son, but we will spare him." Moving away a little, they suddenly crashed down and took all

---

1. Another Indian adduced a different myth, which he said the Sarcee had learned from the Blood Indians. It closely resembled the myth given by Wissler: Anth. Papers, Am. Mus. Nat. Hist., vol. VII, 1912, p. 173 (footnote).

the buffalo meat. After they had departed the whale said to the hunter "Make a bundle like this one"; and it showed him a bag made from the scrotum of a young buffalo. "Hereafter," it continued, "I shall always help you because you have saved my life." The hunter led the whale back to its home in the lake. It said to him before it plunged in "Hereafter always throw something into this lake as an offering to me. Now return home and make the bundle, and place inside it a skin of every living creature upon this earth. Place also some tobacco in the bundle, and keep some berries in this little bag as food for me. On the inside of the bag draw my picture, on the outside the thunders. Do not forget my instructions, and never give the bundle away to any other tribe." The whale then sang the beaver songs for him and went into the water.

Years after the hunter made up the beaver bundle according to the whale's instructions, and, at his death, bequeathed it to another man. So it has been handed clown among the Sarcee through the generations.

Every summer, before the societies gave their 4-day dances and the whole tribe celebrated its Sun Dance, the owner of the beaver bundle held his own ritual dance. His wife enlisted the aid of relatives to join two tents together and to cook a large quantity of food, which they laid out in the middle of the floor space. The bundle-owner then called in all the people, inviting first the old men; and while he painted the faces of the men, his wife painted the women, until every Indian bore a red mark across his forehead and another around his lower jaw. The bundle-owner then resumed his place at the back of the tent, with his wife to his right, and, to his left, eight old men to sing and shake his beaver rattles when he opened his bundle. Next to his wife sat a woman to support her in the ritual; and a smudge of sweet-grass burned behind the fire in the centre of the lodge, as in nearly all religious ceremonies.

The old men chanted a song while the owner opened his bundle, and laid all its contents beside him except the two "buffalo" stones,[2] which he deposited near the smudge. One of the old men then offered up a prayer that ended in a universal *ai,* and two "workers" distributed the food. Before eating every Indian uttered a silent prayer on his own account, and threw away a morsel of food and a few drops of liquid as an offering to the Maker. After the meal a man who sat next to the singers filled every one's pipe with tobacco that the host had provided; and the people smoked. The host's own pipe was handed to him by the bowl, so that he took hold of it by the mouthpiece; in the ritual dance for the medicine-pipe the owner of that bundle always grasped his pipe by the bowl.

After every one had smoked the host rose and produced a bag filled with dried saskatoon berries that he had kept in his bundle, and, beginning with the nearest old man, presented each member of the audience with two or three

2. These stones, and one of the rattles, are now in the National Museum of Canada.

berries; he touched the man's breast with the bag, then circled it around his body to touch his back, and wished him long life and prosperity. On completing the circuit he laid down the bag and threw[3] his eight rattles to the eight singers, one of whom then chanted a prayer for help in remembering the full series of songs; for the beaver ritual called for eight songs, of which only the first had been sung when the bundle was opened.

The old man now chanted the second song while the owner of the bundle danced around the ring sunwise. At the third song his wife and her assistant danced. The fourth, fifth, sixth, and seventh songs were for persons who had vowed to dance with the digging-stick, the beaver skin, the white muskrat skin, and the buffalo tail, respectively. The man who danced with the buffalo tail mimicked the actions of a buffalo and pretended to gore his comrade's wife. For persons who wished to dance with other objects from the bundle the eighth song was chanted and repeated as often as was necessary. Although there was no obligation on any one to rise and dance, individuals often vowed to do so, and always paid a blanket or other object for the privilege, since they hoped by their dancing to receive some blessings from the Maker.

With the chanting of the eighth song the ceremony came to an end. The audience dispersed and the owner rewrapped his beaver bundle and replaced it on the blanket at the back of his tent.

It was not unusual for an Indian to borrow one or more rattles from the beaver bundle when selling a painted tipi, or performing some other ritual. He then approached the owner in the usual way; that is to say, he offered him a pipe filled with tobacco, stated his request, and mentioned the price usually a horse. After signifying his assent by lighting the pipe the owner opened the bundle and threw the rattle at the petitioner's feet.

The Sarcee no longer hold the beaver bundle in the same esteem as formerly. Neither have they maintained the tobacco-planting ceremony in which it played a part. An old man who had witnessed both the ceremony and the planting of the tobacco thus described them:

> Our people joined two tents together in the middle of the camp, and at their centre pegged a buffalo hide over four stakes to make a bag, which they filled with berry soup and stirred from time to time with an elk-bone. The owner of the beaver bundle took his place at the back of the rattles that belonged to the bundle. The remaining Indians crowded round the sides of the tent, or peered in through the door.
>
> Presently three women entered, led by the bundle-owner's wife, who had three large blue beads on her neck and broad streaks of red paint across her forehead and round her chin. While the eight old men shook their rattles and sang these women danced toward the berry bag and rubbed their heads against the stakes like buffaloes.
>
> At the conclusion of their dance two workers brought food of

---

3. The rattles had to be thrown, not handed over; but the writer failed to discover the reason.

various kinds into the tent and distributed it among the audience, when those for whom there was no space inside received their portions on the ends of forked sticks that they thrust through the entrance.

Early the next morning the chief called out "Make haste. Get ready," whereupon all the Indians turned out to burn the grass from a strip of land about an acre in extent. After extinguishing the fire they swept the field with branches, and sprinkled it with white earth to the depth of half an inch. Some one then brought out tobacco seed that had been stripped immediately after the previous harvest, and its husks added to the stalks and leaves for smoking; and a number of women and boys lined up, shoulder to shoulder along one edge of the field, each holding in one hand a sharpened stake, in the other some of this seed mixed with deer manure. At a shout from the chief they marched across the plot, turning up the earth and planting a little seed every one or two steps. The boys then raced over the ground to trample in the seeds, while the men set up stakes at the end of each row, and tied to each stake miniature moccasins, travois or bows and arrows, for the use of the tobacco people, who resemble human beings. Long ago, our people say, an old man fell asleep on the trail four days after the planting, and in his sleep he heard the conversation of some persons approaching him from behind. One voice said "My feet are sore, for my mother was not kind to me and did not make me any moccasins." Another answered "My mother made me moccasins and gave me also a bow and arrows." When the old man reported what he had heard the Indians agreed that his visitors were the tobacco people going on a journey: consequently, ever afterwards, they were careful to tie moccasins and other objects to their stakes.

On the same day as the planting, and on the two following days, the Sarcee moved their camp and spent the evenings singing; but on the fourth day they sent back a swift runner to throw something on the plot.[4] Thenceforward until the harvest everyone who had taken part in the planting buried a little food in the ground before each meal to promote the growth of the tobacco.

In the autumn, when the Indians returned from their hunting grounds and approached the tobacco field they sent forward a scout to examine the plot. He reported that all the rows were growing well except —'s and —'s, who must have forgotten to feed their plants. The people then held a dance and harvested the crop.

The buffalo stones (*tsa'xani:* "rock buffalo") in the beaver bundle figured in a special ritual for discovering where herds of buffalo were grazing; but the

---

4. My informant, One-Spotted, did not know what it was he threw on the plot.

details are unknown. With no other buffalo stones was there any ritual, not even a smudge; they were treated merely as peculiar stones (or fossils), resembling animate objects, that conferred on their finders good fortune and long life. The Blackfoot Indians, holding that these blessings were transferable, bartered their buffalo stones as they bartered other medicine-objects; but the Sarcee rejected this belief. They did, however, retain the popular superstition that buffalo stones kept for a long time in a bag reproduced offspring, and there were two or three Indians on the reserve who claimed to have "parent stones" and "children" in their possession.

THE MEDICINE-PIPE BUNDLE

The blanket-wrapped medicine-pipe bundle hung every day on a travois behind the tipi, that is to say on its west side, since the entrance always faced the east; beside it was the owner's head-dress within its leather case, suspended from a tripod. Both were taken down at sunset, or when rain threatened, and hung inside the tipi, the bundle directly over its owner's head, the head-dress on top of one of his two back-rests; certain accessories of the bundle, such as the food bowl and the fan used in the sweat-lodge, hung on top of the other back-rest. Since the mouthpiece of the pipe had always to face the north, the two ends of the bun-

Plate 8. Medicine-pipe bundle.
(Canadian Museum of History 52789)

dle were distinguished by differently coloured cloths.

The Indian who owned this bundle in 1920, Big Knife, was afraid to tell me what was inside it except that it contained a stone pipe with its stem, a beaver skin, a goat-skin band, and some tobacco; but afterwards a kinsman listed its contents and the objects that went with it as follows:

> The blanket in which the bundle was wrapped. This was painted with juniper twigs on the left hand side.
> Wrappings inside the blanket, viz., a tanned elk hide, a bear skin, pieces of gaily coloured cloth, and some thongs.
> The carrying-strap, which was really a woman's belt, since it was always a woman

who carried the bundle.
A woman's shawl.
A rawhide bag that contained some of the smaller articles listed below.
A decorated pipe-stem.
A small pipe (bowl and stem) used for smoking at ceremonies.
A rattle inside a buffalo-hide bag.
Whistle or flageolet made from the wing bone of an eagle.
Two tobacco pouches, one of loon's skin, the other from the skin of a deer foetus.
Tobacco, a board for cutting it, and pipe-stokers.
Tongs, a small bag of roots and a small bag of pine-needles for the smudge.
Paint bag, and one or more extra bags containing red paint; paint sticks.
The head of a crane.
A mink skin, owl skin, and the skins of some other birds.
Four drums marked with thunderbird claws.
A head-dress of mountain goat's wool; the tripod from which it was suspended out of doors.
An eagle wing-feather worn crosswise on the head.
Two necklaces, each bearing a pendant sea-shell, worn by the owner of the bundle and his wife.
Four wristlets, each bearing one or more blue beads, worn by the owner and his wife.[5]
A white woollen blanket, decorated with three circles of beads, that was substituted for the original buffalo-robe.
A food bowl.
An eagle wing used as a fan in the sweat-lodge.
A whip.
A lariat.

The legend cited by Big Knife to explain the origin of his bundle is follows:

Long ago the Sarcee gathered all their furs and tanned buffalo hides, journeyed to Old Fort Edmonton, and, halting near the fort, sent four or five scouts ahead to inform its factor that their chiefs, councillors and warriors proposed to trade with him. The factor gave the messengers some tobacco in token of his good-will, whereupon the whole tribe entered the fort and traded its furs. As the factor was bundling them together to convey to his home far away he asked them whether any of their chiefs would like to go with him. Two warriors volunteered. Spotted Eagle and Crow Flag, or, as he was also called, Cut-Knife. The factor then prepared two boats; he himself embarked on the

---

5. These and the necklaces on the preceding page, the special insignia of a medicine-pipe owner and his wife, were worn in everyday life.

front boat with Spotted Eagle while Crow Flag followed them on the second.

Now the interpreter on the first boat warned Spotted Eagle that the factor's wife was in love with him, and that he must carefully avoid paying any attention to her. Crow Flag, however, was not warned, and as they travelled down a big river to a great lake he let his glances rest on her so often that the factor became angry and ordered his men to maroon him on an island. So they beguiled him ashore under pretence of obtaining something and sailed away without him. Spotted Eagle, travelling on the front boat, did not know what had happened to him.

The factor conducted Spotted Eagle to the chief factor, and the Big Chief invited both the chief factor and Spotted Eagle to his house. Before they visited it the leader of another Indian party told Spotted Eagle that the Big Chief's house contained many things belonging to Indian societies, and that if their owner asked him what he wanted he should request, not the fine things around the walls, but a certain bundle that hung upon the door; even if the Big Chief repeated his question four times he should give always the same answer. Accordingly, when the Big Chief gave Spotted Eagle some rum and asked what he could do for him Spotted Eagle said that all he wanted was the bundle hanging on the door. The Big Chief told him to choose something more valuable, but the Indian answered "No. Those other things are too good. You have asked me what I want. Well, all I want is that bundle and nothing else." Then the Big Chief said "That bundle belongs to this place and it is very hard for me to part with it. Moreover, it is not worth your trouble in taking it home. Who told you to ask for it?" "No one told me." replied Spotted Eagle; "but I want it for our dances."

Four days he stayed with the Big White Chief. Each day he received some rum and was asked the same question; and each day he returned the same answer. On the fourth day the Big Chief handed him the bundle wrapped in a flag and he started back with the factor for Old Fort Edmonton.

Meanwhile Crow Flag had been picked up by some white men and taken to a different place. They placed him first among some wild animals, which rushed at him to devour him; but when he said "I am Crow Flag" the animals lay down. The white men placed him in another house filled with wild animals of a different kind, and there again the animals lay down at his word. They confined him then in a spot where there were wild animals living in wells of water; and they too he subdued at his command. Even a spotted lynx with which they imprisoned him obeyed his word. Finally the white men conducted him back towards Old Fort Edmonton and marooned him again on an island.

One day, as he was walking along the shore, the factor's boat approached and his friend Spotted Eagle caught sight of him. The factor would have left him alone to his fate, but Spotted Eagle said "He is my friend. Let me join him"; and he jumped overboard as the boat drew near the land. The factor went on his way without them and told their tribesmen that he had left them on an island at their own request. So when they failed to return after many months their people gave them up for dead.

On the island they were starving, for all they could find to eat were a few berries. Crow Flag then said to Spotted Eagle "Have you ever been granted a vision that gave you medicine power?" "Yes," replied Spotted Eagle. "I am a medicine-man. I can take you home. Cut a hole in my neck and close your eyes." Crow Flag obeyed. When he opened his eyes again Spotted Eagle had flown with him to another island a little nearer home. Thence they proceeded in the same way to a third island, and a fourth. Finally, they reached the mainland somewhere far off in the north, in the midst of a terrible swamp. Months and months they walked, living on berries and anything else they could find. At last, late in the autumn, they came to their own country again.

One morning the Sarcee looked up from their camp, and, seeing two men with a flag on a neighbouring hill-top, sent out a rider to investigate. The rider quickly recognized Spotted Eagle and Crow Flag, and, springing from his horse, kissed them. He then signaled the news by waving his blanket, first to the east, then to the west, and preceded them down the hill to the camp.

That same autumn the Sarcee again gathered all their furs and journeyed to Old Fort Edmonton. Crow Flag and Spotted Eagle accompanied them, the latter carrying his bundle on his back. When the scout whom they sent ahead told the factor that these two men were in the party the factor would not believe him, for he was convinced that they had died on the island. When he crossed over on the ferry boat, however, and saw the two men with his own eyes, he was dumbfounded, and his alarm increased when they refused to embark with the rest of the Sarcee, but told him to return for them. Spotted Eagle began to sing as soon as he entered the boat, and his song raised a high wind that threatened to upset them. Nevertheless, they reached the shore in safety, and demanded compensation for their injuries from the now thoroughly frightened factor, who hurriedly gave them guns, powder, and everything else they asked for from his store. He then took Spotted Eagle's bundle into his house, placed fresh tobacco inside it and covered it with a new red cloth, suffering no harm therefrom because the bundle had been derived from a white man. Thereafter whenever the Sarcee carried their medicine-pip^e bundle into a fort the factor made it his first care to renew its tobacco and provide it with a new cover."

Big Knife claimed to own the original bundle obtained by Spotted Eagle, who had given it to a brother-in-law, from whom it had passed to various Indians until it reached Wolf Carrier, Big Knife's father. When Wolf Carrier died another Indian took charge of it for a year, but restored it to Big Knife at the close of the term of mourning. At one period the bundle had been sold to a Blackfoot Indian, who dreamed during a dangerous illness that he was to return it to its proper tribe. The Blackfoot, therefore, held a council about it, and subsequently sent it back to the Sarcee.

All other medicine-pipe bundles, according to this account, were merely copies of Big Knife's, whether they were owned by Sarcee Indians, or by Indians of another tribe; some man would dream about the original bundle, make a copy of it, and purchase the appropriate songs from the owner of the genuine bundle. Whether this be true or not, it is certain that in 1920 the Sarcee attached far greater value to Big Knife's bundle than to their second medicine-pipe bundle, which the National Museum of Canada purchased from its owner, Dick Starlight. Thus Starlight often rested his drum carelessly on the ground outside its case, whereas Big Knife's drums were never allowed to touch the ground.

Spotted Eagle, the legend relates further, had two wives and one son, and whenever he was absent with one wife his son and the other wife took charge of his bundle. In consequence, every succeeding owner of the bundle likewise provided a substitute couple for himself and his wife; in lieu of a second wife or adult daughter he selected a kinswoman, and if he had no son he chose the son of some friend.

The wife or woman partner piously followed a fixed procedure when she suspended the bundle each morning outside the tent. With the ceremonial tongs she placed hot coals on the smudge place, threw some juniper leaves on top of them, and, holding over it the mouthpiece end of the bundle, offered up a prayer before she carried it around the south side of the tent to its travois. At night she went through the same ceremony, but carried the bundle around the north side of the tent in order to keep the mouthpiece of the pipe steadily pointed towards the north. The Sarcee believed that the Maker's blessing rested on the person performing this ritual. Hence, though it was normally carried out by the bundle-owner's wife or her partner, it frequently happened that some lay individual who was troubled by a bad dream, or for some other reason anticipated misfortune, asked permission to undertake the care of the bundle for one day in the hope that he also might share in the Maker's blessing.

The bundle-owner himself had to submit to many disabilities. Whenever he wished to smoke he had first to blow a whiff toward the resting place of the bundle and point the stem of his pipe in its direction, uttering at the same time a brief prayer. He could use no lariat, whip, or food-bowl except those that belonged to the bundle, and were, therefore, forbidden to other people.

When he sat in his tent no one might pass in front of him.[6] Some of the Sarcee considered that it was wrong to bring any part of a bear inside his tent, or
even to utter there the word for bear; but other's rejected this taboo as being
applicable only among the Blackfoot Indians, not in their own tribe. Above all
he might never wash his own clothes, because that would certainly cause a
thunderstorm.[7] On the other hand, the Indians believed that he could stop the
rain by facing the west and flinging out the blanket that covered his head as
though he were parting the clouds.

On two occasions only did he open his bundle ceremonially, when he transferred it to another Indian and when he held his annual dance. He might open
it at other times, without ceremony, to renew the tobacco inside it; yet so great
was its sanctity that even then he generally invited some old man to watch
him pray over the pipe-stem, refill the tobacco bag, and restore the bundle to
its place.

Once in the year, and only once, he held a dance, immediately after the first
sound of thunder in the spring. This was an event eagerly awaited by all the
Sarcee, who no sooner heard the thunder than they tied pots, pieces of cloth,
and other objects to their tents or to trees, and petitioned the Maker for prosperity and long life. The bundle-owner himself hurriedly lit a smudge inside
his tent, brought out his four drums painted with the claws of the thunderbird,
and rapped one of them four times. Then he called in four old men to beat
them and sing the "first thunder" song, raising and lowering the drums four
times that the thunder might hear their voices. As soon as the song ended he
erected a sweat-lodge, placed his medicine-bundle on top and his offering on a
stick behind it, and prayed inside the lodge for help during the coming dance.
Then, returning to his tent, he announced the date of the dance and ordered
his wife to prepare the necessary food.

If the bundle-owner happened to be away from camp at the first thunder-
clap his wife called in the four old men, as the thunder ought not to depart
without hearing its own song. Their reward was a pipeful of tobacco and some
berry soup.[8]

On the eve of the dance an old man made the round of the camp to exhort
the people not to leave. Then, at daybreak, three or four volunteers helped the
bundle-owner to join together two large tents, in whose midst the wife placed
all the food she had prepared for the feast. The Indians crowded inside, every
man and woman adorned with a daub of red paint on each cheek and a streak
of red around the lower jaw. At the back of the tent sat the owner, his bundle
to the left, his wife to the right. He was crowned with the goat-skin head-dress
with its projecting eagle plume; a red buckskin ribbon secured his topknot, blue

---

6. This taboo applied to the owner or ex-owner of any medicine-bundle, but was not observed very
strictly except in the case of the owner of a medicine-pipe.

7. In 1919, when the Sarcee and Assiniboine Indians were helping the white settlers and the
police to fight a prairie fire, some women forced the wife of Big Knife, the medicine-pipe owner,
to walk in the water and to wash her clothes, hoping thereby to cause a thunderstorm.

8. In recent times tea has replaced the berry soup.

beads encircled his head and hung down over each cheek, the white shell dangled on his chest, and more blue beads decorated his wrists. To his left lay the bundle, to his right sat his wife, distinguished by her white shell pendant and blue wrist beads. Next to the wife sat the woman partner, unmarked by any special decoration; but the boy partner seated beside the bundle wore the beaded headband that constituted his special share of it.

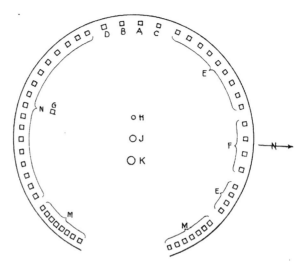

Figure 7. Arrangement at the Medicine-pipe Dance: (A) owner of the medicine-pipe bundle; (B) his wife; (C) the boy partner; (D) the woman partner; (E, E) old men; (F) the four drummers; (G) the official pipe-filler; (H) the smudge; (J) the fireplace; (K) the pile of food; (M, M) women spectators; (N) men spectators.

The drummers, official pipe-filler, and the audience arranged themselves as in the accompanying figure.

Naturally the bundle-owner himself opened the ceremony. He lit the smudge and opened his bundle, while the four men beat the drums and chanted the first medicine-pipe song. The official pipe-filler handed the big medicine-pipe filled with tobacco to one of the old men, who pointed it, with a silent prayer, north, east, south, and west, and handed it back to be lit. It was then passed around for general smoking, but scrupulously kept off the ground.

After all had smoked, two unpaid workers distributed the food, and every person, before eating his portion, prayed in silence. At the end of the meal an old warrior recited from his seat four war deeds, each signalized by the drummers with a simultaneous stroke of the drums.

The drummers now commenced the second medicine-pipe song, in which the bundle-owner joined, shaking his rattle. They repeated it four times, then changed to the third song, which called for a dance by the bundle-owner. Accordingly, he rose to his feet, holding his pipe-stem in his hand, and prayed silently. Then, shaking the stem north, east, south, and west, he danced around the north side of the tent to the east, looked out the door, and continued around the south side to his place.

The boy partner, if present, then danced in the same manner to the same song, but without looking out the door. If he was very young, his father danced in front of him to show him the steps.

To the fourth medicine-pipe song danced the owner's wife and her woman partner. They rose together, and with the wife in front holding the pipe-stem, danced in the same manner as the owner; but whereas the latter had halted every time the song ended, and resumed his dance as soon as the drummers commenced it again, so that it had to be repeated five or six times for his performance, the boy, and after him the women, timed their movements so that they halted three times only, that is to say, on the north, east, and south sides of the tent, respectively. The fourth repetition of the song thus brought them back to their seats.

With the fifth song or songs, for the drummers had several at their disposal, came the lay Indians' opportunity, when all who had vowed to dance with objects from the bundle rose up and performed successively, while the owner rested quietly in his place The Blackfoot permitted laymen to dance with objects from the bundle at any time of the year, but the Sarcee restricted the privilege to the first thunder ceremony, though the dancers often registered their vows months earlier.

The ceremony finally concluded with the chanting of the first thunder song as a "closing" song, and the audience dispersed. Only the bundle-owner, his wife, and the woman and boy partners lingered behind to rewrap the bundle to the accompaniment of a special song.

A medicine-pipe bundle changed hands for one of two reasons. Either some one vowed to purchase it, when the owner could not refuse his assent; or the owner himself grew tired of his possession and foisted it on to some other Indian, for a price.

In the first case the vower filled a pipe with tobacco and, offering it to the owner of the bundle, requested his prayers on the ground that he had vowed to purchase the bundle. Usage obliged the owner to take the pipe and pray, pointing its stem to the four quarters, north, east, south, and west; after which he lit it and smoked. His smoking was the formal sign of his consent.

In the second case the owner invited four old men into his tent one evening and announced to them the name of the man to whom he proposed to transfer his bundle, always taking care to choose some one well able to pay the full price. He then opened his bundle, and the five men slept with its contents spread out beside them. Very early the next morning the owner wakened his companions, and brought into the tent four other men who were familiar with the medicine-pipe songs, and would beat the drums at the critical moment. One old man took up the medicine-pipe stem, a second the owl skin, a third the otter skin, and a fourth the whistle; in that order they marched to the tent of their victim, who was often fast asleep. Slipping the pipe-stem under his blanket they hooted like owls, and the fourth man blew his whistle as a signal for the listening singers to beat their drums. Gathering up the man in his blanket they proceeded to carry him to the bundle-owner's tent, while his wife quietly walked behind. If they had the misfortune to drop him he might walk back to his tent and refuse to go through with the purchase; but once he was deposited in the bundle-owner's tent he had no choice but to submit.

The news spread quickly through the camp, and the Indians prepared for the dance that would see the transfer of the bundle. They joined two tents together to give more space, and the seller's wife gathered a huge quantity of berry soup. At the call of an old man the people assembled inside, and the purchaser sent out a son or relative to bring in his payment, six, eight, or ten horses, and to picket them in front of the tent. The four drummers then started up a song, and the seller, dressed in his special medicine-pipe paraphernalia, danced towards the door and inspected the horses. If he was satisfied, he danced back to his seat; if not, he walked back, and told the buyer what horse or horses he desired from him. The latter could not refuse, and the ceremony was delayed until the buyer received what he wanted.

During a second song the seller transferred his adornments to the buyer and painted his face, while his wife did the same by the buyer's wife. At the proper moment they changed places, and the seller, holding the pipe-stem in his hand, danced around the ring with the buyer following behind him. They halted in four places; at the second halt near the door of the tent the seller blew four times on his hands and passed the pipestem to the buyer, who prayed in silence over it before concluding the dance. Meanwhile, any one who wished to contribute towards the purchase price threw his contribution (usually clothes) on the floor of the tent and danced behind them. The two women followed with a similar dance, after which the buyer's relatives deposited a number of presents on the floor, most of which the seller kept for his own family. The audience then dispersed, and the double tent was transformed again into a single. Throughout the rest of the day, however, the buyer and his wife received instruction from the sellers in the daily ritual of life. Like a child who knew nothing, the buyer had to be shown how to put on his moccasins, to light his pipe, and a thousand other details. He was forbidden to wash himself, or to scratch his body with anything but a special stick. For every item of instruction, repeated four times, lie paid; and throughout the performance the seller chanted and kept the smudge constantly burning.

At evening other men gathered in the seller's tent, and while four of them beat the drums and chanted, the buyer practised the ritual medicine-pipe songs. At the commencement of each song some one walked over to the bundle, received from the seller some object; and, after praying over it, danced around the tent sunwise and handed it back. Thus they continued until some one had danced with every object in the bundle, when the seller closed the proceedings by lighting the medicine-pipe itself and passing it around. Between dances, however, this pipe was not used, but a volunteer filled for the audience another large pipe that every bundle-owner kept in his tent for non-ritual use. Whatever pipe was used it had to circulate, as always, in a sunwise direction around the north of the tent to the east, then around the south again to its owner.

The transfer occupied four days and four nights. Each day the buyer received instruction from the seller, each evening he learned the ritual of the bundle, and each night he and his wife slept in the seller's tent. On the afternoon of the fourth day the seller placed the bundle on top of a sweat-lodge built by some volunteers, and the two men went inside with their wives and rubbed themselves with sage. As soon as they came out and sat down a number of old men took their places within, sang a special medicine-pipe song and prayed aloud in turn. Then the buyer removed the bundle and exchanged tents with the seller, so that the bundle might remain in the same home.

If the seller of a medicine-pipe was comparatively young he often hired an old man to carry out the transfer in order to enhance the dignity of the proceedings. The two men then sat at the back of the tent with the bundle between them, and the actual seller took no part in the proceedings beyond prompting the old man what horses to demand.

After a man had purchased a medicine-pipe bundle he was forbidden to visit the tent of any other Indian until he had received a formal invitation and been presented on his entrance with a horse, for which he later paid in kind. After thus formally visiting one tent, however, he was free to enter others as he wished.

The ceremonies just described relate especially to the main medicine-pipe bundle owned by the Sarcee, the one which they claim served as the model of all others. Very much the same ceremonies, however, attended the second medicine-pipe bundle which the Sarcee sold to the National Museum of Canada in 1920. Under an old torn blanket wrapping this bundle has two others, one a red blanket, the other a blue; and inside, braced by two sticks, are the following objects:

> Medicine-pipe stem wrapped in a red blanket.
> A beaded feather attached to a stick.
> 3 single feathers.
> 2 bunches of feathers, one of them
> thrust into a weasel skin.
> 2 skins of small animals.
> A whistle with pendant feather and strings.
> Tobacco leaf.
> A bird skin.

In a separate bag are:

> The pipe-bowl with its 3 prickers.
> 2 beaded pouches containing tobacco.
> Beaded necklet .and wristlets.
> Rattle.
> Beaded belt.
> White shell sewn to a piece of skin, inside a small' bag.
> Other objects accompanying this bundle are:
> A tripod with 4 legs for suspending the head-dress.
> 1 sets of fire-tongs. one for ritual, one for everyday use.
> 1 drum inside a cover.
> 1 food bowl.
> 1 fans for the sweat-bath.
> 1 everyday pipe.
> 1 board for cutting tobacco.

1 saddle.
1 bags containing red ochre.

BLACK PIPE BUNDLES

The daily ritual governing the black pipe bundle (as stated already, the Sarcee formerly possessed two of them) closely paralleled the ritual governing the medicine-pipe, for, like the latter, it was carried outside each morning, wrapped in a blanket, and suspended above the door of its owner's tent, then at evening carried inside again and hung above his sleeping place. The Indians seemed to remember very little else about it except that it was used only for war.[9] The warrior who wished to gain its protection borrowed it temporarily from the owner, offering him a pipe filled with tobacco and a blanket. The owner smoked the pipe, painted the borrower's face, and tied to his hair a buffalo stone that went with the bundle, after first praying over it at the sweet-grass smudge. On returning from his expedition the warrior restored both bundle and buffalo stone to their owner.

According to tradition, one of the two black pipe bundles originated from a woman's dream. When her husband died, and the other Indians in consequence moved their tents, she remained behind and slept beside her husband's corpse. Many ghosts then visited her, and, showing her a black pipe wrapped in a blanket, bade her rejoin her people and make a bundle like it.

BEAR-KNIFE BUNDLE

The Sarcee have possessed more than one bear-knife medicine-bundle in the course of their history, but their last one they sold to the American Museum of Natural History about 1912. In all of them the principal object was a knife, from whose handle generally dangled two bear's teeth. It was legitimate to open the bag containing this knife and its accessories at any time of the year, but in actual practice it was very seldom opened except when its owner was going on the war-path. He then painted a red line across his forehead, a vertical black line down each side of his face over the eye and corner of the mouth, and red lines across each wrist and hand. Thus adorned he called into his tent all the more important old men, and all who had helped him to purchase the bundle, kindled a smudge, mid solemnly unwrapped the knife to the accompaniment of a special song. Then, holding the weapon in his hands, he prayed that he and his companions on the war-path might meet with good fortune.

As in the case of other bundles, the man who wished to purchase a bear-knife bundle offered its owner a pipe filled with tobacco and stated his wish. At the transfer itself the seller painted his face as above and seated himself at the back of his tent; the buyer, stripped to his breech-clout, sat near the door.

---

9. The Piegan owned a medicine-pipe, used mainly for war, which they claimed to have obtained from the Sarcee. See Wissler, C., Anth. Papers, Am. Mus. Nat. Hist., vol. VII, 1912, p. 161.

After unwrapping the knife the seller painted it with red ochre. Both men then dropped to their knees and held out their arms; the seller, chanting his bear song, and poising the knife between his right thumb and forefinger, pointed it three times at the buyer, and the fourth time threw it. If it dropped from the buyer's fingers the transaction was void; if he caught it he hugged it to his breast and prayed over it. The seller then handed over the rest of the paraphernalia and the ceremony ended. A day or two later the buyer paid the purchase price, a horse, a gun, or some clothes. The Sarcee never used a sweat-bath at the transfer of a bear-knife bundle, nor did they ever roll the purchaser on a bed of thorns, as was the custom among the Blackfoot.

Crow-Collar, who sold the last Sarcee bear-knife bundle to the American Museum of Natural History, received it from his father Feather Head; and Feather Head, according to the tradition, made it himself in consequence of a dream. In this dream he saw a bear which handed him a similar bundle, saying "My son, just as I never turn aside when I pursue some object, so when you give this bundle to any one don't let him turn away. Throw the knife straight at the man's chest. If he catches it in both hands, good; but if it cuts his hands or his chest he will die soon afterwards."

CHAPTER 10
OTHER MEDICINE OBJECTS

PAINTED TENTS

Of equal value with the lesser medicine-bundles, and surpassed only by the beaver and medicine-pipe, were the painted tents, of which the Sarcee claimed at least a dozen. Like the bundles, they originated from visions, could be replaced when worn out, bought, and sold, but never duplicated. Their first owners were always medicine-men who professed to have received from their visions the power to cure diseases, and to have been granted the right to paint certain patterns on their tents after they had practised successfully and established their reputations. Indians who were not medicine-men obtained their painted tents only by purchase.

In 1921 the Sarcee possessed four painted tents, and claimed the right to paint seven others. One, the Eagle, they had sold a few years before to the Cree, and another, the Skunk, had lapsed with the death of its owner; but between 1921 and 1929 they acquired from some source a new tent, the Buffalo (Plate I, frontispiece). The four painted tents they erected and occupied in 1921 were:

> Bee (Plate 4c, page 24).
> Wolf (Plate 4d, page 24).
> Big Stripe Fish
> The seven that they claimed the right to paint were:
> Snake Otter Big Rock Buffalo Head All Black Owl
> Otter Flag

Every owner of a painted tent had to keep a large stone pipe and a board for cutting tobacco, because, being a man of note in his community, he was expected to invite his tribesmen to smoke in his lodge at irregular intervals. This pipe and cutting board he sold with the tent, along with his four medicine-songs, his ceremonial pair of fire-tongs, and, if he possessed them, a drum and the right to paint the face with some peculiar pattern. The medicine-man who first acquired a painted tent, however, could not sell with it his powers of healing, because these powers had been granted for his sole use and perished with him. With most tents went some special custom or taboo; in some, for example, it was customary to set up altars of painted earth whenever they were sold. The owner of the Otter Flag tent claimed the curious privilege of pounding his drum four times when he wished to invite his neighbours to eat or smoke with him; and whenever he lit his pipe, he shook the pole that held up his "Otter Flag," thereby tinkling the elk toes or metal bells suspended at its peak.

At the present time painted tents (and even medicine-bundles) change hands during the ordinary Sioux-Circle dances, sometimes without previous notice, the owner merely announcing that he intends to transfer his tent to some designated person. The purchaser then fixes the payment, and the owner, however small the price he receives, cannot back out of the arrangement. In former times painted tents changed hands only on request, and their owners practically fixed the purchase price. Every bargain was struck in the usual manner; the man who desired the tent filled a pipe with tobacco, visited the owner, and handed him the pipe at the same time stating his wish. The owner, if willing, lit the pipe and smoked; if unwilling (as he might be for two reasons, first, because the price offered to him was too low, and, second, because he believed his ownership was bringing him good luck), he simply refused to take the pipe into his hands.

Let us suppose that the owner agreed to sell his tent. On the appointed day he moved all his property into another lodge so that the purchaser might move in, and while his wife cooked berry soup, he himself took out his ceremonial fire-tongs and prepared a smudge. Towards evening he called in all the old men and any of the younger men who owned painted tents, distributed his food, and waited while they ate and smoked. He then opened the proceedings by adorning the purchaser and the purchaser's wife with his special face pattern, if he had any. After this he took up his fire-tongs, and, with the usual three feints, laid it in the purchaser's hand; then, resting his own hand over the purchaser's, he helped him to place on the smudge a live coal, and juniper or sweet pine on top. The purchaser's wife might participate in this ceremony by holding her husband's arm; should she prefer it, however, the seller guided her through the same movements afterwards.

With the lighting of the smudge the second stage in the ceremony opened. The seller brought out his drum (if he had one; if not, a rattle borrowed from the beaver medicine-bundle) and sang his four songs, in which the audience joined. The audience always knew the songs if the painted tent was an old one; but if it were new, and the songs unfamiliar the company had to rehearse them again and again, because they would chant the same songs at every future sale. Each owner of a painted tent (beginning with the man on the seller's left) then took the drum and led the audience in the songs that belonged to his tent—all four of his songs if the company was small, but one or two only if many men were to succeed him. The audience dispersed at the close of the singing, but reunited the next three evenings to repeat the performance. On the fourth day, too, the seller's wife taught the wife of the purchaser next to the door of the tent, not because it differed in any way from other tents, but merely as part of the ceremony and to extract a little extra payment.

The visions that gave rise to painted tents soon passed out of memory, because there was no reason to recall them when the medicine-powers credited to go with them lapsed. In character they did not differ from other visions, as the two following examples show:

ORIGIN OF THE OWL TENT

Once when I was a young man, travelling alone to another camp, I saw an owl sitting on its nest; and I shot one of the young birds with my arrow. The mother bird disappeared over a hill, but presently returned with a hawk, which flew down to the edge of the creek near the wounded bird and struck its side with its wings. Moving over, it struck its other side, whereupon the young owl stretched out both its wings, healed. A third time the hawk struck it, on the head; and a fourth, on the tail. Then both birds flew away and settled beside the mother owl. Immediately I found myself inside a painted tent like the one I now occupy, with the mother owl sitting beside me. She said to me 'If you had killed my child you yourself would have died; but now that my child is healed I give you the privilege of erecting a tent like this one.' Many years after the vision I painted this tent" (Old Sarcee).

ORIGIN OF THE BEE TENT

"More than fifty years ago, when buffalo were still plentiful on the plains, we pitched our camp a little south of where the Bow and Red Deer rivers join and I rode away to visit some neighbours. Suddenly I passed a nest of bees, that knocked me to the ground senseless. The father of the bees then came to me and said 'My son, come and visit my tent.' I entered and sat down beside him; he looked exactly like an old man, and his wife like an old woman. He said to me 'My son, I give you this tent of mine; but you must never eat the intestine of any animal. He then sang for me four songs, and his wife sang a fifth. The tent disappeared, I came to my senses and found myself lying on the ground under the stars. Now [in 1921] for the first time I am painting the tent which the bees gave me; for though a man receives a vision in his youth, he may not paint his tent until he is well on in years" (Many Wounds).

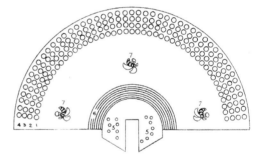

Figure 8. Sketch plan of the designs on the bee tent. The ground of the tent was painted yellow. The bees were represented realistically in green on the tent wall (7), and again by green circular spots on the two ears (5). The beehive was given the form of eight arcs (G), painted, respectively, red, yellow, black, yellow, green, yellow heliotrope, yellow; they formed eight circles near the top of the erected tent, which was painted black above them. The honeycomb appeared as four rows of circular spots (1. 2, 3, 4). painted, respectively, heliotrope, green, black, and red, all around the bottom of the tent.

Many Wounds might never have painted his Bee Tent at all if another Indian named Crowchild, who owned a new white canvas tent, had not asked him to decorate it with his vision, for a stated price. The old man agreed and enlisted his sons and nephews to carry out the work. On the evening before the appointed day he visited Crowchild and his wife to teach them the medicine-songs that went with the vision. At daybreak the two men and their relatives mixed the paints inside—green, heliotrope, yellow, black, and red, all except the last, which was native red ochre, purchased from a store in Calgary; then, with the help of a ladder, they took down the tent and laid it flat on the ground. Many Wounds himself marked out the patterns, using a stick for drawing straight lines, and a wooden hoop for stamping the circles; one large semicircle, which appeared on the erected tent as a full circle near the peak, he traced with the help of a cord. His relatives then filled in the patterns with brushes and rags, and after they had finished he drew in three bees, one on each side of the doorway and one at the back. While the paint was still wet Crowchild and his wife re-erected the tent and moved their property inside again. (See Plate 4c, page 24, and Figure 8, page 101.)

SHIELDS

Every shield possessed religious significance, because no warrior might make or carry one unless he had obtained the right from a vision, or by purchase from a man who himself had obtained it in a vision. Should the vision be revealed the shield lost its virtue and would no longer protect its bearer; hence shields captured in battle were valuable only as trophies. It was not uncommon for a young warrior to vow that he would purchase some old man's shield if he returned safely from a raid.

Since the shield was a religious object, its sale or transfer naturally called for a strict ritual. The seller sat, as usual, at the back of his tent with the purchaser to his right and, to his left, four men holding drums. Between him and the fireplace was a smudge of sweet-grass, and in front of the smudge an altar of white clay. The ceremony went through four stages, each accompanied by its special song.

(1) The seller daubed the purchaser's face with yellow paint, drew a shield in black on his forehead and a new moon in dark red on his right cheek.

(2) The seller placed a knife in the purchaser's hand and guided it while it trace out on the clay altar an image corresponding to the name of the shield— if the buffalo shield, an image of a buffalo's head with the nostrils marked out with red ochre. He then placed the shield in the hands of the purchaser, who held it four times over the smudge before removing its case and resting it, bent inside out, on the ground to the right.

(3) The seller held the purchaser's foot over the smudge four times and pointed it toward the shield, whereupon the purchaser rose and leaped into the shield causing it to spring back into shape. Tradition averred that unless he landed on it properly with both feet he would die soon afterwards. He then danced around the circle and sat down.

(4) The purchaser rose, took up a pot of red paint mixed with water, symbolizing the blood of the buffalo or other animal that first gave the shield, and began drink. Some relative threw down a blanket, took the pot away from him and drank also. Others then followed until all the paint was consumed. Final-

ly the purchaser stepped into the thong of the shield, suspended it over his shoulder, and carried it home.

ORIGIN OF THE BUFFALO SHIELD

A hunter once sighted three buffaloes, a cow leading its calf and the bull following behind. The cow saw him and told the bull, which answered "Don't be afraid, for he will not hurt us. I am going to give him something." Turning to the man, it said "Rise, my son, and don't shoot at us. I will give you my shield, which will enable you to become a great chief and capture many trophies from your enemies. It bade him drink red paint as if it were buffalo's blood, but never to eat the brain of a buffalo. Even though his enemies shot at him as they shot at buffalo, his shield would protect him. That is how mankind obtained the buffalo shield. Other shields came from other animals.

HORN BONNETS

In addition to the shield several other articles worn by warriors were attributed to visions and invested with religious sanctity. One was a bonnet with two upstanding buffalo horns, worn only on the war-path or during the Sun Dance when its owner narrated his four brave deeds, and forbidden on all other occasions. As with the shield, the ritual governing its sale was conducted in four stages, each accompanied by its special song.

To officiate at the ceremony the seller generally engaged an old man who himself had at one time owned a horn bonnet. This old man invited the Indians into the seller's tent and seated the purchaser at the back of the lodge immediately to his right, while four men carrying rattles from the beaver bundle took their places to his left. Between them and the central fireplace was a smudge, beside which lay some white sage covering a lump of buffalo manure; and in front of the smudge was a square altar of white clay. On two opposing sides of the altar the old man outlined with yellow clay the Pleiades and the Dipper, and on the two remaining sides a new moon and the head of a buffalo. He then commenced the ceremony proper.

He daubed the purchaser's face with yellow ochre, and encircled the eyes and mouth with streaks of red.

Placing one of the purchaser's moccasins in his hand, he made him break up the patterns on the altar.

After three feints he placed the horn bonnet on the altar, then took up the white sage and laid it at four places around the tent.

The purchaser danced on each of the four bundles of white sage, therewith bringing the ceremony to a close.

SCALP-LOCK SHIRTS

Certain warriors wore shirts decorated with scalp-locks, a garment that the Indians explain by the same legend that they cite for sweat-lodges and the institution of the Sun Dance. A man who captured a scalp in battle frequently handed it over to an old warrior and offered to pay him two or three horses if lie would make him a scalp-lock shirt. The old man then killed a deer, and while his wife was tanning the hide, he himself intercepted the women at the watering-hole and cut from each of them a lock, saying "Do not refuse me, for this is holy." His wife added the locks he thus obtained to the original scalp-lock, and sewed them on the shirt she made from the deerskin.

The sale of a scalp-lock shirt passed through four stages, as in the sale of a horn bonnet. The principals arranged themselves in the same manner, and there was the same altar of white clay, which on this occasion carried the outline of a new moon, in red paint, flanked by the Pleiades and Dipper in yellow.

The seller (or an old man acting for him) covered the purchaser's face with red paint, then encircled it with a ring of black paint and drew a streak of black down the nose.

The seller removed one lock from the shirt and showed the purchaser how to tie it on again. He next laid an awl in the purchaser's hand and made him punch a hole in the shirt; then, handing him the lock of hair, lie bade him thread it through the hole. The purchaser made the usual three feints attempting to thread it; if he succeeded at the first attempt he gained the blessing of living to old age. The seller received extra payment for his instruction.

The seller held the shirt over the smudge and touched it against the purchaser's shoulder; held it three times again over the smudge and touched successively his back, his other shoulder, and his breast. The purchaser now donned the shirt, and with the feather of a black-tailed hawk that the seller handed him destroyed the altar, praying "May I have long life and many horses." He then planted the feather in his hair.

The seller placed four bunches of white sage in a line leading to the door, and the seller danced on each in turn. This ended the ceremony.

DOG-SKIN BANDOLIER

This was another "medicine charm" used only in war. It consisted of a dog skin split down the centre, and slung as a bandolier in such a way the head of the dog rested on the wearer's shoulder and the feet and tail trailed at the knee. From the bottom hung little bells, bought from the Hudson's Bay Company, that tinkled with every movement. In camp the owner suspended the bandolier inside his tent, but on the war-path he hung it to a tree near his head so that the head of the dog might point towards the enemy and growl if misfortune threatened him. He might not flee in battle, however perilous his plight, unless a comrade whipped him, when his charm would protect him from all bullets.

The Sarcee never possessed more than one or two dog-skin bandoliers at one time and, therefore, prized them very highly. The ritual for its sale followed the usual pattern, but the details were not recorded.

WEASEL-TAIL SHIRTS

Another war garment, commonly worn also at ceremonies, was a shirt (with or without leggings) that was decorated with weasel tails. It was on a garment of this kind only that a Sarcee might paint his war deeds, or hire an old man to paint them for him. Yet no man might make such a shirt because of his valour in war, or in virtue of a vision; he could procure it solely by purchase. Its transfer demanded a ritual similar to that attending the transfer of a horn bonnet or a scalp-lock shirt, although today, when the old customs and beliefs are declining, a weasel-tail shirt may change hands without ceremony.

The seller arranged the usual smudge behind his fire, behind the smudge an altar of white clay and a heap of white sage. Between the altar and his sleeping place he spread out the shirt on a blanket that the purchaser supplied. The purchaser sat on his right, four singers with drums, or with rattles borrowed from the beaver bundle, on his left. The seller then painted the purchaser. He drew two red lines, one right across both eyes and the other across the mouth, or, in some cases, one outward from the corner of the right eye and the other outward from the left corner of the mouth, lie next daubed yellow ochre over the rest of his face, and over his whole body above the waist; and he daubed his legs yellow also, if there were leggings accompanying the shirt. Finally, down each arm, and down the legs if they had been daubed yellow, he painted in red a double track of broken lines intended to represent the tracks of a weasel; for in all ceremonies connected with the weasel its tracks had to be painted on the body or on a blanket, or else marked out on an altar in coloured earth.

The ceremony proper, in four stages, each with its appropriate song, followed the painting.

The seller tied the tail feather of an eagle to the crown of the purchaser's head.

The seller drew the weasel-tail shirt over the purchaser's head, and the leggings, if there were any, over his legs. The blanket on which they had rested he stowed away among his own possessions at the back of the tent, and presented the purchaser with an equivalent blanket.

The seller placed in the purchaser's hand the beaded moccasins that always accompanied a weasel-tail shirt, and guided them in levelling out the pile of white clay. The purchaser then dropped the moccasins, and, guided again by the seller, pressed his forefinger into the clay, making a hole that symbolized a weasel's burrow. Next he made the "weasel's tracks" around the margin by pressing in the clay with his first and middle fingers. Finally, still guided by the seller, he dropped a little yellow paint into each mark, thus completing his altar.

With the seller leading, both men danced sunwise around the tent shouting. The singers chanted their song four times, and at the close of the fourth rendition the dancers sat down again. This ended the ceremony proper, but before the purchaser might leave the seller had to drop bunches of white sage across the north side of the tent, and for some distance outside it, so that his feet might not touch the bare ground.

THE GHOST DANCE

In the latter half of the nineteenth century, perhaps even earlier, there arose among the Sarcee a peculiar dance known as the Ghost Dance, which apparently had no connection with the Messianic phenomenon of the same name that spread so widely throughout the United States. The Sarcee themselves relate the following legend to explain its origin:

One winter when the Sarcee were living in two camps not far apart a young man from one camp went over to visit some people in the other. During his absence a girl in his own camp died. Her people buried her in a tree and moved away, leaving behind only one small tent in which the dogs had sheltered. After they had gone the youth returned, carried a load of wood into this tent, lit a fire, and sat down at the back to remove his leggings and moccasins, which were wet from the journey, and as he removed them one by one he threw them towards the door, exclaiming that, just as though he were married and his wife were sitting there. Hardly had he thrown his last legging when a young girl entered the tent and said "Why, certainly, I will dry them for you"; and she squeezed them out and hung them up to dry. The youth was frightened but she said to him "Why are you afraid? You said 'Dry that,' and I come to dry it for you. Don't be afraid. I shall be your wife." She remained and became his wife.

The next morning they took down their tent and followed his kinsmen's trail to their camp. For a time their lived happily, and she bore him a son. Of one thing she warned him, that, however angry he might be with her, he should never wish that she were a ghost.

One day he killed a buffalo, and carried some of the meat to his tent, where he invited some of his kinsmen to eat with him. The tent became filled with smoke, and he sent his wife out to adjust its ears; but in spite of her efforts the smoke persisted. In his anger he called out "I wish you were a ghost"; then, recollecting her warning, he added "I am sorry I said that." After a time his wife re-entered, put on her blanket, and said to him "Take care not to go to sleep to-night." Soon afterwards she went to bed with her child, while her husband sat up and watched. He became sleepy towards morning and thought that he would lie down and rest without closing his eyes; but as he rested he fell asleep. Suddenly he awoke, stirred up the fire, and drew the blanket from his wife and child. Nothing, remained of them except dry bones. For hours he wept bitterly, but finally he wrapped the bones neatly in the blanket and deposited them in a tree.

With the coming of summer he started out on a long journey, and after travelling for many days sighted on top of a hill some ragged tents, the tents of the shades. A man's shade approached him and said "Human being, our chief invites you to his tent." Following his guide he entered the chief's tent, to which flocked all the other shades in the camp. The chief said to him "You are looking for your wife. She passed here three days ago." They gave him water in a hollow vessel made from the backbone of a buffalo, which he thought he could drain without difficulty; but however much he drank, always a little remained in the vessel. They gave him a little pemmican in a similar dish, and that too he was unable to finish. After he had eaten and drunk he continued his journey.

Now he came to another camp, where he received the same reception, and learned that his wife had passed there two days before. He travelled on to a third; his wife had passed that one only one day before. Then he reached the fourth camp. A shade came out to meet him and conduct him to the tent of his father-in-law, who said to him "Your wife is here."

In the country of the shades day was night and night day. His father-in-law called in all the shades, and, after passing around a lighted pipe, bade them stand while he chanted the "ghost" song. As he chanted he danced four times around the ring moving his left arm as though working a pump-handle, and at the end of the song resumed his seat. When the shades sat down after him the young many noticed that the crowns of their heads had become like those of human beings. After his father-in-law had danced a second time their became human from the waists upwards; after he had danced a third time, holding in his hand a forked stick decorated with two eagle plumes, they became almost completely human; and after he had danced for the fourth time, they changed entirely to human beings, joined in his song, and at its close left the tent.

All through the performance the young man had searched their faces for his wife, but it was not until they had gone that he found her, lying at the side of a tent wrapped in a robe. His father-in-law said to her "Rise, my daughter, your husband has come for you." Her little child rose with her, and, recognizing its father, ran over to him. Thus the man regained his wife. From him first the Indians learned the Ghost Dance and song.

The function of this Ghost Dance was the healing of sickness, yet if was the property of an individual and could be bought and sold like any tangible medicine-object. Its owner, when summoned to the aid of a sick man, painted his face and body with yellow ochre or white clay, according to his fancy, prayed over the patient, and -sang a special song, while the audience remained silently kneeling. He then intoned the ghost song proper, whereupon the audience rose and joined in, holding blankets over the right arms and "pumping" with the left. It then repeated the song while the owner and the patient hopped around the ring, the former leading. Later he received a substantial payment for his services.

The Carrier Indians
of
the Bulkley River
Their Social and Religous Life

by
Diamond Jenness

First published by the Smithsonian Institution, Bureau of American
Ethnology, Bulletin 133, Anthropological Papers No. 25.
Washington: 1943.

Rock's
Mills
Press

PREFACE

This report is the outcome of a visit to the northern interior of British Columbia during the winter of 1924–25,* when I spent 3 months at Hazelton and Hagwilgate, and periods of about a week each at Fort Fraser, Stony Creek, and Prince George. I made no attempt to investigate the material culture or the language of the Carrier Indians, since these subjects had been adequately covered by Father Morice.

The spelling of the numerous Indian names has presented some difficulty. In the field they were recorded phonetically ; but since this report has little value for linguists, and a welter of phonetic symbols would unnecessarily increase the difficulties of the reader, the words have been reduced to their nearest equivalents in English spelling, and only those special characters retained that seemed absolutely indispensable. These characters are: χ, sound of ch in Scotch loch or German ach; χ., sound of ch in German ich; q, the uvular equivalent of k; ł, voiceless l; ω, sound of aw in law; · (period above the line), denotes double length of the preceding vowel or consonant; ' (above or after a letter), glottal stop; and ', breathing. Ch represents the sound of ch in church.

The folk tales collected during the same winter have already been published under the title "Myths of the Carrier Indians of British Columbia." (See Jenness, 1934.)

---

* In fact Jenness actually spent five months there in 1923–24.

LOCATION AND RELATIONS WITH NEIGHBORING PEOPLES

The westernmost subtribe of the Carrier Indians, the Hwitsowitenne, "Clever People," as it called itself, occupied the basin of the Bulkley River, an important tributary of the Skeena in northern British Columbia, together with a block of territory that extended for an uncertain distance to the south (fig. 1). Flanking it on three sides were other subtribes of the same Carrier nation, but on the west were Gitksan Indians of the Tsimshian stock, whose nearest village, Hazelton, lay only 4 miles from the Carrier village of Hagwilgate (plate 1).

After 1800 there were many disturbances of population in this area due to epidemics of diseases, the growth of European settlements, and the greater ease of communication through the building of roads and a railway. Many Carrier families were blotted out and their places taken by immigrant families from other districts; and there was much intermarriage with the neighboring Gitksan Indians. Today the sub-tribe numbers rather more than 300, and has two main settlements, Hagwilgate and Moricetown, while a few families reside at other villages along the

Plate 1. Modern village of Hagwilgate. (Photographs by C.M. Barbeau.)

line of the transcontinental railway. Some of the Indians remain in their settlements throughout the entire year, others cut ties for the railway in winter, or hunt and trap in remote districts where the land is not yet preempted by white settlers and game still survives in fair numbers. Two or three families even roam occasionally as far south as the Eutsuk lake area, which the Bulkley people incorporated into their territory after the earlier inhabitants, who seem to have formed a distinct subtribe, were destroyed by an epidemic of smallpox about 1838. In summer, again, there is generally a slight movement to the coast, where a few natives find employment in the salmon canneries during the fishing season.

EARLIER HISTORY

To recover the history of this Bulkley River subtribe prior to the nineteenth century seems impossible. Its members claim that they originally possessed one village only, Dizkle·, "Dead trees all pointing in one direction," which they locate on a site now farmed by a white man at Mosquito Flat, 12 miles east of Hazelton on the Bulkley River. Here, whither the salmon ascended in huge shoals, the Indians had built houses on both sides of the river, and constructed a dam from one bank to the other. The cluster of houses on the right bank was known as Kwatso, "Excreta," and the larger cluster on the left bank Hahwilamax, "Place where people throw away turnips," because in the vicinity were many wild "turnips" that the Indians both roasted for food and tossed like balls to one another on a large sand bar in the middle of the river. Hahwilamax boasted of one very large house, Tsam'dek' (said to be buried now 2 1/2 feet under the ground), which was the residence of Guxlet, the chief of a small section of the subtribe, the Thin House clan of the Gilserhyu phratry; for though all members of the subtribe, and even Gitksan Indians from the Skeena river, Carriers of the Babine Lake subtribe, and Sekani from beyond Babine Lake, gathered at Dizkle· each year to trap the migrating salmon, the surrounding territory (called Dizkle· like the village) was the hunting reserve of this one section of the Bulkley subtribe, and no one might hunt there except members of the same phratry. The Hagwilgate canyon, then as now, was the boundary line between the Bulkley Carrier and the Gitksan Indians, who had a permanent home of their own at Temlaham, 4 miles below Hazelton; and the dispersal of the two peoples from their respective villages, Dizkle· and Temlaham, led to the establishment of all the modern villages in the area, to Moricetown and Hagwilgate by the Carrier subtribe, and to Hazelton, Kitwanga, and other places by the Gitksan.

So runs one tradition of the Carrier. According to another, Dizkle· was the original home of three distinct tribes, the western Carrier, the Sekani, and the Gitksan. Superstitious fear when two squirrels inspected their dam made them scatter and flee to their present homes; and the passage of years has produced their present differentiation (Jenness, 1934, p. 241).

Plate 2a. Canyon in the Bulkley River, Showing the modern high-level bridge and the ruins of the old village of Hagwilgate below the cliff. (Photograph by D. Jenness.)

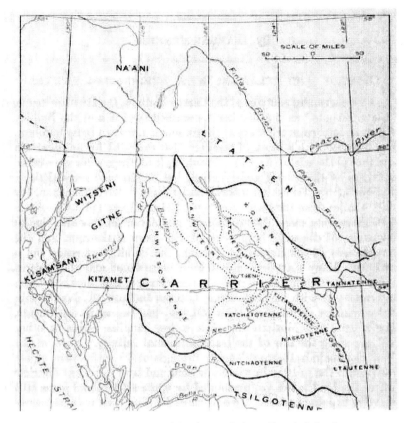

Figure 1 Subdivisions of the Carrier Indians, British Columbia

I have examined the supposed site of Dizkle·, and Harlan I. Smith, archeologist of the National Museum of Canada, has visited the traditional site of Temlaham. In neither place did we discern any traces of a permanent settlement. One may reasonably doubt, therefore, whether the two villages, glorified by similar legends, ever held the prominent place that tradition assigns to them, if indeed they ever existed outside the fertile imaginations of the Indians.

At the opening of the nineteenth century the principal fishing-place and village of the Bulkley Carrier was at Moricetown. Hagwilgate was established only about 1820, when a rock slide in its canyon almost blocked the river and allowed very few salmon to pass beyond (plate 2a). Most of the inhabitants of Moricetown then moved en masse to the canyon and built new homes on a narrow shelf below it; but they abandoned this rather inaccessible site toward the end of the century and established their present village on the terrace above. The last survivor of the migration from Moricetown, Satsa'n, died in 1914 at the age of about 90.

RELATIONS WITH SURROUNDING PEOPLES

Ease of travel in modern times has brought the Bulkley Indians greater knowledge of their fellow Carriers to the east, and revealed to them other Indian tribes in British Columbia of whom they were ignorant in earlier days. This greater knowledge is reflected in the accompanying sketch-map, which outlines their conception of the names and boundaries of their own and other Carrier subtribes in the latter half of the last century. (See fig. 1.)

Of the easternmost Carrier they apparently knew very little until recently; but with their fellow-Carriers of Babine and Fraser Lakes the Bulkley people always maintained close and friendly relations, marred in the case of the Fraser Lake Indians by only one feud of which they retain any recollection. Equally friendly were their relations with the Gitksan Indians; the difference in their speech neither debarred intermarriage, nor hindered the Bulkley Indians from absorbing many culture traits from their more advanced neighbors. The Gitksan controlled the trade route down the Skeena River to the coast that brought to the Carrier objects of shell and copper in exchange for moose hides and various furs. The coast Tsimshian, who were the principals in this trade, tried to eliminate the Gitksan middlemen about 1850, and, themselves ascending the Skeena, established a yearly market on an open flat at the junction of that river with the Bulkley. There for several years they carried on so amicable a trade with the Carrier that a few of the latter ventured to accompany them back to the coast and to pass the winter months in their midst; but about 1866 a quarrel over some transaction led to a fight in which both sides sustained several casualties. One account states that the Tsimshian returned the following summer and demanded the surrender of the Bulkley River valley in compensation for their losses; but that they never took possession of the area, though the Carrier agreed to their terms. More credible, however, is the following version of the conflict and its issue:

Plate 2b. A Fort Fraser family outside its house. (Photograph by D. Jenness.)

> The Tsimshian ascended the Skeena in about 50 canoes and camped at Mission Flat, where that river is joined by the Bulkley. In the course of bartering a Hagwilgate Indian quarrelled with a Tsimshian man over the price of some article and fired his gun to intimidate the dealer. Thereupon the Tsimshian, fear-

ing treachery, seized their weapons and shot indiscriminate-
ly at men, women, and children; and the Hagwilgate natives
retaliated. Finally the latter retreated to their village, and the
Tsimshian, loading up their canoes, hurried back to the coast.
For three years they did not return. Then a large party appeared
in ten canoes, and the two peoples concluded peace at a great
potlatch in which the Tsimshian, as the aggressors in the fight,
paid compensation for every Carrier who was slain.

Besides the Tsimshian proper, Indians from the Nass River visited the
Bulkley Carrier in order to barter oolakan grease for marten and other furs;
and more than once the Carrier, pressed by famine toward the end of winter,
themselves traveled through the territory of the Gitksan to one or other of the
Nass villages in order to purchase oolakan and other food. Yet they have always
disliked the Nass River people, and still remember with bitterness an episode
that occurred about 1864. The story, as related by one of the last survivors,
who in 1924 was a blind old man tottering toward his grave, throws an interesting light on the customs of the Indians at that time.

One winter when our people were starving, my family, together
with my uncle Gyedamskanish, Bini, the chief of the Beaver
phratry, and many others traveled overland to Gitlaxdamks village on the Nass River to buy oolakan grease. Soon after our
arrival my father discovered that one of the inhabitants bore the
same title and crest as himself, and, claiming kinship, ordered
me to lodge for the night with his namesake while he and the
rest of the family lodged elsewhere. He came to the door early
next morning and said to me, "We have bought all we want and
will leave the village before noon." So a number of us started
back for Hagwilgate, and after traveling a few miles camped
near a stump that supported a huge stone. I and some other
youths tried in turn to push this stone over, and when it crashed
to the ground under our united efforts we raised a shout of victory and returned to our camp.

Now, some Gitwinlkul men who were passing heard our
shouts and came to see what was happening. My father said to
them, "Our lads were merely pushing a stone off a stump." But
they answered, "That was the gravestone of the late chief of the
village." Greatly alarmed, my father begged them to keep the
deed secret, but they immediately went on to the village and
spread the news everywhere. Then a woman rushed weeping
into a house where some of our people were eating and cried,
"Why do we feast these wretches? They have disturbed the
grave of our chief." About half our people, led by Bini, retreated
inside another house; the rest hastened after us and told us
to flee, because Nass, Kispiox, and Gitwinlkul Indians were all
mustering in pursuit. We did flee, but the Nass natives overtook
and captured those who were in the rear. One captive, a noble-

woman named Anklo', they proposed to enslave, but she said
to them, "You cannot make me a slave, for I am the daughter
of a chief. If you carry me off as a captive, you must take also
two slave girls for me to lean upon. Besides, why do you want to
make me a prisoner? Neither I nor my family touched the grave,
but Gyedamskanish yonder and his family." They led her away
nevertheless, and with her two slave women to attend to her
wants. A Kispiox Indian then disarmed Gyedamskanish, who
said to them, "Remember that I am a chief. What are you going
to do with me?" "You must return with us," they answered, "to
pay for the insult you offered the grave." "Take my brother also,"
he said, "We will die together"; and when they paid no attention
to his words he turned to his brother and said, "Come. Let us go
together." The two men were led out onto the ice of the river and
ordered to run up and down while their enemies mocked them
and shot at them with guns, Gyedamskanish brother dropped
dead at the first shot, but Gyedamskanish himself, though frequently wounded, ran up and down for nearly half an hour before he fell with a bullet through his thigh. The Nass Indians
then burned their corpses and returned to Gitlaxdamks.

Meanwhile an influential Indian had concealed another of
my uncles inside a large chest, and when the villagers searched
the house sat on top of it and refused to move away; his countrymen dared not disturb him on account of his high rank. My uncle's wife stood near him, grasping a large knife in readiness to
stab the first man who molested her husband or herself, but no
one laid a hand on her. Bini and the rest of our people barricad-
ed themselves inside another house throughout the night, while
their enemies threatened them from outside and occasionally
fired off their guns.

Early the following morning the principal chief of the village sent round word to all the houses that the fighting should
cease and that our people should move over to his house along
a path strewn with the white eagle-down that symbolizes peace.
Preceded by a messenger carrying a white feather, he then conducted them to our camp, a day's journey away, and we returned
home without further mishap.

Some time afterward a party of Nass Indians came to Ha-
zleton to conclude a peace with us. They assembled within the
potlatch house beside a huge pile of blankets, and we went down
from Hagwilgate and stood outside, myself and another youth,
the nearest relatives of Gyedamskanish, in the forefront. After our enemies had presented us with a number of blankets,
we followed them inside the house and ranged ourselves along
one wall while they lined up against the other. Every man was
dressed in his finest clothes and carried a gun and a knife,
but, to prevent trouble, I and my companions sat in front of the
Nass River chief and two Nass youths occupied corresponding

places in front of our chief. As soon as we were thus seated, the two ringleaders in the murder approached us and placed a red-tipped feather on each of our heads to indicate that they intended to pay full compensation. Then one of them delivered a speech declaring that they wanted to make peace, and, shaking a rattle, danced and sang a sonet. The sonet that he sang is a special chant used by Carrier, Tsimshian, Haida, Kitimat, Bella Coola, and other tribes whenever they make peace with each other. Though I know the words, I cannot understand their meaning, because they are in neither the Tsimshian nor the Carrier tongue.

As the man repeated the song, both his Nass companions and my own people joined in. I, for my part, rose to my feet and, to show that he was smoothing out the issue, held flat on my outstretched palm a tail feather from an eagle. But before the singing ended I thought to myself, "They haven't paid us enough," and I turned the feather on its edge. Immediately the man broke off his chant, and his people added more blankets to those they had surrendered to us already. He then began his song anew, and this time I held the feather flat on my hand until he ended. Since we all felt too sad to hold a feast in common, my kinsmen, without further delay, gathered up the blankets and returned to Hagwilgate, while I and my companion, to cement the peace, stayed 4 days in Hazelton with the Nass Indians and danced with them each evening.

Two years after my uncles were murdered some of us went over to the Nass River, collected their bones, and deposited them on top of a pole at Hagwilgate. At the same time we brought back Gyedamskanish' widow, whom the Nass Indians had detained after her husband's death.

Still another coast people with whom the Bulkley Carrier came into conflict were the Kitimat Indians of Douglas Channel, a Kwakiutl-speaking people who sometimes hunted beyond the divide of the Cascade Mountains within the basin drained by the Zymoetz and Telkwa Rivers. It is noteworthy that both the Kitimat and the Carrier Indians were divided into five phratries, one of which was named the Beaver, and that neither a five-phratry division nor a phratry called the Beaver seems to appear anywhere else in British Columbia. This supports the tradition of the Bulkley Carrier that they borrowed several features in their peculiar social organization from the Kitimat Indians (Jenness, 1934, p. 232), and suggests that a few centuries ago the contact between the two peoples may have been more intimate than in recent times, when the Gitksan have lodged between them like a wedge. A well-frequented trail leads from Kitimat to Terrace and there forks, one branch leading up the Skeena River to the Bulkley, and another up the Zymoetz River to the Telkwa, which again leads to the Bulkley. It would seem not impossible that the Carrier Indians once controlled the Skeena River down to Terrace and the boundary of the Kitimat Indians, but were then driven back inland by the Gitksan, who perhaps crossed over from the Nass River. To speculate further in this direction, however, is futile until we know in detail the social organization of the Kitimat Indians and can compare it closely with that of the Carrier.

With the Bella Coola Indians, the Bulkley Carrier had no direct relations, although they may have met a few individuals when visiting the Carrier sub-tribes in the Eutsuk lake and other areas to the south and southeast. They were better acquainted with the Sekani of the Findlay and Parsnip River Basins who often visited the north end of Babine Lake during the nineteenth century, probably also in earlier times; and they vaguely remember the now extinct T'set'sa'ut as another Athapaskan-speaking tribe, living behind Gitwinlkul, that was destroyed by the Tsimshian or Nass Indians. Some assert, indeed, that the inhabitants of Gitwinlkul itself once spoke the T'set'sa'ut tongue, and that a T'set'sa'ut woman was a slave for many years among the Tsimshian of the coast. Concerning the Tahltan of the Stikine River Basin they had little knowledge until the middle of the nineteenth century, when the two peoples sometimes met at Bear Lake or at Old Fort Babine; yet it was doubtless a vague rumor of the Tahltan that gave rise to the legend of a semihuman race far to the north, the Na'ani, wonderfully skilled in hunting (Jenness, 1934, p. 242). Today the Bulkley Carrier call both the Sekani and the Tahltan Itateni, or, more rarely, by their Tsimshian name T'set'sa'ut; but neither tribe has ever influenced them appreciably, or promoted any changes in their material culture, or their social and religious life, comparable with the changes promoted by the nearer Kitimat and Gitksan.

Among these surrounding peoples the Bulkley Indians, like a many-tentacled cephalopod, had wandering feelers gathering sustenance that enriched the community's life. Yet there was no central nervous system to coordinate the movements of the feelers and to assimilate or reject their booty, no ruling chief or established council to control the actions of the different families and govern their relations with the outside world. Like other Carrier subtribes, the Bulkley natives were divided into a number of fraternities or phratries, each intimately associated with the others, yet politically independent. The phratries assembled and lived together at the same fishing places each season, they joined in common feasts and ceremonies, and they united at times to repel a common danger; but they all owned separate hunting territories to which their members repaired for the winter months, and they associated at will with foreign peoples even when these might be hostile to others of their countrymen. Since there was no regulation of foreign intercourse and trade and no hindrance to marriage outside the community, foreign ideas and foreign customs could take root in one family or phratry without permeating the others. It was only the constant association, the ties of kinship and marriage, the uniform dialect, and the pressure of common interests that counteracted the strong centrifugal tendencies and knitted the phratries into a definite, though headless, unit justifying the name of a subtribe.

POLITICAL ORGANIZATION
PHRATRIES

The Bulkley Carrier recognized five phratries, which they named Gitamtanyu, Gilserhyu, Laksilyu, Laksamshu, and Tsayu. The suffix *yu* or *shu* in these words means "people," and the prefix *gi* in two of them has the same meaning in Tsimshian. Only one of the five names, Tsayu, "beaver people," is a true Carrier word, the rest being derived apparently from other sources.[1]

Of the other Carrier subtribes, the Babine Lake, west end of Fraser Lake, Cheslatta Lake, and Fort Fraser, recognized the same five phratries under exactly the same names,[2] except that the Babine Indians called Laksilyu, the third phratry, Kwanpe'hwotenne, "People of the fire-side," while the Cheslatta Lake and west Fraser Lake subtribes gave to the second phratry, Gilserhyu, the name Tso'yezhotenne, "the small spruce people."

The Stony Creek subtribe, on the other hand, recognized two phratries only, Gilserhyu and Yesilyu (= Laksilyu). With regard to the Stuart Lake subtribe there is some uncertainty. Father Morice (1892–93, p. 203) states that it possessed only four phratries, Lsamacyu, Tsayu, Yasilyu, and Tam'tenyu; but a Sekani Indian of Fort McLeod, who was related by marriage to the Stuart Lake people, said that there used to be five, and gave names for them that coincided with Morice's names, except that he substituted Eske for Tam'tenyu and added the fifth phratry Kwanpahotenne. I suspect, therefore, that there were originally five phratries at Stuart Lake just as elsewhere, but that in Morice's day two of them had amalgamated, as happened to two phratries among the Bulkley Carrier about 1865.

Hagwilgate, the westernmost Carrier village, lies only 4 miles from Hazelton, a village of the Gitksan Indians, and the two peoples commonly intermarry and participate in each other's ceremonies. The phratries of the one subtribe then equate with the phratries of the other; and a man or woman who at Hagwilgate belongs to the Gitamtanyu phratry is attached to the Laxgibu phratry at Hazelton. But the Gitksan Indians have only four phratries to balance the five of the Carrier, so that one phratry has to equate with two. The following table shows how the two systems amalgamate:

---

1. Lakselyu is evidently laxse'l, the name given by the Gitksan Indians of Hazelton to the Frog-Raven phratry; and laksamshu is probably the same as laxsamillix, the Hazelton name of the Beaver clan In the Eagle phratry.
2. Apart from minor dialectal differences

Carrier	Gitksan
Gitamtanyu	Laxgibu (Wolf phratry)
Gilserhyu and Laksilyu	Laxse'l (Frog-Raven phratry)
Laksamshu	Gisra'ast (Fireweed phratry).
Tsayu	Laxsamillix (a clan of the Laxski'k
	or Eagle phratry).

The phratries were the most important units within the sub-tribe. Though each was divided into two or more clans that had their own chiefs and distinctive crests, the phratry overruled its clans in many ways. Thus it regulated marriage, for no man could marry a woman of his own phratry, even though she belonged to a different clan in that phratry, and to another subtribe or nation. It took an active interest in all the relations of its members with the members of other phratries, supporting them in their grievances and bearing the responsibility of their misdeeds. Through its chief (who was always a chief of one of its clans) it controlled the division of the hunting territories among its members and acted as a unit in resisting aggression by other phratries. If the members of one clan erected a totem pole, the members of other clans within the phratry contributed generously to the expense and regarded themselves as part owners, so that it was not merely a clan totem pole, but belonged in a measure to the whole phratry. Furthermore, the phratries extended beyond the boundaries of the subtribe far more widely than the clans, so that a man's phratric affiliation gained him support and help where his specific clan was unknown. The first question asked of a stranger (if it were not apparent from his dress or tattooing), was not "what clan does he belong to," or even "what subtribe does he belong to," but "what is his phratry?" And any Laksamshu man, for example, who found himself in a strange Gitksan village looked for a house belonging to the Fireweed phratry (the phratry corresponding to his own) and sought there the protection that he could claim on no other ground, perhaps, than membership in a common phratry.

CLANS

The following table shows the clans into which the phratries were divided, and gives the title of the chief who ruled each clan.

Phratry	Clans	Title of Chief
Gitamtanyu	A, Grizzly House (Kyas-ya')	Wω.s ("Whale")
	Bl, House in the Middle of Many (kaiyawinits)	Giste·hwa
	B2, Anskaski	Medi'k ("Grizzly Bear")

Gilserhyu	A, Dark House (ya'tsaolkas)	Netipish ("Crane or Heron")
	B, Thin House (ya'tsowitan)	Guxlet
	C, Birchbark House (kai-ya')	Samuiχ
Laksilyu	A, House of Many Eyes (giner-klai-ya')	Hagwilnexł
	B, House on Top of a Flat Rock (tsekal-kai-ya')	Widaxkyet (Big Man)
	C, House Beside the Fire (kwanper-ya')	Widak'kwats.
Laksamshu	A1, Sun or Moon House (sa ya')	Smogitkyemk.
	A2, Twisted House (ya'hostiz)	
	B, Owl House (misdzi-ya')	Klo'mkan ("Forest Slide")
Tsayu	Beaver House (djakan-ya')	Kwi·s

Notes:
Sun or Moon House (sa ya'): The word *sa* means heavenly luminary, either sun or moon.
Beaver House (djakan-ya'): According to one old man, the clan (and the chief's house) was called Skeyuya': Eagle House, after its other crest. Possibly it had both names, the second, Eagle House, being more familiar to the neighboring Gitksan Indians.

The interpretations of these clan names are in some cases obscure. The Grizzly, Sun or Moon, Owl, and Beaver Houses derive their names from their principal crests; and the House of Many Eyes from an incident in the legend attached to its crest.[3] House in the Middle of Many was so-called because the house of its chief was once erected in the middle of a village; and House on Top of a Flat Rock because the house of a former chief at Moricetown was built upon a rock. The meaning of the word Anskaski, and the origins of the names Birchbark House and Twisted House, seemed unknown. For Kwanperya the Indians offered two different interpretations, "House Beside the Fire" and "House of a Small Bird named Kwanpe." The title "Dark House" refers to the custom of quenching the house fire on the eve of a pot-latch, when the chief of the clan sang and danced in the gloom. The Thin House boasted leadership by two chiefs, one of whom had moved up from Hazelton when the village was established in the Hagwilgate canyon. His old home (and section of the clan?) in Hazelton had borne the name "Robin's House," because tradition stated that its founder had once visited the nightly home of the robins in the land of the dead (Jenness, 1934, p. 144); but when he moved up with his people to

---

3. For the legends concerning these crests, see Jenness (1934, pp. 214, 225, 232).

Hagwilgate, the clan name was changed to Thin House, because the pillars in the new home were flattened on the inside instead of rounded.

The clans have been listed in the order of their recent standing within their respective phratries. Yet the system was not absolutely rigid, for it underwent changes even during the last hundred years. About 1865 the Tsayu phratry was so decimated by smallpox that its members voluntarily incorporated themselves in the Laksamshu phratry, where they now rank merely as one clan. The Twisted House of the Laksamshu phratry was really a part of the Sun or Moon House that separated off under its own chief when the Sun House became very numerous. Similarly, the two clans in Gitamtanyu phratry, House in the Middle of Many, and Anskaski, had a single origin, though which was the earlier is now uncertain; a member of the House in the Middle of Many claimed priority for his clan, but at the present time the chief of Anskaski clan occupies a higher seat at potlatches.

The head man of a clan was called tene·za', "chief;" his wife (or the principal wife, if he had more than one), zegaiz·a. He was supported by a body of nobles, skez·a, most of whom were close kinsmen. Below the nobles were the common people of each clan, auxtaten'e, and below the common people the slaves, eɬne, who seem never to have been as numerous as among the coast tribes, and, indeed, owned by few Indians except the chiefs. The chief of the leading clan was the recognized head of the phratry, and the heads of the different phratries were coordinate in rank, though the one who had the largest following might possess more power and influence.[4] The principal settlements, Moricetown and Hagwilgate, contained representatives of all the phratries, usually also of all the clans. In such places the maintenance of peace and harmony rested on both the clan and the phratry chiefs. Each clan chief normally settled disputes that extended no farther than his own little unit; when they involved another clan in the same phratry, the head of the phratry, counseled by his clan chiefs, settled them; and when they involved other phratries the heads of the phratries consulted, first with their clan chiefs, then with each other, decided the issues at stake, and arranged for any necessary compensation.

In early times, when Moricetown was still the best place in the district for catching salmon, every clan had there its individual fishing stands, and every clan chief a permanent home. The settlement declined when the landslide 20 miles below partially blocked the Bulkley River, and the majority of the sub-tribe established the new village, Tsekya, "Rock-foot," beside the Hagwilgate canyon. How many houses this new village contained originally is not known, but after the smallpox epidemic of 1862 it possessed not only 9 large houses, each of which provided a home for perhaps 20 people, but also a number of smaller houses that sheltered on the average 5 or 6. The 9 large houses were the homes of the clan chiefs and their nearest relatives, and bore the same

---

4. The strongest phratries at Hagwilgate today are the Laksilyu and the Laksamshu, which rank about equal, although the latter has the larger membership. At Moricetown the strongest phratry is the Laksilyu.

names as the clans. Grizzly House, etc.; but while the Gitamtanyu and Gilserhyu phratries were represented by a large house for each clan, Laksilyu had
only 2 large houses, House of Many Eyes and House beside the Fire; Laksamshu only 1, Owl's House; and the Tsayu or Beaver phratry no large house at
all, having abandoned its dwelling when the epidemic carried away nearly all
its members (see Plan, fig. 2).

DESCRIPTION OF PLAN OF OLD CARRIER VILLAGE AT HAGWILGATE CANYON

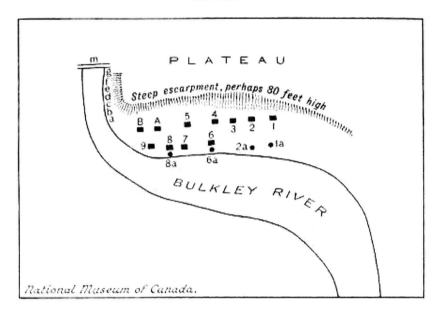

Diagrammatic Plan of old Carrier Village Tse'kya, "Rock-Foot," beside the Hagwilgate Canyon on
the Bulkley River, British Columbia (*a–g* mark the fishing places of the various phratries.)

1. House of Many Eyes, Laksilyu phratry. This clan house was partly preserved
in 1924.

la. Totem pole of this house, known as kaigyet.

2. House in the Middle of Many, Gitamtanyu phratry. Partly preserved in 1924.

2a. Totem pole of this house, known as esrił, "fungus."

3. Anskaski, Gitamtanyu phratry. In 1924 there remained of this house only
two pairs of beams supporting a ridge pole. It had no totem pole.

4. House beside the Fire, Laksilyu phratry. Of this house there remained only
a few logs rotting on the ground. A flat stone that lay on the threshold served
as an unusually fine doorstep.

5. Dark House, Gilserhyu phratry. This house also was reduced to a few rotten

logs. It had no totem pole.

6. Grizzly House, Gitamtanyu phratry. Its site was hardly discernible.

6a. Totem pole of the Grizzly House, known as Grizzly Bear.

7. Thin House, Gilserhyu phratry. There remained on the ground a few logs. It had no totem pole.

8. Owl House, Laksamshu phratry. A few rotten logs remained.

8a. Totem pole of the Owl House, known as Fireweed, though today sometimes called Owl. It really belonged to the Beaver phratry.

9. Birchbark House, Gilserhyu phratry. In 1924 its site was hardly discernible. It had no totem pole.

A, B. Two houses of recent date, owned by Gitksan Indians of Hazelton.

a–g. Fishing places owned by different clans but open to use by a member of any clan or phratry.

m. Modern suspension bridge.

Since the phratries were exogamous units, so also in consequence were the clans, although the decline of the system in recent years has permitted several marriages within the phratries. Children belonged to the clans and phratries of their mothers, not of their fathers, for inheritance and descent followed the female line.

All the hunting territory of the subtribe was partitioned among the different phratries, and trespassing on the territory of another phratry without the consent of its chief led to quarrels and often bloodshed. Within the phratric territory each clan had its recognized hunting grounds that were theoretically subject to endorsement by the phratric chief and to any limitations and changes he might make in the interests of his phratry, but were practically inviolate as long as the clan was strong enough to resent encroachment. The families made mutual arrangements where each would hunt, and two or three generally traveled and camped together. The country was too thinly settled to give occasion for many disputes, and such as did arise were settled by the clan or phratry chiefs. It is said that the phratry chief sometimes remained in the village all winter and did not go out to the hunting grounds, but was supplied with beaver, caribou, and other meat at irregular intervals by returning hunters.

At the present time, individual noblemen who are not even clan chiefs claim possession of one or two small hunting grounds, and their claims are recognized by the rest of the Indians even though they admittedly violate the principle of phratric and clan ownership. But the clan and phratric chiefs have lost their authority, and game has become so scarce that many families do not find it worth their while to hunt, so that no one wishes to stir up trouble by disputing claims which, after all, have little value. How they first came to make these claims is not quite clear. Apparently they were instigated by the growth of individual rights in other directions brought about by the decline of the phratries and clans, and by the indifference with which they had been permitted to reoccupy the same areas winter after winter for many years in succession. The division of the fishing grounds corresponded to the division of the hunting grounds. Each clan had the exclusive fishing rights over the lakes and streams within its hunting territories, subject theoretically to the jurisdiction of the entire phratry, exercised through its chief. Before the landslide occurred on the Bulkley Kiver at Hagwilgate, the best place in the whole district for trapping the migrating salmon was at Moricetown, the common center of the phratries; and on the dam built there across the river most, if not all, of the clans had special stations where they could ply their gaffs or set their traps and baskets. The part of the subtribe that moved to Hagwilgate after the landslide subdivided among its clans, in exactly the same way, the various fishing stands in the Bulkley canyon; but the space was so limited, and fish so plentiful, that a member of any clan, in any phratry, might fish at any of the stands whenever it was not actually occupied by its proper owners. (See Plan, fig. 2.)

Fishing places, and portions of the hunting territories, were often sold or given away in payment for certain services. If a chief or nobleman of one phratry contributed generously to the expense of a potlatch given by a nobleman in another phratry,[5] the phratry that had received help, acting through its chief, might publicly "deed over" its fishing rights on a certain stream, or its title to hunt over a particular mountain. The new owners might retain these rights in perpetuity, but in most cases the transfer was regarded as a mortgage only, and the phratry that had originally owned the areas bought them back after three or four generations. In all such transactions the phratric chiefs played the leading roles, but they could not act without consultation with their clan chiefs and principal noblemen.

The hunting grounds are now greatly restricted through the growth of white settlement, the construction of roads and a railway, the leveling of large areas of forests, and the blocking out of the land for villages and farms. It seems impossible today to map the original hunting areas of the various clans. Those that they now claim are widely scattered, and often of very small extent; yet it may be useful to list them in an appendix (see Appendix 1), if only to illustrate, what seems to have been true in earlier times, that the hunting territory of each clan was not a single strip of country, but a number of discrete strips scattered here and there throughout the territory under the subtribe's dominion.

---

5. Such a contributor was called antoma'na'k. Formerly the man who was giving the potlatch threw all contributions from outside his phratry into the fire, but since 1910, or thereabouts, they have been incorporated with the main pile of goods set aside for distribution.

TITLES OF NOBLES

Every clan boasted the exclusive ownership of a number of titles which carried a more or less definite ranking and alone bestowed on their owners the
hallmarks of nobility. Women as well as men were eligible for all these titles,
and a few, of no great importance, were even restricted to women. In general,
accession to a title depended partly on inheritance, partly on the ability to
give the potlatch necessary to make its assumption valid. The usual successor
to a man's title was his sister's son or daughter; but if he had no children, or
misfortune prevented the validation of the child's claim by a proper potlatch,
the title might pass to a more distant kinsman in the same clan, even one who
previously had ranked among its commoners.[6] The boundary line between
nobles and commoners was therefore fluid. The son of a chief never became
a commoner, because his parents, if only for their own prestige, invariably
financed or contributed to the potlatch that gave him a title and opened for
him the gate to nobility; but a grandson or great-grandson might easily descend in the social scale, if his parents neglected to ensure his succession
by a potlatch and he himself lacked the necessary means. Descendants of
nobles below the rank of chiefs naturally glided into the abyss more readily,
because their parents' means were limited and kinsmen did not always rally
to their support. To climb the ladder again was difficult but not impossible, if
we may trust the statements of present-day Indians, and the traditions that
recount how friendless orphans through their own achievements married the
daughters of chiefs and received the titles of nobles. Doubtless Carrier society,
like many others, placed obstacles in the path of an aspiring nobody, and it
was only through exceptional circumstances that a commoner could amass
enough goods to give the one or more potlatches necessary for his elevation.
Yet the history of Satsa'n, a nobleman in the Gilserhyu phratry, bears out the
traditions of the Indians that the barriers were not insuperable.

Satsa'n's ancestors, a century ago, were commoners without ge-
nealogical history or prominence who occupied at potlatches
any place they could find in the vicinity of their fellow phratrymen. In the first half of the nineteenth century, however, one of
them proved so skillful a carpenter that Widaxkyet, a chief in
the Laksilyu phratry, engaged him to carve a totempole, promising him a rich reward. The man worked on the pole all winter
while the rest of the people were hunting; and when he had
finished the carving he covered the pole with birchbark to hide
it until the day of erection. The pole was duly raised into place
at Moricetown, and stood there until about 1870 when it fell

---

6. Whether it could pass to a commoner of the same phratry, but in another clan, is not clear. The
clan affiliation of a commoner seems to have been less fixed than his phratric affiliation, so that
few objections would be raised if the title were relatively unimportant, and the man could make
out a plausible genealogy. Even if he had no kinship claim, he could probably "jump" the title,
provided he possessed sufficient influence.

and was burned. At the close of the festivities connected with its erection the carpenter found himself possessed of so much property (partly gained by gambling) that he decided to give a potlatch on his own account. He therefore invited all the people, and before distributing his presents stood up and proclaimed, "Hereafter let me not sit in a corner like a nobody, but in front of my phratry in a special place beside the fire. And let me be known, not by my own name, but as Satsa'n." The chiefs of all the phratries consulted together and acceded to his request. He thus acquired a special rank that was neither a nobleman's nor a commoner's; but his niece, who succeeded to the title, ranked as a noble, though she retained the special seat beside the fire. Why the carpenter chose the title Satsa'n, which belonged to a Gitksan chief of Kitselas, on the Skeena River, the present-day Carrier do not know; they merely deny that there was any bond of kinship between the two families.

Although a title never passed, apparently, from one phratry to another, it was sometimes transferred temporarily, and perhaps permanently, from one clan to another within the phratry. Thus, a few years ago, when a member of the Dark House clan in the Gilserhyu phratry died, the clan transferred one of its nobles, Axal'kan, to the Thin House to repay that clan's members for their contributions to the funeral expenses. Under present conditions it really makes no difference whether Axal'kan's successor returns to the old clan or remains in the new, for the big semicommunal dwellings that used to be the chief outward signs of the clan have disappeared. The Indians seemed to think that Axal'kan's transfer was temporary only, and that the title would be "bought back" on some future occasion; but that permanent transfers had formerly occurred for special reasons, such as compensation for murders.

At the present time there are more titles in each clan than there are people qualified to fill them, so that nearly every man or woman who wishes to adopt a new one can choose between several; but whether this was the case in earlier years also is not certain. With the decline in population many titles seem to have found no claimants and dropped from memory. Others, again, may have been superseded by newer titles; for just as Sir Arthur Wellesley, after his victories in Spain, became the Duke of Wellington, so a Carrier nobleman could commemorate some event in his life by adopting a new name and establishing it among his countrymen by a potlatch. His earlier title then dropped out of use, or, more often perhaps, was bestowed on his probable heir, who passed it on to his own heir whenever he himself succeeded to the new-found name.

At feasts the clan chiefs sat together, the chief of the second ranking clan on the right of the phratry chief (i. e., the chief of the principal clan), and the chief of the third clan, if there were more than two, on the phratry chief's left. The nobles then stationed themselves nearer or farther from their chiefs in accordance with their rank; and directly in front of each man or woman sat the probable successor, nearly always a nephew or a niece. The commoners and such slaves as were admitted lined up at the back or wherever they could find room.

We are not unfamiliar, in our own society, with the serious disputes that have resulted in the course of state functions whenever the Ambassador of Timbuctoo has ventured to claim precedence over the Minister of Tierra del Fuego. Among the Bulkley Carrier similar quarrels arose over the order of seating at feasts and ceremonials, for this order was liable to change from one generation to another. At the present day they recognize the following arrangement, or "table of peerage," as it may be called, but a hundred years ago it was certainly rather different.

TABLES OF PEERAGE,
OR TITLES AND SEATING ARRANGEMENTS

GITAMTANYU PHRATRY

Clans: A, Grizzly House; B, House in the Middle of Many, and Anskaski

Rear row:

B8	B7	B6	B5	B4	B3	A2	Bl	Al	B2	A3	A4	A5	A6

Second row:

B3a	A2a	Bla	B2a

Front row:

B9	B10	B11

Titles

B8, Hʊlits (Skunk).[7]

B7, Sowi·s.[8]

B6, Hoigyet.

B5, Wʊ'silop'.

B4, Kano'ts.

B3, Na'ok.

A2, Djolukyet.

Bl, Medi·k (Grizzly Bear), chief of Anskaski clan and 2nd ranking chief in

---

7. Since the last holders of these titles died a few years ago, none have come forward to take their places.

8. Since the last holders of these titles died a few years ago, none have come forward to take their places.

the phratry.

Al, Wws (Whale), chief of the leading clan Grizzly House, chief of the phratry.

B2, Gistehwa, chief of the clan House in the Middle of Many and third ranking chief in the phratry.

A3, Skalił.

A4, Samsmahix̣.

A5, Gu'kyet.

A6, Guxwoq (Sleepy).

B3a, Ismediks (Grizzly cub), who is tlie legal successor to B3, Na'ok, and therefore sits directly in front of that nobleman.

A2a, Baxchan (War-leader), the legal successor of A2, Djolukyet.

Bla, Goqaiuwil, the legal successor of Bl, Medi-k.

B2a, Atne (Bella Coola or Kitlope Indian), the legal successor of B2.

B9, Dettsan (Raven), who must sit somewhere in front to the right of the chiefs.

B10, Hwille·wi, who must also sit in front to the right of the chiefs.

Bll, Nagwa'on (Long Arm), who must sit in front to the left of the chiefs.

A title Anklo', belongs to the clan House in the Middle of Many, but the position of its holder is not known.

At the present time there is attached to the phratry a Gitksan man bearing the Gitksan title Axgotdemash (Heartless, Cruel). Having no proper seat at potlatches he finds a place near the door, although he is trying to enroll himself in the Anskaski clan and recognizes its leading man Medi-k as his chief.

GILSERHYU PHRATRY

Clans: A, Dark House; B, Thin House; C, Birchbark House

Rear row: XI B6 B5 B4 A4 A3 A2 B3 Bl Al B2 CI X2 C2

                                     /\   /\

Third row: Ala Alb Cla Clb

Second row: C3 C4 B7   B8 B9 A5

Front row: C5

Titles

X1, Altu·z, a nobleman of little importance whose clan was not ascertained.

B6, Bita'nen.

B5, As'ten (Fraser Lake Indian).

B4, Gwatsikyet (He Who Cuts off Heads with a Knife).

A4, Anabel's.

A3, Nustel (Wolverine).

A2, Well (Back-pack).

B3, Ne'k (Slave).

Bl, Guxlet, chief of the Thin House clan.

Al, Netipish (Blue Heron), chief of the Dark House clan and chief of the phratry.

B2, Chaspit, second chief of the Thin House clan.

CI, Samuix. (Species of Small Bird), chief of the Birchbark House clan.

X2, Sama't, whose clan was not ascertained.

C2, Gwitsin'alu (alu, bunched together, but the meaning of the full name was unknown).

Ala, Mas'gibu (White Wolf), who sits directly in front of Al, the head chief, as one of two possible successors.

Alb, Gułta': the second possible successor of Al for the chieftainship.

Cla, Chani (Marten): a niece and possible successor of CI for the chieftainship of the Birchbark House.

C3, Guxkalkalas.

C4, Nenesenoxłkaix. (Let Some One Ferry Me Over in a Canoe).

B7, Tenez ik (Dead Man): more often called by the equivalent Gitksan work, lulak.

B8, Kana'u (Gitksan word, Frog).

B9, Axal'kan (Gitksan), or Wusnik (Carrier) (Crazy).

A5, Mistu's (Buffalo or Cow).

C5, Satsa'n, who occupies a special position near the fire in the center of the house.

LAKSILYU PHRATRY

Clans: A, House of Many Eyes; B, House on Top of a Flat Eock; C, House Beside the Fire.

Rear row:	X	B3	B2	Bl	Al	C1	A2	A3	A4
Front row:		B3a	B2a	Bla	Ala	Cla			

Titles

X, Dikyanteltam, whose clan was not ascertained.

B3, Hataxkumex.

B2, Dzi.

Bl, Widaxkyet (Big Man), chief of the clan House on Top of a Flat Rock and second chief of the phratry.

Al, Hagwilnexł; chief of the clan House of Many Eyes and principal chief of the phratry.

Cl, Widak'kwats (Grizzly's Big Dung), chief of the clan House Beside the Fire and third chief of the phratry.

A2, Kela.

A3, Maxlaxlexs.

A4, Dikyannulat (Grizzly that Bites and Scratches Trees). The present holder of the title, since becoming a Christian, does not attend potlatches, and his seat has been taken by Gwinu', a Tsimshian Indian from Gitwinlkul, for whom there was really no seat.

B3a, Stalo'p (Rain of Stones), who as the legal successor of B3 sits directly in front of that nobleman.

B2a, Wiste·s, the legal successor of B2.

Bla, Gowiehan (He Who Pays the Blood-price), the legal successor of Bl for the chieftainship of the clan.

Ala, Gyedamskanish (Mountain Man), nephew and legal successor of Al for the chieftainship of the clan and leadership of the phratry.

C1a, Axgot (Heartless), the legal successor of Cl for the chieftainship of the clan House Beside the Fire.

There are three other titles in this phratry. The title Klbe'kansi (kibe, "dentalium"), which belongs to the clan House Beside the Fire, has been assumed by a woman who sits anywhere behind the other nobles; Xa ("Goose"), which belongs to the clan House on Top of a Flat Rock, entitles its owner to sit anywhere that he can find room; and Negupte, which belongs to the same clan, has dropped out of use and the seat taken by its last possessor is not remembered.

The Hagwilnexl who preceded his nephew, the present Hagwilnexl, as chief of the House of Many Eyes and chief of the phratry, lived originally at Trembleur Lake, where he was either a nobleman in the same phratry, or its chief. When he moved to Hagwilgate in the latter half of the nineteenth century he succeeded, on the strength of some marriage connection, in wresting the title and chieftainship from its proper heir, Kela. There is consequently much ill-feeling in the House of Many Eyes clan, kept alive by the former and present chiefs' use of the clan hunting and fishing territories, to which as strangers from another subtribe they had no legal right.

COMBINED LAKSAMSHU AND BEAVER PHRATRIES

Clans; A, Sun House, including Twisted House; B, Beaver House; C, Owl House

Rear row:	B5	B4	B3	B2	Bl	Al	C1	A2	A3	C2	XI
Second row:							Cla				
Front row:						X2					

Titles

B5, Wigetumstchol (a Tsimshian word meaning "Large Beaver Man").

B4, Namoksu (Tsimshian word).

B3, Wila't (Tsimshian word meaning "Echo").

B2, Mat (Tsimshian word meaning "Mountain Goat").

Bl, Kwi·s, chief of the Beaver phratry and now second chief in the combined phratries.

Al, Smogitkyemk (Tsimshian word of which the last syllable means "Sun"); chief of the Sun House and principal chief in the combined phratries.

CI, Klo'mkan (Forest Slide), chief of the Owl House.

A2, Gutseut (Short Belly).

A3, Amgyet (Resurrected).

C2, Sa'pek (Tsimshian word).

XI, Biste'i (Tsimshian word meaning "Grouse"); the clan that owned this title was not ascertained.

Cla, Kitsilchak (Picks up Weapon Hastily); should succeed to the chieftainship of Owl House, but the title has fallen into disuse. The man who would normally inherit it has taken the title Axkis (Bald-head).

X2, Skokamlaxa (Tsimshian word); the possessor of this title came from Gitsegyukla (Skeena Crossing), and has no proper seat in the phratry.

There has been much confusion and dissension in the Laksamshu and Beaver phratries, since their fusion about 1865. Because the Laksamshu Sun clan was at that time the strongest, its chief became the dominant chief in the combined phratries and occupied the highest seat. The chief of the Beaver phratry then became the second ranking chief in the combined phratries, and the chief of the Owl House, or clan in the Laksamshu phratry, the third ranking chief. The last position (CI), however, was inherited by a woman who has few relatives to support her and at potlatches generally finds her seat usurped by the next ranking noble in the phratry, Gutseut (A2). Her husband claims that she should legally be the ranking chief of the combined phratries; that Smogitkyemk (Al) was originally chief of the Beaver phratry, and Klo'mkan (CI), ranking chief in Laksamshu phratry, with Gutseut (A2), the second chief, and Amgyet (A3), the third chief; and that Klo'mkan, after acquiring Amgyet's title also when its former owner died without descendants, has been pushed aside by Smogitkyemk and Gutseut. Other natives denied this, however, and asserted that Smogitkyemk had always been the title of the leading chief in Laksamshu phratry, the head of the Sun House. In addition to the dissension on this score, there is ill-feeling between Kwi·s (Bl) and Smogitkyemk (Al), the former wishing his phratry to have the precedence and himself to be the leading chief, as was his predecessor and uncle, a man named Kwi·s or Bini, who led a strong religious movement in the subtribe. The Beaver phratry, its present chief claims, is rapidly increasing in numbers, while the Laksamshu is now declining. It seems probable that the two phratries would separate again if the social system retained its old life, but the younger generation of Indians holds it in slight regard.

A cursory perusal of these peerage tables will indicate that many of the titles are in the Tsimshian tongue; in some, perhaps most, cases they coincide with titles actually in use among the Tsimshian. Yet only about a third of the Bulkley Carrier seem to have understood and spoken the Tsimshian language, so that the bearer of a title often knew little or nothing about its origin and real significance. This does not mean, however, that the Bulkley natives slavishly copied and borrowed from their Tsimshian neighbors. Their own system, though extremely fluid, was so full of vitality and life that it was capable of absorbing numerous elements from abroad without impairing its essential vigor. A more detailed examination of its structure will substantiate this point, which is deserving of some attention because it indicates that the system, far from being a recent growth among the Bulkley Indians, has a history extending back over several generations.

CRESTS, CLAN AND PERSONAL
CLAN CRESTS

The Bulkley Carrier, like our forefathers in medieval Europe, publicly represented their division into "houses," or clans, by the display of certain crests (nettse·), of which every clan boasted at least one, and usually several. Such crests were carved on the clan totem poles, painted or carved on the fronts of the chiefs' houses, painted on chiefs' grave-boxes, represented at times on the ceremonial hats and blankets the chiefs wore at dances (plate 3), and tattooed on the chests of the clansmen, on the wrists of the clanswomen, by close kinsmen of their fathers, who, of course, belonged to other phratries. Occasionally an individual was tattooed with his father's clan crest instead of his own, although this required permission from the chief of his father's clan. With nearly every crest went an origin legend that was not regarded as clan property, and might be related by any member of the

Plate 3. A Fort Fraser Indian wearing a cloth replica of the ancient costume, that shows his clan crests on the back. (Photographs by D. Jenness.)

tribe except at potlatches, when a sense of propriety restricted its narration to a clan member, generally to the highest-ranking member of the clan. Over the crests themselves, however, there was a jealous feeling of proprietorship, so that their representation by another clan in the same phratry without the consent of their owners led to serious friction, while their usurpation by a clan in another phratry was almost unthinkable. In clans that had several crests, one (or occasionally two) generally ranked very much higher than the rest, because it was more deeply rooted in the local history and traditions. This crest was then as permanent as the clan, and deeply concerned the entire phratry, which felt toward it the same proprietorship as it felt toward the clan. On the other hand, the minor crests, being of comparatively slight importance, could conceivably be alienated or even dropped.

Clan crests were not restricted to natural objects, but included mythical beings and manufactured articles. The Indians paid no special regard to them when they were birds and animals, but, if the creatures were edible, killed and ate them without ceremony. They did, indeed, ascribe a certain kinship between themselves and two or three of the most conspicuous crests, conceiving that the relationship gave them a certain measure of protection. Thus, if a man of the Laksamshu phratry encountered a whale that seemed likely to endanger his canoe, they believed he had merely to call out that he belonged to the Laksamshu phratry (which reckons whale as one of its principal crests) and the whale would leave him unharmed; even if he belonged to another phratry, but his father had been a Laksamshu man or his mother a Laksamshu woman, he could obtain the same immunity by calling, "My father (mother) was a Laksamshu," which was equivalent to saying, "I am one of your children." Similarly, a Laksamshu man, or the child of a Laksamshu man, was credited with power to stop continuous rain by waving a piece of burning birchbark and calling for sunshine, because the sun also was an important crest in the phratry.

A Bulkley Indian named Saiyella, while hunting with his wife some 40 years ago, came upon two grizzly bears eating berries on a hillside, and, in spite of his wife's warning that two grizzlies were too dangerous for one man to hunt, loaded his flint-lock and went after them. By careful stalking he drew close enough to shoot one animal, but as its body rolled down the hillside, the other grizzly clambered the slope to attack him. Unable to retreat, he rolled some big stones down on top of it, but still it continued to advance. He shouted, "Ha-a," and the bear stopped to listen, but after a moment moved towards him again. Then half weeping with fear, he shouted, "Why do you want to kill me, you grizzly. I am a Gitamtanyu man and you are my crest. Let me alone." Hurriedly ramming two more bullets down his muzzle-loader, he climbed a big rock, and when the grizzly came directly below him, shot it in the head. It rolled over and over down the hill, and as it rolled, he mocked it, shouting, "Why are you rolling down and down? I told you that I was a Gitamtanyu man and you persisted in attacking me. Why are you rolling down now?"

In spite of these instances, however, where one or two crests appeared to carry a totemic flavor it would be a mistake to look upon the system as really totemic. More correctly the crests were emblems, serving much the same purpose as the coats-of-arms adopted by the nobles of feudal Europe; and the representation of a clan crest on the house of a chief closely corresponded with the coat-of-arms carved over the gateway of a baron's castle, and the national flag that waves over our embassies.

TABLE OF CLAN CRESTS

GITAMTANYU PHRATRY

GRIZZLY HOUSE

Grizzly (kyas) and Wolf (yis).—A Gitksan Indian specially engaged for the task carved these two crests on the clan's totem pole in the Bulkley canyon. Below the summit, which was uncarved, was the figure of a wolf head downward; beneath the wolf was the grizzly standing up; and at the base of the pole, the grizzly seated. To explain the origin of both crests, the Indians invoke a single legend, "The Woman Who Married a Grizzly" (Jenness, 1934, p. 129), although the wolf does not appear in the recorded version of that legend.

HOUSE IN THE MIDDLE OF MANY, AND ANSKASKI CLAN

Raven (Dettsan).—This crest was represented in the Bulkley canyon by a carved image of a raven above the large dwelling of the clan House in the Middle of Many, and by two images, one above the other, on the totem pole in front of that house. The Carrier deduce the origin of the crest from the legend of the raven that perched itself on top of a totem pole in the land of the dead and gave warning of the approach of enemies (see Jenness, 1934, p. 234), a legend that they also cite to account for the origin of Guxlet, the title of the second chief in Gilserhyu phratry.

Fungus (esril).—Below the two ravens on the totem pole just mentioned is the figure of a man to whose back was formerly attached a large hollow ball of wood made in imitation of an enormous fungus. This represented the crest Fungus. Tradition states that the Hagwilgate members of the clan House in the Middle of Many once contributed very generously to a potlatch given by Nelli, a chief of the Gitamtanyu phratry among the Nitchaotin or Alkatcho subtribe to the south. At that time Nelli owned and was using as his crest an enormous ball of fungus, the right to which he transferred to his Hagwilgate helpers. They did not take the ball north with them, but hired a Moricetown Indian of another phratry, the Laksilyu, to carve a wooden imitation and attach it to their totem pole, which in consequence received the name esril, "fungus."

Weasel.—This crest was represented on the ceremonial headgear worn by the chief of the Anskaski clan, perhaps also by the chief of the other clan House in the Middle of Many.

GILSERHYU PHRATRY

DARK HOUSE

Logs Carved as Men (tutlemale·t).—This clan, like the other two clans of the Gilserhyu phratry, did not erect a totem pole, but at Hagwilgate displayed its crest inside the clan dwelling of the chief, which formerly had a row of carved images opposite the door.

THIN HOUSE

Three Stars (of no special constellation).—This crest was represented on the old house of the clan in the Hagwilgate canyon by three holes in the front wall. Today the chief, who lives in a modern frame house on the terrace above, has only one star painted above his door. The natives seemed to have no explanation for the crest.

Frog.—On the old clan house in the canyon, a frog was painted on the outside of the door. There was some disagreement concerning the origin of the crest. The majority of the Indians cited the legend of the "Girl Who Married a Frog" (Jenness, 1934, p. 168); but one man cited the legend of the "Woman Who Married a Grizzly" (Jenness, 1934, p. 129).

Small owl (deltsa).—This crest was painted on the outside of the door, beside the frog. Its origin seemed unknown.

Fire.—The front of the old clan house was painted red like fire. The crest is explained from the legend of the mythical chief of the clan, Guxlet, who came out of the ground (Jenness, 1934, p. 234),

Sidewalk (ye'n).—An early chief built a sidewalk in front of his house and, sitting there with his head covered with swansdown, issued invitations to a potlatch. When the people gathered for the feast he proclaimed that "side-walk" was to be regarded henceforth as his new crest, and endorsed his assumption of it by presenting each guest with a bowl of berries covered with mountain-goat fat. Thus only the Thin House possesses the right to build a platform or sidewalk in front of its clan dwelling and to regard it as a clan crest.

tsim'yak'ijak (meaning unknown).—This is the name of the mythical totem pole in the land of the dead (Jenness, 1934, p. 143), and would be the name of the clan's totem pole, if it ever erected one. Hence it ranks as a crest.

gitamgiye'ks (meaning unknown).—This crest would be represented on the clan totem pole by the figure of a man with uplifted palms and an image of a boy on his head. Legend states that it was acquired by a former chief of the clan who ate devilsclub for a year in order to have good luck in his hunting. He then met in the woods a strange woman carrying on her back a baby that cried, "wa wa wa." He snatched the baby away and, without placing it on his back, since it would have scratched and killed him, planted it in a tree beyond her reach, but finally restored it to her for a suitable reward. Thus the clan obtained the crest gitamgiye'ks: and if a man wandering in the woods should hear an unseen baby cry, "wa wa wa," he will be lucky thereafter.

Crane (dił).—The chief of the clan sometimes impersonated this bird at ceremonies. It was classed by the Indians as a clan crest, though it might equally well have ranked as a personal crest of the chief. No legend seemed extant.

BIRCHBARK HOUSE

Woodpecker (mansil).—This crest would be placed on the clan's totem pole, if one existed, but it now receives adequate representation from its use by the clan chief as a personal crest. It is based on a legend of a pileated woodpecker that was killed by a Carrier chief (Jenness, 1934, p. 236),

LAKSILYU PHRATRY

HOUSE OF MANY EYES

Kaigyet (a mythical monster). This is the principal crest portrayed on the clan's totem pole in the Hagwilgate canyon, and gives its name to the pole.

The chief of the clan also impersonated it at potlatches, when he put on a long-nosed mask of wood, hobbled with bent knees into the potlatch house, and stared at the audience. Its mythical origin is a subject of controversy; some Indians invoke one legend (Jenness, 1934, p. 214) and others another (Jenness, 1934, p. 220).

Mountain Man (gyedamskani-sh).—This crest appears upon the clan's totem pole, near its middle, as a human being wearing a collar of twisted cedar bark. The heir of the clan chief bears the title Mountain Man and impersonates that being at potlatches, thus using a clan crest as a personal crest. Its origin is attributed to a well-known legend (Jenness, 1934, p. 229).

Otter (nilzik^w).—This crest is represented on the clan totem pole, near its summit, by the figure of an otter. It is also the personal crest of a noble in the clan, Maxlaxlaxs. The Indians could give no explanatory legend.

HOUSE ON TOP OF A FLAT ROCK

Many Small Frogs.—Half a century ago or more the clan erected a totem pole at Moricetown on which it carved both this crest and a second one, "Big Man"; but when the pole rotted and fell it was burned and never replaced. The Indians ascribe the crest's origin to the same legend, "The Girl Who Married a Frog" (Jenness, 1934, p. 168), as is invoked by the Dark House of the Gilserhyu phratry to explain its crest frog, stating that, when the latter phratry adopted the big father frog as its crest, the Laksilyu phratry adopted the baby frogs because the mother had belonged to the Laksilyu phratry.

Big Man (denitcho, or, in the Gitksan dialect of Hazelton, widaxkyet).—This crest was represented on the now vanished totem pole at Moricetown. The Indians knew no origin legend.

Swan.—The Indians do not now remember how this clan crest was represented, if at all, and could give no legend to explain its origin. A nephew of the clan chief, named Negupte, used it as a personal crest, but after he died no one took over the title or adopted the crest.

HOUSE BESIDE THE FIRE

It was said that this clan had no crest until recently, when it adopted as its emblem a flag obtained from the Hudson's Bay Company; but since there seems no evidence that the clan is less ancient than others, it probably possessed a crest, like all the rest, and for some reason dropped it.

LAKSAMSHU PHRATRY

SUN HOUSE AND TWISTED HOUSE

Sun or Moon (sa).—If these two clans had erected a totem pole, this is the crest that they would certainly have carved upon it. At the present time they occasionally display it at potlatches in the form of a glowing plaque or ball that slowly moves across the ceiling of the house after the lights have been extinguished. The people greet its passage with a song, chanted in the Gitksan dialect;

> Behold the sun just rising;
> Behold the sun in the middle of its course;
> Behold the sun going down.

They ascribe its origin, and the origin of the clan name Sun House, to a widespread legend (Jenness, 1934, p. 215).

Whale (nehł).—The chief of the Sun House, Smogitkyemk, impersonates this crest at potlatches. After sprinkling swansdown over his head, he marches to and fro outside the feast house, clad in a ceremonial skirt and garters, and wearing on his back a blanket decorated with a bone figure of a whale. Two heralds enter the house to announce his coming, and two men enveloped in a wooden model of a whale crawl in behind them. Finally, the chief himself enters, walks around the house and withdraws from sight behind a curtain. After an interval he re-emerges, crawling with three other men inside an enormous whale that conceals them from view. Slowly the monster moves around the house, opening and closing its stupendous jaw; and, as it disappears behind the curtain, the chief of some other phratry sings Smogitkyemk's private chant (Soneł). Smogitkyemk then appears for the third time, wearing now the mask of a grouse, the third crest of his clan. With bent knees, and hands on hips, he jerks his head from side to side like a bird and begins to dance. At some stage in the ceremony he may, if he wishes, relate the origin legend of the whale crest (Jenness, 1934, p. 225).

Grouse (chaddzat').—When the chief enacted this crest as described above, he called it a clan crest; but occasionally he portrayed it in a different way and considered it his personal crest (***see p. [44]511). Some natives claimed that it belonged originally to the Beaver phratry, and that it arose from a forgotten adventure with a being that had the body of a man and the head of a grouse.

Weasel skin decorated with the neck skin of a mallard duck.—The chief of the clan, if he chooses, may wear this crest at potlatches. Tradition derives it from an encounter with the Indians of Kitimat, at the head of Douglas Channel (Jenness, 1934, p. 232).

OWL HOUSE

Owl (misdzi).—This is the crest that would be carved on the clan totem pole, if one existed. The base of a front post in the old clan house in the Hagwilgate canyon bore a large carving of an owl; the doorway, in fact, was merely a hole in the owl's body. The Indians attributed the crest to the same legend as the clan name (Jenness, 1934, p. 239).

Moose (denni).—This crest is said to have been derived from the Babine Lake subtribe. It seems to carry no legend, and must have been acquired in fairly recent times, since the moose did not reach this part of British Columbia until the latter half of the nineteenth century.

Sapsucker.—Tradition states that the Laksamshu phratry adopted this crest from the legend that gave rise to the woodpecker crest in the Birchbark House of the Gilserhyu phratry (Jenness, 1934, p. 236).

BEAVER PHRATRY

Beaver (tsa) and Eagle (ske).—Both these crests were represented on the totem pole of the combined Laksamshu and Beaver phratries in the Hagwilgate canyon, a pole erected about 1865 by a chief of the Beaver phratry, Kwi·s, or, as he renamed himself, Bini. This man promoted a strange religious revival that established his leadership over the two phratries, and indeed over the entire subtribe. His influence even extended to the neighboring Gitksan Indians. Hence, when he erected a totem pole he named it Firewood (gila·s), after the principal crest of the Gitksan phratry that equated with the Laksamshu,[9] caused the figure of an eagle to be carved on its summit, and an image of a

---

9. There is a tradition that before the founding of the village in the Hagwilgate canyon, the Moricetown members of the Laksamshu phratry sometimes wore at potlatches robes of groundhog skin patterned on each side with fireweed leaves.

beaver to be attached at about mid-height. The Indians removed the beaver after his death and placed it on his grave.

The chief of the phratry sometimes impersonated the beaver at potlatches, regarding it then as his personal crest. It arose, the Indians say, from an encounter with the coastal people of Kitimat (Jenness, 1934, p. 232).

PERSONAL CRESTS

In addition to the clan crests every chief, and most, originally perhaps all, of the nobles in each clan, owned at least one personal crest (chanka), which gave him at feasts the exclusive right to wear certain paraphernalia and to act in a certain way, for example, to imitate the movements of a caribou or robin. Whenever a man's personal crest coincided with his title it belonged to the permanent structure of the clan and was therefore inalienable; otherwise it ranked as purely personal property and could be sold within or without the clan like a garment or a piece of furniture. It was, therefore, much easier for a man to acquire a new personal crest than for a clan to adopt a new clan crest; the noble merely devised or purchased one that pleased his individual fancy, and established his right to ownership at a potlatch.

When a man (or woman) gave a potlatch, the object or theme that he dramatized, and alone had the right to dramatize, was his personal crest. It was only in this manner, through dramatization at a potlatch, that he made it publicly known and obtained the public endorsement of his ownership. (See plate 4.) But if a chief chose to drama-  tize one of his clan crests, as often happened, was he thereby entitled to count it as his personal crest also? Actually the Indians were not consistent in this regard. Thus one of the two clan (or phratry) crests in the Beaver phratry (which contained only one clan) was the beaver, which was represented by the figure of a beaver on the phratry's totem pole; but at potlatches the chief of the phratry dramatized the actions of a beaver and considered it as his personal crest. On the other hand, the chief of the clan House of Many Eyes, in Laksilyu phratry, who dramatized in a similar manner two of his clan crests. Mountain Man and Kaigyet, did not consider them his personal crests, but clan crests only. Generally only the chief of a clan might dramatize a clan

Plate 4. Hawilgate Carrier dramatizing his personal crest. (Photograph by Harlan I. Smith.)

crest, whether he called it his personal crest or not; but in at least two instances a noble below the rank of chief has claimed and been allowed the same privilege. Such an anomaly might easily happen if the chieftainship changed hands, for then the deposed chief (or his legal successor) might continue to use at potlatches the clan crest he had used before his eclipse; but one receives an impression that any noble might adopt a clan crest as his personal crest, provided no other member of the clan was using it and the chief gave his consent. Probably, too, what was at one time only the personal crest of a chief might come to rank as a clan crest, particularly if the chief gained unusual prominence and frequently displayed his crest at potlatches. Since a personal crest was a mark of distinction, and a noble could hardly give a potlatch without displaying or dramatizing one, it tended to become hereditary, like the title, and a man normally adopted the crest of his mother's brother when he inherited that uncle's title. In such a case he could validate both badges of distinction in a single potlatch. To lighten the excessive cost, three or four individuals often adopted crests (and, if they wished, titles) simultaneously; and parents, clansmen, and friends contributed to the expense, knowing that they would be repaid later. Every noble, who could afford it, bestowed titles and crests on his children while they were still young, for though these early distinctions did not confer high rank, they gave the children definite places in the peerage and marked out their lines of advancement. A typical example was the career of Dikyannulat (European name, Denis), of the House of Many Eyes, Laksilyu phratry, in 1924 a blind old man of perhaps 70.

When Denis had not yet reached his teens, his mother's brother invited the people to attend a potlatch at which the lad blackened his face and danced. His uncle then distributed many blankets among the guests, and announced that his nephew, being descended from the nobility, would later acquire a title and a crest.

Two or three years later, Denis' kinsmen decided to give another potlatch for him and enroll him definitely in the peerage. At this potlatch he was to assume a personal crest, Throwing Dirt, which his grandfather also had assumed in boyhood. Whether it was derived from a legend Denis did not learn, for his grandfather merely instructed him how to dramatize it without explaining its origin. The guests gathered outside the potlatch hall at the appointed time, flung out their arms and shouted, "hau hau," whereupon Denis, naked to the waist, ran in among them and scattered them with showers of dirt. Later they all gathered inside the hall so that Denis might sing and dance before them; and the ceremony ended with a feast and distribution of blankets.

When Denis reached manhood, he gave still a third potlatch and adopted, again without learning its origin, the personal crest, Gun, that had belonged to his mother's brother. Three relatives of his father went among the crowd to announce his coming, and two others hovered on the outskirts of the village, one dressed in a grizzly skin and the other in a black bear's skin.

Denis himself then appeared and pretended to shoot the two "animals" with a gun. Subsequently he confirmed his new crest with the usual distribution of presents.

The neighboring Gitksan always narrated the legends attached to their crests when they dramatized them; but the Carrier troubled so little about the legends that many of them have dropped from memory. The owner of a crest had the right to decide how it should be dramatized, and although most men slavishly followed the methods of previous owners, an ingenious individual often contrived some new device to increase the pleasure of the spectators. The two examples that follow fairly represent the general pattern.

(a) Guxlet, the present-day chief of the Thin House in Gilserhyu phratry, owns two personal crests, laba'on, "the Snatcher," the origin of which he does not know, and the more important crest, guxlet, which goes with his title and is based on a legend of a person Guxlet who emerged out of the ground (Jenness, 1934, p. 234). Of his predecessors, the earliest, who had another title, Boikyet, is said to have lived at Mosquito Flat, where he was the principal chief in the Gilserhyu phratry; the last, born of a Gitksan father and Hagwilgate mother, also bore the title Boikyet but lived at Hazelton, where he ranked as only the second chief of the phratry. The present Guxlet was born at Francis Lake, but moved to Hagwilgate when he was a young man, and, on the score of a rather distant relationship, obtained the title Guxlet, and the personal crest that went with it, when the previous incumbent died in 1918.

Whenever Guxlet gives a potlatch he dramatizes his crest, Snatcher, outside the dance hall in the afternoon, and his principal crest, guxlet, within doors in the evening. Being the chief of his clan, he wears his chiefly regalia, a shirt of cloth covered with tinkling bells, a blanket, decorated with buttons, that partly conceals his trousers, cloth leggings, moccasins, and a coronet of grizzly bear claws. This, of course, is a modern dress that has superseded the older costume of skins. Three heralds announce his approach to the throng outside the dance hall. Finally he himself comes, and, snatching from the people everything that takes his fancy, hands them to his heralds, who carry them to his home and subsequently to the dance hall, where each object is returned to its owner together with a present of one or two dollars.

When darkness closes in and the people have gathered in the potlatch house, Guxlet dramatizes his principal crest. He marches in full regalia around the central fire, singing his sonel or personal song[10] and vigorously shaking a rattle. At intervals

---

10. The words are Gitksan, and the present Guxlet does not understand them, but this is of no significance.

he stops to lay his hand on some chief, who must then rise and dance; for thus honoring Guxlet he later receives a reward. After this has continued for an hour or more a chief calls out, "Guxlet, why do you just sing all the time?" Then four men lay Guxlet on his back on a moose hide and pretend to throw him into the fire. His predecessor, the Indians claim, actually was thrown into the fire, which consumed all but his bones; but the present Guxlet merely steals away behind a curtain. After a brief interval 8 or 10 men who sit behind this curtain raise his song, and one of them calls, "O Guxlet, Guxlet." Then the chief comes out again (his predecessor is said to have risen from the floor, unharmed), and joins in the song. A herald sprinkles swansdown over his head and crowns him with a special headdress representing one of his clan crests; and Guxlet closes the ceremony with a dance and song that he has prepared especially for the occasion.

The following day is devoted to feasting, to the giving of presents, and the payment of all those who have assisted Guxlet, except the members of his own phratry, who make personal contributions to the pile of presents, assist in distributing them, and receive their reward at some later date.

(b) In 1921 a noble named Dzi, who belonged to the clan House on Top of a Flat Rock, in the Laksilyu phratry, adopted as his personal crest Caribou. He dressed his uncle and two other kinsmen on his father's side as hunters, equipping them with snowshoes, guns, and packs, and sprinkling their heads with flour to simulate snow. Shortly after noon on the first day of the potlatch the men marched through the village in this array, telling the people they were going to hunt caribou; but when they reached the first ridge above the village and were still in plain view, they removed their snowshoes and packs, lit a fire, and pretended to camp. Soon four gunshots resounded in the woods behind them, and a fictitious caribou—Dzi covered with a caribou hide that had its front legs padded with two sticks—bounded into the open and headed for the village, closely followed by the hunter who had fired the shots. All four hunters took up the chase, and now and then, as they pretended to shoot the animal, tumbled over, to the amusement of the crowd. Finally the "caribou" leaped inside the potlatch house, and everyone trooped in after it.

The people gathered again in the potlatch hall at dusk. As they sat there, talking and laughing, a herald entered with a gun, and said to one of the chiefs, "Have you seen any caribou?" The chief answered, "No, I have not." Presently a second herald came in and shouted, "You are crazy. There are no caribou here." Then came a third herald, who said, "I saw a caribou. It will soon come in." Last of all, Dzi entered the hall with his face concealed beneath a wooden image representing a caribou's head. After displaying his mask to the audience, he retired to rid himself of its cumbrous weight, and, reentering, danced and sang his personal song. The people lingered in the hall a little longer, then went home to prepare for the feast and gifts of the following day. (See plate 5.)

Plate 5. Scenes at a Potlach held by the Laksilu Phratry at Hagwil-gate. (Photograph by C.M. Barbeau.)

TABLE OF PERSONAL CRESTS

GITAMTANYU PHRATRY

GRIZZLY HOUSE

Whale (Ww's).—This crest naturally belonged to the chief of the clan who bore the title "Whale." At potlatches, after the people had gathered inside the feast house, a woman belonging to some phratry other than Gitamtanyu threw outside the door a hook attached to a long line of which she retained the other end. As she drew it slowly in again she drew with it a huge wooden model of a whale that concealed the chief and an assistant, who retired behind the curtain after being "dragged" round the room. Subsequently the chief came out again, danced, and, if he wished, narrated the legend on which his title and crest were based. (Jenness, 1934, p. 225.)

Crazy Man (hwisnik).—This crest, which also belonged to the chief Whale, was said to have come from Kitwanga, a Gitksan village lower down the Skeena River. Whether or not it was based on some legend, the Carrier did not know. The chief used indoors only the crest Whale, but out-of-doors he dramatized this crest Crazy Man by dressing himself and his heralds in the oldest clothes he could find, and pretending to tear them to pieces.

Wolf (yis).—This crest, which coincided with one of the two clan crests, and was sponsored by the same legend, belonged to Djolukyet, the second ranking noble in the clan. At feasts he dressed in a wolf skin and pretended to bite the leading chiefs and nobles.

Old Woman (se.te).—Neither Djolukyet, who owned this crest also, nor any of the other Carrier seemed to know its origin. When dramatizing it at potlatches, the owner dressed and acted like an old woman who could hardly walk.

The Man Who Pinches Others (eni dso·kis).—Djolukyet purchased this crest, his third, in 1923 from a Carrier of Babine Lake, but without enquiring into its origin. He dramatized it by pinching the arms of the leading nobles with two sticks each about 5 feet long.

Sculpin (saskwa).—Another crest belonging to Djolukyet, though how he dramatized it was not recorded. It was derived from a well-known legend of a great flood (Jenness, 1934, p. 141).

Fox.—Belonged to a kinsman of Djolukyet, whose title was not recorded. It was derived from a legend of a fox that stole fire for mankind (Jenness, 1934, p. 239).

Seated in the Dirt (klestaste).—Belonged to another kinsman of Djolukyet. It was derived from the same legend as the next crest and title Sleepy.

Sleepy (guxwoq).—This crest belonged to the noble who bore the same title, at the present time a woman. When dramatizing the crest at feasts, she lay on the ground, wrapped in a blanket as if asleep. When "awakened" she moved off a few paces and lay down again. The crest was derived from a well-known legend (Jenness, 1934, p. 219).

Dance (Gitksan: miłłamelu).—Belonged to a sister of Djolukyet, whose title was not recorded. This crest was obtained from a Gitksan Indian of Kitwanga, but nothing further was known about it.

War Leader (baxchan).—Belonged to the noble of the same name. To dramatize it he carried a stick in front of two men, whom he urged forward by raising the stick and crying, "he he." Tradition states that it originated from a fight with the Indians of Fraser Lake (Jenness, 1934, p. 239).

Grouse (gwitakak).—Belonged to Gu'kyet, who obtained it a few years ago from a Gitksan chief with whom she and her husband were traveling to Kit-kargas. They camped in the snow when they were overtaken by night, and the woman strewed boughs for their beds and cooked their supper and breakfast. In acknowledgment of her diligence, the Gitksan Indian gave her this crest, but did not explain its origin. When dramatizing it, she fluttered her blanket and pretended to fly like a grouse.

Black Bear (sas).—Two nobles, Skalił and Samsmahix., shared this crest between them. They dramatized it by wearing black-bear skins and imitating the actions of the bear. The crest derived its sanction from the same legend as the clan name Grizzly (Jenness, 1934, p. 129).

HOUSE IN THE MIDDLE OF MANY, AND ANSKASKI

Grizzly (medi·k).—Belonged to the chief with the same title, who covered himself with a headless grizzly skin and acted like a grizzly. The Carrier did not seem to know the legend on which it was based.

Club of Antler (dzan'xał).—Belonged to the same chief Medi·k. It originated from an incident in a fight with the *Witseni*, or Nass River Indians (Jenness, 1934, p. 231) . To dramatize it the owner danced with an antler club whose knob was carved to represent a wolf's head, and sang, in the Gitksan dialect;

Soon the wolf will eat the Witseni.

Prancing up to another chief, he tapped him lightly on the shoulder with the club, and subsequently gave this pretended enemy a gift, in one instance a rifle.

Grizzly Cub (ismediks).—Belonged to the noble of the same name, who impersonated the animal by wearing its skin and imitating its actions. Its origin was unknown.

Atne· (*Kitlope or Bella Coola Indian*).—Belonged to the noble of the same name, who dramatized it exactly as his chief, Medi·k, dramatized the grizzly except that he retained the head on the grizzly skin that enveloped him. Tradition states that this crest was presented to a Hagwilgate Carrier by a Carrier of Ootsa Lake in payment for help at a potlatch; but its further origin was unknown.

Grizzly Cub's Head (*gulakkan*).—Belonged also to Atne, who clad himself in the front half of a grizzly skin and impersonated the animal. One tradition states that it arose from a man's adventure in the woods; as he slept beneath a large tree something fell on him and a few minutes later a monster, half grizzly and half human, descended the tree beside him. More generally, however, it is credited to an incident in a raid on some coast Indians (Jenness, 1934, p. 237).

Raven (*dettsan*).—Belonged to the noble who bore the title Raven, which at present is unclaimed. Its origin was attributed to the same legend as the clan crest Raven. In dramatizing it the owner wore a dark blanket, flapped two mimic wings of moore-hide, and cried, "ka ka."

Arrow.—Belonged to Gistehwa, chief of the clan House in the Middle of Many, who dramatized it by pretending to shoot the people gathered at the potlatch. Its origin was derived from the legend of the two boys who burst a mountain with their arrows (Jenness, 1934, p. 229).

Spring salmon.—Belonged to Hⲱlits, who clad himself in white clothes to match the color of the salmon and walked in a stooping posture outside the dance house. There seemed to be no origin legend.

Skunk.—Another crest belonging to Hⲱlits, of unknown origin. Its dramatizer wore a skunk skin when impersonating the animal.

Avalanche (*entlo*).—Belonged to Na'ok. It was credited to a legend about a man who emerged from a mountain and caused an avalanche by sliding down its flank. At potlatches the owner of this crest announced his approach by sending out a herald to sprinkle flour in imitation of snow and to warn the people of the impending avalanche. Na'ok himself then appeared and, like an avalanche, flung aside every one he encountered.

Shaking the Head (*Gitksan: qale·*).—Belonged to Na'ok also, but its origin was unknown. At potlatches people cried, "e," and lay down as he approached them wearing a large wooden mask. One after another then raised his head and cried, "qale." At each cry Na'ok turned his head until it was moving so fast that he became dizzy.

Kano'ts.—Belonged to the noble of the same name. It commemorated the adventure of the girls in the canoe and the two medicine boys, or, in another version, the medicine man Guxlet (Jenness, 1934, pp. 175–77, 235). When

Kano'ts, dressed in whatever paraphernalia he happened to possess, appeared outside the potlatch house, the people fell down and cried, "e," then rose, clapped their hands and cried, "wɯ," after the manner of the girls in the canoe.

White Man (nid·o).—Belonged to Kano'ts also, but its derivation was unknown. Its owner, wearing a long moustache and a beard, strutted among the people with his hands on his hips and a stetson hat on his head. The present Kano'ts happens to be a woman.

Shameless (aχata·t).—Belonged to the noble with the same name, its most recent owner being a woman who preferred her other title Hogyet. At potlatches she stared shamelessly into the faces of the chiefs and nobles outside the potlatch house, and, within, stared at them again from behind a large wooden face mask. The origin of the crest was unknown.

Nasko River Indians (nas'kuten).—Belonged to the same woman Hogyet, and, like the last crest, of unknown origin. At potlatches five women supported Hogyet, two on one side and three on the other, and all six swung adzes fastened by bright ribbons to their wrists while they chanted;

> We don't know where this man comes from.
> A Nasko man is coming.

Rain (Chan).—Belonged to *Sowi·s, a noble now dead who has left no successor. At potlatches he sprinkled water on the people in imitation of the rainstorm that formed an incident in a well-known legend (Jenness, 1934, p. 219).

Mosquitoes (detku).—Belonged to Hwille·wi, a woman now dead whose title remains unclaimed. At potlatches she covered her head with a blanket and pricked the arms of the people with a needle held in her mouth, imitating the mosquitoes of a legend (Jenness, 1934, p. 220).

Long Arm (nagwa'on).—Belonged to the noble of the same name, who stretched out each arm alternately and cried, "Long Arm." Tradition says that it was derived through the Hazelton Indians from the Indians of the Nass River, but the Carrier knew of no story connected with it.

Jump Inside (wittsen).—The owner and the method of representing this crest were not recorded.

Heartless (axgotdemash).—Belonged to the noble of the same name, a Gitksan Indian now living among the Carrier. Legend states that a grizzly once crushed a dog, whereupon its owner exclaimed, "The grizzly is a heartless animal," and adopted Heartless as his personal crest.

GILSERHYU PHRATRY

DARK HOUSE

Blue heron (netipish).—Belonged to the chief, since it accompanied his title Netipish. When dramatizing the crest, the chief enveloped his head in a blue blanket and fluttered his arms up and down. No legend recorded.

Hook (sax).—Belonged also to Netipish, the chief. When dancing, he caught the skirts of various men in a small hook at the end of a long pole and made them dance in turn, for which he paid them later. No legend recorded.

Wolverine (nustel).—Belonged to the bearer of the title Wolverine, at the present time the niece of the chief. She dramatized it by covering her head with a wolverine skin and biting people as she hopped over the floor on her hands and toes. Those whom she bit had to rise and dance with her. The crest probably owes its origin to one of several legends about the wolverine.

Back-pack (weli).—Belonged to the bearer of the same title, who dramatized it by carrying a pack on his back. No legend recorded.

Cow (mistu·s).—Belonged to the bearer of the title. At feasts a herald called to the people outside the dance house, "Has anyone lost a cow?" A second herald with a rope then asked, "Where is the cow? I want to rope it." Last of all came the "cow," Mistu's and a paid helper covered beneath a large blanket decked with a tail and horns. The herald roped this cow and dragged it into the dance house. No legend recorded.

Sekani Indian (łtaten).—This crest belonged to the mother of the chief, who has long been dead. No one has revived it since.

Fast Runner (nitchaten).—Belonged to Anabel's, who dressed as for a race, and in dancing leaped high into the air, one step forward and one back. No legend recorded.

Crazy Man (wusnik).—Belonged to the owner of the title, who pretended to be crazy and to beat the people with a stick. No legend recorded.

THIN HOUSE

Guxlet.—Belonged to the bearer of the title, the chief of the clan. (For details, **see p. 503.)

Snatcher (laba'on).—Belonged also to Guxlet, the chief. (For its dramatization, see **p. 503.)

Crane (dił).—Belonged to Tcaspit, the minor chief of the clan, who merely mimics the bird when giving a potlatch. No origin legend was discovered.

His Heart Tastes Bad (Gitksan: kaskamqot; Carrier: bet'sidzal'kai').—Belonged to Bita'nen, who clawed at his heart, did everything wrong, and chanted a song in the Gitksan language. The last owner of the title and crest was a woman. No origin legend was discovered.

Slave (etne).—Belonged to Ne'k, who dramatized it by wearing old clothes and shuffling about among the people like a wretched slave. No origin legend was discovered.

Gidamgiye'ks.—This was a personal crest as well as a clan crest, but its owner's name and the method of dramatizing it were not recorded.

Axweakas (a Gitksan word of unknown meaning).—The owner of this crest has long been dead and his title was not recorded. The Indians remember that he flourished two knives when he dramatized the crest, but knew no legend about it.

Thunder.—The unrecorded owner of this crest dramatized it by fluttering a blanket and beating a drum. Its origin seemed unknown.

He Who Cuts Off the Head with a Knife (gwatsikyet).— Belonged to the noble of the same name, who dramatized a tradition relating how a hunter cut off the head of his wife's paramour (Jenness, 1934, p. 215). A pre-European Gwatsikyet is said to have enacted the crest in a more dramatic way during the evening performances in the potlatch house. Dressed in his regalia he danced and sang his personal song, flourishing a large knife. A man shouted to him, "Why are you flourishing that knife?" whereupon two men forced Gwatsikyet to his knees, and while one jerked back his head by the hair, the other cut right through his neck. They then laid his body on a moose skin, placed the head against the trunk, and summoned a medicine man to sing and rattle over him. Finally Gwatsikyet rose up whole and unharmed.

Dead Man (Carrier: tenez·ik; Gitksan: lulak).—Belonged to the noble of the same name. It was based on a tradition that a dead man once entered a house where some children were playing, gave them a present, and departed, leaving them unharmed. The dramatizer covered himself with a black cloth and, after walking a few paces, fell to the ground in the attitude of death.

Fraser Lake Indian (asten).—Belonged to the noble of the same name, but its origin was unknown. Its owner wore the costume of a Fraser Lake Indian, carried a pack on his back and brandished a spear.

Frog (Gitksan: kanau).—Belonged to the noble Kanau, and was derived from the same legend as the clan crest Frog. Its owner, when dramatizing it, hopped along the ground like a frog.

BIRCHBARK HOUSE

Pileated Woodpecker (mansil).—Belonged, to the chief of the clan, *Samuiχ.*, who dramatized it by standing in a tree, covered with a blanket, and pretended to fly. The legend is the same as for the clan crest woodpecker.

Small Bird, sp.? (samuiχ.).—Belonged also to the chief, being his title. To represent this bird he wore a very small blanket beneath which he fluttered his hands to imitate the fluttering of wings. No legend was recorded.

Satsa'n.—Belonged to the noble of the same name. It was derived from the myth of a being, Satsa'n, who was able to swell and contract his body at will (Jenness, 1934, p. 141). When giving a potlatch, Satsa'n sat on the ground with a large circular cloth fastened around his neck. Assistants then crawled under the cloth to "swell" his body, and the people pushed them out again to make it "contract."

Porcupine (tetchok).—Belonged to Su'tli, who covered himself with a blanket, crawled like a porcupine among the people, and whipped them with a "tail." It was based on a mythical contest between a porcupine and a beaver (Jenness, 1934, p. 240).

Marten (chani).—Belonged to the noble who bore the name, which was said to be restricted to women. As usual she mimicked the actions of the animal. Name and crest were derived from a myth about a marten that ate a youth who was seeking medicine-power (Jenness, 1934, p. 239),

Ferry Me in a Canoe (nenesenoxɬkaiɯ.) .—Belonged to the noble who bore the name, always a woman. When giving a potlatch, she carried a paddle and sent out three heralds, the last of whom announced her approach with the words, "Here comes a woman who wants to cross the river. Let some one who owns a canoe ferry her over." The crest was derived from the myth of the two boys who visited the land of the dead (Jenness, 1934, p. 99).

guxkalkalas (Gitksan word, meaning unknown).—Belonged to the holder of the same title, who was always a woman. When dramatizing it she waved each hand in front of her as though turning two handles. No legend was known.

gwitsin'alu (Gitksan word, meaning unknown).—Belonged to the holder of the same title. After sending out three heralds to dance, he himself arrived dancing, laid hold of a chief, and invited him to dance with him. No legend was known.

LAKSILYU PHRATRY

HOUSE OF MANY EYES

Otter (nilzik^w).—Belonged to Maxlaxlexs, but the present holder of that title has given it to his nephew, who dramatized it by dressing in an otter skin and imitating the movements of the animal. No legend was known.

Dog (klak).—Belonged to Kela, who similarly imitated the actions of a dog. No legend was known.

Throwing Dirt (Gitksan: suwiyit; Carrier: klesgett'lat).—Belonged to Dikyan-nulat, who threw dirt at the people outside the potlatch house. No legend was known.

The Man Who Pays the Blood-Price (gowittcan).—Presented to the present Hagwilnesł about 1870 (before his accession to the chieftainship and while he bore the title Gyedamskanish), by a Gitwinlkul (Gitksan) Indian, whom he assisted in gathering skins and food for a potlatch. Subsequently Hagwilnexł gave it to a cousin. The dramatizer covered his head with swansdown and danced with one or two other men. No legend was known.

gwinu· (Gitksan, meaning unknown).—Obtained by Hagwilnexł from the same source as the last crest. Nothing further was discovered about it.

HOUSE ON TOP OF A FLAT ROCK

Old Man (dene' te).— Belonged to the chief of the clan, Widaxkyet. The Indians referred it to a story about an old man who stole some boys, but they had forgotten the details of the legend. Widaxkyet dressed as an old man, concealed his face under a wooden mask, and, carrying a long stick, toddled among the people and squatted down in front of a chief. Then, pointing the stick at the chief, he slid his hand down it, causing four branching points to open at the top. He slid his hand up the stick and the points closed—the chief was trapped.

Caribou (witsi).—Belonged to Dzi. (For its dramatization, see p. [p. 35]503.) No legend was known.

Goose (xa).—Belonged to the noble of the same name, who imitated a goose. No legend was known.

Rain of Stones (stalo'b).—Belonged to the noble of the same name. When giving a potlatch he wore a mask and threw stones and sand on the roofs of the houses; and in the evening he scattered stones on the floor of the dance house. The noble who now possesses the title caused considerable excitement at a potlatch he gave in 1918 by substituting nuts for stones. The crest is attributed to an incident in the legend that gave rise to another crest, Sleepy (Jenness, 1934, p. 219).

Swan.—Belonged to Negupte, but no one has taken either the title or the crest since the last incumbent died. At potlatches he wore a white blanket and imitated a swan. No legend seemed known.

HOUSE BESIDE THE FIRE

Heartless (axgot).—Belonged to the chief of the clan, Widak'kwats, who beat the house with a big stick when he gave a potlatch. No legend was known.

Water-grizzly (te'ben).—Belonged to the same chief, who dramatized it by wearing a grizzly robe and roaring. Legend states that the Indians once heard a water-grizzly roaring in a small lake on the top of a mountain near Smithers and saw the animal rise to the surface. Hence they adopted it as one of their crests.

djudalatju (Gitksan word, meaning unknown).—Belonged also to the chief. When dramatizing it he wore a large human mask and pretended to grasp people, waving each arm alternately and shouting, "djudalatju."

Big Medicine Man (Carrier: diyin'intcho; Gitksan: wi'hale).—Belonged to Axgot, the chief's heir. In dramatizing it he wore a headdress of grizzly claws, shielded his face with his right arm, and shook a rattle. No legend was known.

Gambling (Gitksan: gu'he').—Belonged to Klbegansi. When giving a potlatch he sat down with his assistants and pretended to gamble.

Something Devours It All (Gitksan: dzełlas).—The title of the owner of this crest was not recorded. In his potlatch he pretended to claw the people. No legend was known.

LAKSAMSHU PHRATRY

SUN OR MOON HOUSE

Grouse (tcaddzat".—Belongs now to the chief Smogitkyemk but formerly to the chief of the Beaver phratry, according to several Indians, or to the chief of the second clan in the Laksamshu phratry, the Owl House, according to the woman who now ranks as its head. In his potlatch Smogitkyemk, clad in a special blanket, struck his elbows against his sides and fluttered his fists as a grouse flutters its wings. He then retired indoors and sent out three heralds to announce his return. The last of the heralds set a log on the ground and announced that the grouse was approaching, whereupon some man in the crowd pretended to set a noose for it. The chief then reappeared, and, kneeling down beside the log, pretended to be caught in the snare.

Slave (Gitksan: an'ka').—Belonged also to Smogitkyemk, who dramatized it by wearing old clothes and acting like a slave. No legend was known.

Short Belly (Gitksan: gut'seut).—Belonged to the noble of the same name. When giving a potlatch he seized everything that came in his way and afterward restored it to its owner and gave him a present.

OWL HOUSE

Forest-Slide (klo'mkan).—Belonged to the chief with the same title. The present incumbent is a woman. At her potlatch she sent out three heralds, the first to announce an impending forest-slide, the second to ridicule the first, and the third to repeat the warning excitedly. Then she herself appeared carrying some sticks in each hand, and followed by a number of youths carrying brushwood with which to push over the people who thronged around them. At the evening performance in the potlatch house, Klo'mkan wore an owl mask and danced. Tradition states that when the Indians were clearing a site for a house at Hagwilgate they uprooted a big stump and sent it sliding down the hill. As they watched it descend, a man said, "Let the chief take this as his personal crest."

Moose.—Belonged to the chief of the clan, Klo'mkan, who dramatized it by imitating a moose. No legend was known.

Cannibal (deni tsa'at).—Belonged also to the chief Klo'mkan, but was derived along with a strip of hunting territory from a Cheslatta Lake Indian in payment for help at a funeral potlatch. When dramatizing it, Klo'mkan covered her back with a blanket which she swung up and down on each side as though engulfing the children who came in her path. The crest refers to a legend of a cannibal woman who carried off all the boys in a village (Jenness, 1934, p. 164).

Sa'bek (Gitksan word, meaning unknown).—Belonged to the noble with the same title. When he gave a potlatch he waved his left arm and shook a rattle after the manner of a medicine man, crying, "I am a medicine man from Wista (said to be a village on the coast)."

Picks up Weapon Hastily (kitsilchak).—Belonged to the noble with the same title, who pretended to strike with a stick anyone who spoke to him while he was dramatizing the crest. No legend was known.

BEAVER PHRATRY

Beaver (tsa).—Belonged to the chief Kwi·s, who dramatized it in the following manner. After the usual three heralds had announced his approach to the throng gathered outside the potlatch house, he himself appeared, garbed in a beaver skin and crawling like a beaver in flight from two or three men who pretended to spear him with long sticks. When this pantomime ended, the people entered the potlatch house, where they were confronted with a pile of wood near the fireplace (the "beaver's food"), and two or three "beaver lodges" of brush and cloth, in one of which the chief lay concealed. The chief of another phratry approached this lodge and exclaimed, "Why, here is a beaver lodge. Did you not notice it? There must be a beaver inside. Watch the water and the other lodges while I knock it over." As he pushed the lodge over the "beaver" ran out, and, after being pursued by two or three men armed with spears and guns, retreated behind a curtain. There he was permitted an interval to dress, after which he came out again and danced, while the people, led by one of the chiefs, chanted his sonet or personal song.

Drunken Man.—Belonged also to the chief Kwi·s, who imitated a drunken man and sang, "Give me that whisky." It is said to have originated from a dream of the present chief's predecessor, Kwi·s or Bini.

Mountain Goat (mat).—Belonged to the noble with the same title, who dramatized it by imitating a goat. It is attributed to a legend that presumes to account for its use as a crest by Guxsan, a Gitksan Indian of Gitsegyukla (Jenness, 1934, p. 240).

Tree Floating Down the River (gwiksuks).—Belonged to Wilat, who carried a long stick to sweep people aside. No legend was known.

The tables just given suggest a marked decline of the crest system under the influence of European civilization. After tattooing went out of favor a hundred years ago, and the large clan houses disappeared a generation later, the clan crests were in evidence only in the graveyards (plate 6a), and on the four totem poles still standing in the Hagwilgate canyon (plate 6b). They linger even today in the Hagwilgate graveyard, on two headstones that were made in Vancouver according to the specifications of Indians anxious for the usual Christian burial and marble monument, yet conservative enough to wish their bones to lie beneath representations of their clans and phratries; so their headstones have bird-figures engraved on their faces, and one a life-sized figure of a bird on its summit. About 1913 the Hagwilgate Indians, prompted by their missionaries, gathered together most of the stage material they had used in dramatizing their personal crests—the wooden masks and other objects that they had religiously preserved from one potlatch to another—and burned them in a great

Plate 6a. A Hagwilgate Indian's tombstone, depicting his crest. (Photograph by D. Jenness.)

Plate 6b. The four totem poles at Hagwilgate. (Photograph by Harlan I. Smith.)

bonfire. Since then they have acquired one or two masks from the Gitksan, who in earlier years gave them many crests and crest paraphernalia in exchange for the skins of beaver and other animals. Nearly every summer they display these masks in what are still called potlatches; but so little do most of them regard their old clan and phratric divisions that they no longer insist on phratric exogamy or pay any respect to the clan chiefs and leading nobles. The very distinction between nobles and commoners has broken down, for any one who wishes may now become a noble, and the chiefs are often poorer and less esteemed than the nobody who has pushed the past behind him and is successfully carving out a career under the new economic conditions. So the acquisition and dramatization of the personal crests is fast becoming a mere entertainment divorced from its old social significance, and ready to adopt new ideas, and new methods, that are more abreast of modern life.

CHIEFS

The chieftainship of a clan was highly coveted, although the authority conferred by the position was in most cases comparatively slight. A son could not succeed his father because of the marriage rules, which compelled a man to marry outside of his phratry and made his children members of the mother's phratry and clan. Hence, the most usual successor to a chief was the son of a sister, or, if his sisters had no sons, a brother; in default of both nephews and brothers a niece could inherit the title provided her kinsfolk backed up her claim, otherwise the position passed to the leading noble in the clan. To prevent disputes a chief generally indicated his personal choice some years before his death by conferring on a nephew the title and crest he himself had used in his younger days, and seating him in front of himself at ceremonies.

The accession of a new chief was a long and expensive affair, involving in former times no less than six potlatches (dze til). Within an hour or two of the old chief's death, the candidate for his place sprinkled swansdown over his head and, standing in front of the corpse, shook the dead man's rattle and chanted its owner's soneł or personal songs. He then summoned all the people in the vicinity to join in the same songs, chanted without dancing to the accompaniment of a drum. The chanting and weeping continued till late at night, when the candidate and his kinsmen brought in food for the mourners, who retired soon afterward to their homes. The people mourned for 2, 3, and sometimes, if the chief (whose corpse was meanwhile rotting at the back of the house) had enjoyed great prestige and influence, for as many as 15 days; and the feeding of the mourners during this period constituted the candidate's first potlatch, known as the yeni'hatittse, "He Falls Down," i. e., is dead.

After the due interval, the candidate finally called on the clanspeople of the dead chief's father to gather firewood and cremate the remains. A day or two later he again summoned the people to his house and gave his second potlatch, habaraninne awilli, "Arranging the Arms and Legs (of the dead chief)." Aided by his kinsfolk, he set food before them all and distributed gifts of skins and other articles, taking care to offer most of his presents, first to the clan that had cremated the corpse, in payment for its services, and second to the chiefs of other clans and phratries in order to win their support for his candidature.

His four succeeding potlatches followed each other at long intervals, because even with the help of kinsmen he could hardly gather the food and presents necessary for one potlatch alone in less time than a year. In the middle of the nineteenth century, the third in the series, called neokwan tesk'an, "Make a Fire" (on the theory that the old fire had been extinguished by the tears of the mourners), generally gave rise to two distinct ceremonies, the erection of a wooden grave-hut over the cremation place of the dead chief by his father's clansmen, and the definite appointment of a successor. If there were two candidates for the position, they gave a potlatch jointly, and the chiefs of the other clans and phratries decided between them after each in turn had entertained the people and distributed his presents. If, on the other hand, there was only one candidate, and general agreement to his succession, he often assumed at this potlatch the title and a personal crest of the late chief, and encouraged some of his clansmen to assume crests also. An old man thus described the installation of a new phratry chief as he witnessed it in his early manhood:

> On the appointed evening the candidate wrapped round his shoulders the skin of a grizzly bear, his predecessor's personal crest, and with three or four fellow phratrymen similarly clad to represent the new crests they were assuming, awaited in the potlatch house a visit from the men of the other phratries. They meanwhile were painting their faces, covering their heads with swan's-down, and gathering at the houses of their respective chiefs. First, the phratry of the dead chief's father marched to the potlatch house, sounded drums and rattles outside it, and beat on the walls with sticks. The door opened for them, and they marched around to the right behind their chief, halting in a long file behind the waiting candidate. He conducted them outside again and through all the other main houses in the village, after which they retired to spend the night under some trees while the candidate returned to the potlatch house to superintend the conducting of the other phratries on the same peregrination by his fellow clansmen. He and his phratry then provided an ample supper for the men camped under the trees, and retired to their homes to sleep.

The next morning they carried more food to their fellow villagers, who had spent part of the night composing playful songs about the new chief and his phratry in order to wash away all traces of sorrow for the loss of its former chief. About noon one of the candidate's assistants, dressed to represent his new personal crest, conducted them one behind the other to the potlatch house, where the phratries ranged themselves in order round the three sides, leaving an open space in the middle for dancing and for the coming and going of the members of the candidate's phratry. Each in turn then danced to the chants it had composed the night before, and after they had resumed their seats the candidate's phratry retaliated by offering pails of oil to the composers of the songs, who were obliged to drink as much as they could. Some became very sick, but others flourished the empty pails over their heads and victoriously repeated their chants. The candidate and his phratry feasted the entire assembly, paid the phratry that had just erected a gravehouse over the cremation place of the late chief, and distributed moose hides, beaver skins, and other valuable presents among all the guests. Then the candidate stepped forward and described where he had killed the moose, the beaver, the bear, and the other animals that had furnished the feast, and a prominent noble of his phratry listed all his helpers and the quantity of food and skins each of them had contributed. Finally, the entire phratry mustered behind the candidate and one noble, speaking for them all, announced, "Bear witness, all of you, that this man has assumed the title, the crest, and the personal songs (soneł) of our late chief and is now chief in his place." After a short delay to enhance the solemnity of the occasion, the chief of another phratry rose to his feet and said, "It is well that he should be your new chief. He is a nephew of the old chief; he has provided us with much food and many skins. Hereafter let him take the place and bear the titles of his uncle." The other chiefs spoke in the same strain and the gathering then dispersed.

Occasionally a rival candidate did not submit to the decision of the other chiefs and presumed to direct his clan or phratry as though he himself had been elected. The chiefs of the other phratries then mustered the people at the house of the man they had appointed and reaffirmed his chieftainship, at the same time warning the defeated candidate to drop his pretentions lest he stir up enmity and ill-will. If he still refused to submit, some partisan of the new chief killed him, and the people united in protecting the murderer from blood revenge.

The new chief was expected to give three more potlatches before he could claim the same dignity as his predecessor. The first of the three, his fourth potlatch, was called ni'habaatałtai, "Place the Corpse at the Back of the House;" and the next, tsar yin hatata'ai, "Cease the Song of Mourning," because it ended the ritual connected with the dead chief. His sixth and last potlatch, called taraiyełtił (meaning unknown), was the greatest of all if he erected a new totem pole, for then he invited Indians from all the surrounding country, even from other subtribes and nations. The mere preparation for the potlatch extended over 2 or 3 years, for first he had to hire his father's phratry-men to cut the tree in the woods and drag it to his house, then engage a skilled crafts- man (in nearly all cases a Gitksan Indian) to carve the clan crests on it during the winter months when the people were absent at their hunting grounds. Yet apart from the erection of the pole, the ceremonies at this potlatch closely paralleled those at the others; and actually most chiefs either did not care to erect a pole, or were unable to afford the expense. There seem, indeed, to have been no totem poles at all in Carrier territory before the nineteenth century, with the possible exception of one at Moricetown. The oldest pole that the Bulkley Indians remember stood at Moricetown, where it fell about 1870 and was buried. One, about 25 feet high, uncarved, was erected at Francis Lake about 1875 and fell about 1919; and four, that were erected at various dates during the second half of the nineteenth century, are still standing in the Hagwilgate canyon.[1]

By the end of the nineteenth century, when European settlement had caused the confinement of the Indians to certain reserves, six potlatches to become a chief were far too heavy a burden for any individual to undertake, especially since a chieftainship now carried no shred of authority and very little prestige. The present-day chief of the Thin House in the Gilserhyu phra- try, Felix George, gave only four potlatches when he succeeded his uncle in 1918, and none was as elaborate as the potlatches of earlier years. For his first potlatch he merely distributed a little tobacco among the villagers who assem- bled at his uncle's home on the day of that kinsman's death. For his second he summoned all the people to his own home immediately after the funeral and presented them with tea, sugar, apples, meat, biscuits, and other foods bought at the European stores in Hazelton. To help him out, his kinsmen and fellow-clansmen purchased some of the food for him, and also placed contributions of money into a bowl so that he could both pay his father's phratrymen for burying his predecessor and distribute a few dollars among the leading chiefs and nobles. Then his mother's brother rose up and proclaimed that Felix George was now the chief of the clan and would bear the hereditary title, Guxlet, together with the personal crest that accompanied it. Everyone understood, of course, that Felix would signalize his appointment by a more liberal feast as soon as he was able to raise the necessary funds.

Two years later Felix summoned together all the phratries and distributed among them 75 sacks of flour, 40 of which had been purchased by himself, 10 contributed by his brother, 10 by his brother-in-law, and the remaining 15 by various members of his own phratry. Since neither at this potlatch, nor at the two preceding, had any dancing occurred, and he still lacked the second per-

---

1. For descriptions of these poles see Barbeau, C.M. (1929, pp. 132–33, 143–46, 149).

sonal crest, Snatching (**p. 503 [p. 33]), that had belonged to his predecessor, he determined to save up his money for a fourth potlatch, which would go under the same name, taraiyeteɫtɨɫ, as the sixth and last potlatch of earlier times. Within 3 years he accumulated between $700 and $800. He then approached three fellow-phratrymen who were erecting grave monuments for themselves and were anxious to celebrate the occasion by giving potlatches. The four men agreed to join forces, and in the middle of summer announced the date of their common potlatch and sent out the formal invitations. Felix George himself bought from the stores in Hazelton 10 moose-hides, 4 cases of biscuits, 40 sacks of flour, several cases of milk and soft drinks, some soap, tea, meat, and a few other items. His eldest son gave him 12 sacks of flour; his brother-in-law and a cousin, each 10 sacks; Netipish, the chief of his phratry, and his brother, 4 sacks each; a kinsman, 3 sacks; a woman relative whose home was at Babine, 1 sack; and a friend from Burns Lake, 1 moose-hide. In addition, he paid a Hagwilgate native $5 to compose a song for him, and reserved a little money to distribute during the feast. His three colleagues bought other hides and food at the same time, but in less quantity.

The potlatch lasted 4 days. On the first the three men adopted crests which they impersonated in the potlatch house during the evening. Then followed the unusual incident of a raid by the members of the kaluɫlim society (***see p. [114]577 *et seq.*), who invaded the hall and carried off four neophytes. The rest of the people lingered and danced for a little while longer, then quietly dispersed about midnight to their homes. They passed the next 2 days in idle feasting, and the evenings in dancing. On the fourth day Felix and his colleagues distributed their presents and the guests from other places prepared to depart.

Important potlatches brought many guests from other places, such as Hazelton, Gitsegyukla, and Babine; and the Bulkley Indians often attended Gitksan potlatches. Two or three young nobles, delegated by the chief who was giving the potlatch, traveled together and conveyed the invitations to the surrounding villages. In each place they looked for the house of a phratry chief, who entertained them at a meal and received their message. They then visited any other phratry chiefs in the place, repeated the invitation, and passed on to the next village. On the opening day of the potlatch, again, the chief sent round a young noble to summon the people together. The youth entered every house, stood in front of each adult and, tapping the floor two or three times with a stick, said, "'Come to the potlatch hall." Gradually the people mustered outside the hall, where the members of each phratry waited for their chief to lead them inside. The giver of the feast guided every person to his seat, a delicate operation that required both a good memory and good judgment, for any error in ranking was certain to breed serious dissension and ill will. His own phratrymen either remained outside the building, or stood within wherever they could find room to assist in distributing the food and presents piled up in the middle of the floor.

It is clear that whether he was the head of a phratry, or of only a clan within a phratry, a chief had to expend much labor and wealth to gain his position.

Even after he had established himself firmly in his seat, he had to keep open house, as it were, to all members of his phratry, to relieve the wants of the poor, and to support his people in their relations with other phratries. His dwelling had to be instantly recognizable, to shelter his immediate family, the families of his nearest of kin, and visitors from other districts, and to serve as an entertainment hall at feasts and ceremonies. It was, therefore, much larger than the dwellings of the other villagers, its roof was supported by two rafters instead of one, and a crest of the clan was often carved or painted on its doorposts. Animal claws and shells suspended at night from the ceiling rattled at the touch of an intruder and guarded the inmates against attack.

A stingy chief who sought only his own profit soon lost his influence; if he were a clan chief, his own clan and the phratry chief would look to one of his nobles for leadership; and if he were a phratry chief, one of his clan chiefs might push him into second place. Only a chief could lead a war expedition, because no one else possessed the means to gather the stores of food necessary to feed the warriors from different places who assembled to take part in it; but if it succeeded, he was given all the captives, who thenceforward became his slaves. These slaves, who were generally well treated and well dressed, performed most of his menial work, and even assisted him in the chase, so that he was able to acquire two or more wives, whereas the ordinary native could seldom support more than one. Yet he, himself, was expected to share the hardships of the chase as long as his strength lasted, when he might pass the rest of his days in quiet state within the village, supplied with all necessities by the able bodied hunters, and receiving with his fellow-chiefs the largest gifts at every potlatch. One of his special perquisites at feasts was a strip of bear fat about a foot long, which was handed to him at the end of a long stick.

If the Indians demanded from their chiefs liberality, protection, and leadership, they in turn could demand that voluntary submission to their rulings without which the phratries and clans would have lost their coherence and the chiefs their prestige. Hence, when two families quarreled, the leading chief of any phratry might summon the people to his house, strew his head with swan's-down, the time-honored symbol of peace, and dance before them to the chanting of his personal song and the shaking of his rattle. After the dance he would deliver an oration, recounting all the wealth that he and his clan or phratry had expended in order to confer on him his title, his personal song, his rattle, his ceremonial leggings (xas), and his headgear (amali), all of which indicated their desire that he should be their leader and mediate in all their quarrels. Turning then to the disputants, he would exhort them to settle their strife, and warn them of the troubles that would overtake their families and clans if they persisted. In nearly all cases he was able to carry his audience with him, and the quarrelers, seeing that popular opinion was opposed to them, distributed moose skins in token of submission. So, although the authority of the chiefs was not codified, and they often ranked little or no higher than some of the nobles, an energetic and tactful man could occasionally guide the actions not only of his own clan and phratry, but of the entire subtribe, and become its official spokesman and leader in the eyes of all the surrounding subtribes.

The four (or five) phratric chiefs did not constitute a definite council, but discussed informally with one another matters that affected more than one phratry. Thus, if a man of one phratry murdered a man of another, the two phratric chiefs, supported by their clan chiefs, cooperated to avoid a blood-feud by arranging for satisfactory compensation. It was they who enjoined on the murderer a fast that lasted sometimes for 25 days, and they presided at the ceremony in the potlatch hall when the murderer and his clans-people handed over the blood-price. The ceremony held at Hazelton, when the Nass River Indians atoned for the murder of the Bulkley chief Gyedamskanish (see p. [5]479 *et seq.*), illustrates the usual procedure at such a ceremony. Besides handing over an enormous quantity of skins, blankets, stone adzes, and other goods, the murderer's kinsmen nearly always surrendered some fishing or hunting territory, usually, too, a marriageable maiden, who thenceforth could claim no protection from her clan or phratry, but became the unqualified property of the clan to which she was surrendered.

THE CYCLE OF LIFE

The Bulkley River child, like other Carrier children, started its career in life swaddled in sphagnum moss and warm furs inside a birchbark cradle that its mother carried perpendicularly on her back, or hung to a tree-limb or a lodge pole when she was working around her home. Not until it could run about did it receive clothes like its parents', first of all a tunic, longer or shorter according to its sex, then leggings and moccasins, and, in winter, a cap, mittens, and a little robe to wrap around its shoulders. Within the cradle its legs hung perfectly straight, from fear that even the gentlest flexion might impair its speed in running when it grew older. If it cried continually, or was restless and troublesome, its mother believed that it was anxious for a brother or sister to follow it into this world and that she would soon give birth to another child.

For the first few weeks or months it bore no other name than baby; then it received a name that suggested one of the crests in its father's clan or phratry. Thus the daughter of a man who belonged to the Gitamtanyu phratry received the name "Fierce Grizzly," because the grizzly was a crest in that phratry. Though the parents might confer any name they liked provided it suggested a paternal crest, they generally selected one that had been borne by a grandparent or other relative in childhood years. Commoners rarely changed this name in later life, and even a noble often retained it for everyday use. It conferred no rank of any kind, yet it possessed enough social significance to demand a potlatch—at least when the child's parents were nobles, and perhaps, too, when they were commoners, for it is so long since all caste differences disappeared that the Bulkley natives are uncertain on this point. (Plate 7.) Nobles summoned all their neighbors to the house of the chief of the mother's phratry, where the chief, taking the child in his arms, publicly conferred the name, mentioned its previous bearer, and usually related any story that was connected with it. The mother then carried the child home again, the guests ate the food provided by the parents and by the mother's phratry, and the father divided among his family and nearest kinsmen such gifts as her phratry had contributed for the occasion.

According to the amount of property that the parents were willing to give away in potlatches, a child between infancy and manhood might assume three or four names that had been previously held by different relatives. He obtained his first definite rank among the nobles, however, between adolescence and manhood, when he assumed the title of his mother's brother, or, if that brother were still alive, a title

Plate 7. A Carrier family at Alkatcho. (Photograph by Harlan I. Smith.)

that he had borne in his earlier days. The child's first name had signalized his relationship to his father's clan and phratry; but this later name marked him out as a member of his mother's clan. Thenceforward he sat directly in front of his uncle at all ceremonies, and was publicly recognized as the favored successor. A mother might have several brothers, or none at all; in any case she was related more or less closely to all the men in her clan. Hence, there was always a choice of titles, some marking a line of advancement higher than others; and parents naturally chose the more promising titles for their sons. Yet they did not neglect their daughters, and, in the absence of nearer male heirs, a woman might obtain the most honored titles and succeed to the highest positions.

Children, from the time they could walk, underwent systematic training along two lines, which the natives distinguished as geretne and gidet'e. Geretne was instruction in the various manual tasks that would fall to their lot when they grew up. The girl learned to carry wood and water, to cure and cook fish, meat, and berries, tan the various hides, design and sew the clothing, make birchbark baskets, sinew thread, and many other objects required in the home. The boy helped to build the houses, learned to manufacture tools and weapons, snow-shoes and canoes, and especially to hunt and fish for the daily supply of food. When he killed his first game, even if it were only a robin or a squirrel, his father entertained his phratrymen and told of his son's deed. Each sex had its own duties; if the men provided most of the necessities of the home, the women organized them and worked them up for use. So while the girl was helping her mother in the camp or village, the boy, as soon as he was old enough, followed his father to the chase, or plied a fish-rake beside him when the salmon were ascending the rivers.

Gidet'e, religious and ethical instruction, was the natural complement of this manual training, but followed a more indirect method. Its medium was the folk-tale, narrated in the evenings by the oldest man in the camp when the Indians were scattered in their hunting-grounds, and, in the villages, by the chief of the clan as he lay on his couch at the back of the big clan dwelling. Nearly every story carried with it the explanation of some phenomenon (e. g., the moaning of the trees, the shape of a certain rock), or else a moral (such as the penalty involved in the violation of a certain taboo). While the parents or their brothers occasionally thrashed a child that had committed some breach of etiquette, or violated an important taboo, they generally suffered the offence to pass without remark until the evening, when the oldest man narrated a story just as the inmates were retiring to their beds. After developing the plot until it applied to the particular occasion, he turned to the culprit and asked, "Did you do such and such a thing today?" and the child had no option but to confess. Then the old man resumed his story, and stressed the punishment meted out by Sa, the sky-god, or by the animals, for a similar breach of morals or of the customary law. If we may believe the present-day Indians, the shame and humiliation inflicted by this method were harder to endure, and more efficacious, than the severest thrashing.

It was only in the evenings that the Bulkley Carrier narrated their folk-tales, and then only from the beginning of November until mid-March, fearing to continue storytelling after that date lest it should lengthen out the winter. Very often they followed up a story with direct instruction about the habits of the game animals, the proper methods of hunting and fishing, the numerous rituals and taboos, and the etiquette that governed the relations between nobles and commoners, and between elders and children. The child, they taught, should be respectful to his elders, especially to the widowed, the aged, and the infirm, whether of equal or lower rank; and they pointed to four stars in the Dipper as a warning of the efficacy of an old woman's curse (Jenness, 1934, p. 137). Misfortune should never be mocked nor sorrow ridiculed. When a widower mourned his loneliness, weeping inside his hut, the boy should softly draw near and ask in low tones whether a little food would be acceptable, or a few sticks of wood to replenish the fire. He should never ridicule the animals, or gloat over success in hunting, remembering that the mountain goats destroyed a whole community because a few youths had cruelly tortured a little kid (Jenness, 1934, p. 155). In his play he should never be uproarious, but observe a certain dignity and moderation; for did not Sa, the sky-god, once carry a whole village into the sky and drop the lifeless bones to earth again, merely because the children, refusing to heed the warnings of their parents, had raised a tumult around their homes (Jenness, 1934, p. 125). Regulations such as these, promulgated by the old men at night through folk-tales, had to be observed by every child, but especially by the nobler born, because their parents were expending much property in potlatches to give them high standing, and filial obligation demanded obedience. Often the degenerate son of a

noble father had been eclipsed in fame and honor by a poor orphan who had
drunk in the words of his elders from a seat behind the door.

The Indians laid down some special rules of etiquette for young girls. A
high-born girl was expected to look straight ahead as she walked, turning her
head neither to right nor to left; girls of lower rank had to keep their eyes
modestly fixed on the ground. While the dentalia shells attached to the ears
of a chief's daughter, and the labret inserted in her lip, indicated her high
rank, they reminded her also that she should never speak ill of any one, but
guard her words and talk slowly, as befitted the daughter of a chief. Mothers,
of course, kept strict watch over their daughters, and taught them all these
necessary rules; but the folk-tales drove home their lessons, and also warned
the children beforehand of the special regulations and taboos that would be
incumbent on them as they approached maturity.

Adolescence brought an intensification of the training to boys and girls
alike. At that period some girl friend (what clan or phratry she belonged to did
not matter) tattooed the boy's wrist to make him a straight archer. From the
moment his voice began to change, he was instructed to refrain from many
foods that were thought to lessen his speed in running, impair his sight, or
hinder in other ways his success in the chase. He might not eat the heart of
any animal, lest it should give him heart trouble; nor the head, especially the
head of a mountain goat, lest it should make him dizzy and half-paralyzed,
and children born to him should fall sick and die; nor tripe, lest it should
make him cough violently when running after game; nor marrow, lest his
legs become sore; nor the meat of a bear cub, lest his limbs become stiff; nor
the meat of a young beaver, which travels so slowly that he too might become
slow at everything; nor caribou leg-meat that enclosed the sinew, lest his legs
become tired or suffer cramp; nor the leg of a black or grizzly bear in which
the bone lay embedded, lest it make his own legs sore; nor the paws of a black
or grizzly bear, lest his feet swell; nor the spruce-partridge, whose slow, short
flight might make him short-winded and slow of foot; nor eggs, lest his children have sore eyes, or he himself be sluggish like newly-hatched birds. Not
until he reached middle-age might he neglect these taboos, and eat such foods
with impunity. One further admonition his elders gave him; he should run up
hill, but never down, so that he might become a fast and steady runner. At
Hagwilgate several paths led from the high shelf above the canyon down to the
water's edge; boys were forbidden to run down these paths, but encouraged to
race each other up them.

More rigid still were the regulations for girls at this period. The Indians
thought that the adolescent girl was fraught with mighty powers for good and
evil; that if she carried a little child on her back the child would cease to grow,
or grow extremely slowly; that if she drank from a stream that the salmon
ascended they would appear there no more; that if she touched a hunter's
snowshoes, tools, or weapons he would capture no game; that if a man so
much as saw her face he might die, especially if he were a medicine man,
though, if his medicine were very powerful, it might kill the girl instead. She
herself was in grave danger; her parents' blood was coursing to and fro in her

veins, and only after a year or more did it yield to her own pure blood that would give her health and long life. So for at least 1 year, and generally 2, she might not contaminate her blood with the "blood" of fresh meat or berries lest it should bring on sickness and early death; dried fish and dried berries, roots, and barks became her only foods. On her head she wore a skin bonnet that had long fringes in front to conceal her face, and a long train behind. If her parents were noble, she wore over it a circlet of dentalia shells, and attached dentalia and other shells to three strands of her hair, one in front and one on each side, to make it seem long and trailing; girls whose parents were too poor to afford these shells merely bound their hair in two braids. Suspended from her neck, or fastened to her belt, were a drinking tube of goose or swan bone so that her lips would neither touch liquid nor any vessel that contained it, and a comb or scratcher to use on her head instead of her fingers. To prevent her hair from falling out, as might happen if she herself combed it, her mother or sister combed it for her. For about 2 years she lived in a tiny hut out of sight of the village or camp, and avoided as well as she could the trails of the hunters. When her people were traveling she followed far behind them, in the same trail, if it was easier, for she was not required, like Sekani girls, to break an entirely new trail. If the party came to a stream, her father laid a log across it so that she might cross without touching the water, or else her mother lingered behind and carried her across; and as the girl passed over, if possible without looking down, she dropped a few twigs into the water. The entire community knew of her condition, for, when the first few days of seclusion had expired, her parents took her home, and, setting her at the back of the house, announced her approaching maturity at a potlatch. If her father was a chief, his sister then pierced the girl's lower lip with a bone awl to hold a labret, and after the presents were distributed she retired once more to her hut, where she was supplied each day with food and drink by her mother, sister, or grandmother. The neighboring Gitksan Indians, who were rather more sedentary than the Carrier, built the girl's hut half underground, and connected it by one, or more often two cords to the parents' house, so that she could signal in case of need. The Bulkley natives seem occasionally to have built similar lodges, but the practice never became usual.

All these restrictions on the girl's liberty were of a negative character, designed to protect herself and the community from fancied harm; and they recurred, for a few days at a time, throughout the whole of her subsequent life. The 2 years' seclusion at adolescence, however, was a period also of positive training, when the mother or other near female relative gave the girl regular instruction in the duties of married life. They supplied her with birchbark to fashion into baskets and trays, hides to tan (plate 8) and sew into moccasins, and rabbit skin to weave into blankets. If at certain times she was advised to lie down and rest continuously, most of her days were fully occupied with tasks that she would be performing in later years.

Although the Bulkley natives no longer seclude their adolescent daughters in separate huts, they still subject them to various taboos, and warn them against eating fresh meat. A middle-aged woman can still remember how she

caused her brother to lose a valuable
beaver net. Her family was moving to
another camping place, and, as she
followed behind it, she found the net
hanging forgotten on a tree. Not daring to touch it, she hooked it over the
end of a long pole and deposited it in
the evening near her mother's lodge.
Her brother used it for several days,
but failed to catch any beaver, though
all his companions were successful. He then concluded that she had
spoiled the net, even though it had not
touched her, and in his anger he threw
it into the fire.

Sometimes the Indians tried to use
the mysterious forces operating in the
adolescent girl to prevent the constant
dying of infants in a family, which they
attributed to the violation of some taboo by one of the parents during his

Plate 8. Carrier girl dressing a hide. (Photograph by Harlan I. Smith.)

or her youth. When a woman who had lost two or more babies gave birth to
another child, she would ask an adolescent girl to bend a twig to the ground,
tie down its end with a cord, and then cut the cord with a knife. Thus, the
mother hoped, she could remove the curse that had overtaken her and raise
her child in safety.

After about 2 years, boys and girls emerged from the adolescent stage and
were ready to take their places among the adults of the community. The girl
laid aside her special costume and put on new garments; to keep her hair from
falling out later, she cut off the three long strands to which she had fastened
dentalia shells; and she held herself in readiness for her marriage, which
usually took place very soon afterward. Boys, however, did not marry until at
least 3 or 4 years later, when they had proved their skill in fishing and hunting
and their ability to support a wife. In Carrier subtribes farther east they were
expected at this time to undertake a diligent quest for guardian spirits that
would help them in emergencies, enable them to heal the sick or to obtain
game when the people were starving; but the Bulkley Carrier, believing that
guardian spirits and medicine powers came to men unsought, did not insist on
a definite quest, although they encouraged their young men to dream, and to
pay the greatest attention to their dreams as likely to give them medicine power. They did require each youth, however, to practise a certain ritual (**see
p. [79] 545 f), both before and after marriage, in order that he might thereby
achieve greater success in the chase.

Most young men tried to enhance their appearance by eradicating the eyebrows, moustache, and beard, although a man's good looks counted for little in
comparison with his rank, prowess in hunting, swiftness of foot, or reputation

for medicine power. With girls, too, rank and conduct theoretically counted for more than beauty. The well-bred girl seldom or never stumbled; if she were a chief's daughter, she looked straight in front of her; if a commoner's daughter, she looked modestly down; whatever her rank, she refrained from turning her head frequently to one side or the other; and when she sat down, she kept her feet together, not stretched one in front of the other. A slender face and figure, well-developed eyebrows and long hair were very desirable, but neither in woman nor man was beauty considered of prime importance.

The Bulkley Indians preferred a marriage between cross cousins, because it retained the family titles and privileges within a close circle and was more conducive to harmony. For the same reason, when a man's wife died, he regularly married her younger sister, if she had one; and a woman whose husband died went to his unmarried brother. Men who married more than one wife generally chose two sisters.

The distinction between cross and parallel cousins appears in the terms of kinship and relationship given below, where it will be seen that men had one term for the daughters of their fathers' sisters and their mothers' brothers, who were eligible for wives since they necessarily belonged to other phratries, and another term for the daughters of their mothers' sisters, who necessarily belonged to the same phratry, and of their fathers' brothers, who must frequently have belonged to it also. Similarly women distinguished between the sons of their fathers' sisters and mothers' brothers, on the one hand, and of their fathers' brothers and mothers' sisters on the other.

TERMS OF KINSHIP AND RELATIONSHIP

an·e', my mother (be-n, his mother).

sbeb, my father (bebeb, his father).

siyi', my son.

stse', my daughter.

sa·k'ai, my mother's sister (man or woman speaking); sister's daughter (man or woman speaking).

stai, my father's brother, my mother's or father's sister's husband, my wife's sister's daughter (man or woman speaking).

sbits, my father's sister, my mother's brother's wife, my mother-in-law (man or woman speaking); my brother's daughter, my husband's sister's daughter (woman speaking).

sezets, my father-in-law (man or woman speaking).

sre, my sister's husband, my brother's wife (man or woman speaking); my wife's brother, my wife's sister, my husband's brother, my husband's sister.

salt'en, my husband's brother's wife.

sla, my wife's sister's husband, my husband's sister's husband, my wife's brother's wife.

saz'e, my mother's brother (man or woman speaking).

sezi·t, my father's sister's daughter, my mother's brother's daughter (man or woman speaking); my father's sister's son, my mother's brother's son (woman speaking).

so·n'di, my father's sister's son, my mother's brother's son (man speaking).

saɬsen, my mother's sister's son, my father's brother's son (man or woman speaking).

saɬte'tse, my father's brother's daughter, my mother's sister's daughter (man or woman speaking).

stso, my sister's son or daughter (man or woman speaking) .

stchal, my brother's son (man or woman speaking), my wife's or husband's brother's or sister's son.

stitɬ, my younger sister (man or woman speaking), my brother's daughter, my wife's brother,s daughter (man speaking).

sa·t, my older sister (man or woman speaking).

songri, my older brother (man or woman speaking).

stchatll, my younger brother (man or woman speaking).

sranten, my son-in-law (man or woman speaking).

siyes'at, my daughter-in-law (man or woman speaking).

sti'ɬ, my husband's brother's daughter (woman speaking).

stchai, my grandchild (man or woman speaking).

stsets, my grandfather (man or woman speaking).

stsani, my father's mother (man or woman speaking) .

stso, my mover's mother (man or woman speaking) .

The choice of a husband rested with both the girl and her parents, who generally respected her wishes unless a chief asked for her in marriage, or required her surrender to atone for a murder or other crime. Occasionally the suitor, or one of his parents, suggested the match to the girl beforehand in order to sound out her inclinations, though she herself could neither accept nor reject the proposal. The youth then offered a large quantity of furs, moccasins, arrows, and other property to her mother and kinspeople, and if they rejected the amount as insufficient, gathered still more to add to the price. If they finally accepted, the father invited the suitor to join his household and to help him in hunting and other enterprises. The young couple did not marry immediately, even though they now lived in the same house or lodge; but they tested each other out, as it were, by carefully watching one another's actions and listening to all the conversation that went on in the home. At last one night, when everything seemed propitious, the bridegroom silently crept under his bride's robe, and remained seated beside her when the family arose in the morning, thus openly declaring their marriage. For a year or so longer they remained with her parents, handing over to them everything they acquired except the few skins they themselves needed for clothing. Thereafter they could build their own lodge and hunt by themselves, though the girl's parents still had a claim on their services, and largely relied on their son-in-law's help at potlatches.

A widowed chief (for a man could hardly become a chief until long after his first marriage), or a chief who desired to take an additional wife, was exempt from any period of servitude. He merely notified the girl's parents through a kinsman or kinswoman, who at the same time delivered the bride-price. The parents naturally coveted the honor for their daughter and rarely refused. Shortly afterward the girl, however reluctant she might be to wed an elderly or middle-aged man, was escorted by the same kinsman to her new home.

Neither was there any period of servitude for a girl surrendered in compensation for a murder or other crime. Her parents resigned every claim to her when they handed her over, with other property, in payment of the blood-price, and the brother or near kinsman of the murdered man who took her to wife enjoyed absolute authority over her. However harshly she was treated, she could not return to her parents, for she now belonged, body and soul, to her husband and his kin. Nevertheless, it does not appear that she was treated very differently from other girls, for every hunter needed a wife to handle the meat and hides he secured, to prepare his food and make his clothing; and an efficient and contented wife increased his own comfort.

The Indians strongly discountenanced marriage outside the caste. If a nobleman married a commoner woman his children were commoners, and only with the greatest difficulty could he secure their elevation, because his wife's brothers and kinsmen could offer no appreciable aid. On the other hand, a girl of noble rank who married a commoner incurred general disapprobation, and was constantly mortified by the lowly position he occupied at all feasts and ceremonies. Her children, too, would in most cases remain commoners, unless her parents and brothers took pity on them and undertook the expenses of the potlatches necessary to raise their standing. If a commoner greatly distinguished himself by his prowess in hunting, or gained a reputation for great medicine power, he might aspire to marry even a chief's daughter, but in that case the chief would certainly wipe away the stain of his birth and confer on him a title in a magnificent potlatch. The ordinary mésalliance was liable to turn into a tragedy.

> Several youths of noble rank were rivals for the hand of a noble-man's daughter, and enlisted to serve her kinsfolk in the chase. The girl herself, however, favored a commoner, and in spite of her parent's admonitions, refused all her authorized suitors and encouraged his addresses. One night he stole into her lodge and shared her sleeping robe, giving her parents no choice but to recognize their marriage and dismiss the other youths. Soon afterward a nobleman announced that he was holding a pot-latch and invited all the people to attend. The chiefs and nobles occupied their accustomed places in the seats of honor, but the girl's husband had to squeeze in among the commoners in one corner. Her old grandmother said to her, "Let us peer through that hole in the wall of the potlatch house and see where your husband is sitting." They looked, and saw him squeezed among the rank and file in the corner. "We warned you about that," the old woman said. The girl was so mortified that she returned home, tied a rope to a tree, and hanged herself.

In a polygamous household, the first wife ranked above the others, who were in a measure her servants and did such cooking, drying of fish, clean-ing of hides, and other duties as were not done by slaves. If they quarreled among themselves, their husband thrashed them soundly with a stick. A man could divorce his wife for misconduct, idleness, or, indeed, any reason at all by sending her back to her father or nearest kinsman, and either retaining the children or sending them with her. To be divorced by a chief in this way was so disgraceful that the woman's father or brother might publicly censure her in a potlatch. For that purpose he stationed her in the middle of the hall with a woman on each side of her, and stood behind with three or four men hired to chant satirical songs, such as, "I did not cook for my husband; I sought after other men, etc." At each song the two women compelled the divorced wife to dance while the audience mocked her. Afterward her kinsmen, to blot out the disgrace, distributed presents to all except their own phratrymen and took the woman home.

Divorce by a chief needed no justification; but a nobleman who divorced his wife generally felt impelled to ventilate his reasons by engaging his father and some men in his father's phratry to satirize the woman in the same way; and a woman who left her husband on account of ill-treatment or neglect sim-ilarly satirized him through her own father and kinsmen. The guilty person stayed away on these occasions, but might retaliate in a later potlatch. The divorce, however, was complete, and both the man and the woman were free to remarry whom they pleased.

Before the birth of her child, a mother submitted to nearly as many taboos as an adolescent boy or girl. Old women cautioned the expectant mother that if she lay down too much her child's head might become elongated and impair its health, whereas constant activity would increase both her own strength and her baby's. She was to be sparing in her diet, lest the child should grow too big and make delivery difficult. Neither she nor her husband should eat eggs, which would give the child sore eyes; nor the head of any animal or fish, particularly the head of a beaver, which would make the child's eyes small like a beaver's eyes, or of a rabbit or salmon, which would make the child cry continually; nor the meat of any animal that had been caught in a noose or snare, for it might produce a constriction in the child's neck that would strangle it as it grew up. After the delivery of her first child, the mother should use a drinking-tube, and abstain from fresh meat and fresh fish for a whole year; with later children she could use a cup, if she wished, and eat fresh food after 1 month. To insure her baby being a boy (or girl) she should make a noose and repeat continually, "I want a boy (girl). If a girl (boy) is born I'll hang it with this noose."

As the hour of childbirth approached, the husband built for his wife a special hut which no man save himself dared to enter through fear of becoming lame. Here he attended to all her needs, or else he engaged a female relative to look after her, for a homicide who attended his wife in labor might render her incapable of bearing more children. The helper cut the umbilical cord, placed the baby in its cradle, and wrapped in bark or fur the afterbirth, which the mother herself later concealed in a tree where neither bird nor animal could touch it and by so doing destroy her fertility.

Domestic life varied considerably with the seasons of the year, periods of isolation alternating with periods of intense social activity when the family was almost swallowed up in the clan and phratry. Dominating everything was the necessity of securing an adequate supply of the principal foods, meat, and fish. Consequently the man and his sons (as soon as the latter were old enough) spent most of their time in hunting and fishing, while the woman and her daughters carried home the meat, set snares for small game such as rabbits and marmots, collected berries and roots, cooked the food, dressed the skins, made the clothing, the bags and the baskets, and performed the many miscellaneous duties that are inseparable from a home. Very few women used the bow and arrow or the fish spear, but they shared the line fishing in the lakes and rivers.

The Bulkley natives recognized four seasons, spring (kω·łił), summer (kyen), autumn (ta'kait) and winter (xait). They counted by winters, and watched for the appearance of each new moon, which commonly evoked the cry, "Look" (ho biye) and the stereotyped answer, "The little moon" (sa inai). They seem to have divided the period from one winter to the next into 12 moons, beginning the cycle with the "little white fish moon," which fell around September–October. At Fraser Lake, the Indians used a similar calendar, but had different names for certain moons.

CALENDAR

Moons	Bulkley Indians	Fraser Lake Indians
Sept.–Oct.	Little white-fish moon (xlʊts uzze', because the fish spawns about that time)	Little white-fish moon (xlus uzza)
Oct.–Nov.	Time of little cold (binin'hozkatsyez)	Big white-fish moon (xlu'uzza)
Nov.–Dec.	Gyint'ek (meaning unknown)	Hankyi (meaning unkown)
Jan.–Feb.	Big sun (sa·kyo)	Big sun (sa·cho)
Feb.–Mar.	Moon inverted like a cup (?) (minkyes)	Black specks on the snow (takasstil)
Mar.–Apr.	Fish month (t'lo'gaxt'si uzze')	Fish month (t'lu'gas uzza)
Apr.–May	Month of suckers (guskyi uzze')	Month of suckers (taggus uzza)
May–June	Time when ducks moult (bininkyetkyas)	Thumb (ne.chaz)
June–July	Time when salmon come up the river (biningyist'lex)	Sock-eyed salmon (ta.lok)
July–Aug.	Time top-of-mountain hunting people go out (bininziłk'ats tsetattił)	Char month (bettuzza)
Aug. –Sept.	When the full moon comes up over the last line of trees on the mountain side (sky-anlere·pes)	(?)

In July the entire subtribe used to gather at Hagwilgate (prior to 1820, at Moricetown) to intercept the migrating salmon, which were dried and stored away for the autumn and early winter (plate 9). This month, and the month following, were periods of abundance, when the diet of salmon could be varied with fresh berries, with wild rice (djankatł), and with the roasted roots of the wild parsnip (djanyankotł) and of the djinitłrets, an unidentified plant whose root attains the size of a pumpkin. Near relatives of each chief then shared with him the big clanhouse, while the other families in the clan occupied small individual dwellings round about. Many days and nights were given over to ceremonies and potlatches, attended not only by all the villagers, but by numerous guests from neighboring subtribes. Since every man and woman

participated in these ceremonies, the individual families
seemed for a few weeks nearly submerged.

Before any snow settled
on the ground, however, the
subtribe broke up and the
families dispersed to their
hunting territories in search
of beaver, caribou, bear,
goats, and marmots. Tribal
activities then ceased, and
for a time the families lived
solitary, or else one or two together, eking out a precarious
existence by the chase. In the

Plate 9. Fish-traps in the canyon at Hagwilgate. (Photograph by Harlan I. Smith.)

autumn, and again in the spring, they snared hundreds of marmots, whose
skins the women sewed together into robes and socks; but during the winter
proper they secured very little game except bears and caribou. Surplus caribou
fat they melted and poured into the long intestine of the animal and carried as
a food ration on their journeys; and surplus meat they preserved in boxes or
baskets, sealed with the grease that dripped from strips of bear fat laid sloping
over a fire.

In March the snow melted rapidly, and living by the chase became more
difficult. After their long winter isolation, the families eagerly gathered on the
lakes and rivers to fish through holes in the ice, making use of both the spear
and the set line. The latter carried a barb of bone lashed at an angle of about
45 degrees to a wooden shank and baited with a lump of fat. When using the
three-pronged spear, the Indians commonly encircled the fishing hole with a
low wall of spruce boughs, roofed the shelter with a blanket, and scraped away
the snow outside so that the light penetrated through the ice to the water beneath; then, peering through the hole, they observed the fish approaching the
lure, and struck them when they disappeared within the shadow of the shelter.

In some years March brought them famine; their stocks of dried salmon
were exhausted, the lakes yielded few fish, and the game seemed to keep
out of reach. A few families would then cross to the Nass River to join in the
oolachan fishery, but the majority supported themselves on the inner bark of
the hemlock, which they wrapped in spruce bark and roasted for several hours
on hot stones. Then they crushed the fibers with stone hammers and dried
the pulpy mass in large cakes that could be softened in water and eaten with
fat. As soon as the ice broke up in the lakes, the various households generally
scattered again to hunt until summer reassembled them for the salmon fishing at Hagwilgate or Moricetown.

Despite their permanent settlements at Moricetown and Hagwilgate, therefore, the Bulkley Indians were constantly on the move, driven from place to
place by the vagaries of the food supply. In summer they used canoes of spruce

bark (after the fur-traders came, of birchbark also), but even at that season they traveled mainly on foot, carrying on their backs the meager furniture of their homes. Down to the nineteenth century they lacked even snowshoes and toboggans, though they sometimes improvised a toboggan from an animal's hide, and, in crossing wide expanses of glare ice, dragged their loads on sticks and branches. Present-day natives say that the man always carried the heaviest load, unless he was called away by the chase; but that even the little children bore burdens proportionate to their strength. Their tump-lines were of babiche, with a broad head band of skin, though for other purposes they often used ropes of twisted cedarbark. Torches of birchbark lighted their footsteps in the darkness; and two lumps of pyrites, or sometimes a stick rapidly twirled in the hands against another stick, gave them fire. A stake planted in the ground and pointed toward the sky told passers-by the hour at which friends had preceded them along the trail; and a crude grass image of a human being lying on his side, tied to a tree, indicated that some one had died recently in the vicinity.

Yet life was not all toil and hardship for a Bulkley household. Whenever food was plentiful and three or four families settled down together, they indulged in many games and pastimes. The most popular was a gambling game played with two short sticks of bone, one of which was marked. Two rows of men sat opposite, and over at one end someone beat a drum. Amid frenzied singing and drumming each side in turn passed the sticks from hand to hand and the other side guessed where the marked stick was concealed. It is probable that this game, so widespread in Canada at one time and still common in the Mackenzie River Valley, did not reach the Bulkley River until the fur-trading days of the nineteenth century. There was, however, an older game, in which the marked stick was known as chat and the unmarked stick ke. The player seems to have thrown one of his sticks on a board of leather; but the further details are no longer remembered.

Formerly, as today, jumping and racing were popular with the children and younger men. Other games now seldom or never played were:

1. *Snow-snake.*—The players gambled on the distance to which they could "skip" a long wooden dart off a hard snowbank. Players at Fraser and Stuart Lakes did not use an elevated snowbank, but merely skipped the darts over the natural surface of the snow. Their darts were only about 4 feet long, whereas the darts used by the Bulkley Indians averaged 6 or 7 feet.

2. *na'hatilko.*—Each player hurled a 3-foot dart with a disk on the end against a thin slat of wood 1 1/2 inches wide set upright in the ground, and tried to catch the dart as it rebounded. If he failed to catch it, or missed the lath, he yielded place to his opponent.

3. *Hoop and stick.*—The players hurled short spears through a small hoop as it rolled along the ground; or else one side shot an arrow through it, and the other tried to shoot the arrow at its resting place.

4. *Retrieving with a line.*—The players rivaled each other in retrieving a bundle of twigs sent floating down the river, each hurling a short hooked spear tied to a long line.

5. *Rough and tumble.*—Two small holes were dug in the ground a few yards apart, and the girls lined up at one hole, the boys at the other. A man then waved a strong 4-foot stick between them and chanted, "By and by I shall eat blueberries," i. e., cause many bruises. The children rushed to catch the stick as he threw it into the air, and while the girls struggled to register a "touch" with it against their hole, the boys tried to register a touch at their own.

6. *Tug of War.*—Men and women took opposite sides and tugged on a stout Rope of twisted cedar bark. If the front man could pull the opposite woman over to his side, she had to face round and help her adversaries. There were other forms of this game for two people only. Sometimes two men tugged on a swan's bone about 9 inches long; at other times they sat on the ground, feet against feet, and tugged on a stick or rope until one or other was lifted to a standing position.

So life jogged along for the Bulkley Carrier until at last old age overcame him or some catastrophe cut short his career; either he perished in a raid or while hunting, or he succumbed to one of the ailments that afflicted the natives even before the white man introduced new plagues to increase the toll from disease.

The Indians ascribed most of their ailments to supernatural or psychological causes, and tried to combat them by the same means (*** see Medicine men, p. [96]559). Yet this did not prevent their employment of many herbal remedies, some of which, e. g., the use of balsam gum for wounds and burns, and of fernroot for worms, possessed true therapeutic value. For coughs and colds they inhaled steam, or drank decoctions of wild-rose roots or juniper tips; and to check bleeding they applied a poultice made from the green roots of the Cottonwood. Juniper tips, the root of the red-fruited elder, and the barks of the balsam and devilsclub supplied them with purgatives; and for biliousness they injected a decoction of red-alder bark, using the crop of a bird as a syringe. The prescription for a certain tonic called for the drinking, morning and night, of two tablespoonfulls of a decoction made from a handful of each of the following ingredients; Needle-tips of the Jack-pine and of another pine, inner barks of the wild gooseberry and of the wild rose, bark of the red osier dogwood, inner pulp of raspberry canes, and stems of the bear-berry. To this and many other prescriptions might be added a sweat bath, taken, as usual, inside a bee-hived lodge where the bather generated steam by pouring water on red hot stones.

Sooner or later sweat baths, herbal remedies, and the frenzied chants of the medicine men were bound to fail the Indian, and the day came when his father's phratry dressed him in his finest clothes and laid him on the funeral pyre. On top of him lay his widow, who had to embrace her dead husband until she could no longer withstand the smoke and the flames. Even then his kinsfolk, whose servant she now became, pushed her repeatedly into the flames until she was severely burned, if for any reason she had incurred their displeasure. The people sat around in a circle and wept till evening, when they retired to their homes and either left the widow to spend the night at the pyre, or led her to some house of her husband's kin. The neighboring Gitksan made her mourn at the pyre and weave a net to prove that she had passed the night in sleeplessness; but the Carrier, apparently, set her no task. The day after the cremation, the father's phratry gathered the calcined bones in a box and handed them for safe keeping to the phratry of the deceased, who then repaid them in a potlatch. About a year later, the father's phratry built a wooden grave-house over the cremation site, and deposited the bones on top of a post carved with the crest of the deceased's clan or phratry.

If a man died at his hunting grounds, his widow cremated his remains and carried the bones to the village when the hunting season ended. Among the more eastern Carrier, she was obliged to carry them on her back for a year or more, whence the early French voyageurs called these Indians porteurs, i.e., Carriers; but the Bulkley natives have no recollection of the custom in their own district.

A widow had to serve her husband's kinsmen for at least a year, at times much longer, if they were unwilling to release her; indeed, if she was content with her position, and too old to remarry, she sometimes continued to serve them the rest of her days. She slept in any part of the house that they assigned her, and preserved the strict semblance of mourning, wearing old clothes, keeping her hair short, and refraining from washing her face. In most cases her servitude was light—invariably so if her kinsmen were powerful—and she could secure her release and remarry after the 12 months ended. She usually married a brother or near kinsman of her dead husband, although she was free to exercise her own choice.

A widower underwent exactly the same servitude as a widow, though he, of course, served his wife's kinsmen, and was more immune from ill-treatment; thus, he was not forced to embrace his dead wife during her cremation. At the end of the mourning period, he washed his face and held a potlatch, if his kinsmen were influential; if not, he moved without ceremony into one of the houses of his own clan or phratry. He then generally married any sister of his dead wife who was still unwed, although, like the widow, he was not restricted in his choice.

Today each Bulkley Indian family has its individual frame house, and a widower (or widow), though expected to aid the kinsmen of his dead wife in minor ways, is not obliged to live with them. He refrains from remarrying, however, for at least a year, and generally terminates the period of mourning by giving a small potlatch, at which he hires some one to compose a new song. All the guests dance to the new song, and after eating, return to their homes with trifling presents.

Like other peoples, the Bulkley Indians did not look upon death as the ultima rerum, the final goal of all things. They believed that every human being possessed three parts besides his corporeal body; a mind or intelligence (bini, "his mind"); warmth (bizil, "his warmth"); and a third part, called while he was living his shadow (bitsen, "reflection in water, shadow cast by the sun or moon, ghost or apparition of a living person"), and after death his shade (bizul). These three parts were indispensable to give the body life and health; but whereas the warmth, being a mere attribute, as it were, of the body, perished with it, the mind probably persisted after death, though whether it then became identified with the shadow, or what happened to it, the natives held to be quite uncertain. Neither the mind nor the warmth left the body during life, but the shadow frequently wandered abroad, especially in sleep or in sickness. Too lengthy an absence, however, caused the owners's sickness and death. To see an apparition of someone—his shadow—was a sure sign that the person to whom it belonged would soon fall sick and die. If a man chanced to see his own apparition, he placed a little bird's down in his cap or moccasin, and hung it over his bed; if in the morning it still felt warm, his shadow had returned and he would live, but if it felt cold he would die. A dog was able to see a wandering shadow, and the barking of a dog at night indicated that such a shadow was roaming in the neighborhood. At times it threw a stick or a stone at someone, who knew at once that, unless he could obtain help from a medicine man, both he himself would die and also the person whose shadow was molesting him. A medicine man, in his dreams, could discover a wandering shadow and imprison it in his own body until, in a public ceremony a few hours later, he could restore it to its rightful owner. It was not infrequent, indeed, for one medicine man to accuse another of stealing a sick person's shadow, and the accused had then either to restore the patient to health by returning it, or else be adjudged a murderer. More frequently still, powers in the animal or spiritual world captured and imprisoned men's shadows, and such men, after recovering them, became imbued with special gifts of foresight and of healing not granted to the ordinary layman.

After the death of the body the shadow, or, as it then became, the shade (bizul), journeyed to a City of the Dead somewhere toward the rising sun. It did not know that its body was dead and decaying, being conscious only that it was traveling along a broad smooth path through a pleasant land warm with the breath of summer. It began its journey the moment it left the body, but occasionally it returned an hour or a day afterward, and, reentering the lifeless form, revived the dead man, who was able to explain what his shade had seen.

My cousin Gudzan lay dead one day for an hour, and during that time his shade fared forth along the path that leads to the City of the Dead. The warm, summery air was tinged with a faint smokelike haze, and the landscape was very beautiful. His shade had gone but a short distance through this country when it thought, "Why am I traveling along this path. I will return." But as it started back a black streak moved across the path and barred its passage. Vainly it endeavored to circle round the obstacle, and at last, in its terror, it tried to leap over it. The object moved back, and the shade landed right on top of it. It was its own body that it lighted on, and straightway my cousin came to life again.

In August 1923 a Babine Indian named Nettsis died for a day and also returned to life. He told me that he too found the broad path that leads to the City of the Dead. It ran through a gently undulating plain clothed with summer verdure, and was lined on either side with bushes of ripe blackberries. At the summit of a low hill bubbled a spring of pure clear water. Many footsteps had marked the road, all pointing eastward, but he saw no people. He halted at the spring, thinking to himself, "The people will laugh at me, for I have no clothes. I had better turn back." So he returned to life again.

Two persons, and only two, the Indians relate, have ever reached the City of the Dead and returned to life again to describe their experiences. One was a youth, the hero of many strange adventures (Jenness, 1934, p. 99); the other a medicine man who, like Orpheus, followed his dead wife to bring her back to earth (Jenness, 1934, p. 143). The Indians derived all their notions of the after-life from these two myths, principally this section of the myth concerning the medicine man.

As the two shadows traveled along the wide, smooth road, the man ahead and his wife behind, they saw many tracks of un-moccasined feet, all pointing in the same direction, and none returning. On either hand were berry bushes, but all the berries were black. The medicine man refrained from eating them, for he was still alive; and when his wife attempted to eat them, he took the berries from her hand and threw them aside. Soon they came to a spring of water. Here the woman wished to drink from the small basket of birchbark that lay beside it; and again her husband forbade her. When he himself dipped the basket into the spring, all the water flowed through it, although he could see no hole; for he was still living, and the basket was intended for the dead alone. People are often thirsty when they die, and this place, a little above the road, is the last drinking place of the dead.

Now they came to a great precipice, down which, in one place, led an easy road. The dead, trying to return to earth, often come back to this precipice, but they can neither find the road again nor can they scale the cliff. Beyond the cliff was a river, and on its farther bank a city, divided into two parts. On the one side all the houses and canoes were black, on the other red; and between them stood a totem-pole named tsim'yak'yak. The black houses were the homes of the dead, the red the homes of the robins, which dwell on earth during the day and depart to the underworld at evening. Here the dead woman yawned, and immediately a black canoe put off from the farther bank and began to cross toward her. The medicine man shouted, and the people in the red houses, hearing him, put off in a red canoe. Both canoes reached the bank together. The woman wished to enter the black one, but her husband told her to embark with him on the red canoe. When they reached the opposite shore she wished to enter a black house, but he constrained her to follow him into a red one. There he was given some good dried fish, which he ate.

Behind the house which they had entered stood a smaller house inhabited by a little old woman. She informed the medicine man that the red houses were the homes of robins, the black the homes of the dead. "Presently," she said, "the dead will invite you and your wife to visit them. Go, but do not eat the food they offer you. Warn your wife also not to eat, for otherwise she will never retarn with you to the land above. I will stand behind your back, and whatever food they offer you, pass it back to me, for I am dead and can eat with impunity. They will seem to give you huckleberries, but the huckleberries will be dead men's eyes."

After a time the occupants of a black house called to the medicine man, "Come over to our house." When he entered with his wife, a man set a blanket on the floor for them to sit on, and offered the medicine man a wooden dish filled with seeming huckleberries. His wife grabbed them up, but he forced her to release them, and in spite of her anger passed them back to the old woman behind him. Then they set before him the dried flesh of frogs and snakes and lizards. These, too, he handed to the old woman, and, when the meal had ended, led his wife back to the village of the robins.

In the morning the old woman said to him, "If you wish to return to earth alive you must pass over the cliff again. There are two trails that lead to it, besides the broad road for dead people that you followed hither. One trail is very filthy, for it is the path taken by dead dogs. The other is a faint trail, not easy to find, that leads to a place where a huge snake spans the river of death. The snake undulates up and down so that any one who tries to cross on its back falls flat and cannot rise again."

Good and bad alike, the natives thought, shared the same fate; both made their way to the City of the Dead, where they dwelt in idleness, never hunting, and eating nothing but dried frogs, dried snakes, and other loathesome foods. Each morning the robins deserted them and flew back to earth to enjoy the sunlight and the society of man. The living Indian who heard a robin singing during the daytime would say, "yo'hodinne (I am grateful to you)," but when evening drew near, and it sang its departing note, "so so so so," the note that it sings in the City of the Dead, he carefully said nothing, lest his shade should follow after it. He hoped, perhaps, that his own shade would be among the more fortunate that for some unknown reason did not journey to the City of the Dead, but lingered near the grave and sooner or later obtained reincarnation.

The inheritance of physical characters provided the Indians with seemingly solid grounds for their belief in reincarnation. One man's sister-in-law had six toes, and his son, born after her death, likewise had six toes, whence the conviction that the aunt had been reincarnated in the child. Strangely enough, the second son had a crooked thumb that was said to resemble its grandmother's. Another man had a birthmark on his foot similar to one on his mother's uncle, and, believing that he possessed the same shadow, he adopted that uncle's title. The Indians thought that deep and prolonged morning often induced the shade of a dead relative to enter into the next child, and if such a child cried frequently, its mother, believing that the desires of one life were carried over into the next, would search out something that had been prized by its predecessor. A child credited with being a reincarnated relative was sometimes referred to as hwatchan e'kaidittsut, "a person who travels everywhere," because its shadow seemed peculiarly liable to rebirth generation after generation.

Like many Europeans, the Indians claim that they often see the shades of the dead haunting old burial places. Thus, one man stated that a few years ago, when traveling near Quesnel, he observed a woman emerge from a grave, wander away for two or three hundred yards, and return to the grave again. Being a fervent Christian, he went up to the place and prayed for her.

When Simon Fraser and his party reached Fraser Lake in 1806, the local Indians, who are closely related to the Bulkley River people, looked upon them as the reincarnated shades of cremated Indians, because they not only came from the east, up the Nechako river, but they blew smoke from their mouths (Jenness, 1934, p. 257).

RELIGION

John McLean, who spent several years among the Carrier in the first half of the nineteenth century, states that "the Takelly" (Carrier) language has not a term in it to express the name of Deity, spirit, or soul. When the Columbia religion was introduced among them, our interpreter had to invent a term for the Deity—Yagasita—the "Man of Heaven." The only expression I ever heard them use that conveyed any idea whatever of a superior Being is, that when the salmon fail, they say, "The man who keeps the mouth of the river has shut it up with his red keys, so that the salmon cannot get up."

The Bulkley natives, however, assert that they at least recognized a superior Being long before Europeans penetrated to their country. At Stuart Lake he was called yutarre; at Fraser Lake, yutakki; and by the Bulkley people themselves, utakke, all meaning "that which is on high." He was a typical sky god, and indeed the Bulkley natives often called him sa, "sky or sky luminary." They regarded the sky as another land abounding in lakes and forests like this earth, but neither very warm nor very cold. Sa and his children had their dwelling there, but occasionally he came down to earth to help some unfortunate man or woman (see Jenness, 1934, pp. 183–84, 215–18, 229–31), and once he sent his son instead (Jenness, 1934, pp. 164–65). Thunder the natives attributed to the flapping wings of a bird, about the size of a grouse, that lived on top of a mountain; but whenever the sun and sky were obscured by heavy rain or snow they would say, "utakke nenye" (Utakke is walking on earth), concealed in the storm. Whenever, again, the sun went under something (sa wi'inai), i.e., was eclipsed, they thought that Utakke was punishing them for some transgression and that the phenomenon foreboded sickness. They still recall the terrible epidemic of smallpox that ravaged the Skeena River Basin in 1862, shortly after a total eclipse of the sun.

Although this belief in a sky-God probably dates back to pre-European times, it was not until elements of Christianity had penetrated to the Bulkley Carrier that it gradually assumed a prominent place. Before that time the Indians had looked mainly to powers in the animal world for explanations of life's phenomena and for assistance in life's journey. They thought that animals possessed warmth, mind, and shadows equally with man; that they differed from man only in their corporeal forms, in possessing certain powers that man lacked, and in lacking other powers that man enjoyed. Thus, they could assume at will the shapes of human beings, and somewhere or other had their individual homes where each species lived very much the same life as human beings. Legend recorded that the wolf, the caribou, the bear, and even the frog had carried people away and married them, or else sent them home with special medicine powers; and even today the Indians believe that such happenings are possible, although now, they claim, the animals usually abduct only the shadows of men. It was from the animals that man acquired much of his knowledge, and on the animal world he depended for his daily food. Every word that was spoken, every act that took place in a village or camp, the animals knew. Hence the Indian needed to be extremely careful in all his relations with them; if he were wise he scrupulously obeyed all the time-honored regulations and taboos, and never treated an animal with contumely or said a disparaging word about it. An old man well summed up their attitude thus:

We know what the animals do, what are the needs of the beaver, the bear, the salmon, and other creatures, because long ago men married them and acquired this knowledge from their animal wives. Today the priests say that we lie, but we know better. The white man has been only a short time in this country and knows very little about the animals; we have lived here thousands of years and were taught long ago by the animals themselves. The white man writes everything down in a book so that it will not be forgotten; but our ancestors married the animals, learned all their ways, and passed on the knowledge from one generation to another.

In the earliest times, the Indians continue, many monstrous animals disputed with man the lordship of the earth. There was a lynx larger and more savage than the existing lynx, grizzlies that attacked the Indian villages, huge snakes that destroyed all passers by, and frogs that killed from a distance. Although various heroes long ago rid the world of these creatures and left the fauna as it is today, even now the Indian who wanders in remote places harbors a lurking fear that some appalling monster may suddenly spring up to bar his path. Should a stranger approach his lonely camp he stands on his guard, partly from a traditional fear of human enemies, and partly because he is not sure that the visitor may not prove to be an animal in human guise. He firmly believes that the otter sometimes transforms itself into a youth or maiden and seduces an Indian to his destruction.[2] The hooting of a small owl night after night near his camp fills him with dismay, for it is warning him that a relative will soon die; although the first time he hears it hooting he may throw a little fat into the fire and pray, "As I now give you this fat so do you provide me with abundant fat hereafter"; or else he may divide his fat into three pieces, and sacrifice the first piece to the owl, the second to the raven, and the third to the blue jay, in order that these birds, rejoicing in the feast, may deliver the game into his hands.Whenever he kills a black bear, he kneels beside its carcass and chants this song, on the vowel "e"; to please its departing shade and ensure his killing other bears thereafter.

About 20 years ago, when I was traveling with my uncle and other Indians east of Moricetown, my dog scented out a black bear, which I killed quite easily, for I had often dreamed of killing bears. Six days later my uncle fell sick, and said to me, "I'll eat some of that fresh bear meat, and rub some of the grease over me. Then perhaps I shall feel better." That evening a young Babine girl joined our camp and said to him, "I should like to eat some of that bear meat too." At first my uncle refused her, because she seemed to be at the adolescent stage when fresh meat was forbidden her; but when she still pleaded he at last gave her a little. At midnight he died, and we discovered that the

---

2. The Indians therefore advised their young men (and young women) not to think much about the other sex, lest they be deceived by the otter. They believed that a woman became insane if she merely touched the tail of a dead otter, or if someone wrapped one of her hairs round its tail; but that, contrariwise, she would conceive a violent attachment for the man who wrapped one of her hairs round the sweet-smelling hummingbird.

girl really was adolescent and should not have eaten the meat; it would have killed her had it not killed my uncle first. I myself was unable to kill any more bears for a long time afterward, for they were angry with me; in my dreams I sometimes saw them on the far bank of a river or lake, and always they seemed very angry. Within the last few years, however, I have managed to kill one occasionally.

Bearing this attitude toward the animal world, and being entirely dependent on it for his daily food, it was hardly strange that the Bulkley Indian should turn to that quarter for protection and guidance in the affairs of life. He conceived that he possessed a special gift lacking in white men, the gift of communing with the animal world in dreams, when his shadow wandered abroad and associated with the shadows of the animals. Dreams were therefore tremendously significant. If a man dreamed frequently of black bears, or of beaver, his shadow acquired special knowledge and power that enabled him to kill those animals more easily than other men.

I have never dreamed a great deal, so I have never been a very successful hunter. One season I caught a beaver, not in the jaws of the trap, but with the chain, which became wound round the animal's legs. I do not know why this should have happened, because I have seldom dreamed about beaver, and never of catching a beaver in that unusual manner.

Kela, who died last winter, was always dreaming, and in consequence he was an exceptionally good hunter. He dreamed frequently of meeting three beaver girls, and sometimes, shortly before the beaver season opened, he would say to his wife, "I dreamed I saw the three beaver girls last night. They were laughing, so I know I shall catch many beaver this season." At other times he would say, "I saw the three beaver girls last night and their heads were drooping, so I shall not catch many beaver this season." In the autumn of 1923 he told his wife that the three beaver girls had spoken to him and warned him that he would die if he sat down to a meal with an unclean woman. Two months later some relatives from Moricetown visited him and stayed the night at his house. The following morning Kela said to his wife, "The beaver girls visited me in the night and reproached me for eating with those women. I think I am going to die." Half an hour afterward he complained of pain in an elbow joint. The pain spread rapidly all over his body and within a few days he died.

Carrier Indians to the eastward, at Fraser Lake and beyond, made every youth seek an animal protector or guardian spirit, and taught him how he might gain it. Night after night during the summer months the youth wandered away, alone or in company with another, to sleep in solitude on a hillside, or beside a lake or a river, where an unbroken silence promoted dreaming and the contact of his shadow with the world of animals. The weirder or more dangerous his sleeping-place the more hope he entertained of achieving his quest. Some youths therefore slept on boughs overhanging the water, or hung, head downward, over a rock-slide, secured from falling by a thong around one leg; some slept in graveyards, which the Indians tended to avoid on other occasions. Not every dream betokened a significant visitation from the animal world, but only a dream so vivid and intense that it printed itself indelibly on the memory. Then the bird, the fish, or the animal so revealed became the youth's guardian spirit, which he could summon to his aid in times of crises. Of the various methods of acquiring guardian spirits and medicine power three were in especially high repute, partly perhaps on account of their difficulty.

1. Find a log on which a cock grouse stands and "drums" during the April mating-season, purify your body by bathing, and crawl underneath at dusk. Even though the grouse seems conscious of your presence and stays away for several nights, repeat the process until at last it comes and "drums" on the log above you. If nothing happens except that the noise keeps you from sleeping go home, for you have failed and will never become a medicine man. But if you are fortunate, when its wings begin to flap they will seem to embrace the whole world, and fire will shoot from under them, impelled by a mighty wind. You will lie as if dead, but your shadow, traveling away to a mountain or a river, will encounter a fish, a bear, or other creature and learn from it a song. Return to your home in the morning, but at evening sleep under the log again in order that the grouse may repeat its visit and your shadow may perhaps acquire a second song. When the third night comes beat your drum and practice the two songs, for now you are a potential medicine man and will have two guardian spirits at your command.

2. Catch a number of live frogs, make a tub of birchbark, and lie in it stripped to the waist. Protect your eyes, mouth, and armpits with moss and let the frogs crawl over your chest. Lie thus night after night until a vision comes to you, and your shadow wanders away inside a cliff or a mountain where it sees a duck, a bear, or other creature, and hears a song and the beating of a drum. You will remember the song when you awake and must practice it each evening just after sunset.

3. Go at evening to a swamp where frogs are numerous, remove your clothes and lie naked in the water. Repeat this evening after evening until at last a frog comes and settles on your body. Many others will follow it. As soon as they cover your body catch the first frog, go out of the water, and dress. Then lie down to sleep under a tree with the frog suspended by its leg only a foot or two above your head. In your dream your shadow, returning

to the swamp, will find under the water medicine men chanting a song inside a big house whose door is coated with moss. This will be your medicine song.

The Stuart Lake Carrier, like the Sekani and other Indian tribes to the eastward, seem to have believed that every youth obtained a guardian spirit, but that only a few favored individuals, through dreams of a special character, apparently, acquired definite medicine power and ranked as medicine men. Thus Morice says:

> They also attach to dreams the same importance as did most people of antiquity. It was while dreaming that they pretended to communicate with the supernatural world, that their sha-mans were invested with their wonderful power over nature, and that every individual was assigned his particular nagwhal or tutelary animal-genius. Oftentimes they painted this genius with vermilion on prominent rocks in the most frequented plac-es, and these rough inscriptions are about the only monuments the immediate ancestors of the present Dénés have left us. [Morice, 1888–89, p. 161.]

At Fraser Lake and Stony Creek, however, this doctrine underwent a signif-icant modification (plate 10a). There the Indians conceived that most youths were unsuccessful in their quest, that only a favored few acquired guardian spirits, and that these few became the medicine men able to cure diseases and to foresee the future. The Bulkley Indians modified the doctrine still further, probably through the influence of the Gitksan. They knew their kinsmen's methods of obtaining medicine power, and stated that they too followed the same practices in earlier times. At a later period, however, they developed the notion that guard-ian spirits and medicine

Plate 10a. Village of Fort Fraser, on Fraser Lake. (Photograph by D. Jenness.)

power were not amenable to search, but came to man unheralded; that animal spirits took possession even of unwilling Indians, causing dreaminess and a wasting sickness that only the medicine men could diagnose and cure. The medicine men fortified the patients with some of their own power, and trained them to perceive and thereby control the animal spirits inside their bodies until, gaining the mastery, they recovered their health and themselves acquired the power and status of medicine men.

In this revised doctrine of the Bulkley natives, persons who seldom dreamed, or whose dreams had no coherent content, were not attuned to the supernatural world and could never acquire medicine power, however earnestly they might desire it. For the first symptoms of approaching medicine sickness, or of possession by an animal spirit, were frequent dreams, especially dreams that centered about one or two animals. Often the man marked out for that possession was totally unconscious of his destiny; he merely knew that every now and then he dreamed of a black bear or a beaver, and following his dreams had unusual luck in killing those animals. Sooner or later, however, by slow stages or with a sudden onset, a languor overcame him, and he lay in his hut, too listless and weak even to rise to his feet. The people used three expressions to describe his malady: eyiɫsin, "something is inside his body" (sasiɫsin, "he has a black bear inside him"); "he is caught by a dream," because dreams were the gates to the spiritual world and persisted like spirits, so that a man was frequently beset by the same dreams as his predecessors; and "he is caught by a medicine song," because a medicine song invariably issued from every contact with the world of spirits.

A later section will describe in fuller detail how medicine men acquired their status, and how they practiced their art. In no sense did they constitute a priesthood or interpose a barrier between the laity and the supernatural world. The lay Indian did not cease to dream, or to believe that his dream opened up contact with the spiritual world and thereby brought him substantial benefits; for even the layman's dreams gave him power to accomplish whatever they signified. If he was swift of foot, his swiftness came from dreams in which he seemed to pursue and overtake the fleeting caribou; if unusually successful in his salmon fishing, his success came from dreaming about the salmon.

> When I was about 12 years of age I often dreamed about a tailed man, which surely signified an otter. While still a lad, I dreamed that I was standing on a mountain-side gazing into a bear's den among the roots of a giant Cottonwood tree. I broke off a stick and thrust it down the hole. Then I awoke; but the dream, and subsequent dreams like it, brought me good fortune, for I was always finding black-bear dens along my trap-lines. Often I would dream at night about a bear and kill one the very next day.
>
> One winter when I was trapping with my uncle and his son our supplies of food gave out, and my uncle said to me, half jestingly, "You are such a wonderful hunter. Why don't you bring us in some meat?" At daybreak, with two dogs, I went out to visit my traps, leaving my flint-lock in the camp and carrying only my knife. I came to a bear's half-finished den, and, searching about, found the bear itself hiding inside a real den beneath a fallen tree. I tied my knife to the end of a pole, lashed two other poles crosswise across the mouth of the den so that the animal would have to push its head above or below them, and urged on

my dogs to scratch through the roof. When the bear, disturbed by their scratching, poked its head outside, I stabbed it in the back of the neck and killed it.

In time all the people recognized that I was an unusually successful bear hunter. Then one day Djolukyet, who is a powerful medicine man, came to me and said, "The bears are angry with you. They have been visiting you in your dreams, they have been entering your body and helping you to find their dens. Soon you would have become a powerful medicine man; but because you stay with your wife at certain seasons they will no longer come near you and before many years you will become blind. If you wish, however, I will catch the bear, put it back in your body, and make you a medicine man. Then your sight will remain unimpaired." I refused him, because the priest had told us that it was wrong to practice medicine and I wished to do what the priest said. Consequently, before many years I lost my sight.

Nevertheless, dreams were so erratic, visitations from the animal world so ungovernable, that no Indian hunter cared to stake all his fortunes upon them. He believed that in ancient days the animals themselves had delivered to him a powerful weapon by disclosing certain "medicines" and rituals that would deliver the game into his hands.

Long ago wolverine was always successful in its hunting, but man and the other animals always unlucky. If a hunter cached his meat, wolverine stole it; if he baited a trap, wolverine stole the bait and escaped scot-free. At last a man caught a wolverine alive, tied it up and threatened to beat it to death unless it revealed the secret of its luck. Wolverine said, "I eat such and such a grass." But the man struck it with his stick saying, "You lie. I, too, have eaten that grass, but derived no luck from it." Then wolverine wept bitterly and said, "Far up on the mountain, and there alone, grows a tiny grass. That is what I eat." The man killed the wolverine, found the grass on the mountain and ate it. Thereafter he was always successful in his hunting. Many other medicines besides this one the Indians learned from the animals, though it was Estes, the Trickster, who first revealed their existence to man.

Hunting medicines of this type were called yu; the ritual that always accompanied their use, xał; and the hunter who employed the "medicine" and performed the ritual, xałete. Apparently every hunter knew at least one such medicine, and the majority several. Although the rituals all conformed to one general plan, the Indians carefully preserved their details secret, believing that the man who revealed his "medicine" to another transferred also its efficacy and deprived himself of its further use. Older hunters imparted their knowledge to their sons and nephews, and occasionally men purchased hunting medicines from one another at considerable cost. The "formula" of one Bulkley native illustrates the general type.

> Cut a bundle of devilsclub sticks and, in the evening, after you and your wife have bathed, remove the outer bark of two sticks and from the scrapings of the inner tissue make two or three balls about the size of marbles. Chew these thoroughly and swallow them. Repeat the same procedure every evening for a month, and carefully refrain from touching your wife. At the end of the month bathe, let your wife bathe, and sleep with her during the following month. Alternate in this way for six months. Then you will be able to trap all manner of fur-bearing animals, and kill all kinds of game. But beware of immorality, lest the animals, smelling your corruption, keep away and compel you to purify yourself again by repeating the entire ritual, or another ritual of similar character.

This was a formula for the "wolf" ritual, practised, with individual variations of detail, by many Bulkley Indians, and by a few Carrier of Fraser Lake. Some men limited its duration to the month immediately preceding the hunting season, others extended it over several months, although tradition states that one man who extended it over a full year made his medicine so powerful that it killed him. The "wolverine" ritual was similar to the "wolf," but, according to one formula at least, required the use of hattak leaves instead of devilsclub[3] until 6 days before the hunting season opened, the sleeping for alternate periods first on one side of the body, then on the other, complete continence before and during the hunting season except on the night preceding its opening day, and the bathing of husband and wife four times during the early morning of that day, after the analogy of the wolverine, which was reputed to end its ritual by diving four times into a swamp. In still another ritual unmarried men, and a few married men who had observed continence for a period, bathed each evening and rubbed their faces and bodies with the smoke of burning "poison-weed" (kanye). In every hunting district the Indians built at least one sweat-house for the practice of these rituals, and for use in cases of sickness.

The early religion of the Bulkley natives that has just been outlined contains many obscure features very difficult to unravel today owing to what we may call the reformation brought about by Europeans and Europeanized natives during the nineteenth century. Before 1850 Christian teachings, or garbled versions of them, had so leavened the aboriginal doctrines as to occasion their drastic reinterpretation. Dreams still retained their ancient significance, the animal world still held a prominent place in the Indians' minds, but dominating them both was the once shadowy and neglected sky-god, Sa or Utakke, now identified with the God of the Christian religion and considered the ulti-

---

3. Both are laxatives used by the natives for certain ailments.

mate power behind all dreams, the ruler of everything on earth and in the sky. If an animal continued to quiver after it was shot, the hunter raised his eyes to the sky and said. "Utakke, this is yours. You have granted me this trophy"; for it was Utakke rather than the animal world that now demanded propitiation. If game was scarce, he threw a little meat or fat into the fire, as his ancestors had done, but instead of praying to the animals he prayed to Utakke, saying, "Utakke, this is yours. Increase this food for us. Grant us long life." When he carried out the long hunting ritual, xaɬ, he was not propitiating the animals so much as striking a bargain with Utakke, who would deliver the game into his hands if he underwent proper penance. It was Utakke, too, not the animal world per se, that according to the new doctrine exacted punishment for the violation of taboos, for the wasting of food, for mockery of the animals, laughter while eating their flesh or the idle throwing-away of their bones; and the onlooker who rebuked such wrongdoing adopted new expressions such as, "Beware, Utakke made that" or "Don't laugh. Utakke may hear you and give that animal power to harm you." Similarly it was Utakke, not the animal world, that raised the poor and depressed the proud and wealthy; whence the old and needy now blessed their benefactors by saying, "Thank you. Utakke will reward you," and the chiefs warned their children, "Do not laugh at that poor orphan, for Utakke, who governs everything, may make him rich and you poor." The expression mi, "it is taboo, take care," took on a new sanction when the Indians thus invested their sky-god with supreme rank and made him the controlling force in the animal and human world alike.

Once the sky grew very dark, the rain poured down in sheets, and the wind howled in the tree-tops. Then a woman called to her boy, who was shouting outside to his playmates, "Come in. You are making too much noise. Sa will hear you and send such heavy rain that no one will be able to go out."

Many years ago the Indians gathered in March to set their nets under the ice of Francis Lake. They caught and dried large numbers of fish, while the children played happily round the camp. Then a boy named Mek made a girdle of some fish-heads and began to dance with them. An old man scolded him, saying, "Don't do that. Sa will see you and by and by you will be hungry." A year passed, and the people gathered again at the same lake; but this time they caught no fish at all. The men left the women to tend the nets and went away to hunt, but the game too had vanished. Before long they were starving, and the first to die was Mek. No sooner was he dead than the lake seemed to teem with fish and the people had no difficulty in catching all they needed.

The elevation of an obscure sky-god to the rank of a supreme deity was not the only readjustment occasioned by the impact of Christian teaching. It led also to a reinterpretation of man's relationship to the supernatural world, and produced a crop of reforming prophets who attempted to graft on the stalk of the older religion various Christian ideas and rituals. The first impetus in this direction came from other Carrier subtribes, themselves stimulated by certain fur-traders, by two Oregon Indians who had been educated at the Red River settlement in southern Manitoba, and, a few years later, between 1842 and 1847, by visits from two Roman Catholic missionaries, Fathers Demers and Nobili.

> Two young men, natives of Oregon, who had received a little education at Red River, had, on their return to their own country, introduced a sort of religion, whose groundwork seemed to be Christianity, accompanied with some of the heathen ceremonies of the natives. This religion spread with amazing rapidity all over the country. It reached Fort Alexandria, the lower part of the district, in the autumn; and was now embraced by all the Nekaslayans (Stuart Lake Carrier). The ceremonial consisted chiefly in singing and dancing. As to the doctrines of our holy religion, their minds were too gross to comprehend, and their manner too corrupt to be influenced by them. They applied to us for instruction, and our worthy chief spared no pains to give it . . . [M'Lean, 1849, pp. 263–64; see also Morice, 1904, chap. 15.]

The Bulkley natives caught the infection from two sources, from their kinsmen at Old Fort Babine and from other relatives around Fraser Lake. At Old Fort Babine, they say, a white man named Misamombin, an employee of the Hudson's Bay Company,[4] dressed in white clothes and white shoes, strung a rosary around his neck, hung a cross to his side, and sang and danced among them. He then ordered them to throw sundry skins and clothes into the fire as an offering to God, forbade them to work on Sundays, and warned them against "black coats" who would come after him to corrupt them with false teachings. If the Indians followed his instructions, he told them, they would become white men when they died; but if they listened to the "black coats" they would turn black.

Soon afterward a Babine Indian named Uzakli, head chief of the Gilserhyu phratry, became afflicted with the medicine-dream siclmess and, on his recovery, announced that he had visited God's home in the sky and obtained a new medicine-song with power to heal the sick. He conferred new names on his followers and distributed tin crosses among them. Two years later he had a recurrence of the same sickness and acquired another song, which ran;

> ane-e nipili soll yilkyot
> ane-e nipili, solle yilkyot
> ane-e-yin betlol ustan a.
>
> (Nipili (an angel in the sky), hold my hand.

---

4. Probably William McBean. See Morice, 1904, p. 221.

Nipili, hold my hand.
I hold the rope that holds up the earth.)

Contemporary with Uzakli was Senesaiyea, a medicine man who lived at Fraser Lake. One summer, when the salmon were late in appearing, the Indians asked Senesaiyea to summon the fish up the river. Gathering his countrymen inside a smoke-house, he shook his rattle, sang a medicine-song, and lay down as if to sleep. After half an hour he arose and announced that his soul had traveled to the home of the salmon and that they would reach Fraser Lake within a few days. Subsequently he claimed that his soul made other visits to the salmon country, and also to the home of God in the sky. So often did he dream of wandering about in sky-land that the people grew skeptical, and he promised to bring back a piece of the sky as evidence. Then one night, as he slept in a smoke-house, he again dreamed that his soul ascended aloft through a hole in the sky, and, after wandering around for a time, returned to the same hole and broke a fragment from its edge. He slept until the sun had risen. When at last he threw off his blanket he found in his clenched fist only a scrap of spruce bark from the cabin roof. Laughingly he showed it to his countrymen and said, "I have been deceiving myself all this time; and other medicine men who claim to visit the sky are deceiving themselves also."

These earliest manifestations of the new ideas that Christianity was quickening in the minds of the Indians deviated only slightly from the old religion; but succeeding prophets introduced further innovations that altered its entire complexion. Among the first was a Fraser Lake woman named Bopa. Tradition states that she said to her daughter, "When I die don't bury me, but leave my body in the house and keep watch from a distance." When she died, therefore, her daughter covered her body with a blanket and moved into a small hut at the edge of the woods. For three mornings she visited her mother's corpse and nothing happened, but on the fourth morning, though it was already decaying, a song issued from its mouth and a voice said, "Wash my body and cook me some food, for I am hungry." The woman washed the body and cooked food, whereupon her mother came to life again and ate. She then announced that she had traveled to a large town on the shore of a sea and entered a house where people offered her fresh apples, which she had refused in order that she might return to life. They then offered her some bread, and she refused that also. Finally, on the fourth day, a man said to her, "Do you want to return to your body?" and when she answered, "It is too far away, the road is too difficult," he replied, "No, it is not difficult." So she returned to her body and lived for another 20 years. She taught the Indians that the dead become white men on the far side of a great sea, and that the whites, who were then beginning to enter the country of the Carrier, were their own kinsmen returning to their old homes. Hence the Fraser Lake Indians gave to Europeans the name nauniɬ, which means "ghosts of the dead."

Another Fraser Lake woman named Nokskan (a Gitksan word meaning Kan's Mother) is reputed to have died while she was fishing alone beside a lake or stream. She lay on the ground many days, but at last came to life again and returned to her village, where she told the following story:

> I lay on the ground dead, and one side of my body rotted. My shadow did not go to the city of the dead, but to sky-land, where it met Sa and Sa's son. Murder, theft, adultery, and swearing are displeasing to Sa, who bade me tie the hands of offenders and purify them with the lash lest they go after death to an evil place. But whoever avoids these sins, and lives a pure life, will go to Sa's home, a happy country where people neither work nor eat, but idle away the days in song, or, when inactivity becomes monotonous, ride around the country on horses.
>
> White men will soon visit Fraser Lake, bringing with them horses and cows (or buffaloes). At first they will eat dried fish and dried berries as we do, but after a time they will bring various foods of their own. Then the Indians will have abundance of food and prosper as they never have before.

Nokskan showed the Indians how to make the sign of the cross, and to dance with uplifted palms while they chanted her songs, one of which ran;

> sa bez'kai asendla cho wasassałte
> ai ya ha-a ai ya he.
>
> (Sa's child took and carried me aloft.)

This and her other songs the people chanted inside her lodge at the fishing camp, stretching their palms towards heaven and slowly moving round in a circle, while Nokskan, carrying a small wooden cross, stood in their midst. On certain days she called out one man after another, made him kneel in front of her, and whispered in his ear, "What sins have you committed?" After he had confessed, she called for a rope, tied his hands in front or behind according to the gravity of his sins, and sometimes whipped him on the back 10 or 12 times to cleanse him. She treated the women in the same way as the men. Unlike some of her successors, she never baptized the Indians, though she herself submitted to baptism many years later when a European priest visited Fraser Lake.

The first Bulkley River Indian to take up the craze was Lexs, a man of the Beaver phratry. One old native said that Lexs claimed to have visited the sky and received there a new song and a new name, Sisteyel, "I, a man, visited the sky"; but that the people did not take him seriously because he was very poor. A still older man, however, who was a youth of about 14 when Lexs died, regarded him as the real founder of the religious movements which, through the influence of his younger brother and successor Bini, completely gripped the western Carrier and many of the neighboring Gitksan during the middle years of the nineteenth century. According to his account, Sisteyel fell sick and died, but after 2 or 3 days came to life again and declared that he had visited God in the sky and been sent back to earth to instruct his people. He warned them that God was displeased with evil actions such as theft and murder, and that wrong-doers would go to an evil place when they died, whereas the good would ascend to the sky. From his visit he brought back one song, which his countrymen chanted as a prayer:

> sisteyal netaiyel sisteyel netaiyel
> he he he he he beyin.
>
> (Sisteyel walked down from the sky. His song.)

Not content with adopting a new name himself, he conferred new names on the members of his family and on one or two near kinsmen. Thus he called his wife Sutal, after a woman he claimed to have met in the sky. Soon afterward he became blind, but before he died he enjoined his younger brother to visit the sky as he had done in order to gain authority and knowledge to carry on his mission.

This younger brother who took up Sisteyel's mantle was Bini, who far eclipsed in fame and influence all his predecessors and successors. Although he died about 1870, within the memory of men still living, his name is fast passing into legend and every description of his life and teachings differs from every other. The following account is a composite one, based on the joint testimonies of three old Bulkley Indians, who had been with him in their childhood and were old enough to hunt when he died. One was his nephew and successor as chief of the Beaver phratry, another his sister's nephew, and the third had accompanied him on his last journey and was present at his death.

Bini's boyhood name was Sami, derived from the name of a deceased uncle; and the name he acquired in early manhood Mat, a title in the Beaver phratry. Subsequently he became the chief of that phratry and assumed the title Kwi·s together with the two personal crests, Beaver and Drunken Man, that went with it.

One spring, when he and his kinsmen were hunting near Decker Lake, he lay down in his house as though indisposed and mysteriously disappeared. His kinsmen searched all round the camp for him, and at last, with the aid of his dog, found him buried in the ground with only his arm protruding above the surface. They carried him home, seemingly dead, and sent for all their relatives in the vicinity; but, while they crowded round his body a man named Omak heard a voice issue from his chest, and listening intently, discovered that Bini was singing.

> ane-e anesenle-e so anesenle-e-a
> anea aneneskye meneskye.
>
> (Someone healed me, made me well again.
> I came down from the sky.)

All night Omak continued to watch beside him, and the next day Bini, grown a little stronger, spoke to him and bade him interpret to the people as follows:

"I died and ascended to heaven, but God made me alive again and sent me back to earth to teach you what you must do. You must chant my songs, for they are prayers; and you must make the sign of the cross. Things are going to change. Soon you shall eat dust that is white like snow (flour), and shall hunt and fish for 6 days, but refrain from all work on the seventh. Many horses will come to this country and you shall use them. But now you must cut out a smooth plank and write on it for me."

The people cut out a smooth board and under his direction one man made one letter, another another, until they had carved out his prayers. Quickly his strength returned, and he was able to proclaim his mission without the aid of an interpreter. As soon as he could walk he rose to his feet, and, supported by a man on each side, took a few steps forward. Then he said "Let me go. I will walk alone." But as he walked his feet sank into the hard ground as though it were soft snow. For years afterwards the Indians pointed with awe to these footprints.

When the fishing season opened, Bini and all his people moved down the Bulkley River to Hagwilgate. Both during and after this journey he lay down several times and died for a few hours; and each time he brought back from the sky a new song. Every evening he gathered the people around him and preached to them, using Omak to interpret and amplify his words. "On top of the sky," he said, "is a happy land filled with happy people who told me to make you all new so that after death you too would go to live in the sky. Then a song issued from my body and I came back to life again in my hut." Rising to his feet he would dance before them, feet together, arms outstretched, and his body swaying up and down; and as he danced he sang one or other of his songs. The best known, still used by Hagwilgate medicine men, ran:

> yisiłkli yaneketłsai-a
> he he hi ha.
>
> (Horses stamp the ground as they gallop.)
> Others were;
>
> ni pa·kyo yatettso'til atso'te
>
> (People entered the great father's house
> and became proud and wealthy.)
>
> ee e e a
> noxdzi to·bi eyinlea
>
> (Their hearts he (God) baptizes.)
> and

The great father had a cross.
Let someone make a cross for me.

After he taught them this last song, his followers made one large cross for himself and many small crosses to distribute among his disciples.

When the fishing season ended, the prophet and his disciples toured the country to gain new converts; but during the remainder of the year he hunted, fished, gathered furs, and participated in potlatches like other Indians. A few years later he caused the totem pole called Fireweed to be erected in the Bulkley canyon (see **p. [30]500) and himself gave a great potlatch for the occasion. He then built in the canyon a frame house furnished with a chimney and decorated with a cross; it was modeled, he said, on a house he had seen in the sky. His costume did not differ from that of other Indians, but in his later years he carried a small bell that he obtained from the Hudson's Bay Company's trading post at Old Fort Babine. During his lifetime he was generally known by his phratric title, Kwi·s, not by the name Bini, which he adopted after his first visit to the sky, or Samtelesa, which he assumed after a later visit.

Bini carried on his mission for about 15 years, gradually gaining so many adherents that at last he summoned them to his house and selected a number of men to maintain order and prevent wrongdoing. To these "watchmen" he gave sky names, Teluza, Nebezti, Samali, Chali (Charlie), Oyali, Nantali, Maskali, Sazzali, etc. The first three, Teluza, Nebezti, and Samali, took precedence over all the rest and became his principal aides. He performed also one or two miracles in confirmation of his powers. Thus, while sitting with his followers on a hillside overlooking Long Lake, he put some twigs (or flowers) into his mouth and drew out berries. On one occasion, however, he gathered all the Hagwilgate Indians inside his house and ordered them to confess their sins and be purified with whippings from his aides; but, most imprudently, he allowed the confessions to be made openly in full hearing of the entire gathering, and thereby stirred up so much discord in the village that he never dared to repeat the ceremony.

Often the sick appealed to Bini rather than to the regular medicine men. He would then set a basin of water beside the patient, and, after dancing and singing one of his songs, would lie down and gaze intently into the water to discover, apparently, what would be the issue. Finally, while attending a potlatch at Old Fort Babine, he was asked to heal a certain woman who was sick. That night, as he slept, a voice from above warned him that if he complied with the request he would die. He was very troubled the next morning, but when the people carried the sick woman out of doors and laid her down in front of him he placed a pan of water beside her, danced around her once, and, lying down, gazed into the water or perhaps drank some of it. Immediately he fell on his face dead—through a judgment of God, the priests said afterward, though many Indians believe there was strychnine in the water, for at that time they were using strychnine in their hunting. Whatever the real cause, his death caused a great commotion, and a large crowd of his disciples, flocking to Old Fort Babine, conveyed his body to Hagwilgate and buried it in the village.

Folklorists have long recognized that tribal traditions have not the same historical value in all parts of the globe. In Polynesia, where the world of dreams and visions did not merge with the daily life so inextricably as in North America, where there were professional schools for preserving a correct memory of tribal occurrences and rights, and where we can compare the genealogies and tales of islanders who were isolated for several hundred years, we may employ the native traditions with considerable confidence (though not, of course, uncritically) to recover the main sequence of events in the centuries preceding European penetration into the Pacific. But our Canadian Indians seem to have lacked the historical sense, as we interpret history. Many of the plains' tribes embellished with impossible myths so recent an event as the acquisition of horses; the Five Nations of the Iroquois failed to preserve any credible account of the formation of their great confederacy about 1580; and the Ojibwa narrate fantastic fairy tales about the part they played in the War of 1812. The Indians of the British Columbia coast and hinterland, who evolved a complicated caste system in which the inheritance of rank and property depended largely on kinship and the memory of kinship rights, have so interwoven fact and fancy in their legends that, unless we can confirm them from other sources, we cannot trust them even for the events of the early nineteenth century. The many conflicting accounts given of Bini's career strikingly illustrate this "romanticism" in traditional lore. One version

Plate 10b. Grave of Bini at Hagwilgate. (Photograph by Harlan I. Smith.)

has been given above—a composite account derived from the statements of three old men who discussed the subject together. It should be compared with the "history" of Bini published by Father Morice in 1904 (pp. 235–36), and with the following accounts given by two old Bulkley Indians who also had associated with the prophet in their youth.

1. Bini's home was at Moricetown, but, in the spring following Sisteyel's death, he and his people went to fish near his brother's grave about 15 miles west of Burns Lake. I was then 14 or 15 years of age, and living with my uncle 20 miles to the eastward.

Bini, or, as he then called himself, Samtelesa (the sky-name given him by his brother), walked several times around Sisteyel's grave, and feeling dizzy, lay down in his house. He lay there for 3 days, apparently dead, but his people made no attempt to bury him, for he had told them that he would die and come to life again. After watching over him for three days they heard a song mounting inside his body until at last it issued from his mouth. He then rose up and began to speak:

"I went up to the sky and talked to God, who told me that his house would come down to this world and make it a happy place to live in. He ordered me to teach you this song, which you must continue to sing day after day, until God's house descends;"

gitaksiya asenla kyo sałyinkai'o-nai
e hye ha . . .

(Big house up above. We two come down together.)
That evening the people danced and sang his song.

Next day Bini died again, but only for about 3 hours, when he recovered as before, breathing another song:

yiziłkli e e yaneketiltsai.

(Horses stamp the ground as they gallop.)

He explained his new song thus: "By and by many horses will come to our country, and there will come also priests who will teach you what I teach you now."

On the third day he fell down and died for about 2 hours, bringing back the song:

niba hanzu li'sta.

(Our good father has many good things.)

When he died on the fourth day, he produced the song:

e ye he noxlen e.

(Look at him (God)); and on the fifth day;

sba kyo tagałkwas ele e'kat nesoltse.

(My great father caused me to be born on top of a cross.)

After he had danced and taught the people this last song, he made a number of little tin crosses, and, calling out the men and women one by one, tied a cross round each person's neck and baptized him by sprinkling water over his head with a stick also shaped like a cross. He then made the sign of the cross over the disciple and conferred on him a new name.

Bini moved his home to Hagwilgate when the Gitamtanyu phratry erected its totem-pole esrił, and scores of natives from all the surrounding villages had gathered to attend the ceremony. He warned them that a great sickness was approaching the country, but that if they danced and chanted his songs it would not harm them. Many of the Indians, however, refused to believe him. When smallpox did attack the Carrier in 1862, Bini gathered the Hagwilgate people at an open spot about 2 miles from the village and made them dance round in a great circle, the children on the outside of their elders, all holding boughs shaped like crosses. He then ringed in the dancers with a long rope, and proclaimed that if the rope broke many of them would die. His prophecy came true, for a woman inadvertently touched and broke the rope while she was dancing, and soon afterward many of the villagers fell sick and died. I was a lad at this time and danced with them.

Before and during the epidemic, Bini's disciples had danced for an hour or more every day, but after the epidemic he announced, "Hereafter you shall work for 6 days and dance only on occasional days; but on the seventh day you shall abstain from hunting and fishing and dance three times, at morning, noon, and night; because there are three gods, and you must pray to each, your prayers being dances. Furthermore, because there are three gods, three men must serve them, myself, Male (a man of the Gitamtanyu phratry), whom I have baptized Samali, and Gyedamskanish (of the Laksilyu phratry), whom I have baptized Teluza." People say that he also ordered 10 commandments received from God to be carved on a board; but I myself never saw this board, though I remember that three of the commandments were, "Do not steal; do not kill another by violence; do not kill another by sorcery."

Thereafter Bini preached on the 7th day only. At such times he wore the everyday Indian costume, but often carried a bell in each hand, for he said that by and by people would be summoned to prayers with a bell. While dancing, he held his arms nearly horizontal and fluttered his hands. Occasionally he fell down as if dead. Then the people would quietly sit in a circle round him and await the issue, while Samali, his official interpreter, placed his ear against Bini's mouth to catch the new song that came from above. As soon as the disciples learned it from Samali's lips, they rose and danced to it; and Bini joined them a few minutes later. The last song that Bini brought back ran:

e ya huballi hube nesiltchot.

(Light, light, took hold of me (so that I came to life).)

The prophet now traveled with his disciples all over the country, and appointed Samali and Teluza as his watchmen to punish wrongdoers. If anyone ventured to laugh when the people sang Bini's songs, these two men struck the offender with whips of caribou hide. Whenever, too, Bini summoned the people to confess, they stood one on each side of the sinner with their whips and inflicted whatever punishment the prophet ordered. Once Teluza ordered away a certain woman who came to confess, saying to her, "You are only a poor woman and don't need to confess. Go outside." The woman, however, stood her ground and said loudly, "Why should I go outside? I want to confess to Bini that you seduced me." Both disciple and master were thus put to shame, but Bini had to let the incident pass because he dared not dispense with Teluza's services.

Bini's travels throughout the country sowed the seeds of a great revival, which came to fruition when he erected the Fireweed totem-pole in the Hagwilgate canyon. The potlatch that he and his phratry held on that occasion attracted a large concourse of people who carried his songs and dances far and wide. Nevertheless, it was among the Hagwilgate Indians that his mission gained its chief stronghold; elsewhere there were many Carrier who refused to recognise his authority. Whenever he traveled round the country four strong young men always attended him to carry him over streams; for he had declared that heavy rain would inevitably follow the wetting of his feet. On one occasion, when his party had crossed a creek near Barret station and was waiting for him to overtake them, someone suggested that they should let him wade through the water and so find out whether his prophecy would really come true. No sooner had Bini stepped out on to the bank than the clear sky became overcast, the rain poured down in torrents, and the stream rose so rapidly that the fearful Indians thought the whole world was to be covered with the deluge. At Bini's command they hastily built a lodge of spruce bark and frenziedly danced to his songs. Then the rain ceased, the stream subsided, and a warm sun dried up the land.

After Bini had been preaching for a number of years, he had a contest at Hagwilgate with three medicine men, Widak'kwats, Gukswot, and Akyewas (the two last were Hazelton Indians), who resented Bini's vaunt that their power was insignificant compared with his own. The medicine men shook their rattles and sang their medicine songs, while the prophet danced and chanted the songs he had brought back from the sky. Soon afterward the three men died, and last of all, but in the same year, Bini died also.

The true cause of his death is uncertain. During a visit to Old Fort Babine he was asked to heal a man who was sick. He sipped up some water from a basin, intending to spout it over the patient; but suddenly he fell on his face dead. Some people say that he had used a medicine man's rattle over this patient, and conducted himself in other ways like an ordinary medicine man, though forbidden by God under penalty of death. But I myself believe that someone had poisoned the water.

2. Bini's wife quarreled with his sister, who was living in their hunting camp, and when Bini ordered her to give his sister some food she refused. Very angry, he carried off the two caribou hides that served him for bedding and went away to sleep in the woods. At sunset his wife looked for him, but found only his empty bed-skins. Anxious and contrite, she looked for him again in the morning, and when he was still missing, notified some relatives who were hunting in the vicinity. After a long search they found his shirt, still buttoned at neck and sleeves, high up in a tree, and on the ground some distance away, faintly breathing, his naked body, which they carried to his lodge. He remained there motionless all through the day and night. Next morning he began to utter strange guttural sounds, and when the people failed to understand him—for he was speaking in the language of the dead—he opened his eyes and beckoned to his nephew Samali. Samali, to everyone's amazement, understood what he was saying and interpreted his message. Bini declared that he had ascended to the sky and returned to teach them what was about to happen and what they themselves must do. Heaven, he said, had promised that the poor should be made rich and the rich poor; that the Indians should become like white men and speak a new language; and that great dogs (horses) would descend from the sky and raise a tumult as they ran about on earth. He himself was to unite in marriage, with fitting ceremony, every young man and young woman who had attained the necessary age; and the people were to dance with him day after day.

His relatives then conducted Bini from his hunting lodge to the village, where I myself saw him, being then about 8 years old. He was still unable to talk in our language, but used the language of the dead, which Samali interpreted for him. Yet he danced among the people, and they danced with him. One day he sent some young men to bring him a blossom-laden branch of a saskatoon tree, and as he danced with the blossoms in his mouth, ordered the people to dance their hardest with him. Presently he withdrew the blossoms from his mouth. To our astonishment they had changed to ripe berries.

Later a large crowd escorted him to Hagwilgate, and, at his command, assigned 12 young men to carry him over every stream. As we traveled along with packs on our backs (being very small, I myself did not carry a pack), some of the older people discussed what would happen if Bini wet his feet, and told the young men to let him wade through the next stream. When Bini saw his bodyguard walk over without waiting for him he said, "Very well. I'll wade across. It was only to save you trouble that I made you carry me." Hardly had he set foot on the opposite bank when a terrific thunderstorm burst over us, though previously the sky had been cloudless. After this the Hagwilgate Indians believed all that Bini told them, and everything he prophesied has come true. He regained his ability to speak our Carrier tongue when we reached Hagwilgate.

Bini made only one mistake in his whole career, but that was a fatal one. He used a medicine man's rattle to heal a dying Babine native, and through thus contaminating the ways of heaven with those of the medicine men he brought about his own death.

The discrepancies and impossibilities in these biographies of the same reformer, all furnished by contemporaries and eyewitnesses of some of the events, show how little we can rely on Carrier traditions for reconstructing their earlier history. The natives have always lived in an age of miracles, and even today they look upon the interference of the supernatural world as an everyday affair, and see supernatural forces at work in the most trivial events. The mundane details of these events signify little compared with the necessity of maintaining a proper rapport between the Indian and the unseen world so that he may enjoy long life and successful hunting. To most of the Bulkley natives Christianity (and today they all adhere to the Roman Catholic church) has not abolished the supernatural world of their forefathers, but merely added a second one that has increased life's complexity because its teachers and missionaries condemn the old principality and demand undivided allegiance to the new. Some of the elder Indians, therefore, try to compromise. Christianity, they say, has introduced nothing that is radically new. Bini and his fellow prophets were ordinary medicine men, as others had been before them. Their shadows visited the sky in dreams, as other men's shadows had visited the homes of the animals; and they acquired from their dreams the usual medicine songs and medicine power. The dream-force that attacked Bini was not really different in kind from other dream-forces, though its "content" was different. The same dream-force had attacked Bini's uncle, Sami, then his brother, Sisteyel; that is why Sisteyel spoke rather crazily and at the last became blind. Bini happened to be made of sterner stuff than his predecessors; he gave full sway to the dream-force and thereby acquired the power to establish his gospel in the land. After Bini's death the same dream-force attacked his relative, Louis, but it was too strong for Louis, who could not obtain a medicine song and consequently became crazy and died. Last of all it attacked Jim Michel's wife, but,

Plate 11a. Old Paul wearing his top hat and purple sash. (Photograph by D. Jenness.)

when the priest forbade her to voice her song, she also became crazy and died from the pent-up force to which she gave no outlet.

These struggles of the modern Bulkley Indians to reconcile their old religion with the religion that has been brought to them from without stand out quite clearly in the career of an old Indian named Paul, who distinguished himself at Hazelton every Sunday by wearing a top hat, and a broad sash of purple satin thrown over one shoulder like a bandolier and decorated with gold rosettes and his name in gold letters, "Ease Paul" (plate 11a). The following incidents in his life were taken down from his own lips in 1924, the year before he died.

My father was Guxwoq, "Sleeper," a Hazelton Indian, but my mother was a Hagwilgate woman and my hunting grounds are at Mosquito Flat, 12 miles east of Hagwilgate. As a child I bore the name Sowetinye, "Walking Away," but when I was about 14 I was given another name Axweras, "Persistent Person," and again, when I was about 19, Watex, "Land Otter." Finally when I became a man I took the name Skagilth, "Grizzly Bear That Sleeps Across the road;" but I prefer myself the "baptismal" name, Ease Paul, that was given to me in a vision.

When I was a boy my father, who had recently been made chief, invited the Hagwilgate, Hazelton, and Babine Indians to a great potlatch that he proposed to hold in a meadow near Babine Lake. Many Hazelton and Hagwilgate families traveled with my own family, and we camped together for the night at a place known as "Gitksan camping-place." There a nephew of Satsa'n named Aiyuwindet, who was too poor to marry and consequently had no wife to arrange his bed, sat up in the night and called to the moon, "Travel fast. It is uncomfortable sleeping here alone." Several people shouted to him to stop, because it was not right to speak thus to the moon; but he kept on calling until at last he became tired and fell asleep.

Next evening we reached the meadow where my father was to give his potlatch, and the women busied themselves in collecting fir boughs for our beds. Aiyuwindet's nose then began to bleed copiously. He scooped out a hollow in the ashes of a fireplace and let the blood drip into it; but the hollow soon became full. Someone brought him a root-basket, and that also he filled with his blood. He sat there silent, while messengers went from house to house summoning the people to witness the fate of a man who had dared to talk disrespectfully to the moon. Some one said to him, "Why do you sit there and bleed to death? Stand up and ask the moon to heal you." Aiyuwindet did not answer. Presently blood began to pour from his eyes and from under his nails; and at last he toppled over and died. His relatives drew his body to one side and debated what they should do with it. But that night nearly every one in the camp fell sick and many died, including my father; for smallpox had broken out among us.

After my father's death, my uncle became head of our household and we returned to Hagwilgate. He said to me, "So many people are sick that there are not enough left to hunt and we are starving. You are young and active. Take this gun and go with my son up Rocher Deboulé mountain, where you may come upon some mountain goats."

My cousin and I traveled all day without seeing any game, and at night we took shelter in a hunting-lodge on the slope of the mountain. Before dawn I woke my companion and said, "Get up. We must kill a goat today"; but he answered, "It is too early yet. Wait till dawn." So I lay down again.

As I lay there, just before the dawn, a strange man appeared and said, "Why have you come hither?" "There are many sick in our village," I answered, "and we are in need of meat." "I know that," he said. "Have you any powder?" "Yes," I replied. "Give it to me," he then said. "It is your own fault that sickness has broken out amongst you. You have sinned and used rattles." Taking some of my powder in his hand, he poured on it pure water from his mouth and rubbed it over my neck. "This will keep you from becoming sick. Can you make the sign of the cross?" I made it with my whole hand, but he corrected me, saying "That is not the proper way. Make it with the two middle fingers only, for the thumb and the other two fingers are small. It is useless for you to hunt goats up here. I am the spirit of fish and can give you fish. Go home now and fish; and stop the medicine man from using his rattle, for it is he who has brought the evil spirits that are killing you."

The spirit vanished, leaving in my hand a little water, which I rubbed over my neck. As I rubbed, a numbness crept over my body and my breathing became troubled. I said to my cousin, "Help me back to the village. A great sickness is coming over me." In the village I lay ill for many days, and during that period I was able to foretell who of all those struck down by the sickness would die.

After my recovery I became an excellent hunter, and could kill as many as 20 caribou in a day. Our hunting lodges at Mosquito Flat were crowded with relatives dependent on me for meat. One night when all my household was asleep a great light suddenly filled the cabin and slowly concentrated over my head, leaving the rest of the house dark. Within the light I saw the figure of the Great Spirit holding a little child on his breast. It did not speak to me, nor could I speak myself, but when I moved my foot a little it disappeared and the light vanished. The Great Spirit visited me several times thereafter, even though I married, but only when perfect silence reigned. Once, too, white spirits visited me and told me that my name should be Ease Paul; that is why I wear those letters on my chest, though I have added my chief's title below them to appease my family. Now for 3 years no spirit has visited me, perhaps because my brain is growing weak. I have been a faithful Christian for 30 years, have never attended a ceremony where the Indians were using drums or rattles, and have constantly implored my countrymen to put away those instruments.

MEDICINE MEN

Among the Bulkley Carrier, as we saw in the last chapter, the old doctrine that every youth could, by seeking, acquire a guardian spirit and medicine power underwent radical revision through the influence of new ideas that seeped in from the coast. These new ideas largely reversed the previous attitude of the Indian toward the supernatural world. He still depended on that world to guide him through the vicissitudes of life, but he no longer regarded himself as the active agent in bringing about the necessary contact. Rather he believed that the spirit world itself selected its intermediaries (whether they willed it or not), and that it revealed its selection by producing a state of dreamy phthisis ending, unless properly treated, in death. While the intermediary lay inert and listless, unaware of the reason for his condition and, therefore, unable to cure himself without aid, his sickness evoked from his kinsmen contradictory explanations as earlier ideas struggled with new to hold their place. Some natives, the conservatives of their group, maintained that during his dreams the shadow of the patient had wandered to the home of the eagle, the salmon, or the bear, beneath some lake or mountain, where it had remained imprisoned, unable to return; that the body in consequence languished, and the sick man could not regain his health until a medicine man recaptured the shadow and restored it to its home. Others conceived that the shadow returned from the spirit world, indeed, but acquired there a medicine song which remained below the threshold of consciousness pent up like an ill-digested meal, sapped away the man's strength, and caused a slow languor and decline; these Indians, therefore, described him as being afflicted with the medicine-song sickness, and sought his cure through a revelation of the buried medicine song and its out-welling from his lips. Quite different was the interpretation favored by the majority of the natives. They asserted that entrenched within the patient's body lay some super-natural force—the shadow of a bird or an animal; that without reinforcement from the power in other medicine men, the sick man lacked the ability to throw off this incubus or to transform it into a source of strength; and that while the communion of the man's and animal's shadows certainly induced subconscious dreams and one or more medicine songs, no cure was possible until the patient was relieved of his burden or beheld with his own eyes the supernatural shadow within him and acquired from without the additional power necessary for its control. These variant theories led to three slightly different schools of practice. One group of practitioners claimed to recover the shadow from its supernatural prison house; another to open the patient's eyes to his dreams and release his pent-up medicine song; while a third sought to discover and extract the incubating shadow, then either to reinsert it, if the patient was fitted to receive it again, or else to dispose of it in some other way. In their actual treatment of individual cases, the first and third groups of practitioners looked for the ebullition of a medicine song just as much as the second group; but they regarded the song as an invariable concomitant of the sickness rather than its primary cause.

When a man became ill, therefore, his wife or kinsmen called in a medicine man, who brought with him a bag containing his outfit—a rattle (into which some practitioners summoned their guardian spirits), a coronet of grizzly-bear claws, a bone or skin image (bea) of his guardian spirit, animal or fish, to suspend from his neck, and a skin cloak, usually the hide of a bear or wolf. After donning this paraphernalia and seating himself beside the patient, he demanded a bowl of water, sipped up a mouthful and blew it out again to lubricate the passage of the "sickness." He then shook his rattle and chanted one of his dream, or medicine songs, in which the audience joined. Sipping up more water he chanted a second song, sometimes a third. Finally, he sat silent with his eyes closed, but with his mind searching out the innermost recesses of his patient's body to discern, if possible, the shadow.

Any practitioner, whatever his school, might declare the shadow missing, for all natives believed that medicine men commonly used their powers to steal the shadows of their enemies. If this was the doctor's diagnosis, he returned home, and during the night sent forth his own shadow to secure the release of the captive, or to regain it by force and lodge it for safekeeping in his body. In the morning he visited his patient again, proclaimed his success, and, dipping up a little water from a basin, sipped it into his mouth and spouted it over the sick man. The audience then drummed and chanted the doctor's medicine song while he shook his rattle and danced vigorously round the room. After several minutes he stopped, rapped himself from stomach to chest, vomited the errant shadow into his cupped hands, and, laying them on the patient's head, blew it into his body. Thus he restored the vital spark, dispelled the cause of the sickness, and set the patient on the road to health.

A practitioner of the first school, however, might find that the shadow was imprisoned in the home of an eagle or a bear; that the patient's malady arose, not from sorcery, but from enforced contact with the supernatural world. He then restored the shadow in exactly the same way as if it had been stolen by a medicine man, but his patient forthwith burst into song, the medicine song that his shadow had learned during its imprisonment. This outburst of song marked the first step in his recovery, and also in his acquisition of medicine power and elevation to the rank of a medicine man.

It was not possible to ascertain what special symptoms, if any, the medicine men correlated with the loss of a shadow. Every practitioner claimed the power to discover (though not always to release) a shadow held captive by another medicine man; but he also maintained, whenever the sickness seemed attributable to enforced contact with the spiritual world, that only a medicine man who had experienced the same contact, i. e., contact with the same supernat-

ural being, was able to effect a cure. Hence, he often declared himself unable
to discern the cause of a man's illness, and advised the relatives to call in other
practitioners. Several in turn might shake their rattles and chant their songs
over the sick man before one of them would undertake his cure.

We have seen how the practitioner of the first school operated; he pretended to bring back the shadow from the home of the animal or fish that
had imprisoned it. The practitioner of the second school adopted a different
method. Sitting beside his patient with a bowl of water in front of him, he dis-
cerned and disclosed the sick man's dream, and bade him recall the medicine
song that went with it. The revelation of the submerged dream released the
song, which escaped as by explosion from the patient's lips. As it died away he
belched out his accumulated sickness and obtained relief.

> If a man falls ill with a medicine song that does not come out of
> him he wastes away and dies; but if it comes out of him and he
> sings it night after night, he recovers his health and becomes a
> powerful medicine man. Just as eating bad food causes a pain
> in the stomach, and, unless vomited, sickness and death, so it
> is with the song; unless it comes out of you, unless you sing it
> to the accompaniment of a rattle, and vomit after singing, you
> become very ill and die. The missionaries now tell us that this
> singing is wrong, so today people who are stricken with songs
> are afraid to let them issue and in consequence fall sick and die.
> My own daughter has this malady; she has spells of craziness,
> because she is afraid of the priest and seldom allows her song
> to issue. Whenever she does allow the song to come out of her
> for a few nights she feels better, and if she would only sing every
> night for a year she might recover completely. But she has an-
> other sickness also, for she was caught by kyan (***see below, p.
> [103] 567); so I am afraid it would be very hard for any medicine
> man to cure her of both maladies.
>
>   For many months young Djolukyet lay on his back, afflicted
> with a medicine sickness that no one seemed able to diagnose.
> Finally, his parents called in a famous medicine man named
> Wisauwan, who brought to assist him about a dozen other prac-
> titioners. The boy lay in the middle of the room beside the fire,
> the medicine men sat in line facing him, and the large audience
> lined the walls. Each medicine man in turn walked round the
> patient, singing and shaking his rattle; and the laity swelled his
> song with their voices, while his comrades, with closed eyes and
> pounding rattles, concentrated their thoughts on the case before
> them and prayed for a cure. Last of all Wisanwan rose and said,
> "Djolukyet here lies near to death, absorbed in his dreams. I will
> reveal those dreams to him; I will bring the object before his
> eyes." "Good," ejaculated his assistants; "We will help you with
> our prayers." Wisanwan placed a beaver hide on his own chest,
> and another on Djolukyet's, for the beaver was not only his own

eyilseni, the object of his own dreams, but of Djolukyet's also, though the boy did not know it. He then removed from his back the hide of a mountain goat, another eyilseni that he possessed, and laid it on the floor beside the fire, where it waved up and down of its own accord as he shook his rattle. With his free right hand he raised the beaver hide on Djolukyet's chest—raised it just a little, for it clung as though it were the patient's own skin. Instantly Djolukyet obtained release, became conscious of his dream, and, opening wide his mouth, exploded with the medicine song that he still uses today;

> sa·bekyo asinler setelner aiyakke.

> (A big Dolly Varden trout did it to me;
> it tried to swallow me. O my.)

Waving his hands in the air he rose to his feet and sang this song again and again. Every evening for about a year and a half he sang and danced until at last he was completely cured, and able himself to practice as a medicine man. During his convalescence and training, another medicine man made for him a wooden image of the Dolly Varden trout, his eyilseni, to suspend from the ceiling over his head; and whenever Djolukyet danced and sang beneath this image it swayed to and fro of its own volition.

The practitioner of the third school began like the others; he sipped a mouthful of water, blew it out, and sang one of his medicine songs to the shaking of his rattle. After repeating this procedure two or three times he exclaimed, "Now I see what is wrong with you. I see the shadow of a bear (or other animal) inside your body. You have been dreaming of bears so often that at last one has taken possession of you. Or you have done wrong, eaten fresh meat in the company of an unclean woman, and the angry bear has lodged itself inside you." His assistants called out, "Remove it from his body." The medicine man chanted a few minutes longer, working himself into a state of ecstasy that brought out the perspiration on every limb; he then laid down his rattle, beat a tattoo on the patient's chest with both hands, and pulled out (or sucked out and caught in his hands) the obsessing bear-shadow. Holding it firmly aloft like a bayonet, he cried, "What shall I do with it? Shall I put it back inside him? Shall I make it enter my own body? Or shall I send it away?"

Often it rested with the patient himself to decide the shadow's future. If he said, "I am too weak and ill to endure it. Put it inside your own body," the medicine man laid his hands on his own chest and blew the bear shadow into himself. Being already gifted with bear medicine, or, in other words, having the bear as his guardian spirit, he sustained no harm, and his patient, relieved of the incubus, gradually recovered his health. He recovered also if he requested the shadow to be sent away, and the medicine man blew it into space. But if he said, "Put it back inside me," then he signified his desire to retain the bear as a guardian spirit, and required help from the medicine men to endure and control it. Accordingly they rose to their feet, still singing, and gathered round the fire, where each in turn received the bear shadow and warmed it over the hot coals before handing it on to his fellows. Thus shearing it progressively of its strength they passed it again, after two or three rounds, into the hands of the principal medicine man, who waved it to and fro before the patient's eyes that he, too, might see and recognize it, although it remained invisible to the laity. He then laid it against the patient's chest, blew it into his body, and bade him sing his dream song. With the singing of the dream song the ceremony ended for the day, unless the medicine man discovered a second shadow lurking within the sick man's body and treated it in the same manner.

In most cases a medicine man, whatever his school, had to work over his patient, night after night, for several weeks or months. Theoretically, his powers of healing increased with the amount of skins and money he received in payment, although the resources of a Carrier family were very limited, in spite of contributions from its kin. Moreover, whether a patient regained his health quickly or slowly, he needed several months of training before he was ready to graduate as a fully qualified medicine man. So usually 1 or 2 years elapsed between the time of his submission to treatment and the date of the final potlatch when his "physician" publicly inducted him into his new station and allowed him to hang out his shingle.

All the people of the village were invited to this potlatch. While the laity crowded against the walls, the medicine men who had assisted in the cure sat in line facing the ex-patient, who lay in the middle beside the fire. The procedure varied a little according to circumstances. Sometimes the ex-patient merely danced a few times round the room behind his healer and instructor, both shaking rattles and chanting the ex-patient's song or songs. On other occasions each medicine man arose in turn, shaking his rattle and chanting a song of his own that was taken up by the audience. Rubbing the novice's chest, he caught in his hands the incubating shadow, inserted it into his own body with a prayer that it might receive some of his strength, and restored it to the novice again. So strenuously did he labor in his task, so vehemently did he strive to impart some of his own supernatural power, that the perspiration poured down his face and he returned to his seat well-nigh exhausted. After each of his assistants in turn had carried out his part, the principal medicine man raised the novice up, placed a coronet of grizzly-bear claws on his head, and exhorted him to chant his medicine song. The novice then walked round the room, shaking his rattle and chanting his song, all the medicine men fell in behind him, and the entire gathering joined in the singing. A few presents distributed at the close of the ceremony concluded the potlatch. A new medicine man had made his debut.

In outward appearance these medicine men—now called diyinne, but in earlier times niłkin—were indistinguishable from other Indians except at ceremonies, when they wore the coronet of grizzly-bear claws, the special cloak, and the necklet with the bone image of the guardian spirit, that were mentioned on a previous page. A few, to ensure success in the chase, painted or carved the images of their guardian spirits on their snowshoes and arrows.

Morice states (1904) that Carrier medicine men farther east, especially those of Stuart Lake, painted them also on rocks, but the Bulkley Indians deny this practice, asserting that such pictographs as occur in their own territory were made for pastime only.

Of the special powers credited to a medicine man through his possession of guardian or dream spirits, first and foremost was his ability to restore human shadows that had been lost or stolen, and to cure persons obsessed by the same spirits as himself, or, as some Indians expressed it, afflicted with the same dreams. Many thought that the violation of a taboo rendered a man peculiarly liable to obsession by an angry spirit, and that confession aided the medicine man in his diagnosis, though it could not alone effect a cure. Since the spirits were numerous, and a medicine man could control only those with which he himself had communion, the Indians needed a specialist for every class of spirit (bear, beaver, etc.), and required many medicine men to keep their communities in health. They still remember another theory of disease, namely, that it arose from a stick, a stone, or other object magically implanted by a sorcerer, and removable only by a medicine man's discernment and suction; but this theory they discarded many years ago in favor of the doctrine of a lost shadow or of obsession from the world of spirits. Today, they say, the medicine man who practices witchcraft does not implant something in his victim's body, but steals and imprisons his shadow; and though this occurs quite commonly, being partly responsible for the high mortality from which they suffer, they no longer dare to kill the suspected sorcerer, as happened not infrequently in the nineteenth century. As late as 1885, indeed, Kwi·s, the chief of the Beaver phratry, shot a medicine man whom he suspected of stealing his brother's shadow; for his brother had intrigued with the medicine man's wife, and both the woman and her lover had died soon after the aggrieved husband composed and openly chanted a song, "My wife shall die."

> The most powerful of all Hagwilgate medicine men was Yip, who died during that great epidemic which we now know was smallpox. As it carried off one man after another he could see it traveling through the air, and dreamed that he should catch it in a salmon basket. He said to the villagers, "If I can hold this sickness in a salmon basket until the cold weather comes we shall be saved; but if the basket explodes I myself shall die 2 days later." The people set the trap on the dry ground and watched over it all night. Shortly before daylight it shook and burst. Yip died 2 days later; the smallpox was too powerful even for him.

The medicine man whose guardian spirit was a bear, a beaver, a caribou, or other animal enjoyed, the natives say, unusual success in killing that species of game. He was permitted to eat its flesh, and did so quite freely, although

among the Stuart Lake Carrier, according to Morice, it would have been taboo
to him.

> Two Hagwilgate brothers who were hunting bears one summer
> sat down beside a small lake and watched two loons swimming
> round and round in the placid water. Presently one man turned
> to his brother and said, "You have told me that you are always
> dreaming about loon. See the wakes of these two birds, stretch-
> ing like ropes toward us. Take hold of one wake and capture the
> bird at its end. Then I will believe you." His brother answered,
> "You know that no one has ever done that before. Nevertheless,
> I will try." He rubbed his hands in the water, and the end of the
> wake approached him. He pulled on the wake as though it were
> a rope, and the loon drew nearer and nearer until he captured
> it in his hands. Then he laid the dead bird at his brother's feet
> and said, "Here is the loon. Let us eat it." But his brother was
> afraid and answered, "If I eat it I may die. Truly you are a med-
> icine man."

Some medicine men were credited with power to control the weather.
Dressed in their special costumes they would shake their rattles, chant their
songs, and call for rain or sunshine. In a droughty summer such a man could
cause the rain to fall by merely washing his body in a creek.

There are many eyewitnesses still living who attest the marvelous feats
ostensibly performed by these medicine men through power derived from
dreams. One man, they say, ripped open his stomach while he was dancing,
and by merely passing his hand over the gaping wound made his body whole
again; another allowed his head to be split open with an axe, and after a brief
interval rose up unharmed; a third rubbed his finger over a hard boulder and
produced a deep groove visible to this day; and several swallowed fire from
blazing torches of birchbark.

> About 40 years ago, at a time when many Indians from Hag-
> wilgate, Hazelton, and other places had gathered at Old Fort
> Babine, a number of medicine men gave a display of their
> powers. Some pushed porcupine quills deep into their bodies,
> others, knives that had been heated in the fire. Then someone
> scornfully asked George, a young Babine medicine man, what
> he could do. George answered, "Bring me two dishpans and fill
> them with clear water." When the pans had been set before him,
> he shook his rattle and danced till the perspiration streamed
> down his body—for a medicine man's powers always increase
> as he perspires. He then raised his hand in the air and prayed
> for power to fulfill his dream, a dream that his stomach filled
> with black fluid for 3 days, emptied itself, filled with blood, and
> emptied itself again. Still praying and leaping he approached
> the two pans, lifted one in his hands and carried it round for
> inspection. The clear water had turned to blood. He spilt a little

beside the fire, laid the pan down, called on the people to sing faster and louder, and, after more dancing and leaping, raised the second pan. In this one the water had become thick and black like tar. Suddenly he swung around and emptied it over his fellow medicine men, who crouched and covered their faces in fear. The black fluid, as it fell, changed to eagle down, which lighted gently on their heads like soft snow.

A spectacular but not uncommon feat was fire-walking, of which perhaps the latest exhibition occurred at Hagwilgate in 1918. An eye-witness on that occasion stated that after the unconsumed logs from a large fire had been rolled to one side, leaving a bed of red-hot coals and ashes, the medicine man, a Moricetown Indian, walked four times barefooted through the glowing embers and emerged unscathed, although his feet sank nearly 5 inches into the ashes. Two other natives who had witnessed a similar performance some years earlier declared that the medicine man was wholly unconscious of his movements, and that, without the testimony of his countrymen, he would have regarded the episode as a dream.

We have seen that the Bulkley Indians, under influences that seeped in from the coast, obtained the notion that medicine power came from the spiritual world not by man's seeking, but through sickness that attacked him even against his will; yet that they still clung to their earlier ideas in regarding this spiritual world as inseparably associated with the world of animals, birds, and fish. It was still the beaver, the eagle, or the salmon that imprisoned a man's shadow in its mysterious home and taught him a medicine song; or else it was the shadow of one of these creatures that took possession of his body. There were, however, other influences, coming in from the same source during the first half, apparently, of the nineteenth century, that gave rise to a slightly different class of medicine men, a class that introduced among the Bulkley Indians features that properly characterized the widely spread Cannibal Society of the Pacific Coast. These new medicine men received their "call" not through the usual form of sickness, but through a violent hysteria that recurred every few hours or days, when it induced in the subject cannibalistic cravings that made him a menace to his fellow men, even his own kin. In the eyes of the Indians he was kyanilkyot, seized by one of those mysterious forces called kyan that have their home in the mountains; and he could be cured only by a kyanyuantan, a man who had experienced a similar affliction and acquired the power to control his kyan. The cure came slowly, in from 1 to 3 years, but on his recovery the patient also became a kyanyuantan, an accredited member of the loosely organized group or society whose specialty was the treatment of this strange complaint.

About 32 years ago, i.e., about 1892, Old Sam, who is now our principal kyanyuantan doctor, was camping out in his hunting grounds when he heard a cry, "hu hu," from a neighboring mountain. The cry was repeated, and though he had never been ill in his life before, a burning fever spread over his body, passed away, and came on again. He prepared his bed for the night and was about to lie down when he heard other sounds from the mountain, the beating of a drum and the thumping of sticks on sticks, that brought to his mind thoughts of kyan and its incursions. Suddenly there came a whistling noise, and something, he knew not what, lifted him from his feet, and hurled him to the back of his lodge, lifted him again and hurled him almost into the fire. There he lay in a daze, but after a few minutes he rubbed some cold, wet snow over his face and cleared his brain.

In the morning he returned to the house where he had left his wife and children. Hitherto he had been very fond of them, but now he was conscious of a deep antipathy and would not go near them. As the inmates were preparing for bed they heard a queer sound from something that had accompanied Old Sam; but no one paid any attention to it, and in the morning the whole party started out for Hagwilgate several days' march away. Throughout this journey Old Sam's brain seemed to cloud at intervals, and he nourished an impulse to devour his children; but he offered no open violence, and the party reached Hagwilgate without mishap. I was then a lad in my teens, and can remember seeing them arrive late one afternoon, men, women, and even children carrying packs on their backs.

Three or four days after their arrival Old Sam cleaned four steel traps and prepared to set them along Bulkley River. His wife, knowing that he was not feeling well, remonstrated, but he answered her, "The winter is long and the children need more clothes. A foxskin or two will help us." "I will go with you then," she said, "and stand back when you set the traps." So the two went out in the morning, set their traps about 2 miles from Hagwilgate, and started home together in the moonlight. As they walked along, there came from the mountains a peculiar sound like the whir of wings or an approaching tempest. It drew nearer, and from the woods rose an answering clatter as of a medicine man's rattle. Old Sam trembled violently, for he could see the kyan that to his wife's eyes remained invisible; and when a whistle shrieked he fell flat in the snow, his clothes dropped from him, and he vanished from sight. His wife fled in panic to the village, where she gasped to my mother and others, "My man was telling me a hunting story to shorten our homeward walk when he fell to the ground, shed his clothes, and disappeared."

About half an hour later Old Sam himself arrived. He was stark naked, his eyes were gleaming, and his quivering lips gave forth wild shrieks of "hu hu hu." Gnashing his teeth, he tried to seize one of his children, but the people restrained him and forced some garments on him. One of his relatives hastened away immediately to Kispiox, whence he returned on the following afternoon with a kyanyuautan doctor named Djolusanak and his assistants.

Old Sam had been quiet during the day, but as evening approached the frenzy attacked him again. He tore off his clothes, broke open the door, and raced about in the snow. Djolusanak and his kyanyuautan assistants pursued him, while the members of the cognate kaluɬlim society inside the house pounded long planks with sticks and chanted medicine songs. Old Sam knocked down several of his pursuers and tried to bite them, but Djolusanak caught him by the hair and with the help of others dragged him indoors. So contagious was the malady from which he suffered that no one was allowed within except the kyanyuautan and kaluɬlim people; but listeners outside the house heard Djolusanak remark, "I have discovered what is wrong with him. He desires human flesh. Tomorrow I shall give him dog to eat"; and late that evening Old Sam's brother bought six fat dogs.

The villagers prepared a great feast for the following day. Soon after dawn Djolusanak sent round word that they should stay in their homes, and that when he escorted Old Sam through the houses, one after another, they should cover their heads with blankets and pray that Utakke would cure him. At the same time he warned them that Old Sam was so dangerous he might break loose and bite the face of anyone who neglected to cover himself. In spite of this warning I peeped through a little hole in my blanket, and saw him, stark naked, devouring an unskinned dog that he clutched in his arms; and people say that he devoured six dogs as he visited from house to house. His guardians finally led him back to the potlatch hall, where they danced around him, and shook their rattles. Then he woke up sane, and said "What is the matter with me? I must have been dreaming." Since that time he has experienced no further attacks.

Old Sam had what we call Indian sickness, that only an Indian doctor can cure. It is most prevalent in the vicinity of Kitimat, where many kyan haunt a neighboring hill. Once a man caught in that district by kyan became so violent that the people, afraid to wait for a doctor, put hot stones on his stomach and burnt a hole right through him. He jumped to his feet and ran shouting towards the mountain, where he disappeared without leaving a trace. Kyan took possession of him permanently.

One old Bulkley Indian cherished the idea that kyan was but a collective term covering all the spirits of the animal world, and that possession by kyan was not a new phenomenon, but merely a variation of the old relationship that had always existed between the Indian and this spiritual domain. The shadows of the grizzly, the otter, the owl, the salmon, and other creatures, he claimed, dwell in houses beneath lakes or inside mountains, and when a man is seized by kyan, becomes kyanilkyot, his shadow wanders away to one of these houses during his dreams and becomes imprisoned there. Smoke or water then seems to swoop down into his body at intervals, rendering him crazy, and he cannot recover until a kyanyuantan travels in his dream to the same house and recovers the shadow. The most violent form of insanity arises from the otter, which sometimes (in dreams) takes the form of a girl or youth, seduces a man or woman and carries off its victim's shadow; insanity from this cause is well-nigh incurable. He himself, he believed had been kyanilkyot, caught by kyan; and he actually shook with incipient hysteria as he described his experience. He was traveling to Babine, and had camped for the night under a group of trees when he began to tremble violently and was seized with a mad impulse to run away. Unable to eat or sleep he lashed his body to a tree and lay down on the ground. Then a black eagle shouted to him from the top of a mountain, and, swooping down, settled with a loud explosion on a tree above his head. He swooned, and did not recover until nearly sunset the next day. During this trance he seemed to enter a great tunnel in the mountain, where two songs came to him from opposite directions. One ran:

he ye nesateltsai eyesenlea he ya he ya.

(A noise that moved away into the distance took hold of me.)

And the other;

he ya he ya tsilyak wate eyesenlea.

(A man who remained in the mountain took hold of me.)

Now and again, even today, the same strange feeling comes over him, but it always vanishes as soon as he takes his rattle and chants these songs. Because he has been caught by kyan, he ranks as a medicine man, and is sometimes called in to heal the sick. When he sings and shakes his rattle over his patient, night after night, he can generally see within the patient's chest the shadow of the grizzly, the beaver, or whatever creature it may be that has caused the sickness. Then he withdraws it into his hands, forces his own power into it, and restores it to the patient's body. But he is not a kyanyuantan, is not a member of that society, because the kyan that attacked him was not powerful enough to bring on insanity or to call for treatment by the kyanyuantan

The majority of the Bulkley Indians flatly rejected this interpretation. To them this old man was an ordinary diyinne or medicine man, and his visitation from the animal world was quite different in character from an attack by kyan. Some distinguished three kinds of sickness (apart from wounds and ailments obviously brought on by material causes); The ordinary medicine sickness induced by contact with shadows of the animal world and characterized by phthisis and dreamy languor; violent insanity caused by an otter in human form; and possession by kyan. Still more limited the number to two, regarding the otter sickness as only an aggravated form of possession by kyan. They often spoke of kyan as though it were a formless, indefinite but living force, as when they described it as a devouring sickness that travels invisible, though just as much alive as a man or animal; yet quite as often they insisted that there were many kyan, not all possessed of equal powers, whence some of their victims became violently insane and others only mildly deranged. What primarily distinguished seizure by kyan from every other sickness was a periodic hysteria or dementia associated with a craving for human flesh.

There can be no doubt that this kyan sickness, and the kyanyuantan society based on it, was copied from the cannibal society of the neighboring Gitksan, itself derived from the tribes of the coast. Among the Gitksan, too, the initiates concealed their rites from the laity and devoured human corpses and dogs as they paraded through the villages—or at least pretended to devour them, for in recent times they have not actually eaten the raw flesh, but chewed alder bark instead and let the red juice drip from their lips. The lay Indians in both tribes stand in such awe of the society that they commonly propitiate its members with trivial gifts in order to retain their goodwill; and at Hagwilgate any one who enters a member's house by mistake, even though he is himself a medicine man, atones for the error with a small sum of money. Their awe of the society rests mainly on fear, for they credit its members with power to drive kyan into any person who offers it affront. Hagwilgate natives have heard that at Skeena Crossing—and what happened there might easily happen in their own community—

A man once ridiculed the cannibal society and accused it of deceiving the people; but a short time afterward he himself, through the agency of the society members, was seized by kyan and became demented. The society escorted him through the village and worked over him until his condition became more normal, then ordered him to stay alone in the mountain all winter and eat devilsclub. When he returned at the end of the winter the kyan gripping him was so powerful that though they bound him with ropes he broke away, killed and ate two or three men and threw away their bones. The society then said, "We can't restrain him. Let him loose." Instantly he vanished toward the mountain and was not seen again for a whole year. Then one night the villagers heard loud shouts of "hu hu" from the top of the mountain. The laity hid in their houses, while the members of the kyanyuantan and kalullim societies hastily put on their head bands, necklets, armlets, leglets, and skirts of red-cedar bark, sprinkled their heads with swan's-down, and gathered in an open spot, beating a drum. Then the man flew through the air crying, "hu hu hu," and, lighting in their midst, said, "my kyan is so powerful that if I remain among you I shall devour you all. So I shall not come back again." As he spoke feathers sprouted from his arms and face and he changed to an eagle that flew away and disappeared over the mountain. This was his fate for ridiculing the kyanyuantan society.

Today, nevertheless, whatever may have been the case in the past before European influences began to break down the social order, there is an important difference in the attitudes of the two peoples toward the phenomenon. It may mean nothing that the Bulkley Carrier, who now considers everyone a noble, at least potentially, believes that in his community any individual whatsoever may be seized by kyan and ultimately gain entrance to the society, whereas the neighboring Gitksan limits membership to persons of noble rank and regards that class alone as liable to invasion by the supernatural force. The Carrier, however, looks upon the kyan sickness as a calamity that he would gladly avoid, even though recovery makes him a member of the society and brings him prestige and profit; but the Gitksan, except insofar as he is modernized and scorns his old customs, regards membership as highly desirable and the qualifying sickness as a matter of little concern. Indeed, if he is of noble birth, he may even offer himself as a candidate, indicating that in many cases the sickness is either simulated or self-induced. To the one people the society is primarily a group of medicine men joined together to treat a peculiar and dangerous disease; to the other it is an organization for conferring prestige and influence on a limited section of the community by means of a spectacular initiation rite that invokes the sanction of the supernatural.

The following episode will illustrate this attitude of the Gitksan:

About 1913 a low-born youth of Kispiox (a Gitksan village 16 miles from Hagwilgate) acquired a little wealth through working in the coastal canneries, and became so ambitious that he determined to enter the wilala society, the name by which the kyanyuantan, or cannibal society, is known among the Gitksan. He made his ambition known, but the members of the wilala and kalułlim societies, at a joint meeting, decided that his low birth debarred him from the wilala society, but allowed him to enter the inferior kalułlim. This, however, did not satisfy him. He invited the villagers to a potlatch at which he imitated in his dance the frenzy of the wilala member, and, before distributing the huge pile of skins, coats, and money he had heaped on the floor, made his grandmother step forward and announce, "This huge pile of goods belongs to the poor young man whom you refused to make a wilala." The members of the society said nothing, but the next time the people gathered in the potlatch house they set side by side near the fire a goose with level outspread wings and a small duck that had one wing stretched high in the air. Then a wilala man rose up and asked, "What is the meaning of this? Is not this goose a noble bird?" "Yes, it is indeed a noble bird," responded his fellow members. "But this duck here, of what use is it?" he questioned. "It is a worthless bird that no one wants." they answered. "If that is the case, why does it stretch its wing so high above the goose?" And the answer came amid laughter, "It wants to be a wilala." Thus they humiliated the presumptuous youth.

Such an incident could hardly occur among the Bulkley Indians, where the kyan sickness seems never to be fictitious or consciously self-induced, but is looked upon as fatal unless treated with unremitting care. In the winter of 1924–25, during my visit to Hagwilgate, Old Sam's wife was smitten by the disease, although she was well advanced in years, short, stout, and apparently healthy. An attack of hysteria overcame her each evening toward sunset, and she whistled shrilly and cried, "hu hu." In her dreams she had seen a stick about 4 feet long wrapped in three places with cedar bark; and throughout the day, as she lay on her couch against the wall of her house, a copy of this stick lay beside her. At times she would wander painfully to the kitchen behind, using the stick to lean upon.

The sickness had lasted for several days until her husband, devoid of confidence in the neighboring white physician, determined to use his own power as a kyanyuantan doctor and to treat her in accordance with the old-time custom. The noise of his drumming and singing disturbed the white school teacher on the reserve, who ordered Old Sam and the fellow members of his society to cease their humbug; but since he was afraid to enter Old Sam's house, his exhortations from without passed unheeded. He complained to the white policeman at Hazelton, and to the Indian agent there. This alarmed Old Sam and his people, for they feared that the sick woman, deprived of proper treatment for her malady, would grow worse and die. They recalled two similar cases within the preceding 10 years when the Indians had listened to the priest and had refrained from using their old-time method; and two other cases when the priest and the white doctor had sent the patients to the insane asylum at New Westminister, near Vancouver. All four of these patients had died within a few months, whereas their own treatment, they believed, had nearly always succeeded. Old Sam himself had been cured, and the wife of Felix, my interpreter; and there were two other women in the village suffering from the same malady who were almost cured.

The Indians, therefore, invited me to attend one of their performances that I might substantiate their protest that it was neither improper nor harmful. It might begin at 4 o'clock, they said, or at 6 o'clock, whatever time the symptoms overtook the sick woman. I reached Felix's house at 4 o'clock and went over with him to interview Old Sam. His wife seemed quite normal at that hour, but he promised to send us word as soon as her ailment developed. We therefore returned to Felix's house and waited. The account that follows is taken directly from my notes, written during the ceremony and revised the following morning.

Just before 6 a messenger put his head inside the door and announced that the patient was becoming restless. Felix had gone to visit a neighbor for a few minutes, but his wife, who, as a member of the kyanyuantan society, was to play a leading part in the performance, hastily dressed, combed her hair, and placed in a flour sack the head band of cedar bark that she would wear throughout the ceremony. Her brother and I followed her to Old Sam's house, a new building consisting of a large, rectangular living room with a kitchen behind. In the center of the living room was a camp stove, along the right wall half a dozen chairs, and on the opposite side, against the other wall, Old Sam's wife, lying on a pile of blankets. In three corners were some wooden chests, while in the right-hand corner nearest the door lay a blind old woman, wife of Netipish, chief of the Gilserhyu phratry, who was slowly dying in the Hazelton hospital. There she lay throughout the entire evening, helpless and apparently unconcerned.

Two other Indians, a man and a woman, had entered the house just ahead of us. The woman, who was dressed entirely in black, had been stricken by the kyan sickness 2 years before, but her cure was now almost complete. In her hand she carried a stick about 18 inches long, representing the stick that had appeared in her dreams. The man, like the brother of Mrs. Felix, belonged to the kalułlim society, whose members assist the kyanyuantan society in their rituals.

We sat on the chairs at the side of the room, quietly talking. From time to time Old Sam's wife emitted from her bed a shrill whistling sound, and at intervals a "hu" like a distant wolf. The two women sitting near me caught the infection and broke their conversation with similar sounds. Presently the woman in black rose and drew down the blinds on all the windows so that no one could peer in from the outside. Then she lit a lantern and went out, returning a few minutes later with a young Indian woman, the wife of a Chinaman who was living on the edge of the reserve. This Chinaman's wife was convalescing from the most dangerous of all ailments, violent dementia, caused by constantly dreaming about the land otter.

After a brief conversation together, the three women removed their moccasins and unbound their hair, and the woman in black drew off the moccasins from the feet of the principal patient, Old Sam's wife. Mrs. Felix took out of her bag the head band of red-cedar bark, the woman in black produced similar bands from a chest in the corner, and every person in the room (except myself) placed one on his or her head. The women then sprinkled eagle down over their hair, while Old Sam brought out a tambourine and pushed in front of our chairs two planks 7 feet long by 4 inches wide, which we were to pound with sticks. Finally Mrs. Old Sam shuffled from her bed into the middle of the room and squatted there; the woman in black squatted behind her, and the Chinaman's wife placed herself third in the line. Old Sam, Mrs. Felix, her brother, and the third man remained seated on the chairs against the wall, Mrs. Felix's brother holding the tambourine, the others short sticks with which to pound the planks. Thus we waited in silence.

Suddenly a whistle shrilled, blown by Old Sam, though none of us saw it. To the Indians it blew kyan into the room. The Chinaman's wife flung her head to the floor with a shriek and beat a wild tattoo with her hands on the bare boards, while her two companions sighed loudly "hu hu hu," and swayed their bodies up and down and from side to side. Old Sam from his chair began to shout his medicine-song, and his assistants joined in, beating the tambourine and pounding the planks. The three women in the middle were seized with violent hysteria; their eyes were staring and dilated, their bodies swayed, their hands quivered as with a palsy. Old Sam's wife, holding her long stick before her in both hands, raised it up and down jerkily; the woman in black swung her shorter stick first to one side, then to the other; while the Chinaman's wife, more violent than either, shuffled along the floor, her head down and her hands beating the boards or clawing the air rhythmically in front of her. Occasionally this woman raised her head and faced the singers in an attitude of wild adoration, trying, like her companions, to join in the song, but, like them, able to utter only shrieks, or whistling sounds, or loud sighs of "hu hu hu."

The song, repeated over and over again, louder and with more frantic drumbeats and pounding of sticks whenever the women's frenzy threatened to break out into greater violence, lasted some 15 minutes. It contained two or three significant words, but from lack of an interpreter I could not follow them. Suddenly it stopped, and there was an interval of about 10 seconds during which the women sighed loudly and repeatedly "hu hu."

Old Sam now started up another song, translated thus by Felix, who came in at this moment and sat down beside me.

A big beaver's nose goes inside the mountain.

The music stirred up the women again, causing them to resume their frantic gestures. Sometimes they faced the drum and executed a kind of squatting dance in front of it, their waving arms and swaying bodies reminding me strongly of Malayan dances. The extreme paroxysm of their first frenzy, however, had passed over, and their movements seemed more controlled by the rhythm of the chant. As the song continued Mrs. Old Sam began to "hu hu" vigorously again, and Mrs. Felix, who herself had caught the infection and "hu hued" once or twice while pounding her plank, rose and slowly danced on her toes toward her. Stretching out her hand, she raised Mrs. Old Sam to her feet, braced her arm with her own, and led her round the room in a slow rhythmic dance, during which the patient continued to bow her head over her horizontally held stick and toss it backward again. The woman in black danced on her toes behind them, flinging out her short stick first on one side, then on the other. Last of all, after two or three futile efforts, the Chinaman's wife struggled to her feet and danced in their train, with her head lowered, her face almost concealed by her hair, and her hands waving gracefully to right and left alternately. As they passed me, so close that I had to move back my chair, I could see their fingers quivering as if palsied; but both their feet and their hands kept perfect time with the song and the drumbeats.

At the close of this song, which also lasted about a quarter of an hour, Mrs. Felix retired to her seat, the three patients sank slowly to the floor, breathing heavily "hu hu," and Old Sam hobbled over to them to shout the same cry "hu," in their ears, one after another. His wife, only half-conscious apparently, pushed back the hair from her forehead, then pulled out a pan of water from beside the stove and mechanically washed her hands, while the other two women squatted in an attitude of exhaustion. In less than half a minute Old Sam started a third song, which Felix translated as

Something goes into the water,

explaining that old Sam, by "hu huing" in the women's ears, had expelled some of the kyan from their bodies into the air and was now driving it into the pan of water. The three women remained squatting, swaying their bodies as in the earlier songs, but less violently; and when the song ended Mrs. Old Sam pushed the basin of water under the stove again.

The fourth song was in the Carrier language also, being, like the three preceding, one of Old Sam's own medicine-songs. It ran:

Many wolves come for something to eat.

The women continued to squat throughout its repetition, but the Chinaman's wife shuffled a little around the floor.

The fifth song was wordless; the sixth a song of the kaluḷlim society, in the language of the Haida Indians of the Queen Charlotte Islands, which my interpreter could not understand. As soon as it commenced, Mrs. Felix rose and slowly hopped in front of Mrs. Old Sam to lead them in another dance. They stood in line one behind the other, Mrs. Felix facing them and moving her arms like a band conductor to make their feet and bodies keep time with the slow music. Mrs. Old Sam waved her stick up and down in front of her, the woman in black swung her stick from side to side, and the Chinaman's wife waved her arms gracefully to left and right alternately. The dance was perfectly timed and would have found favor in any music-hall. When it ended Old Sam again hobbled forward to "hu" in each woman's ears, even in Mrs. Felix', since she also seemed to have become infected and cried "hu hu" occasionally with her patients. The last song, also a chant of the kaluɬlim society, was in the Gitksan language. It ran:

The strong man afflicted by kyan is eating something.

The women still breathed "hu" occasionally as they repeated their dance, and Mrs. Old Sam emitted one or two whistling sounds. So when the song ended and they squatted on the floor again, Old Sam hastened over to "hu" into their ears, and to beat them upward on chest and back with a bundle of eagle feathers in order to expel any kyan that still remained in their bodies. Each woman gave a loud-breathed "hu" as it left her and Old Sam blew it away from the crown of her head. But from the woman in black it seemed very reluctant to depart; even though Old Sam beat her vigorously with his eagle feather and shouted "hu" in her ears, she still "hu hued" hysterically. At last he dropped his feathers and rubbed her vigorously with his hands, when with one dying shriek "hu-e-e" she subsided and sat quiet.

The performance was now over. It had lasted a full 2 hours, and every one was weary. The patients, to all appearance perfectly normal again, pushed back their disheveled hair, rubbed their eyes, and retired to the walls to rest. The tambourine and planks were hidden away, the cedar-bark head bands replaced in the chest, and all traces of the eagle down carefully removed. Presently the woman in black replenished the fire and examined the kettle to see if the water was boiling, for we were all to share in a light supper before returning to our homes. Then the men gathered around me to ask whether their remedy for the dream-sickness was not perfectly reasonable and proper. I told them that I could see nothing wrong in the ceremony, but advised them either to muffle the tambourine a little or to hold the performance in a house farther away from the school teacher and thus avoid any further complaints.

The performance just described dissipates all doubts concerning the reality of the kyan malady among the Bulkley Indians, for clearly the morbid condition of each woman was neither fictitious nor consciously self-induced, although Old Sam deliberately provoked a temporary paroxysm. It would seem reasonable to conjecture that the Indians, generally speaking, are somewhat unbalanced mentally. They believe that the world around them is full of supernatural beings or forces that are constantly interfering in human affairs, and they readily fall victims to their hallucinations. The notion of a supernatural force or forces lurking in the mountains that may strike them down at any moment induces a condition of periodic hysteria. Since kyan is supposed to be most active in the evenings when darkness begins to close in, it is at that time that auto-suggestion brings on the first signs of hysteria. The blowing of Old Sam's whistle was the spark that ignited the smouldering fire; the women became frantically hysterical, but in a manner conditioned by their beliefs and by the many cases of hysteria they had seen previously. The beating of the drum and planks, the rhythm of the music, checked their frenzy in its first stages, and gradually governed all their movements until they danced, swayed their bodies, and moved their limbs in perfect time with the slow and measured notes. Mrs. Felix' leadership in the dance also helped to bring them under control; and the hysteria was forced to express itself in slow, rhythmic movements until the patients became physically exhausted and their minds cleared. During periods of normality they encountered no social barriers or restraints, and incurred no feeling of inferiority, because they believed their malady unavoidable and fully expected permanent cure. So in time (some cases, the Indians say, require 3 years), they might well outgrow the mental and pathological conditions that induced the hysteria and become fully normal again.

The kyanyuantan, or cannibal society of the Bulkley Indians, then, consists of a group of men and women who are credited with power to heal a peculiar type of hysteria or dementia because they themselves have recovered from the same malady. The society appoints no definite leader, apparently, but one man usually stands preeminent over the rest by reason of his social standing or of the unusual medicine power he is presumed to derive through overcoming the dementia in its most violent form. There are no formal meetings apart from the clinics at which new patients are treated, and certain sessions at potlatches when candidates are initiated into the subordinate kalułlim society. From these meetings outsiders are excluded because the dementia is deemed to be contagious, and no one would voluntarily expose himself to its onslaught. Members are entitled to charge for their services, and enjoy a certain amount of prestige; but their standing at all ordinary ceremonies and potlatches remains unaffected, and today not a single chief belongs to the society, though some may have been members in earlier years.

The kalułlim society of the Bulkley Indians is younger than the kyanyuantan. The Indians said that it came from the Gitksan when Old Sam was stricken with the kyan sickness some 40 years ago, but did not take firm root until about 1900, and then only among the Indians of Hagwilgate and Moricetown. Membership is limited to the nobles, that is to say, to the men and women who have assumed titles and claim definite seats at potlatches. Many of the younger Indians are, therefore, ineligible, not because they are debarred from assuming titles, but because they no longer value them enough to scatter their wealth on the necessary potlatches. While they fear to speak disrespectfully of the society, they tend to regard it as a profitaking organization, because its members regularly assist the kyanyuantan doctors in treating patients afflicted with the kyan sickness, and the patients, or their relatives, naturally pay for their services, though on a smaller scale than they pay the kyanyuantan. The majority of the villagers, however, hold the society in higher esteem. To them it is a true medicine-society, for its members have actually experienced the mysterious force of kyan, albeit in a weakened form, and thereby acquired power to assist in the treatment of kyan sickness, though unable themselves to effect a cure. Indeed, they are considered the only people who dare assist in the treatment, because the disease is highly contagious and dangerous, and their past exposure has given them immunity. Moreover, even if some of the members have enrolled deliberately, submitting themselves of their own free will to a kyan infection induced either by a qualified member or by a kyanyuantan, others have caught the infection involuntarily, and only failed to become eligible for the kyanyuantan society because their malady was so slight. Consequently, the kalułlim society is really a lower order of the kyanyuantan, though the societies are mutually exclusive and members cannot pass from one order to the other.

A man (or woman), we will presume, is indisposed, and the ordinary medicine men or diyinne diagnose his ailment as a slight infection by kyan, and consequently outside of their scope. The patient's relatives approach the members of the kalułlim society and entreat their aid, which is promised for the next feast or potlatch. His initiation into the society then follows the same general course as if he is in perfect health, but merely aspires to become a member. On the first evening of the feast, when the man is sitting quietly in the potlatch hall among the audience, one of the leaders of the society (or else a kyanyuantan doctor), slipping outside unnoticed, suddenly bangs on the door and shrieks a wooden whistle. The candidate falls prostrate to the floor, for the thoughts of every member are concentrated on him and the whistle is theoretically charged with kyan. A member may now raise one of the society's songs, to which his co-members beat time by pounding on wooden planks. They encircle the candidate, lift him to his feet, and lead him round the fire, with loud shouts of "hu hu hu" or "hap hap hap." Any kyan that has infected him now supposedly flees before the kyan blown into the room by the whistle, and the force that resides in the cries of the members. Once only they circle round the fire, then they go outdoors, leaving the spectators silent in their places, afraid to follow lest they too be stricken by kyan, or else seized and mulcted a heavy fine.

Now from without comes the sound of a chant, and, at its conclusion, a clapping of hands and cries three times repeated of "pr pr pr." The candidate has been "wafted" to kyanberhya, the "house of kyan," some empty dwelling as far from the village as possible which the laity scrupulously avoid for the time, if indeed they are aware of its use. There the society members sing with the candidate all night, leaving him just before daylight to return to their homes. Sometimes they allow him to walk as usual about the village during the daytime; if he is wealthy, and therefore certain to pay liberally for his initiation and to distribute much largess among the people, they may even escort him to the potlatch hall so that the laity may join in their prayers for his recovery to health (a ceremony called by the Gitksan name gela·ls). More often, however, they keep him secluded for 3 or 4 days until the potlatch is drawing to its close.

On the third or fourth night of the potlatch all visiting chiefs dance in succession until nearly dawn. Then the head chief of the candidate's phratry steps forward, holding a spoon of sheep horn whose handle is wrapped with red-cedar bark. Slowly he marches, singing his own special song, and, standing beside the fire, thrice raises the spoon aloft and cries, "hu." Then, at the shout "kalułlim" from a leader of that society, he pours the grease into the fire and says, "May this grease be as a bridge whereby you (the candidate) may return to us." All now retire to their homes to await the reappearance of the vanished man.

Before noon the next day a kalułlim member makes the circuit of the village and invites the people to stand at their doors and watch for something to happen. A near relative of the candidate (usually his father's brother) dresses up in full dance regalia, dons a wooden mask representing one of his clan crests—we will say the grizzly—and, imitating the gait of that animal, searches round the outskirts for the missing man, who has concealed himself in some prearranged hole in the ground or in a crevice among the rocks. The members of the society follow the "grizzly," and, as soon as he noses out his quarry, drive him away, or, if he is himself a kalułlim member, remove his mask and merge him in their throng. Then, singing, they escort their new member inside all the houses in the village, where every inmate who is not a member covers his head with a blanket lest he be rushed off to the same hiding place, initiated into the society, and forced to pay a heavy indemnity.

After the novice and his escort have vanished from sight, the villagers resume their usual occupations for an hour or so, when a repetition of the procession again sends them hastily to their blankets. Only when the procession approaches for the third time are they free to gaze their fill.

The society now secretes itself in the novice's hiding place, and toward evening sends a messenger to gather the villagers in the potlatch hall. The audience lines the walls of the room while the kalułlim members conceal themselves just inside the door behind a curtain guarded by two men, one of whom is a near relative of the novice. Drawn out by these two men, the novice emerges from under the curtain, prances with his relative round the room, gesticulating with his hands, and vanishes from sight again. He reappears a few minutes later, shaking a rattle, and executes a formal dance with his relative. Then his helpers bring in the food that has been provided by his phratry, and, when the audience has eaten, the blankets, strips of moose hide, and other goods that are to be given away. A fellow kalułlim belonging to the same phratry as the novice distributes these goods, after which the people return to their homes. But an hour or so afterward the members of the society reassemble in the potlatch hall for a private feast, from which they carry away as their own booty the dishes and cutlery furnished by the novice.

For 2 or 3 days more the novice must secrete himself in the vacant house and each evening learn from his fellow members the society dances and songs. Some one composes one or two new songs for his use, and these also they practice in the evenings. The villagers are then invited to attend the final ceremony in the potlatch house, to which the leader who blew the whistle brings a rattle and an extra head band made of cedar bark, and another member of the society an extra cedar-bark collar. The head band and the collar they place on the novice as he sits in front of them, and the leader, shaking his rattle, announces that his protege is now a fully ordained kalułlim and

Plate 11b. Hagwilgate Indian in Kalułlim costume, viz., cedar-bark head bank and neck-ring; leather coat with pearl buttons; cloth aprong with pendants of beads, thimbles, and deer hoofs; and cloth leggings. (Photograph by Harlan I. Smith.)

privileged to enjoy that title (plate 11b). The ceremony then closes with a distribution of food. Later the new member quietly pays everyone who has played a prominent role in his initiation, his payments varying from as much as $30 to the leader who blew the whistle down to a single dollar, perhaps, to the men who encircled him with the collar. His total expense, including what he spends for food, often runs to as high as $500.

Such is the general method of initiation into the kalułlim society, but the exact details vary on nearly every occasion. Thus in 1921, for the first time, the society used the potlatch hall for the opening ceremony only, and held its other public ceremonies out-of-doors during the hours of daylight. It possesses perhaps a dozen whistles, all purchased originally from the Gitksan Indians by a chief of the Laksilyu phratry, who subsequently sold most of them to three men in the Gitamtanyu phratry. It may be worth adding that the leaders are not elected, but are simply the ranking men and women of their respective phratries.

Besides the kyanyuantan and kalułlim, the Bulkley Carrier have still a third society known as the komitt'ła, which was borrowed from the Gitksan Indians about the same time as the kalułlim. Unlike the latter, however, it exists for purely social purposes, and has no connection with religion or with the healing of the sick. Initiation, which takes place in a potlatch, is comparatively inexpensive. Members are entitled to blow a certain type of whistle, and to wear head bands and collars of cedar bark dyed red in a solution of boiling maple bark. The whistle has a different shape from that used by the kyanyuantan and kalułlim societies, whose cedar-bark head bands and collars, too (as well as the wristlets worn by the kyanyuantan doctors to protect themselves from the frantic biting of their patients) are not pure red, but mingled red and white, the latter being the natural color of the bark. In their dances the members of the komitt'ła society do not gesticulate with their hands, like the members of the kalułlim, but swing a wooden paddle. Some years ago it held private entertainments similar to those held by the kalułlim people, but latterly the two societies have held their meetings jointly. Their combined membership is small and apparently decreasing, so that both will probably disappear within another generation. The kyanyuantan society, being more deep-rooted, may last a few years longer, but it too has passed its hey day.

APPENDIX 1: HUNTING TERRITORIES

GITAMTANYU PHRATRY
GRIZZLY HOUSE

1. An area about 20 miles long by 15 miles wide around Tayi (=Maclure?) Lake, near Telkwa, known as chꭐchꭐt.

2. A strip about 3 miles square at Lamprey Lake, between François and Morice Lakes. This belonged originally to a clan of the Gilserhyu phratry, the Dark House, but was surrendered to the Grizzly House when the brother of its chief was mortally wounded by the sister of Netipish, the chief of the Gilserhyu phratry. The area was known as cha pe'kaz.

3. An area of unspecified extent around a creek north of Moricetown, known as xał tatsali kwa, "the river in which people place their packs of meat to protect them from flies."

4. Two small lakes for trapping beaver in the Babine Mountains north of Barrett station, known as uwitak.

HOUSE IN THE MIDDLE OF MANY, AND ANSKASKI CLAN

1. A tract about 20 miles long by 15 miles wide along the middle reaches of the Morice River, known as tsamik'aitchan, "the bottom of the mountain on which tsami berries grow."

2. An area of undetermined extent around Trout Lake, between Owen Lake and the wagon road running to François Lake. Formerly there existed on Trout Lake a large potlatch house surmounted by the figure of a raven, the principal crest of conjoint clans. The area was known as t'ak'as'lenli, "where the water flows into t'ak'az lake."

3. The territory around a creek that flows into Owen Lake, known as tazgli kwa, "tazgli river."

4. A tract around Rose and Old Woman's Lakes, just west of Burns Lake, known as djakaz, "middle place."

5. A tract about 5 miles square on Buck Creek, near Houston, known as tsan-ko·sai, "he remains in a graveyard."

GILSERHYU PHRATRY
DARK HOUSE

1. An area about 60 miles long by 30 miles wide around Tagetochlain Lake, between Morice and François Lakes, known as tagitsoxlen, "the place where the hunter watches for caribou to swim across."

2. An area about 25 miles long by 15 miles wide between the foot of Morice Lake. Morice River, and two creeks that join this river from the southwest and northwest. It belonged originally to the Tsayu or Beaver phratry, but was exchanged for a fishing station at Moricetown. It was known as talbitskwa.

THIN HOUSE
(Chief Guxlet's section of the clan)

1. The area from Hagwilget canyon to Moricetown, about 35 miles long by 28 miles broad, known as dizkle, "dead trees all pointing in one direction in the water."

2. A tract about 25 miles square around Owen Lake and Nadina Mountain, known as pitwinni.

3. A tract about 8 miles square halfway between François Lake and Houston, known as tatak, "creek joining two lands."

THIN HOUSE
(Chief Chaspits section of the clan)

1. A tract about 20 miles square around Atna Lake, near Morice Lake, known as gilenepin diltan, "place around the head of the lake."

2. A tract about 50 miles square just south of Morice Lake, known as neneka.

3. A tract about 35 miles long by 15 miles wide at the west end of Ootsa Lake, known as taiłla, "swampy place where brush grows in the water,"

4. A tract about 40 miles square on both sides of François Lake, known as t'se konakaz, "one-eyed woman," because there is a tiny lake in the middle of a wide plain.

BIRCHBARK HOUSE

1. A tract about 30 miles long by 25 miles wide around the west end of Ootsa Lake, known as netanli, "waterfall."

LAKSILYU PHRATRY
HOUSE OF MANY EYES

1. An area about 20 miles square around Topley, known as aɫk'at, "beaver dam on top."

2. An area about 10 miles square at the head of the Telkwa River, known as tse'tseniɫa, "much cottonwood coming down the river."

HOUSE ON TOP OF A FLAT ROCK

An area about 15 miles long by 20 wide on each side of the Bulkley River around Moricetown, known as ta'perte, "trail beside the water."

HOUSE BESIDE THE FIRES

1. A tract on the Zymoetz River below McDonnell Lake, known as kaskłał k'watlat, "many grizzly at its end."

2. The Bulkley Valley from Barret Station to about Telkwa and McClure Lake, known as chost'let.

3. The lower part of Buck Creek and the country around Houston, Recently this has been given to the clan House of Many Eyes in the same phratry,

LAKSAMSHU PHRATRY
SUN OR MOON HOUSE, AND TWISTED HOUSE

1. A tract about 15 miles long by 10 miles wide at the head of a creek flowing from the southeast into the Zymoetz River, together with the mountain at its head. It was known as uiyeni, "far across."

2. A tract around a small lake and mountain at the head of Reiseter Creek that flows into the Bulkley River west of Smithers. It was known as guskibewinni, "lake containing suckers."

3. A tract about 8 miles long and 2 or 3 miles wide along the Morice River just east of Barret Station, known as neɫtsikyet, "source of neɫtsi or Bulkley River."

OWL HOUSE[1]

1. A tract about 10 miles long and 5 miles wide at the head of the Suskwa River, wedged between territories belonging to the Gilserhyu phratry. It was

---

1. Hunting territories of this clan have been seized by the Sun or Moon clan, because the chieftainship of the Owl House, in the absence of male heirs, has descended to a woman who cannot maintain her rights against the chief of the Sun House, who is also chief of the phratry.

known as alkane·te, "a trail crossing a beaver dam."

2. A tract about 40 miles long by 20 miles wide around the end of François Lake, known as nestikyet, "source of Nesti Creek."

3. A tract around two small creeks flowing from the south into Tahtsa Lake.

TSAYU PHRATRY
BEAVER HOUSE

1. Area around Telkwa River and Mooseskin Johnny Lake, known as taltsewi-yez.

2. A small area around Day Lake, near Forestdale, known as ndettsane.

3. An area around the head of Buck Creek, known as nełtsisklat.

4. An area around Decker Lake, known as ndettlat.

APPENDIX 2. PHRATRIC ORGANIZATIONS OF OTHER CARRIER SUB-TRIBES

The phratry-clan system of organization seems to have extended no farther inland than the Bulkley River and Babine Lake, the two districts that bordered on the territory of the Gitksan. Some Carrier subtribes to the eastward ranged themselves into phratries whose chiefs bore hereditary titles; and they even adopted crests for these phratries, or for the chiefs who presided over them. Nowhere, however, did they subdivide their phratries into definite clans, nowhere did their chiefs erect large semicommunal houses or giant totem poles, nowhere was society clearly demarcated into the three strata, nobles, commoners, and slaves. The nobles comprised only the chiefs and their nearest relatives, who were far outnumbered by the common people; and the only slaves were prisoners of war, usually, if not always, women and children, who married their captors and obtained the same rights and status as other Indians. So unstable even were the phratries that today they are almost forgotten, and only resuscitated when members of these subtribes visit the Bulkley River or Babine Lake. The easternmost subtribe around Prince George, indeed, the Tannatenne, may never have adopted phratries at all, although its neighbors on Stuart Lake acquired the system, presumably through association with the Babine Indians. Father Morice (1892–93, p. 203 *et seq.*) has outlined the Stuart Lake system, which need not, therefore, be repeated. Here I shall merely append some brief notes on the phratries of certain other Carrier groups, whose locations may be found on the map on **p. 476.

(A) FRASER LAKE SUBTRIBE (NATTLEWITENNE)

Phratries	Crests of Phratries
Tamtanyu	Grizzly, black bear, entire weasel, leaf
Gilserhyu	Big frog, crane, small owl
Laksilyu	Raven, big frog
Llsamashu (Łsamashu)	Owl, grouse, whale, sun or moon, half of weasel
Tsayu	Beaver, owl

The phratries in this subtribe coincide with those of the Bulkley Indians, and the chiefs of the Bulkley phratries were regarded as the real chiefs of the Fraser Lake phratries also. Nevertheless, the Tamtanyu and Gilserhyu phratries each acknowledged a local chief, and the Llsamashu had two local chiefs of coordinate rank. A man could not marry a woman of his own phratry unless she belonged to another subtribe; a Laksilyu man, for example, could marry a Laksilyu woman of Hagwilgate, but not of Fraser Lake. (**Plate 25, fig. 2.) Children belonged to the phratries of their mothers, but were not considered nobles unless their fathers were nobles. Thus the nephew (sister's son) and logical successor of the old man who claimed the chieftainship of Gilserhyu phratry did not rank as a noble because his father had been a commoner; yet

322

he expected to be the next chief of the phratry, if it still continued to exist.

(B) ENDAKO RIVER SUBTBIBE (NU'TSENI)

Phratries	Crests	Chiefs' Titles
Tam'tanyu	?	?
Tso'yezhotenne (small Woodpecker spruce people)	?	?
Yiselyu	Frog	1. Naselti·ał.
		2. Tsekokak (Woman's Skin)
		3. Pilancha (Big Hand)
Llsamashu	Grouse	1. Usakkye
		2. Guzkli'
Tsayu	Beaver	?

An epidemic is said to have destroyed the Tam'tanyu phratry early in the nineteenth century. About the end of the century Naselt**ial, one of the three chiefs in Yiselyu phratry, adopted a personal crest, Frog, and about the same time the chief of Tsayu phratry, whose title was not recorded, adopted the personal crest, Wolverine.

(C) CHESLATTA LAKE INDIANS (TATCHATOTENNE)

Phratries	Crests	Chiefs' Titles	Chiefs' Personal Crests
Tamtanyu	Grizzly	1. At'na	Old Grizzly, Wolf.
		2. Nelli	
Tsu'yaztotenne	Woodpecker	1. Kles'al	Marten, lułlim.
		2. Anaintil	?
		3. Ne'tsan	
Yesilyu	?	?	?
Llsamashu	Grouse	Tsakwiłtai (Butterfly)	Butterfly?
Tsayu	Beaver	1. Ayuna'tle	Eats Man.
		2. Nustel (Wolverine)	Wolverine).
		3. Tapise'yin	?

About 1900 Kles'al, the chief of the Tsu'yaztotenne phratry, participated in a potlatch at Stellaco, at the west end of Fraser Lake, and seized the opportunity to dramatize his personal crest lullim. Under the pretext that he was going away to hunt he disappeared for 3 or 4 days. His fellow phratrymen then discovered him hiding near the village, adorned with the cedar-bark head band and wristlets that on the Bulkley Kiver signify membership in the Kaluɬlim society; and when they conducted him to the potlatch hall he chanted a song that is still used by that society in Hagwilgate. Probably he had observed its initiation rite at Hagwilgate, or else among the Gitksan, and after he returned to his own district converted it into a personal prerogative; for the society itself has never taken root around Cheslatta or Fraser Lakes.

(D) STONY CREEK SUBTRIBE (YUTA'WOTENNE)

Phratries	Crests	Chiefs' Titles	Personal Chiefs' Crests
Gilserhyu	Small owl	1. Sisarpai	Wolverine.
		2. Yazcho	Sturgeon.
Yesilyu	Frog, crane.	1. Peyeɬ	Frog, crane
		2. Lleanuɬih	Frog, crane

The Stony Creek Indians claim that they never had more than two phratries, that a man inherited his phratry from his mother, and that his rank depended less on his ancestry than on the num.ber of potlatches he was able to give. Anyone could become a chief by giving a certain number of potlatches; a lesser number bestowed on him the status of a noble. His children were then nobles, potentially at least, provided their mother also was a noble, but if either parent was a commoner, the children were commoners until they succeeded in raising their status by the necessary potlatches. In 1924 these Indians counted on their reservation two chiefs, two who had almost the status of chiefs, since each required to give only one more potlatch, about 20 nobles of varying grades, and some 150 commoners.

Before they were confined to a single reserve, they occupied two villages, one on Nulki Lake, the other on the neighboring Tatchik Lake. Some of them asserted that in former times all the Nulki Lake people belonged to the Yesilyu phratry, and all the Tatchik Lake people to the Gilserhyu. This is clearly impossible, since the phratries were exogamous units and every man must have belonged to a different phratry from his wife. It may be, however, that the hunting territory around these lakes was divided between the two phratries, the Tatchik Lake district going to the Gilserhyu and the Nulki Lake to the Yesilyu. Neither lake contained salmon, so the Stony Creek Indians used to merge during the fishing season with the Indians of Fraser Lake.

LITERATURE CITED

Barbeau, Charles Marius

1929. *Totem poles of the Gitksan, Upper Skeena River, British Columbia*. Nat. Mus. Canada, Bull. No. 61, Anthrop. ser., No. 12.

Jenness, Diamond

1934. Myths of the Carrier Indians of British Columbia, *Journ. Amer. Folk-Lore*, vol. 47, Nos. 184–185, April–September.

M'Lean, John

1849. *Notes of a twenty-five years' service in the Hudson's Bay territory.* 2 vols. London.

Morice, A.G.

1888-89. The Western Dénés. Their manners and customs. *Proc. Canadian Inst.*, 3rd ser., vol. 7. Toronto.

1892–93. *Notes on the Western Dénés*. Trans. Canadian Inst., vol. 4. 1904. History of the northern interior of British Columbia. Toronto.

CPSIA information can be obtained at www.ICGtesting.com
Printed in the USA
LVOW10s1924191015

458864LV00002B/697/P